What readers are saying about this book...

Great book. L.A. CA

Great book, I have been looking for a book on the 486 that has technical information. This book answered a lot of questions. Need more input. P.T. LA

Now I feel I can come to grips with this complex, electronic box. L.A. England

Well written. T.W. NJ

Abacus books tell it all how it really is .... good for in depth learning. S.I. Australia

Very well written and helpful thanks. P.J. KY

Excellent book for new owners of 486 machines. I recommend it to clients. F.R. OR

Excellent book. R.R. CT

This type of book should have been written years ago. C.J. NY

Super book. C.C. WI

Good book. S.M. CA

Nice layout, good diagrams. R.R. MN

Excellent! S.I. MI

The 486 Book

User's guide to 486 computer systems

by Joseph Haas and Thomas Jungbluth

Abacus

A Data Becker Book

Managing Editor: Scott Slaughter

Editors: Louise Benzer, Al Wier, Robbin Markley

Technical Editor: George Miller

Book Design: Scott Slaughter

Cover Art: John Plummer

```
Library of Congress Cataloging-in-Publication Data
Haas, Josef, 1954-
    The 486 book / Josef Haas, Thomas Jungbluth.
        p.  cm.
    Includes Bibliographical references and index.
    ISBN:  1-55755-183-9 : $34.95
    1.  Intel 80486 (Microprocessor)  2.  Microcomputers.
I.  Jungbluth, Thomas, 1962-  .  II.  Title.  III.  Title:
Four hundred eighty six book.  IV.  Title: Four eighty six
book.
QA76.8.I29282H32  1992                        92-24958
004.165--dc20                                 CIP
```

Printed in U.S.A.

10 9 8 7 6 5 4 3

The 486 Book

Quick Contents

Contents

7   Graphics   221

8   Interfaces   251

9   Operating Systems   277

10   User Interfaces   295

11   It's A Changing World   319

12   80486 Programs   329

13   **Companion Diskette**   **361**

Appendices: 443

Index 479

Chapter 1
The 486 World

When you purchase a 486 you obviously expect more from your computer. The 486 computers are among the fastest microcomputers. These computers are so fast that, regardless of the operating system, user interface, or program you're using, usually there won't be any delay.

The distinguishing feature of a 486 computer is that its principal component is an i486 processor. However, there is more to a computer than simply a processor. A system's overall performance is determined by the combination of equally important components (motherboard, memory bus, peripherals).

In this case, the computer is only as efficient as its weakest element. So, all the components should be carefully considered.

Because of the peculiarities of computers based on Intel processors, it's important that the operating system that's used be optimally adapted to the system. By loading drivers in the proper sequence and optimally allocating the working memory, it's possible to reach even higher levels of performance.

1.1 In a Class by Itself

Why is the 486 such an important part of the computer world?

A 486 computer takes its name from the model number of its main processor, the Intel 80486 microprocessor. The number 80 is often omitted and is even printed in small characters on the chip itself. The term "i486" is used more frequently.

The i486 is a fourth generation chip, hence the prefix 4.

There are actually two types of 486 processors. The standard type is called a 486DX. A less expensive version is the 486SX, which is functionally the same as its big brother DX but does not have an integrated math coprocessor. It does have, however, all the other advantages of the DX version.

Limitations

When the first computers in the series of MS-DOS compatible computers were being built, the developers established certain characteristics that soon became limitations. Today's MS-DOS compatible computers still struggle with these limitations.

These limitations include limiting general memory to 1 Meg and two-part addressing. The new generation of i486 processors can avoid these problems. The i486 is not only highly efficient but extremely flexible. Whenever it must be compatible with older software, the i486 simply behaves like a standard computer chip. However, when performance is necessary, the i486 is ready to display its capabilities.

Is a 486 necessary?

Obviously, before purchasing a computer, you should determine whether you actually need a 486. There are a few things you should consider. First, as programs become more powerful, they are more demanding on the system's hardware (e.g., processor, memory, mass storage). Also, the 486 provides a secure foundation for future upgrades.

If cost isn't a factor (a 486 based computer is slightly more expensive than a 386), the only question is which 486 to purchase: the standard one or the economy SX version.

If you use processor-intensive applications, such as spreadsheets or CAD, you should use the standard version. In addition to the integrated math coprocessor, the standard DX version provides higher computing performance; the standard 486 runs at higher speeds than SX versions. However, if you don't need a math coprocessor, you should purchase a 486SX and save yourself some money.

The same performance at half the clock speed

Compared to the 386/33 or 386/40, the 486SX is a great value. A 486SX reaches the same performance level as a 386 processor running at twice its own clock speed.

Two upgrade possibilities

Intel's 487SX is also suitable if you plan to expand your system later with a coprocessor. On many boards it's also possible to change the processor and crystal. In this instance, a 486DX is plugged into the 486SX socket and the 20 MHz crystal is exchanged for a faster one.

Competition

If you own a 486, you probably want to know what the competition has to offer. In this price range, there are only four computer models that can compete with the 486:

- Commodore Amiga 3000
- Apple Macintosh

- Atari TT
- The NeXT

Besides these, you can also include the entire range of workstations (e.g., such as those from Sun). However, only the four computers listed above can be considered serious competition, especially if the prices are comparable.

1.2 Personal Computer History

It's amazing how much of our present way of life, both professional and personal, is affected in some way by computers. In this section, we'll discuss how this happened.

Until the late 1970s, only large companies used computers. Small businesses and individual users couldn't use these computers because they were too expensive and there wasn't any software available to meet their needs.

On April 16, 1977, Apple introduced its Apple II at "The First West Coast Computer Fair". This computer cost $ 1,298 and had a memory of only 4K. Since then, the "microcomputer", as the personal computer is sometimes called, has experienced rapid development.

After the Apple II was introduced, the effort to standardize computers began. IBM had already developed several computers for people unable or unwilling to purchase a mainframe (large-scale computer installation). In 1978, when William Lowe took over the job of development, a corresponding project was begun at IBM. During the mid-1980s he was convinced that he had found a comparable computer model.

During this time period, approximately 200 companies entered the market with their own computers. However, few of these companies sold computers in any volume. Besides the Apple II, only Commodore's PET (Personal Electronic Transaction) and Tandy's TRS-80 were widely distributed.

Along with hardware, software also entered private homes. One such pioneering effort was the first spreadsheet, *VisiCalc*, which was written in 1979 by Dan Bricklin for the Apple II. VisiCalc was an electronic worksheet with lines and columns and was used, among other things, for accounting and financial planning.

VisiCalc changed the displayed results automatically whenever one of the initial values was changed. Approximately one fifth of the 130,000 Apple computers sold could be attributed to VisiCalc.

A new market

By the end of 1980, personal computer sales had risen to 900 million dollars. William Lowe of IBM noticed that no one had broken into the commercial market. Tandy, Apple, and Commodore sold their computers primarily to private individuals and small businesses. While other producers of mainframe computers didn't consider the manufacture of small computers worth the effort, IBM assigned William Lowe the task of developing a computer for this market.

The main processor

Developers believed that a computer capable of processing only 8 bits of data at a time was too slow, so they utilized a 16-bit microprocessor in the computer. Intel had introduced the 8086 just two years earlier. The 8086 was a 16-bit processor and met IBM's requirements. However, because the chips used to control the Input/Output devices processed only 8 bits at a time, Intel modified this chip into the 8088. It communicated with the surrounding world using a data width of only 8 bits, but processed the data internally in 16-bit batches.

IBM developed its prototype around this processor. This was a breakthrough when compared with other manufacturers. Only the main processor was fixed. Other components, as much as possible, could be interchanged. The principle of open system architecture (OSA) had never existed in the mainframe computer world, in which it was normal to keep the internal workings of a system secret to avoid competition from other hardware or software developers.

IBM believed that this openness would help promote the popularity of the personal computer. After analyzing the success of the Apple II, IBM was convinced that OSA was partly responsible for some of this success. The Apple II could be equipped with a plug-in card.

The IBM computer was to be market-ready twelve months after the conception of the prototype. The project was given the code name "Chess" and the computer was called "Acorn".

Operating system and BASIC arrive from Microsoft

Besides a few unexpected problems, everything went surprisingly smoothly. A small software firm (Microsoft) in Redmond, Washington was contracted to develop the operating system and a programming language, BASIC, for this new computer. No one, outside of IBM, knows exactly how Microsoft was selected.

One rumor is that Gary Kildall, the manager of Digital Research, which had developed the CP/M operating system for Z80 computers, refused to sign a pledge of confidentiality which solely benefited IBM. However, Bill Gates, manager of Microsoft, was willing to sign this agreement and secured a contract to supply operating systems.

This rumor and many others have been denied by all involved. Nevertheless, Digital Research did produce software for the computer (e.g., GEM and later DR-DOS).

Components from outside suppliers

Despite protests from suppliers within IBM, all the remaining components, including the keyboard, were obtained from outside sources. Disk drives were obtained from Tandon, the power supply from Zenith, and a printer was supplied by Epson.

Even the marketing plan, to sell computers like radios and television sets, was an innovation. The first deliveries were to two chain stores, Computerland and Sears.

On August 12, 1981, after a defect had been discovered and corrected, the first IBM PC was introduced to the public. The computer had 16K of memory, a keyboard similar to a typewriter, and a connector for a cassette recorder. Including the monitor, it cost $1,265.

A deluxe version with 48K of memory, two 160K disk drives, a monochrome monitor, and a printer sold for $4,300. It cost an additional $2,000 to purchase the hardware to expand the memory to 256K.

The first computer

Seven programs, including an adventure game, a word processor, and the spreadsheet program VisiCalc, were available for the IBM PC when it was introduced. Within two years, sales of the IBM PC rose from 20,000 to 50,000 computers.

During this period, more than 150 imitations also became available, which is both an advantage and disadvantage of the open system architecture. Many of these imitations were superior to the original IBM version because of a wide variety of improvements and many were simply cheaper than the original. These copies are called "clones" or "IBM-compatibles".

The BIOS determines compatibility

However, software produced for the IBM PC didn't always run smoothly on these compatibles. Many large companies tried to make their computers independent and weren't concerned with software compatibility. However, certain smaller companies faced bankruptcy if their computers weren't completely IBM-compatible.

Whether a computer is compatible is determined by its BIOS (Basic Input Output System), which is a sort of "mini-operating system" that controls the data traffic between the individual components (keyboard, monitor, mass storage, etc.). Although the computer was an open system and the BIOS was known to everyone, since the BIOS is a "program" (albeit one installed in the system hardware), the clone manufacturers couldn't simply copy the

BIOS. Instead, they had to program one themselves, which (hopefully) behaved exactly like the BIOS from IBM.

Compaq's trick for copying the BIOS

Compaq was one of the first companies to imitate the IBM BIOS successfully. Initially, the founders (Rod Canion, Bill Murto, and Jim Harris) simply wanted to build workable computers. They copied the BIOS by separating the developers assigned to the task into two groups.

The first group analyzed the BIOS program code and described its functions. The second developed a completely new program based on the descriptions supplied by the first group. This procedure is called "reverse engineering".

Other firms (e.g., Eagle Computer and Corona Data Systems) simply copied the IBM BIOS. Ultimately, they lost a copyright suit initiated by IBM.

Phoenix: the BIOS for everyone

Phoenix, a software developer, was the first hardware-independent firm to realize they could earn money by developing a BIOS and reducing the compatibility problem. For a licensing fee of $100,000, any hardware manufacturer was able to use the Phoenix BIOS in their computer, without restrictions.

Competition builds

Once the BIOS problem was solved, an ever-increasing number of companies, anxious to reduce the market share enjoyed by the two powerful computer manufacturers IBM and Compaq, entered the personal computer market.

These companies succeeded not by building computers with better features, but by offering lower prices or by using special marketing strategies. For example, direct marketing, which was introduced by Michael Dell for his company, involved selling computers by telephone. Eventually this marketing method even spread to Europe.

AT - The Next Generation

The next round: the AT

In August 1984, IBM introduced the next generation of computer, the AT (Advanced Technology). This new computer was based on Intel's 80286 microprocessor and was about three times faster than the original personal computer. The AT also had a built-in 20 Meg hard drive.

Although the microprocessor had the capacity to address an area of memory 16 times larger than the original PC, for compatibility reasons, it was restricted to accessing only 640K.

IBM loses market share

Eight months later, Phoenix successfully copied the AT-BIOS. So, IBM was again forced to share the market with numerous producers of compatible computers. This, along with some other mishaps (e.g., the disaster of a domestic model called the "PCjr"), ensured that IBM's market share would continue to decrease. For example, it dropped from 63 percent in 1984 to 53 percent in 1985 and one year later down to 40 percent.

The PS/2 computer system

This decline caused IBM to develop a completely new product line, which was introduced in April, 1987. One model of this new line contained the 8086, a variant of the 8088 used in the original computer and two others used the 80286 processors found in the AT. The basis for the new top-of-the-line model was a new generation microprocessor, called the 80386.

The 386 arrives

Compaq was first

Unlike the personal computer and the AT, a computer using the new Intel generation wasn't first introduced by IBM. The 80386 had already been seen in September, 1986, in the Compaq Deskpro 386.

When the 80386 processor was being developed by Intel during the mid-eighties, Compaq was busy planning a new generation of computers. Even while the new chip was being developed by Intel, Compaq was adapting its system for this new processor.

The Compaq Deskpro 386

The Compaq Deskpro 386 was the first computer with a 32-bit processor.

The 80386 was a true step forward. It could process data that was 32-bits wide (instead of 16-bits, as with its predecessors) and it was also able to behave like one of its predecessors, so compatibility was maintained. This new chip could also address 256 times as much memory as the 80286 and could execute up to four million instructions per second (MIPS).

The big brother and the little brother

During 1988, an "economy version" of the 80386, called the 80386SX, was introduced by Intel. This processor had the same outside connections as the 80286, but inside it was a 386-processor supporting the 386's expanded instruction set and the various operating modes. This allowed manufacturers to use AT-boards in a 386 computer, with only minor changes. The 386SX properly ensured, for the first time, the expansion of the 386s in the market.

Some events, which would influence the future, were occurring even before the 386 was introduced. Early in 1989, Intel displayed the 80486, the more highly integrated variant of the 80386.

Computers using the 486 microprocessor became available during 1989 at reasonable prices. Also, the 80486 provided EISA, a bus standard more suitable for 32-bit processors. (The majority of 386 and 486 computers are still sold with the 16-bit wide AT bus.)

Meanwhile, there's also a variant of the 80486, the 80486SX. It differs from the "true" 486DX because the integrated math coprocessor is inoperable and the microprocessor runs at a lower clock speed.

Operating systems

The operating system of the personal computer has been the DOS (Disk Operating System), developed by Microsoft. DOS was also developed further in parallel with the computer, but even in the most recent version still must fight restrictions that were imposed by the original computer.

Short History of MS-DOS	
Version	**Special characteristics**
1.0 (August 1981)	Operating system based on approximately 4000 program lines, consisting of three files with elementary functions, utility programs, a text-editor and disk-formatting program.
1.1 (May 1982)	Supports double-sided diskettes.
2.0 (March 1983)	Hard drives and hierarchical diskette structure with subdirectories.
2.1/2.11 (October 1983)	International character set.
3.0 (August 1984)	AT diskette format, 1.2 Meg and 20 Meg hard drives.
3.1 (March 1985)	Network compatibility.
3.2 (December 1985)	3.5-inch/720K drives.
3.3 (April 1987)	Hard drives with several partitions, 3.5-inch/1.44 Meg diskettes.
4.0/4.1 November 1988	Larger hard drive partitions, expanded memory, DOS-shell.
5.0 (June 1991)	Removal of DOS drivers into expanded memory, DOS-shell with limited multitasking, 3 1/2 inch /2.88 Meg diskettes, full-screen editor.
6.0 (March 1993)	New improved features including Double-space, File transfer, Antivirus, new DOS- backup, Defragmentor

Alternative operating systems, such as OS/2 or UNIX, have been used on only a small portion of the IBM and compatible computers. However, these operating systems appear to make sense, especially on 386 and 486 based computers. They increase the performance of these processors.

1.3 Purchasing a 486

If you're thinking about purchasing a 486 based computer, the following tips should provide some helpful information. We won't discuss alternatives, such as 286 and 386 based computers. However, many 386 based computers are attractive alternatives, especially if cost is an important factor. Because of the reduced price of 386 based computers, we don't recommend purchasing a 286 based computer.

Determining your needs

To select the proper computer, you must consider your requirements. If you want to use a word processor to write letters or simple documents, a 486SX equipped with a monochrome screen is sufficient. However, if you want to set up a system using DTP (Desktop Publishing Programs) for producing newsletters and brochures, you'll need a more powerful and better equipped 486.

Selecting a computer

Evaluate performance tests to become familiar with the computer that will meet your needs the best. You should pay attention not only to the price and performance of the computer, but also to test results relating to durability.

Basic knowledge is vital

Once you've decided that only a true 486 will satisfy your needs, there are still a few important steps to take before purchasing your new computer. Try to learn some basic information, especially if you're a first time buyer. By doing this, you'll know what the seller is talking about and you won't feel "intimidated" by his or her supposed level of "expertise".

To obtain an introductory knowledge level about computers, use the following sources:

- Computer books

- Computer magazines and journals

- Good advice from friends with sufficient computer experience (especially with 486 computers)

Buying options

There are several options for purchasing a computer. We've listed these options, along with their advantages and disadvantages, below:

Mail order

There are firms who advertise in computer publications and ship their computers by mail, either COD, against prepayment, or on open account. The advantage of these sources is low prices, which the shipper is able to offer because of the limited service. Unfortunately, limited service is a disadvantage you must accept. Also, there is usually limited customer support. So, if you place an order with one of these companies, you should know exactly what you want.

Although most mail-order houses are reputable businesses offering the best prices to informed consumers, others are somewhat questionable. Some mail-order house offer very attractive prices for computers and peripheral devices and require prepayment, either by credit card, check, or money order for all purchases. The company takes your money, then informs you there is a problem with your order, but it will be shipped when possible. But your order is never shipped, your inquiries go unanswered, and the company goes out of business. You lose your investment.

So, before dealing with mail order companies, check them out with the Better Business Bureau. Try to talk with someone who has dealt with the company in the past. Don't make your decision solely on a magazine ad. (They might not have paid for the ad.)

TAKE NOTE

Telephone marketing

Dell sells most of its computers by mail with the telephone marketing method. Prior to the purchase, the customer can seek advice by telephone by using an 800 number. The support equals that offered by a normal dealer; there is free 24-hour service for one year after purchase. As a result, Dell isn't as cheap as some mail-order shippers.

Wholesaler or department store

The wholesaler or department store is another possibility in which computers are sold along with many other items. Since these stores sell more than just computers, the service and support are usually very limited.

Specialized dealers

Specialized dealers sell only computers. However, there are various types of dealers. Generally you can obtain competent advice and service from specialized dealers (some very good firms even work out of their homes). Unfortunately, they cannot offer any real bargains, since advice and service don't come free. However, there are computer dealers that can provide cheaper computers ("discounters") but you must know what you want because only limited service is available.

Computer leasing

For relatively large items, such as the 486 computer, leasing is another alternative. With leasing, the customer pays only for the depreciation of the computer and can, on expiration of the term of the lease, either purchase a new computer or buy the computer for its salvage value.

Guarantee and warranty

Many people don't know the difference between the terms "guarantee" and "warranty". The guarantee on a computer is the assurance from the manufacturer but the warranty is the responsibility of the seller/dealer. In this case, you have three options:

1. Demand that the dealer take the computer back and refund the purchasing price (annulment).

2. Demand the dealer refund to you a part of the purchase price because a defective unit isn't worth as much as one that's intact (depreciation).

3. Have the dealer fix the computer.

Normally the dealer has the option of repairing the computer twice before he is obliged to accept annulment or depreciation, but this may vary depending on the state law and the dealer.

The guarantee is the responsibility of the manufacturer. However, you should always refer to the warranty first. Also, the guarantee usually covers only the defective parts; the cost of the labor is usually paid by the customer. To protect your rights, you should always complete and mail the registration card or guarantee certificate as indicated at the time of purchase. This also applies to any software you may purchase with the computer.

After purchase

When you unpack your computer, ensure that all the items listed in the manual are present. A power cord and a manual are both part of the package and should be included in the price. Determine whether your computer corresponds to the quality of the equipment you bought (i.e., what's described in the purchase agreement).

1.4 Ergonomics

The concept of "ergonomics" relates to the best possible interactive adaptation of man and the materials with which he works. This includes the proper installation of a computer system. The longer you work in front of the screen, the more important this becomes.

Any stress resulting from an unergonomic arrangement of computer components eventually grows from a minor annoyance to a major concern. So, carefully select the place where the computer will be installed and the furniture for your computer system.

Shopping for computer furniture

Usually computers, along with their components, are simply placed on a desk. However, if possible, you should use furniture specifically designed for computers.

This is important because standard desks are about 28 inches high. This is too high for working at the keyboard for a long period of time. The most comfortable position for typing is to have your arms bent at a right angle; your lower arms should be horizontal with the floor and should be only 25 inches above the floor. So, the computer keyboard should be placed on a surface that's 25 inches above the floor. To accommodate different individuals, this height should be adjustable.

A suitable chair is also important. The best chairs are movable, which makes it possible to move to other locations quickly. Arm rests provide additional support for the arms. This becomes obvious after long periods of activity before the screen. Many computer desks also have a rest for the lower portion of the hands and wrists, which provides additional relief and helps to prevent carpal tunnel syndrome.

An alternative to conventional office chairs is the posture chair. Instead of resting only on the spine, the weight of the body is also partially transferred to the knees. This type of chair takes some time to get used to and depends on personal preferences. However, it's recommended for health reasons because the correct posture arrangement greatly reduces fatigue.

Light and shadow

Installing computers and furniture

Once you've selected the proper computer furniture, you must determine the proper installation of your computer. A monitor has a glass screen that reflects external light sources, which may lead to unnecessary distraction. The computer table shouldn't face a window. The light in the room should not come from a single lamp, but from several light sources, which can be switched on and off as needed.

The screen should be positioned horizontally to your line of vision so you don't have to turn your head or tilt your head up or down to see the screen.

The viewing distance doesn't depend only on the size of the screen. It's also important to consider the size of the characters displayed on the screen. Usually, the optimal viewing distance is about 19 inches but the actual distance may vary depending on the individual.

There are other factors that are also important to ergonomics. Ideally, the image on your monitor shouldn't flicker. The monitor should have a non-reflective screen that has adjustable brightness and contrast. It's also very important that the monitor produce a very low level of radiation. A screen filter is also helpful because it protects you from static and glare.

You should set up the system so operating the keyboard and the disk drives doesn't require stretching (i.e., everything should be within easy reach). Also, the peripherals shouldn't be too far away. Ensure that the keyboard cable is long enough so it can be moved when necessary.

Breaks are important

Even when all ergonomic needs have been met, working at a computer for long periods of time can be physically stressful. So, you should take breaks and alternate between working with your computer and performing other non-computer related tasks.

Chapter 2

System Unit

The heart of a 486 is the system unit. It contains the motherboard with the microprocessor, the memory, the graphics card, the interfaces, and any other components. The system unit also contains the mass storage device, which stores data even after the computer has been switched off.

The principal structure of a computer system is always the same, regardless of the type of housing or structure of the motherboard that's used to accommodate the 486. The system unit always forms the heart of a computer. This is true even in special cases, such as portable computers (laptops, notebooks, etc.); this doesn't include the two primary input and output devices (keyboard and screen). You should take advantage of this and search out these components just as thoroughly as the computer itself.

There are also certain features that are so typical of computers that they are essential in all computers. One example is the Reset button.

Reset button

The Reset button is probably the most destructive element in the entire computer world. This button places the computer in its booting mode. Unfortunately, this is frequently necessary because programs can cause the computer to "hang" (i.e., stop without reason and no longer accept input). Resetting the computer is more gentle than using the on/off switch, which can cause a surge of electricity through the system.

2.1 Cases

A review of case types

A case is supposed to "package" the most diverse computer components in a visually pleasing way. These components include different types of system architecture (modular or highly integrated), different formats for the diskette drives and hard drive, and numerous system extensions.

Several case types have been developed; these can be placed into six categories:

- The classic desktop case

- The compact desktop case (mini-desktop)

- The mini-tower

- "Normal size" tower

- Laptops, notebooks, and portables

- Specially designed shapes

Size comparison of desktop, mini-, and standard tower units

Desktop cases

Although the standard desktop case is still the most popular case type, they are being used less frequently for 486 and 486SX computers. Desktop cases are the standard form of a computer's external appearance. The monitor is usually placed on top of the case to save space.

External similarities

Because of ergonomics, a few features, which are identical in all desktop cases, have become important. For example, the disk drives are always positioned to the right because most users insert diskettes with their right hand. The hard drive is placed to the right, between the drives or isn't visible at all in the center of the case. Sometimes smaller hard drives are located elsewhere in the case.

Expansion slots to the left and behind

Instead of being located on the motherboard, the electronics for the interfaces and graphics of many 486s are placed in the plug-in slots of another card. The capabilities of the computer can also be extended by using expansion cards in these slots.

The plug-in slots in nearly all desktop models are located at the back and to the left. Correspondingly, the outside connectors of some of the cards positioned here are also located at the back of the case, to the left.

Internal differences

The similarities between the desktop cases of different computers ends with the position of the disk drives and expansion slots. Depending on whether the computer is highly integrated or modular, the sockets for connecting external system components (monitor, keyboard, etc.) are located in various locations.

The cases are also opened differently. For example, there are flip-top cases, which are removed in an upward direction once the screws have been removed.

486 systems are purposely designed so you can easily access the system's hardware. So, if you're willing to install expansion items yourself, you can save a lot of money. Obviously, you should consult your dealer for help with sensitive and complicated expansion cards.

The motherboard in desktop units is generally mounted against the bottom of the case. The power supply is at the rear, to the right. Either a well isolated cable leads from it forward to the On/Off switch or the computer can be switched on or off by using a switch that's mounted on the power supply itself.

Mini-desktop

Space-saving cases

A variation of the classic desktop case is the mini-desktop case. The external features of this case are almost identical to a normal desktop case except that the dimensions are more compact. A mini-desktop computer isn't much larger than its monitor.

So, the expansion capabilities of these small cases is often limited. More than the available mass memory cannot be built into the housing; even the expansion slots are limited to a maximum of three slots. In many cases, these plug-in expansion cards are mounted in the case horizontally (i.e., parallel to the motherboard).

Tower cases

Upright operation

Some users don't like placing the computer on their desks. So, they place it on the floor beneath or next to the desk. This is helpful when you don't have enough space on your desk.

QUICK TIP

Standing a desktop case on its edge doesn't affect the operation of the electronic components; even hard drives and disk drives can usually be placed upright. However, you shouldn't use the upright position if your system includes a CD-ROM drive with a drawer.

Reasons for the tower

Many users immediately begin with a tower (i.e., a tower case, in which the 486 stands on its edge). This type of case was developed to meet the needs of users who want to turn their computers upright because this arrangement is more professional and saves space.

Also, often the various system components of a powerful computer can no longer fit in a desktop case.

A tower is usually designed to be located under a desk or table, on the floor. With this type of tower, the controls and mass storage are always located as high as possible so the user doesn't have to bend over. However, everything else is rotated 90 degrees from the normal position on a desktop case.

What it looks like inside

The motherboard in a tower is mounted on one of the walls instead of on the floor of the case. For repairs or expansions, a side panel is removed. A tall tower generally has enough space for the various mass storage units.

There is a lot of space even inside a "mini-tower". However, sometimes the 5.25-inch drives must be positioned vertically in narrow cases. Instead of being inserted in the upright position as in a desktop case, expansion cards are inserted horizontally in a tower.

Mini-towers

Mid-sized cases

The mini-tower is a compromise between the desktop and tower cases. A mini-tower is a tower that's no taller than the monitor and can be placed beside it. Most mini-towers are wide enough to accommodate the 3.5-inch and 5.25-inch drives horizontally. In the mini-tower, the motherboard is mounted on its side and the plug-in cards are horizontal.

Laptops and portables

Portable computers

For many users, the portable computer has become a necessity. These computers are widely used by sales representatives and journalists, for example. Notebook and laptop computers are the two general types of portable computers. However, in our discussion of portable computers, notebook and laptop computers will be considered the same type.

Laptop characteristics

A laptop is a portable computer, in which all the essential components are enclosed within a case that's about the size of a briefcase or notebook. The keyboard is part of the console and is very compact. The display screen can be folded down to cover the keyboard when the computer is closed for transportation or storage.

Users that need access to a computer even while traveling use notebook and laptop computers. Since most laptops can be operated with battery power, electrical outlets aren't needed.

Laptop computer

System-dependent disadvantages

Unfortunately, because of the compactness of the laptops, some compromises must be made. The size and style of the keyboard is usually different than AT or MF2 keyboards.

Generally, only an alphanumeric keypad is available. The function keys are usually arranged along the top of the keyboard and a separate numeric or function keypad isn't available. The keys are positioned slightly higher than on a standard keyboard.

Even the mass storage devices must be adapted to the requirements of compactness and portability. On laptops, 3.5-inch drives are always used. Most laptops usually have a hard drive.

Laptop peculiarities

Many laptop manufacturers have had to use tricks to optimally use the available resources. Among these tricks is a screensaver that automatically shuts off the background display of the screen during long periods of inactivity.

An intelligent current switch may be used to switch off the hard drive whenever it isn't accessed for a relatively long period of time. Both of these options conserve precious battery power.

In its computers, Toshiba uses batteries that are easy to change. The contents of the memory are buffered by supplementary batteries to prevent the contents from being lost during battery changes. The computer often doesn't even have to be switched off for this operation.

Portable characteristics

With portable computers, the emphasis is usually on moving a highly integrated computer system from one location to another instead of actually using the computer while traveling. Portable computers have a normal size keyboard that can be detached from the unit and they usually have external 5.25-inch disk drives.

Notebook and palmtop computers

Notebooks and palmtops are even smaller than laptops and portables. Although notebook computers occupy the same amount of space as a piece of notebook paper, they are equivalent to a laptop.

A palmtop, however, is much smaller. When closed, these computers aren't much larger than your hand. Although notebook computers are always equipped with hard drives, disk drives and normal sized keyboards, the style and performance of a palmtop can vary.

Designer cases

To give modern computers a more modern look, a few manufacturers have tried to create a better design for their cases. Computer cases have been designed in the form of a pyramid and even a brick. However, variations of the standard cases are increasingly being praised by users. Unfortunately, a better design usually means a higher price.

The Kyocera Multilight series

The Tandy and the Kyocera Multilight IIIsx (see photograph) above are two examples of a particularly compact case form and good design. The Radio Shack Tandy computer, as an AT, has been available for a relatively long time. Recently it became available as a 486SX computer with an integrated CD-ROM drive.

The Kyocera Multilight has its own design team. In this computer, the keyboard and mouse are integrated for the best possible ergonomic results.

The components of a computer

The complete system

The components located within the case (internal devices) and those attached to the outside (external devices) form a complete system. The system may contain a combination of the following parts:

• Power supply	• Motherboard
• Plug-in cards	• Diskette drives
• Hard drive	

The position of the components differs, depending on the type of case and the type of computer. We discussed the primary structure in the section on the different types of cases.

2.2 Motherboard

The most important component of the motherboard is the main processor. Its either on the motherboard or plugged into the motherboard via a processor plug-in card. Many upgradeable computer models have a processor plug-in card.

The main processor, also called the CPU (Central Processing Unit), is the heart of a computer and is responsible for the performance of the computer. In a 486 computer, the CPU is, as the name indicates, an 80486-processor from Intel. It's abbreviated as the "i486".

The i486-processor is a highly integrated unit with approximately 1.2 million transistors. Its registers, as well as its data bus, are 32-bits wide. It consists of four components:

- 80386-compatible processor unit

- 80387-compatible arithmetic unit

- 82385 cache controller

- Two 4K cache memory

Performance and output comparison

The structure of the main processor alone doesn't determine the performance of the computer. The clock speed, the structure of the motherboard (also called the main board), as well as the interface with the peripheral devices (e.g., the screen or graphics card) are also important.

It's very easy to determine a car's performance. Simply compare the horsepower or mileage figures. However, how can you determine the performance or speed of a computer?

The speed and performance of the main processor is only one aspect to consider. You must also consider the rate of data transfer between the system components and also the availability of a coprocessor.

It's difficult to compare the overall performance of a system because different system improvements increase the system's performance.

Adding a coprocessor or even two coprocessors accelerates a program, such as a CAD program, that executes many numerical calculations. A faster hard drive controller will increase the performance of database applications.

Generally, the characteristics of a computer are used by programs in varying degrees. Whether a given program runs faster on a computer with a faster processor or on another computer with a faster hard drive, is usually hard to determine.

It's very difficult to rank computers according to performance. Predicting the performance of a computer based on its technical data is just as difficult.

This uncertainty can be partially eliminated by running benchmark programs (evaluation programs) on the computers you want to compare. A benchmark program is a standard program for comparing computers.

Benchmark tests

Each user and each program emphasizes different aspects of computer performance, which results in performance evaluations. Different standards have been developed according to use. These differences led to the development of different benchmark programs. The data from the various benchmark tests can be used as references. You can determine the speed with which a certain application runs only by actually working with the computer.

There are ways to optimize the performance of a system. These methods can involve hardware, such as equipping the computer with more RAM or software.

The following table provides an overview of some of the popular benchmark programs. The performance data from these tests are standardized and refer to an IBM AT with a clock speed of 8 MHz. This computer has a performance factor of 1.

Comparing Benchmark Test Programs	
Test name	**Performance area measured by the test data**
Landmark speed	Clock speed at which an AT would have to run to deliver the same performance as the computer tested.
Whetstone test	Test of the speed with which numerical calculations are executed; of predictive value with regard to CAD applications. The result is given in whetstones per second.
Dhrystone	Standard benchmark program testing several aspects of general computer operation. Only floating point arithmetic is not tested by dhrystone.

Computer architecture - types of motherboards

Besides the processor's performance, the working speed of the system is determined by the structure of the motherboard. The most important characteristic is the rate of data transfer between the individual components of the computer system. Data is transferred over the data bus, whose resolution (the number of simultaneously transferable data units) and clock speed (the frequency of transfer measured against time) significantly affect the speed. The address bus, however, doesn't directly influence the speed. However, its size provides some information, at least indirectly, about the maximum memory size.

The AT series (Advanced Technology) introduced by IBM established a standard for personal computers. The AT data bus has a 16-bit wide data bus and an address bus with a 24-bit width. This is practically the standard for personal computers with an 80286 or 80386 processor.

The ISA bus

The computer manufacturers competing with IBM retained most of the AT architecture and called the bus system for their motherboard the ISA bus (Industrial Standard Architecture). The 16 data lines of the ISA bus can transfer a maximum of 8 Meg per second. With the 24 address lines, it's possible to directly address up to 16 Meg.

The EISA bus

The newly developed EISA (Extended Industrial Standard Architecture) bus system has bus master capabilities. This means that the main processor doesn't necessarily have to participate in actions on the bus. For example, an EISA network controller can exchange data directly with memory (RAM). In this case, it has complete control of the bus.

The function division made possible by the EISA technology naturally led to a changed motherboard structure. Since the main processor no longer had the central controlling function for the system bus, it could be removed from the motherboard and placed on a special processor board. This created an open architecture with which it's possible to integrate new processor developments by inserting a plug-in card.

Three motherboard structures are currently used for 486 computer systems. These structures include the following:

- Standard board

- Highly integrated motherboard

- The passive backplane board structure

The highly integrated motherboard architecture is derived from laptop technology, which tries to produce a computer system that occupies as little space as possible. This compact technology is also used in very high-performance workstation computers that are equipped with 486 processors. In this case, the capacity to upgrade the computer with expansion cards or drives wasn't important because they were designed for network use more than for standard applications.

Passive backplane

The third most popular motherboard structure, called passive backplane, is a very open computer architecture. In this case, essentially only the bus system with the structural components needed for bus control and controllers, as well as a basic complement of working memory are located on the motherboard.

The main processor is on its own processor card, which is attached to the motherboard with a plug-in slot. So, new processor developments can be incorporated into this system by simply changing the processor card. These systems often have numerous plug-in slots for expansion cards. So, they are suitable for use as main computers for networks, which are also called file servers.

The development and introduction of the EISA bus took place at the same time the i486 was introduced. The 486 computers were to be delivered with the AT or the EISA bus architecture. Because the EISA bus architecture wasn't available to all computer manufacturers yet, the first 486 computers were equipped with the ISA-bus to get them on the market quickly.

With the newly developed EISA bus now available, computer manufacturers have many more possibilities available for varying computer architecture on the motherboards.

The difference between 386 and 486 systems

One difference between the 386 and 486 computers is that the 486 chip already has an integrated coprocessor (Intel 80387). So this component is no longer on the motherboard and joined to the main processor via bus lines.

Also, the 80486 chip has an 8K onboard memory and an associated 80385 cache controller. Unlike a 386 computer, this component no longer needs to be designed onto the motherboard.

Although up until the introduction of the 80486 processor and the new EISA bus, all 386-equipped computers were integrated on a motherboard with the AT or ISA bus, there are now also 386 computers with the EISA technology.

So, it's possible to use the 32-bit data width on the motherboard in both the 80386 and 80486 processors. This has also led to a new type of program that takes advantage of the 32-bit technology used in the computer.

The Compaq Systempro - A concept for open computer architecture

Compaq's Systempro, which was introduced at the same time as the first i486 computer, set a new performance standard because of its innovative technology. It's one of the first computers capable of multiprocessing.

FLEX/MP architecture

The Systempro is based on Compaq's proprietary FLEX/MP (Flexible Advanced System Architecture with Multiprocessing Support) architecture. This allows you to use two main processors, each on its own plug-in processor card.

The standard Systempro is delivered with 4 Meg of memory but can be equipped with up to 256 Meg. It has eleven expansion slots, of which seven are 8/16/32-bit EISA slots. The remaining four can be used for a 32-bit processor or 32-bit memory plug-in cards.

With a 32-bit IDA (Intelligent Disk Adapter) controller, it's possible to support up to four drive arrays (i.e., the memory capacity of the hard drives amounts to more than 1.5 gigabytes). Compaq designed Systempro primarily as a network server and multiuser host.

Double processor computers

Conventional computer architecture is based on a single microprocessor. Since the introduction of the i486 and i860 processors by Intel, it's now also possible to build computers according to the industry standard, which can use several microprocessors simultaneously.

All the processors developed by Intel, beginning with the 8088 through the 80286 and 80386 to the 80486, are completely downwardly-compatible with each other. So, an 80486 processor can run the object code written for the 8088 without any errors. All these processors, which are called CISC (Complete Instruction Set Computer) processors, have a very comprehensive instruction set.

However, this doesn't apply to the i860. Although this processor can execute only a limited set of instructions, it's much faster because it has approximately the same integration density as the i486. Certain applications, for example processing graphics data, don't require the complete set of operating system commands.

Because of this, processors running these applications are much more efficient. These processors, which support less than the complete set of commands, are also called RISC (Reduced Instruction Set Computer) processors.

One of the first computers equipped with this multiprocessor technology was introduced by BORSU at the 1990 CeBit (an international computer show). This computer is called the BORSU 4860. The two microprocessors in this computer, i486 and i860, were combined on a single motherboard. This resulted in an authentic multiprocessor operating mode, which is compatible with the IBM PC.

Frame buffer

A special internal CPU bus with a 64-bit width enabled internal data exchange between the two processors, the conventional memory, and the peripherals. The frame buffer, which is a special graphics system, is also attached to this bus. This is needed because the i860 must directly access this memory card.

With this graphics system, it's possible to display 65,536 colors with a resolution of 1,260 x 1,024 or 1,152 x 960 pixels. Since the i860 processor was specially designed for graphics applications and can access the graphics card directly, the result is high performance graphics.

A minimum of 4 Meg and a maximum of 64 Meg of memory is supplied. Upgrading is accomplished with SIMM modules. The external bus, according to the EISA specification, takes over the connection possibilities for the peripherals.

The Intel chip set consisting of the 82357 and 82358 effects the connection between the internal bus and external bus, as the EISA bus controller. There are eight plug-in slots available on the motherboard. Six of these are able to act as bus master. Another 8-bit plug-in slot with the ISA specification and the 64-bit wide slot for the frame buffer is also available.

Also available on the motherboard are one parallel, two serial, and one mouse port. A Weitek 4167 floating-point processor can be added for special applications.

2.3 Basic Components of The i486

In this section, we'll discuss the i486 in detail. Although you may think this information is too technical, you should have some basic knowledge of these principles.

Obviously the main reason for the development of the i80486 by Intel was the comprehensive and large amount of DOS software. The 168 pin microchip contains approximately 1.2 million transistors, assembled on a chip surface of about 1.7 cm^2.

This extremely high integration density of millions of components on a minuscule surface was made possible by the CMOS-IV manufacturing process developed by Intel.

This high-tech method of manufacturing permits the production of structures in the 1 micron (= 1 µm or 10^{-6} m) range (1 m = one million µm). In comparison, a human hair has a thickness about 100 times as great and would cover more than 100 of such microstructures.

The microchip is located in a 44.83 mm x 44.83 mm PGA ceramic housing. The maximum current consumption of the i486 processor is 3.8 A.

Because of this ability to manufacture such tiny microstructures, a very high degree of integration of the individual components is possible. This in turn produces shorter data lines and results in smaller capacities in the microstructure lines. Capacities are generated during data transport by changes in line current that retard the flow of the digital impulses. This delay must be kept smaller than the clock speed at which the data are moved along the line to prevent transmission errors.

Obviously, a reduction in the line and current capacities inside the processor is an important prerequisite for increasing clock speed. The i486 is currently available in versions with speeds of 25 MHz, 33 MHz, and 40 MHz. Soon versions with clock speeds 50 MHz and beyond will be available.

CISC architecture

The i486 represents an extremely successful synthesis between two opposite structural principles for microprocessors. Because the i486 has a 100% binary compatibility with the earlier microprocessors of this series, a CISC (Complete Instruction Set Computer) architecture is possible. It understands all the computer instructions of its predecessors like the 80286 and 8088. Since complete downward compatibility has been maintained, it's possible for software developed for the 8088 to run on the i486.

However, because of its 342 different instructions, the i486 has one of the most complex processor architecture's possible today. Its complete instruction set and downward compatibility ensures that software written for computers in this series can be used. So, software doesn't have to be written especially for the i486.

RISC architecture

The most frequently used instructions execute in a single clock cycle. This means, for example, that only one clock cycle is needed to load data into a register, to add registers, or to compare them. This speed is usually achieved only by microprocessors with RISC (Reduced Instruction Set Computer) architecture. However, RISC microprocessors don't have the richness and complexity of commands needed for applications like 3-D graphics.

The i486 combines the advantages of the two computer architecture principles, language complexity, and instructions with the speed of special processors. With the i486/33 MHz it's possible to achieve a maximum transfer rate on the data bus of 106 Meg per second.

Performance

If you compare the calculating speeds of the i486 chip with the performance capability of other computers, you may wonder whether the i486 should be considered a personal computer.

The i486 processor, at a clock speed of 25 MHz, has a calculating speed of 37,000 Dhrystones per second and more than 6.1 million Whetstones per second with double precision. The processing speed is between 15 and 20 million VAX-MIPS (Millions of Instructions per Second).

The 33 MHz version has a processing speed between 20 and 25 VAX-MIPS. The term VAX-MIPS provides a standard of comparison and a point of reference with respect to the famous high-performance VAX 11/788 computer from Digital Equipment Corporation.

FLOPS

MIPS represents only one expression for the processing speed of the microprocessor. You must know the index called FLOPS (Floating Point Operations per Second) to determine the performance of a system. This value is an index of the calculating performance of graphics functions or of scientific/engineering calculations.

The 80386 microprocessor, with its 80387 coprocessor, has about 50,000 FLOPS. With the i486, this amount increases to approximately 400,000 FLOPS, which is about eight times the floating point performance.

WT 1167 math coprocessor

Coupling a 80386 and 80387 processor requires the external bus for data transfer between the processors. This external bus, which becomes a bottleneck, is no longer needed in the i486. Besides the 80387 coprocessor developed by Intel, the WT 1167 math coprocessor marketed by Weitek, which offers significantly improved performance, is also available.

WT 4167

Weitek also has developed a coprocessor especially for the i486, called the WT 4167. Calculation-intensive applications run two to three times faster with this coprocessor installed in an i486 computer.

Prime Computer is trying to market a version of an i486 microprocessor with a processing speed of 100 MIPS. The logic of the i486 processor is realized in terms of ECL (Emitted Coupler Logic) technology and offered as a module assembled on a board with dimensions of 25 x 80 cm. The ECL is currently the fastest microprocessor technology available. It permits clock speeds in excess of 150 MHz.

The performance of the ECL 80486, compared to the version with a clock speed of 33 MHz, is increased by a factor of 5. Intel plans to enter areas of the market previously reserved for mainframe computers with this supercharged version of the 80486.

The four-in-one structure

The architecture of the 80486 microprocessor integrates four components, which have been available only on separate microchips, into a single unit. These components are:

- 80386-compatible processor unit

- 80387-compatible numeric coprocessor

- Cache controller modified into an 82385

- Two 4KBytes cache memory

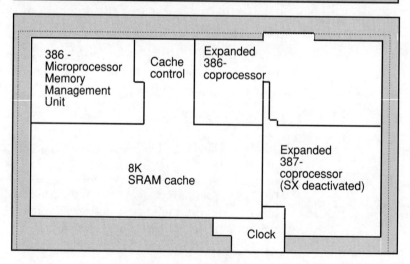

Surface plan of 80486 chip

Because of the CISC architecture in the i486, the 8086/8088 compatible real mode and 80286 compatible protected mode memory access mechanisms, which are needed for multitasking operations, are available to the processor, as with the 80386. The 80386 operating modes, such as "native mode" and "virtual mode", are also available.

New additions include a few status bits and six commands, which support the multiprocessor technology. The i486 has a 32-bit microprocessor architecture and consists of nine functional units.

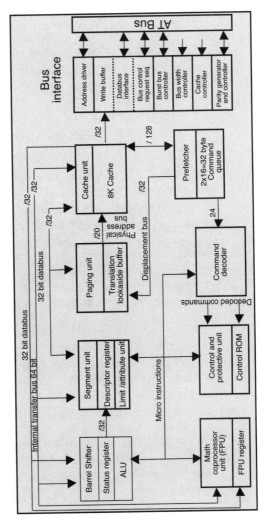

Block diagram of the 80486 processor

The interface for the mass storage units and the interface components of an i486 computer form the bus interface. The 32-bit data bus contains the address lines and the four bus control lines. With these 32 lines it's possible to address 2^{32} or 4 gigabytes (4 billion bytes).

If the processor is run in the virtual mode, 64 terabytes (64,000 billion bytes) can be addressed virtually. Another advantage of this address bus is that it can operate bidirectionally. So, it can not only pass addresses but can also read external addresses.

The internal bus structure is redesigned to perform better. The most important units in the i486 (the ALU, FPU, and cache) are connected to two 32-bit wide data buses. The external bus, which is a hindrance with the 80386 and 80387, was avoided.

The cache memory and the FPU have a 128-bit wide path. So they guarantee a rapid transfer rate for data and instructions. The instruction queue was also expanded to 32 bytes.

The i486 has an onboard clock. A simple pulse generator, which generates a square wave signal, is attached to the frequency input of the i486 chip.

The 80386, however, uses an externally generated clock frequency, which is divided by two, to drive the processor. An 80386 processor driven at 20 MHz requires an external frequency generator that's capable of producing a frequency of 40 MHz.

This is necessary to maintain a balanced duty cycle ratio of 50/50 because only the rising (positive) edge of the clock signal is used to generate the output signal and thus the processor frequency. The i486 uses both edges of the rectangular clock signal to calculate the output signal.

As with all microprocessors, the conventional bus system in the i486 is subdivided into data, address, and control buses. When the 80386 processor is used, you can choose between a 16-bit and a 32-bit wide data bus. In addition to the 16- and 32-bit busses, other bus widths are available with the i486.

The bus interface of the i486 closely corresponds to the 80386. The 80386 operates with a two clock pulse cycle. The bus system of the i486 possesses a single pulse cycle, which allows for a faster system.

An on-chip cache

With memory-intensive applications, such as those involving technical or scientific calculations or CAD programs, the memory access time can sometimes become noticeable. At these times, cache memory is helpful.

A cache enables wait-state-free access to conventional memory. So the microprocessor requires no wait states, as the waiting cycles are called, to receive data from conventional memory.

The conventional memory in a computer usually consists of dynamic memory chips or DRAM chips. These chips require an access time of 100ns or 80ns. However, sometimes only 70 ns (nanoseconds) are needed.

A microprocessor running at a frequency of 10 MHz cannot execute two memory accesses, in immediate succession, to the same 100 nanosecond chip. The memory chip needs time to stabilize before the next address can be accessed. The microprocessor must therefore sit through a few wait loops. This means that it's forced to do nothing for a few clock cycles.

SRAM

By using faster static memory elements called SRAM, these forced waiting periods can be avoided. Unfortunately, these units cost much more than the dynamic chips.

Alternatively, the cache controller can be used to implement communication between the microprocessor and the cache memory (a small amount of memory consisting of static elements). The cache controller also oversees access to the slower DRAM conventional memory.

Cache memory is smaller

Because cache memory is usually much smaller than conventional memory, it requires a very carefully designed method of operation. It contains precisely the data just requested by the processor. This obviously depends partly on the application program.

Measurements made with standard software packages produce success rates in excess of 85 percent, even up to 98 percent, in the case of the i486 computer.

The following table compares a computer with an 80386 processor equipped with an 80387 coprocessor and an i486 computer with regard to the number of clock cycles required for a few operations:

Clock Cycle Comparison of 80386/80387 - 80486		
Task	**80386/ 80387**	**i486**
Read a value from memory	4	1
Write a value to memory	2	1
Transfer a value from one register to another	2	1
Execute a conditional branch	9	3
Conditional branch not executed	3	1
Function call	9	3
Store floating-point value	15 to 20	3

The mixed instruction and data cache, with its 8K memory capacity, is partially responsible for the i486 microprocessor's increased performance. The cache controller with memory occupies a significant portion of the chip. So, Intel wasn't able to integrate the 82385 cache controller with the associated 32K cache memory in the i486.

This cache memory works according to the "buffered write through" write mechanism, which ensures that the data in conventional memory are identical with the cache memory contents. The cache memory of the i486 uses a "pseudo least recently used" or LRU algorithm instead of a 16-bit memory entry.

The cache memory contains 16 bytes, with 128 lines per 2K bank, per line. The LRU process checks the cache lines. If the microprocessor notices that a cache line is rarely used, data is exchanged. This ensures there won't be any unnecessary data in the cache memory.

The transfer of data from and to the cache memory occurs in burst mode. This requires four 32-bit accesses to the address bus to replace a complete cache-memory line with 16 bytes. In the burst mode, the microprocessor must set the initial address only once and is then able to read or write four bytes in a single clock cycle.

This transfer procedure can then be repeated up to four times, without explicitly setting the next address. The only prerequisite is that the data values are located in successive addresses. This access method permits a microprocessor running at 25 MHz to achieve data transfer rates of:

$$\frac{25 \text{ MHz}}{5 \text{ pulses}} \text{ X } 16 \text{ bytes } = 80 \text{ Mb/s}$$

In the case of a 33 MHz microprocessor, a burst speed of 106.5 Mb/s is achieved.

Although the "buffered write through" method, which maintains a balance between conventional memory and cache memory, is time-consuming, it ensures the consistency of cache memory and conventional memory in single-microprocessor systems.

If a multi-microprocessor system is operated according to the same method, the data bus traffic joining all microprocessor cache memory and conventional memory would become jammed. Obviously this would undermine any possible performance improvements of using several microprocessors.

"Writeback" strategy

To solve this problem, a special "writeback" cache strategy is used. Not every write operation, of the microprocessor, to the associated cache memory leads to a write operation in conventional memory.

As long as a microprocessor writes in addresses, whose data only it has in its cache memory, there isn't a writeback. The corresponding address in the cache is considered modified.

Whenever a microprocessor obtains data in its cache memory, the data bus is checked to determine whether the accessed address is characterized as modified in another cache memory. If it is, the address is read from cache memory.

Suitable for multi-microprocessor systems

Otherwise, it's read from conventional memory. Three of the six new computer instructions are devoted to the consistency of the cache memory. This makes the i486 perfectly suitable for constructing multi-microprocessor systems.

Another reason for the significant performance increase of the i486 over the 80386 is the five-stage pipeline technology, which permits five commands, at different execution stages, to be processed simultaneously.

The five-stage processing begins with the prefetch unit. This is followed by a two-stage decoding operation, the execution of the instruction, and, as the last step or slot, the writeback slot.

The prefetch stage has a code and a data port joined to the cache memory via a 120-bit wide bus. The two following decoding slots are addressed in parallel over a prefetcher bus.

The first decoding stage determines the operation type and the second determines the address of the operand. Because the operations of the two stages overlap, one instruction per clock pulse is decoded. Collisions caused by hardware interlocks are avoided.

For example, if a second instruction requires the result of the first instruction, the first decoding stage must wait until the result is available. A multiplexer makes this result instantly available to the ALU (Arithmetic and Logic Unit).

Gate arrays

The following illustration shows a block diagram of a computer system with the i486 microprocessor. This is a UNIX system with 8 Meg of memory and a corresponding DRAM controller. The total system can be built with standard components.

The 82380 DMA controller is responsible for rapid data transfer between the motherboard and the microprocessor. It also controls various peripheral devices.

The 82077 floppy disk controller is 100% hardware-compatible with the AT computer. The RAM controller is controlled over four lines by the i486. Internal connections in the DRAM controller produce four series outlets or CAS (Column Address Strobe) outlets, connected directly with the DRAM. The four line outlets or RAS (Row Address Strobe) outlets determine the respective line.

Through the column and row addresses, it's possible to reach a specific memory cell, of the conventional memory, that's composed of eight 8 x 1M x 1 DRAM chips. Faster access times within a line are possible if only the column address must be accepted.

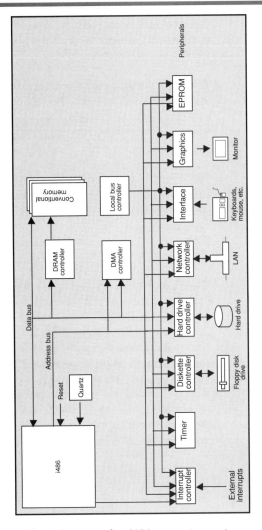

Block diagram of a i486 computer system

Preview of new microprocessors

Around the same time the i486 was being introduced to the public, Intel introduced the 80860 RISC microprocessor. This chip, produced with the same technology as the i486, also exhibits a high degree of integration. Compared to the i486, the instruction set of the 80860 microprocessor is limited.

It was developed for specific applications and has three independent calculation units linked by a data bus with a width of 128 bits and an instruction bus with a 64-bit width.

The computation units are designated as a floating-point multiplication unit, a floating-point addition unit, and a graphics unit, respectively.

The i860 is designed for scientific and engineering computations and CAD applications. The i860, with a clock speed of 40 MHz, can process 40 million integer instructions and 80 million floating-point instructions in a single second because of its parallel architecture.

The result is a maximum floating-point performance of 80 MFLOPS and a system performance of 120 MIPS. The planning phase of the i486's successor is over. The Intel 80586 (or i586) will be a 64-bit microprocessor.

The Intel 80486SX

The recently introduced small format version of the i486, the Intel 80486SX, is connected to the outer world by a 32-bit data bus, like its larger brother.

The layout corresponds to the 486DX, except that the 486SX doesn't have a math coprocessor because it was removed from the chip. If you need a math coprocessor, the 80487SX can be installed.

The 486SX, like the 486DX, has an 8K cache memory and the associated cache controller. Currently it's only available with clock speeds of 16 MHz, 20 MHz, 25 MHz, and 33 MHz.

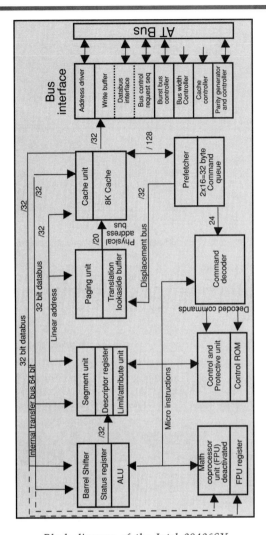

Block diagram of the Intel 80486SX

However, it performs much better than its predecessor, as shown by the following illustration. The 486SX runs about twice as fast as the 386DX microprocessor at about the same clock frequency.

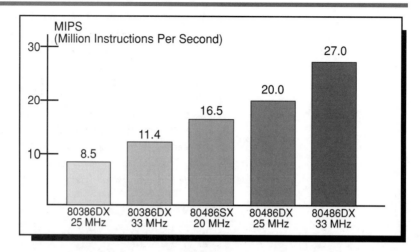

Benchmark test of 32-bit Intel microprocessors

2.4 Understanding Your Hardware

Once you've purchased your 486, you must set up the system and bring it to life. In this section you'll find information that should help you set up your new system easily.

A few hints before unpacking the unit

QUICK TIP

Buy an outlet strip with your unit.

The computer itself isn't the only electrical device you'll be connecting to the electrical outlet. If the monitor isn't attached to the back of the computer case, you'll need an extra outlet. At least one additional outlet will be needed for any output device (printer, plotter, etc.).

You should purchase a multiple-outlet power strip. Many power strips also have built-in circuit breakers and surge protectors to protect your computer. Inexpensive power strips that don't have any built-in protection cost around $10. However, we recommend spending the extra money to purchase a good surge protection power strip with a circuit breaker. This type of protected power strip costs about $30.

It's also possible to switch on all units simultaneously by using a central switch on the outlet strip. Since the individual units are very sturdy, they can easily be switched on simultaneously.

However, more cautious users switch on their computers and attached devices individually (e.g., first the peripherals, such as a printer or modem, and then the computer itself).

Unpack everything

Once you've selected a suitable location, you can unpack your computer. Be sure that all the parts and cables are removed from the packing material. (You should keep the original packing material and box for at least six months in case you have to exchange or return the computer.)

Generally, the procedure for setting up a computer is always the same:

- Unpack the unit

- Check to see that everything is present

- Set up the units

- Connect the various components

- Remove the shipping security devices

- Switch on the units

Usually a washing machine or a stereo system, for example, can be used immediately after completing the steps described above. However, preparing to use a personal computer is slightly more difficult.

Very few computers are delivered ready for use. The user must set it up him/herself. You'll notice this immediately after switching on the computer. In most cases, computers aren't completely configured yet.

A message similar to the following may appear on your screen:

Invalid configuration - Run Setup utility

This message means that you must use the Setup program to set the system configuration parameters.

You may also see the following the message:

No System Disk - Please insert bootable Disk

In this case, the system data is present, but the hard drive hasn't been formatted, partitioned, and loaded with the operating system.

The open system

The personal computer is an "open" system. This means that computers can be expanded in all directions. For example, if you want to install a second floppy disk drive at a later date, you can do so easily. Some day you may discover that your hard drive is no longer adequate. You can expand your system by installing an additional drive or even exchange the present hard drive for a larger one.

Installing expansions

Once you've opened the case to your computer, you'll see the slots where graphics cards or cards for additional devices can be installed. The variety of expansion cards is virtually unlimited. However, you can install these expansion cards without expensive tools and electronics knowledge. With some manual dexterity and common sense, you can install most devices on your computer. We'll present the general steps for installing expansion cards.

The limits of do-it-yourself

However, we must also remind you of your own limitations. Although installing expansion cards is easy, it's not for everyone. Anyone lacking manual dexterity or impatient or nervous individuals should stay away from the hardware. There are also parts of the computer, such as the power supply, on which you shouldn't work.

You'll need the following tools:

- Phillips screwdrivers   • Screwdrivers
- Needle nose pliers   • Tweezers
- Jeweler's screwdrivers

Before opening the computer you must:

1. Park the hard drive.
2. Switch off the computer.

> 3. First remove the power cable from the outlet, then the plug from the back of the computer.
>
> 4. Remove the keyboard cable and all connections to external devices (monitor, printer, etc.).

Location and care are important

Place the computer on an empty table with enough work space. Work carefully and use the proper tools. Phillips head screws should be removed only with the proper screwdriver. The flat-headed screwdriver, which is intended for slotted screws, will ruin Phillips head screws and the blade will be damaged.

If you do a lot of installation work, an electric screwdriver may be a wise investment. Ensure that the torque setting is at the lowest level and stop once the screw is snug.

Case

To access the inside of a 486 (or any other computer), first you must open the case. Since there are various types of cases used for 486s, we'll describe only a few. A flip-top case is the easiest to open. Some 486es' boards may be installed in leftover AT cases, but we aren't aware of any 486s sold like this.

Desktop cases

There are two types of desktop cases. In the first type, the screws are located in the back. Both the screws on the top right and top left sides, and one in the middle of the top must be removed. Then to remove the case, pull forward and up. When it's time to close the system again, ensure that the switches and keys at the front operate properly.

In the second type of desktop case, the top of the computer case is attached to the bottom by two screws on either side. Once these are removed, the cover is usually pushed back along a track.

Mini-tower

One of the most popular mini-tower cases is the one shown in the following illustration. The upper part of the case must be removed to install additional expansion components. First you must remove three screws at the back of the computer. These are located at the top, in the center, as well as to the right and to the left. The upper part, together with the front, must then be pushed forward.

The best method is to get a grip on the upper part with your fingers and then push on the floppy drives with your thumbs. When replacing the cover, ensure that you don't tilt it out of alignment when you push it back. Also, make sure that the On/Off switch and the Reset button operate properly.

The following photograph shows a typical mini-tower. It has a two-part, seven-segment display with the floppy drives positioned further down in the case.

An example of a mini-tower

In the mini-tower case above there is a clock frequency indicator that consists of two LCD 7-segment displays. This indicator can be set to any value by using a jumper. Seven groups of four solder pins each are located beside the two-position 7-segment displays. Each of these four-member groups is associated with one of the 14 segments. This arrangement is shown in the following illustration.

TAKE NOTE

In some cases the pin assignments may be different. You usually don't have to set these jumpers; they're preset at the factory.

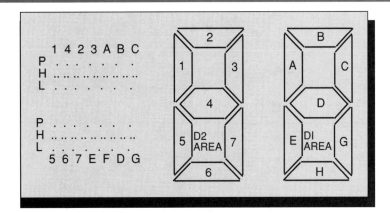

Arrangement of the jumper groups for the segments of a mini-tower

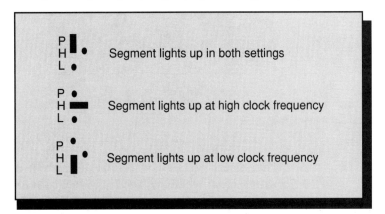

Jumper position options for the clock frequency display of a mini-tower

When do the lights go on?

Each segment can be set to switch on only at a higher or lower clock frequency or not at all. In the latter case, a jumper isn't set. The jumper settings for the other variations are shown in the diagram.

Slim-line tower

There are also several types of tower cases. The tower case in the following figure is a quasi "ancestral" tower, in which the first compatible computers were sold. It has a similar appearance to the case used by IBM for its Model 60 (AT) and its Model 80 (a 386).

Slim-line tower case

This case is very easy to open. Simply pull away the side wall, which is attached with springs from the bottom. Generally you must remove a few screws at the back.

Wide tower

Thick tower cases are generally used for 486 computers. These cases are useful because they have enough room for several different mass storage devices and the motherboard with individual cards. Unlike the slim tower, the thick tower comes in several different forms. In some, the controls are near the top and, in others the controls are located beneath the place where mass storage devices can be mounted.

Special cases

Besides the standard cases, which are identical regardless of the computer, there are also special cases that are used by specific companies for all their computers.

Compaq

Compaq units are arranged so they can easily be serviced. The upper part of the case is attached to the base by three screws at the edge, which can be removed by hand. The upper part is then pulled forward and lifted up.

A part of the motherboard extends under the rack for the disk drive. To remove this, you must take out the screws and move the rack back and forth out of the mounting, once the cables have been removed from the hard drive.

Compaq desktop case in which 486es are offered

IBM

The IBM PS/2 computers aren't much different to operate than a personal computer. This computer is usually delivered completely installed. The PS/2 models were designed to be particularly user-friendly. So, the computer can be taken apart without tools.

First you must remove the two thumb screws at the back, near the top. Pull the cover forward slightly and then lift it off. You'll probably be surprised to find there isn't a single cable connection inside.

Everything in the PS/2 model is simply plugged in and screwed down. The thick screws at the edge can easily be taken out and reinserted by hand.

IBM's 486 generation computer

Tulip

To open the case of a Tulip AT 486, first you must unbolt the key switch at the back. Then you must remove the two screws at the back of the case, near the top. The case is then pulled forward and lifted up. If you want to operate the Tulip in the upright position, you can rotate the LCD display 90 degrees. To do this, simply move the right side out of its mounting with a screwdriver, rotate it one quarter of a turn, and then put it back. When replacing the cover, be sure that you don't pinch the cables.

2.5 Understanding The Electronics

Speeding up computers

Even if you've decided on a computer with a specific microprocessor and clock frequency, there are still some things you can do to speed up or slow down its performance. For example, you could either activate an externally mounted Turbo switch or change the computer's operational mode by entering a key combination from the keyboard.

When resetting the frequency doesn't work

The indicated settings may not work if optional character tables are loaded with the DOS KEYB command. In some very rare instances, you may have to open the computer to adjust the speed. You can "tune" the computer (i.e., increase the performance of the system by installing a better component).

If you don't feel confident about your ability to work on a computer, you should have a dealer do this for you. Many computer manufacturers recommend that difficult operations be performed by a professional repair shop.

However, you can perform the easier jobs yourself. Generally, jobs that don't require soldering can be done easily. Once you've opened the case, then you must become familiar with the layout of the motherboard.

BIOS

One of the most important aspects of your computer is the BIOS, which is an acronym for Basic Input/Output System. The BIOS is a mini-operating system that organizes the basic functions, such as accessing peripheral devices and mass storage.

When the computer is switched on, it performs a self-test called the POST (Power On Self Test) and checks the individual components. Depending on the BIOS in your computer, these tests are indicated in various ways.

386es equipped with the AMI BIOS show only the memory count while those equipped with the Award BIOS indicate each test of the individual components.

Then the bootstrap, which checks whether a boot diskette is in floppy diskette drive A:, is activated. If a bootable floppy diskette is found, the system completes its initialization routine; if a diskette isn't found, the system tries to boot from the active hard drive partition. If this can't be found, an error message appears.

Function carriers

The TTL component groups of an AT system are various component groups that were collected by the manufacturers of gate arrays (Chips & Technologies, Suntac, Intel and others).

These groups were placed into new chips and are present in some form in every 486 computer.

Bus controller

The bus controller produces the signals needed to manage the bus system. The main microprocessor communicates with other system components through the bus. This bus consists of three parts: the address bus, the data bus, and the control bus.

The memory locations to which data are sent or from which data are received is entered via the address bus. The actual transfer of data takes place over the data bus.

The control of data traffic is affected by the control bus, which determines whether the memory location accessed by the address bus should be read from or written to. The bus controller places the appropriate signals on the bus under the supervision of the main microprocessor and guides data transfer over the individual bus systems.

DMA controller

Data is transferred frequently between memory and various peripheral devices. This data transfer can be controlled by the DMA (Direct Memory Access) controller. With the DMA, the component groups directly access memory, without going through the CPU. In ATs and 386es this is handled by two 8237 chips. These units are much faster than the main microprocessor.

If data must be transported from the hard drive to memory, the DMA controller is notified by the hard drive controller through its request line. The DMA controller then processes this request according to its priority logic and passes it to the main microprocessor. If the latter accepts the request, it will signal the DMA controller and give it control of the bus. The DMA controller then sends a start signal to the hard drive controller and begins transferring data.

To use more than the 16 address lines, which can be accessed by the DMA controller, a DMA page register is used. This makes it possible for the DMA controller to access the entire address range (386SX: 24 bits/16 Meg, 386DX: 32 bits/4 GB). This register is contained in the unit with the designation 74LS670.

In an AT/386 there are two components with the designation 8237, each having control of four DMA channels. Data are transferred between these eight DMA channels in 64K packets.

In addition to the DMA controller, a DMA page register, in the form of a 74SL670, is also available to enable it to reach the entire address range of the 386 with its 16 address lines.

Realtime clock

The realtime clock performs an important job in the computer system. This clock stores certain information about the system configuration, which is needed by the 386 after the system has been switched on.

This information (memory size, hard drive type, type and number of the floppy drives, type of graphics card, and possibly some additional system specifics) is stored, along with the correct time, in the CMOS-RAM of the realtime clock component. The time is transferred to the system clock after the start.

> The DOS commands DATE and TIME adjust only the system clock instead of the realtime clock. For permanent changes, run Setup.

TAKE NOTE

The 146818 chip is fed electrical current by a lithium battery so the information stored in this won't be lost when the system is switched off. Instead of a lithium battery, you can also use standard batteries or nickel-cadmium batteries, which are environmentally friendly.

Interrupt controllers

Besides handling computing operations, a microprocessor must also communicate with the outside world. It interrupts its work whenever a peripheral device reports an input or output task. When operations are stopped like this, it's called an "interrupt". When this occurs, a subprogram is called to handle the output device that has just reported. If the operation is terminated, the computer continues working at the place where it stopped.

Interrupts can also be requested by the various peripheral devices. These are controlled by the interrupt controller and passed to the microprocessor. In addition to the hardware interrupts, a series of software interrupts, which can be used by the programmer (see BIOS), are also possible in a 386 system.

The hardware interrupts are controlled by two 8259 chips. Up to 16 interrupt requests can be managed. Internally the two controllers are switched on in succession, over interrupt line 2. The hardware interrupt sequence is located in the Appendix.

Master/slave controllers

The first controller is the "master" and the second the "slave". Direct lines attach the interrupt lines from the timer, keyboard, hard drives, and diskette controllers, as well as the serial and parallel interfaces to the interrupt controller. Over these lines, requests are directed to the interrupt controller, evaluated, and then passed via data lines to the microprocessor.

The interrupt controller communicates with the main microprocessor over two control lines. The microprocessor sends commands for selecting and processing interrupts. If several requests follow one another rapidly, the various requests are assigned a system established priority according to their number and passed to the microprocessor, according to this evaluation.

Frequency generator

The 82284 frequency generator uses the quartz crystal frequencies from the motherboard to generate clock frequencies for the main microprocessor and the other components (system bus, peripherals). It generates the ready signal, which informs the microprocessor that the peripherals are ready to send and receive data. The clock generator is also the source of the hardware reset signal.

Keyboard controller

Today the keyboard is still the most important data entry medium. The 8042 keyboard controller controls the keyboard in the computer system. Whenever a key is activated, the entry is evaluated by the keyboard controller, which issues a corresponding signal to the keyboard interrupt of the computer. Each key is assigned a specific code, called the scan code.

For the scan code transmitted by the keyboard controller, refer to the Appendix.

The keyboard controller receives the serial data over the keyboard cable, it stores these data temporarily, codes them, and then delivers them to the parallel outlet of the component. It also transmits the coded data to the CPU.

The keyboard controller is also responsible for monitoring the key switches and position of the dip switches recording, memory structure, BIOS type, or the graphics card used.

Timer

The timer component 8254 contains three timers and a control register. The first timer generates the signals for the interrupt controller and system clock.

A second timer produces the signals needed for the memory refresh of the dynamic RAM and the DMA controller. The third timer produces the tone frequencies for the system speaker.

The Intel Chipset

The microprocessor manufacturer, Intel, has also developed a set of gate arrays. In 486 computers, these components are included with the Intel motherboard.

The chipset consists of the Intel 82335 High Integration Interface Device and the Intel 82230/82331 logic control chips. The clock frequency of the system can be either 8 or 16 MHz. The frequency can be set by either hardware or software.

The Intel 82230 combines the following components:

- 82284 clock generator and ready interface

- 82288 bus controller for the main microprocessor

- 6818 realtime clock

- Master-slave implementation of the dual 8259A chip

- Programmable interrupt controller

The following chips are included in the Intel 82231:

- 8254 programmable interval timer

- 8284A clock generator

- LS612 memory mapper

- Dual 8237 DMA controller

- Refresh generation and refresh/DMA logic

The Intel 82335 integrates the following elements:

- Ready generator
- Address mapper/decoder
- Parity generator checker
- Clock generator/reset synchronizer
- Bus cycle translator
- Coprocessor/interface
- DRAM controller

Although the main microprocessor usually comes from Intel, the gate arrays can come from other companies. So obviously many companies get more out of their computers by using chips from other sources. Unfortunately, this also leads to compatibility problems.

The position of the jumpers, DIP switches, and other settings are presented only for users who are considering extensive hardware changes. Usually 486 computers automatically recognize the configuration; otherwise it's specified in the setup.

Jumper and switch settings

The jumpers and DIP switches at various points on the motherboard are important for configuration. Jumpers are push-on contacts that can be used to connect two terminal pins on the motherboard. A condition in the computer is activated or deactivated according to how a jumper is set. The easiest way to set or remove jumpers is by using small flat nose pliers.

Jumpers are small shorting blocks that are set with flat nose pliers

Shorting blocks as switches

A jumper can operate like a switch. If there are three pins available on the motherboard, as shown in the above photograph, one state will be active when the shorting block is pushed over the center and right-hand pins and the other will be active when it's on the center and left-hand pins. The other method of adjustment is the DIP switches.

Setting the DIP switches

The term DIP switch refers to the row of tiny switches that can be operated by using a small screwdriver. DIP switches are used to configure various states according to their position.

DIP switches can be easily adjusted with a small screwdriver

When a 486 has a coprocessor, it's plugged into an extra socket that's provided specifically for this purpose. One corner of the socket is beveled so the chip can be installed properly. Coprocessors have pins, on their lower sides, that are inserted into the corresponding holes in the socket. The socket has 121 of these holes. The Weitek chip is the only coprocessor that can be used with the 80486DX.

Only the 80486SX requires a coprocessor, the 80487SX, which is inserted in the corresponding socket of the 486SX motherboard.

TAKE NOTE

> Although the 80486SX is actually an 80386 with an integrated cache, you cannot use the 80387 coprocessors in the 486SX.

Changing microprocessors

Based on pin assignments and data and address bus width, the 80486DX and 80486SX are two entirely different microprocessors. However, the 80486SX differs from the 80486DX only because the coprocessor of the 80486SX is deactivated and that it's run at a lower clock frequency. Some manufacturers, such as Elite Group, produce boards on which you can mount either the 486SX or DX.

To convert the board, simply change the board and the quartz crystal for the clock frequency. Usually you'll purchase the board with the 80486SX and 20 MHz crystal. The 80486DX chips and 33-MHz crystal can be purchased as an upgrade kit.

If you want to perform the conversion yourself, you'll need a flat screwdriver, diagonal cutters, and a cable clip. The crystal is mounted in its socket with a cable clip. To remove this clip, you must cut it with a diagonal cutter. Then pry the crystal out of its socket with the flat screwdriver.

You must pry gently all around the chip to remove it from its socket. Don't bend the pins too much because you may be able to sell the chip to someone who bought a board without the chip and crystal.

2.6 Hardware Problems

Usually problems occur when the computer is new. If you have a problem and the following hints don't help, consult your computer dealer.

■ **Computer won't start**

Faulty power supply

Check the entire power supply chain starting from the power strip to determine whether all the plugs are properly seated and all switches have been turned on.

■ **The monitor does not operate**

Faulty connection

> Check that the cable connecting the monitor to the computer is properly seated in the correct receptacle and that the screws are tight.

■ **Same as above but stripes appear**

Incorrect adjustment of the monitor/graphics card

> Check to see whether the graphics card and monitor have been configured correctly. Some graphics cards require that DIP switches be set. The monitor also has a switch.

■ **The computer counts through the memory, but then "hangs" without reporting any error**

A component isn't working properly, but the computer is unable to determine which one

> This error occurs whenever mutually incompatible adjustments have been made in Setup, particularly in NEAT 486 units. Press the [Reset] button, while holding down the [Ins] key, until the computer reaches the end of the memory count.

■ **The computer completes the memory count, but then "hangs" and beeps or returns a number and an error message**

Some component isn't working properly, and the computer is unable to localize it

> Look up the appropriate component in the Appendix and contact your computer dealer.

■ **The computer boots, but displays an error message and tells you to run the Setup utility**

The system configuration doesn't coincide with the entries in the CMOS-RAM

> Run the Setup program, and ensure that all components have been correctly entered. If they have, then it's possible that one of the components wasn't connected properly. (For example, this may be the keyboard. Sometimes this happens when the computer was opened, for example, to install expansion cards.)

■ **The computer boots, but displays an error message stating that an operating system isn't available**

The hard drive wasn't set up correctly

Boot from a floppy disk and then install the operating system.

■ **The computer boots and loads the operating system, but you are unable to make entries from the keyboard**

Keyboard unattached, but the error was unnoticed by the computer during booting

Reattach the keyboard.

The computer is locked

Unlock the computer by using the key switch.

2.7 Electrical Problems

Experimenting with DIP switches and jumpers isn't for everyone. If you don't know what you're doing, you could severely damage your system. So if you cannot identify the individual switches and jumpers, consult your computer dealer.

Before making any changes to the system, you should always record the original settings. So, if you encounter problems, you can return to these settings instead of starting over completely.

■ **The computer won't run**

The computer won't operate if a jumper/DIP switch has been set incorrectly. So you shouldn't make two or more adjustments on the motherboard simultaneously. Check to determine whether the activation/deactivation of other switches or jumpers may be the cause of the problem.

Occasionally the settings on the motherboard are incompatible with a driver or a program you've loaded. You should deactivate the drivers and program calls in the CONFIG.SYS or AUTOEXEC.BAT files until the problem is found.

■ **Error message**

The computer reports the following error:

CMOS-RAM

after you adjust a DIP switch/jumper. The setting doesn't agree with the configuration of the CMOS Setup. Run the Setup program and change the corresponding entry.

■ **Expansion not recognized**

An installed coprocessor isn't recognized by the system. The corresponding DIP switch/jumper wasn't reset. In almost every computer the presence of a coprocessor must be reported. Do this now; refer to the computer manual for the location of the jumper.

■ **Switching the frequency has no effect**

The clock frequency can be set by using the switch; but this setting doesn't take effect. In this case, the change wasn't recognized by the system. In many computers the changed clock speeds are effective only after a reset. Press the appropriate button or the [Ctrl] + [Alt] + [Del] key combination.

Chapter 3

Memory

After the main microprocessor, the memory has the greatest influence on the performance of your computer. All important information, including the operating system, applications, and data that the programs will process, is stored in memory.

Because the operating system is able to access each location in memory, the memory is also called RAM (Random Access Memory). This term is related to magnetic tapes, which were used to store large amounts of data. On these tapes, data could be accessed only sequentially.

The byte

The number of information units memory is able to accept is represented in bytes. A byte is the basic unit in which a letter or a number can be stored. Since it consists of eight bits, a byte can assume 256 different values. It's possible to define 256 different characters with a single byte.

The memory size indicates how many of the different information units the computer can store. One kilobyte is 2 to the 10th power (2^{10}) or 1,024 bytes.

A megabyte (1,024 kilobytes) is 2 to the 20th power (2^{20}) or 1,048,576 bytes. Much higher capacities can, however, be addressed by an 80486 microprocessor.

The next highest unit is the gigabyte. One gigabyte is equivalent to 1,024 megabytes or 2 to the 30th power (2^{30}) or 1,073,741,824 bytes. The next step higher is the terabyte. One terabyte is 2 to the 40th (2^{40}) power or 1,099,511,627,776 bytes, which is almost an unimaginable amount of data.

3.1 Memory Basics

The memory (its size, type, and speed) is the most important component of a computer system, besides the microprocessor. It's the most significant factor for determining system performance.

Two types of components are used for memory. These are either individual chips or memory modules, which in turn contain individual memory chips.

Chip organization

In the computer, memory chips are arranged according to a specific system. In memory, each byte is subdivided into eight bits and each bit is stored in a separate memory element. So, a single byte is distributed among eight memory elements.

A ninth element, which is an error check, follows these eight memory elements. One such bit is assigned for each byte. In this check element, a bit is either set or not set, depending on whether the sum of the eight bits stored in the byte is odd or even. This ninth bit is also called the "parity bit" because it indicates the parity of the value stored.

Depending on how they are built, memory chips are able to store 64 KBit, 256 KBit, or 1 MBit. To obtain a memory with a 64K capacity, nine 64 KBit chips are needed.

For 1 Meg, you need a series of nine 1 MBit memory chips or 4 rows each containing nine 256 KBit chips. Memory chips with capacities of 4 MBit and 16 MBit are currently being developed. With these chips, it will be possible to store 4 Meg or 16 Meg in a series of nine such elements.

Rows must have nine components

Because of the way a byte is stored, a row must always be completely filled with nine components. The minimum number of rows or banks that must be present depends on the width of the data bus. For an XT computer, with its 8-bit wide data bus, a single row of nine is sufficient.

Two rows of nine are needed for an AT computer with the 80286 microprocessor or even for one with the 80386SX microprocessor, because it has a data bus with a width of 16 bits.

Both the i486 and the 80386DX have a 32-bit wide data bus and need four rows of nine memory chips each, which is also called a memory bank. This is also the source of the computer-dependent minimum memory sizes.

In the case of the XT, this is 64K and in the AT this is 128K if the boards contain 64 KBit chips. Since the i486, and even the 80386DX, don't use 64 KBit chips, 256 KBit produces a minimum memory size of 1 Meg.

RAM chips

The 1 MBit chips have two connectors more than the 256 KBit chips, which can be used only on boards with double sockets. There is also a special group of 256 KBit chips, in which four 256 KBit units are combined into a single chip. Only two of these special units are needed to complete a row and produce a memory capacity of 256K.

SIMMs (Single In-line Memory Module) are being used more frequently on computer motherboards.

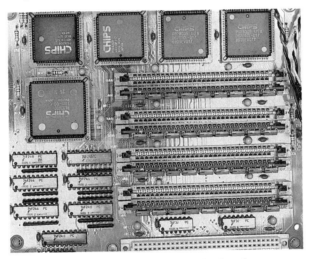

SIMM modules on a motherboard

SMD

SIMMs are memory modules consisting of small boards. Each of these boards has a full set of 256 KBit or 1 MBit memory chips, which are simply inserted into a SIMM socket. The memory chips are either cemented or soldered to the pads on the board; they are positioned on these boards to save space. This is an example of SMD (Surface Mounted Device) technology.

Unlike expansion cards, SIMM memory expansion sockets don't require any plug-in slots. The microprocessor can access the memory chips on the SIMMs at the bus frequency instead of, as with memory expansion cards, at the bus frequency of the card.

A less expensive way to expand memory, without using expansion cards, is by using the SIP (Single In-line Packages) module. In this case, conventional chips are mounted on a small board. These boards, which have one-row arrangements, are simply mounted in plug-in slots on the system board. The board structure based on simple insertion in the system board is called the DIP (Dual Inline Package) mode of construction because the chips have pins on either side.

Memory expansion cards

An important criterion for selecting a computer is whether conventional memory can be expanded on the system board. For example, the memory of the Compaq 486/25 Deskpro can be expanded on the motherboard to a maximum of 100 Meg, although the i486 microprocessor could directly address 4 gigabytes. As we already mentioned, it's possible to address the memory on the motherboard, whether it's located in SIMMs or SIPs, with the clock frequency of the system (i.e., that of the microprocessor). This is the only way to fully utilize the advantages of the i486 microprocessor.

System boards (and the computer) aren't equipped with the maximum memory size addressable by the microprocessor. This is because special chips, called gate arrays, which are designed for conventional memory control, are needed.

Because most application programs and most users would never need the maximum memory size addressable by the microprocessor, computer manufacturers have reached a compromise in the design of their computers. The memory on the system board is constructed according to a specific purpose or the needs of the customers the computer manufacturer wants to reach. To avoid raising the cost of a basic model computer, manufacturers don't include unnecessary components or waste space on the motherboard for the installation of memory chips.

If you have an i486-based computer and you need memory expansion cards, you must use the manufacturer-specific 32-bit expansion bus. Unfortunately, these expansions aren't standardized. So you must rely on a single source, which is usually expensive.

Another option for a 486 computer with the AT bus is 16-bit memory expansion cards. These cards are available from various suppliers. In addition to Intel's Above Board Plus 8, which can be configured for a maximum of 8 Meg, there is also the BOCARAM AT/Plus from Boca Research, which is designed to accept a maximum of 32 Meg.

Also, usually the memory chips on expansion cards, as with the memory on the motherboard itself, can be divided into three structural categories, such as DIP, SIP, or SIMM chips.

Memory speed

Although access times, to the RAM chips, in the 200 ns (nanosecond) range were suitable for the XT, the AT requires 150 ns memory chips. The DRAM chips ordinarily used in computers are too slow for the most recent generations of microprocessors. Initially the problem with slow memory was solved by using wait states.

The i486 or 80386 microprocessors generally require two clock cycles to read or to write. Introducing a single wait state would require three clock cycles for reading and writing, which slows the microprocessor's performance by 33%. The fastest RAM chips currently available have an access time of 80 ns. So an i486 or 80386 microprocessor requiring 2 clock cycles to read or to write could be driven at a maximum clock frequency of 25 MHz, without needing wait cycles.

However, the memory chip requires a certain delay after every access before it can be used again. This time period usually demands a large percentage of the access time. You cannot determine the memory speed only by the access time. Instead, you must use the cycling time, which consists of the access time and the recovery period. So it isn't possible to drive an 80 ns chip at 25 MHz in a 386/486 computer system without wait states.

SRAM and DRAM chips

> • SRAM chips - Static RAM is fast but very expensive.
>
> • DRAM chips - Dynamic RAM is slower but less expensive.

The structure and the logic of the two chips are different. Static RAM chips use two transistors to store a single data bit. These transistors are joined together in such a way that only one of the two transistors can be "in" and the other "out". The member of the pair designated as "in" determines whether a "zero" or a "one" is stored at the memory location. This means that the switching state of the transistors determines the memory content.

With dynamic RAM chips, only one transistor is needed to store a data bit. The transistor functions merely as a switch that stores a small electrical charge in a capacitor. The size of the charge determines whether a "zero" or a "one" is stored.

Because all capacitors leak, the charge on the capacitor is slowly dissipated as a result of insulator losses. Eventually the charge on the capacitor dissipates completely and the memory content, in contrast with static RAM, would be lost.

The solution to this problem is to read the dynamic RAM before the data are lost and to rewrite the RAM chip again with the same data. This procedure is called the refresh of the dynamic RAM.

So, static RAM retains data as long as the current is turned on, while dynamic RAM must be continually reloaded.

To enable the DRAM chips to manage with fewer connector pins, which decreases the amount of chips, these components are addressed in the multiplexing mode. The address of each memory cell is transmitted in two parts.

The first half of the address is called the row address and the second is called the column address.

Access optimization

To avoid decreasing the performance of the microprocessor with too many wait cycles, DRAM chips have been replaced with SRAM chips whenever possible. However, this is a very expensive method and is sometimes impractical. Besides being expensive, SRAMs are as readily available as DRAMs.

As an alternative, a more effective and less expensive method is used. Performance can be significantly improved by optimizing the access times of not only memory, but also the most frequently used programs.

Most programs use only small areas of memory for brief periods, then use another small memory area. It's very possible that a program currently using one memory location will use the same or an adjacent memory location next.

Because of this, static optimization procedures have been used to increase memory access speeds. In this case, four different optimization procedures are specified:

> - Memory interleave procedure (corresponding to a division of memory)
>
> - Page mode operation
>
> - Page interleaving
>
> - Cache memory (supplementary intermediate memory)

Memory interleaving

Memory interleaving is the easiest way to avoid microprocessor wait cycles. The sequence of memory addresses is arranged into two banks; the odd memory locations are in one bank and the even ones in the other. If the microprocessor then accesses the continually addressed memory locations in strict sequence, the zero wait state condition can be achieved. Since this is also the weak point of the procedure, sometimes wait states must be accepted.

The average number of wait states that will occur with this procedure is difficult to predict. The microprocessor will have to process approximately 0.5 wait cycles for an operation that normally requires 1 wait state.

This procedure is possible only if there are two memory banks available. This means that by installing a second bank of memory in a computer that already has one megabyte of RAM, you can increase the computer's speed. Although the interleave procedure can also be extended to more than two memory banks, this may not result in a proportional increase in performance. Often as many as four banks are supported. These banks are addressed by using different interleave procedures.

Page mode operation

Page mode operation uses a property of the DRAM chips. The second access to a memory location on the same page takes about half as long as the first access. The page size depends upon the respective DRAM chip, which is usually about 2K. If the memory accesses take place in sequence, a wait state occurs during the first access, for access operations within a single page.

This process doesn't produce impressive optimization results. Programs normally use only two active memory regions (one for the program code and another as the data region). These regions are usually on different pages, reducing one wait state to about 0.8 wait states.

Page interleaving

Page interleaving is a combination of the two optimization procedures described above - the memory interleave procedure and page mode operation. A wait cycle can occur only if a memory access is made to a page in the same bank in which the active page is located.

With the page interleave mode it's possible to reduce 1 wait state to about 0.3 wait states. This procedure is very easy to use and provides a good solution for a relatively slow memory. The standard memory controller chip for 386/486 systems produced by Chips and Technologies supports this process.

Cache memory

The cache memory is an expansion of page mode operation. A supplementary block of fast SRAM memory is used as a working memory for the microprocessor. In this case, the cache acts as an intermediate memory stage for the microprocessor. If the cache memory was as large as the primary memory, microprocessor wait cycles could be completely eliminated.

Since these chips are very expensive, typical cache memories are 16K, 32K, or 64K. As you can see, they are very small when compared with the normal memory of a 386/486 system. An 8K cache memory has already been integrated into the microprocessor chip of the i486.

How cache memories differ

Cache memories differ in the way they store and find data and in the way they use cache memory. There are three cache types: the directly modeled cache, the partially associative cache, and the completely associative cache. As the number of rows increase, so does the complexity of the structure and the level of efficiency.

Actually the size of the cache memory is more important than the cache memory procedure. Most manufacturers use the directly modeled cache or the partially associative cache.

Another important difference among caches is the quantity of data stored at each cache location. This is called the word length of the cache memory. In a 386/486 computer, the basic word length of the microprocessor is either 32 bits or 4 bytes.

The word length of a component cache memory should be expanded so the next memory location in sequence can be transferred to the cache. Often it's possible to organize memory so read and write operations are executed with a complete cache length, which accelerates them even further.

Problems can occur

Sometimes problems involving the balance between cache memory and standard memory can occur, especially if a unit or a second microprocessor accesses and changes the data in memory. This problem is generally referred to as cache consistency; the cache controller hardware solves this problem.

The following procedures are used to ensure consistency:

> • Declaring the entire cache contents invalid whenever another unit accesses the working memory. This process is simple, but not very efficient.
>
> • A better procedure involves marking only the locations in the cache memory, that have been changed, as invalid.
>
> • The cache controller checks which memory locations in conventional memory were changed and continuously updates the cache memory. So, none of the cache memory locations have to be marked as invalid.
>
> • Another possibility is treat the cache memory as a part of the memory. By doing this, every access to memory will take place via the cache memory. This simplifies maintaining the cache consistency.
>
> Unfortunately this procedure isn't widely accepted by the manufacturers. Under normal operating conditions it's possible to reduce 1 wait state to 0.03 wait states or less by using a cache memory.

Cache memory, along with its associated cache controller, is integrated into the i486 microprocessor chip. This offers the most easily optimized possibilities for conventional memory access. The word length of the cache memory integrated into the i486 is 16 bytes long, which is twice as long as the usual 8 bytes.

Quadruple associative cache memory

The next four locations in conventional memory are stored in a cache memory location. This is called a quadruple associative cache memory.

Even when ensuring cache consistency, the i486 uses the most effective procedure, in which data changed in the working memory are successively updated.

Although the cache memory of the i486 is better than its 8K size would seem to indicate, many computer manufacturers enhance this memory even further.

One method involves a supplementary cache memory consisting of fast SRAM chips. However, an external working memory with DRAM chips, driven with the page interleaving process, can produce the same results in conjunction with the internal cache as a supplementary cache memory.

Burst operation

A new memory accessing procedure, called burst operation, enables the i486 to transfer one memory location per clock cycle. In burst operation, the i486 can transfer 16 bytes or four 32-bit words into sequential memory cells, in the cache memory, in only five clock cycles.

The 8K cache memory is divided into two banks, each containing 4K. This can be used as interleave memory.

3.2 Memory Management

Not all the memory in the computer can be used with the DOS operating system. This hasn't changed with "modern" 486es. Memory is divided into conventional and extended memory.

0 to 640K = conventional memory

DOS can use only 640K of the 1 Meg of addressable memory. All DOS programs can easily address this region. This memory is also called "conventional memory".

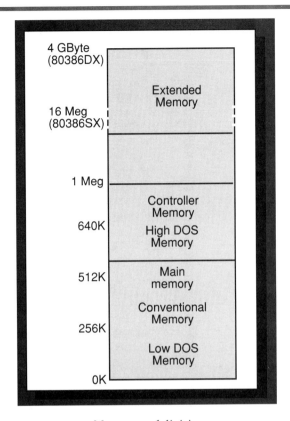

Memory subdivision

Upper memory

Reserved zones

The 8088, which was used in the first computer models, cannot address more than 1 Meg of memory. This address space was divided by the developers into 640K for the conventional memory and 384K for system-internal purposes.

This upper memory area contains the memory for the video card and the ROM BIOS routines. However, some areas of upper memory aren't used because the developers reserved them for future expansions.

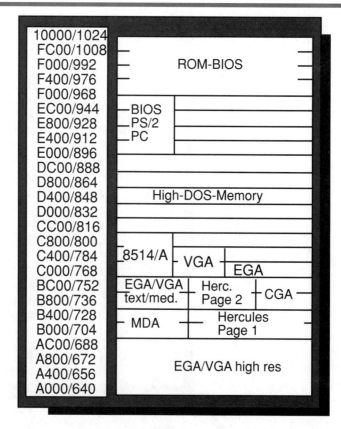

10000/1024	
FC00/1008	
F000/992	ROM-BIOS
F400/976	
F000/968	
EC00/944	BIOS
E800/928	PS/2
E400/912	PC
E000/896	
DC00/888	
D800/864	
D400/848	High-DOS-Memory
D000/832	
CC00/816	
C800/800	
C400/784	8514/A VGA
C000/768	EGA
BC00/752	EGA/VGA Herc.
B800/736	text/med. Page 2 CGA
B400/728	Hercules
B000/704	MDA Page 1
AC00/688	
A800/672	EGA/VGA high res
A400/656	
A000/640	

Controller region of memory

The barrier

Working memory consists of the addresses from 0 to 639K; the upper memory block is located at the upper end of the address space. What had seemed practical with 1 Meg became an obstacle to further development. This 384K memory block prevented the linear use of all addressable space.

In many 386es and 486es, the extended memory between 640K and 1 Meg is referred to as high DOS memory or upper memory. This area must be used as extended memory because the internal system addresses described above are located between 640K and 1 Meg. However, this memory cannot be used as extended memory in all computers. With some computers, it isn't possible to extend the memory space from 640K to 1 Meg.

Because of this, an attempt is made to free the memory between the remaining ROM areas for other purposes. However, this isn't always easy to do. In some computers, this region can be used only as "shadow RAM".

Limited use

This means that 384K must always be subtracted from the memory capacity. For example, a 2 Meg 486 has only 1.6 Meg that can be used by DOS. However, this 384K of memory isn't wasted. It can be used for other purposes.

It's usually possible to copy the ROM routines into RAM at the same address (shadow RAM). The computer is then able to access these routines more quickly. The area between the routines is free because DOS addresses, which are never used, are located there. This area is called high DOS memory (not to be confused with high memory).

Special memory manager programs (e.g., 386LOAD from Qualitas) can be used to locate drivers and memory-resident programs in this area. Such programs also allow DOS programs to use this memory under certain circumstances.

The DOS program must be able to use the memory. Many applications crash when they have so much memory available. MS-DOS 5.0, MS-DOS 6.0, and DR-DOS 6.0 are all able to load their drivers into the high DOS region by using the appropriate commands.

Whenever a computer (AT, 386, or 486) has more than 640K of conventional memory, everything beyond 640K is called extended memory. This memory cannot be directly addressed by DOS. This memory can be accessed as either extended or expanded memory.

Extended memory

AT and 386 computers work under DOS only in the real address mode. In this mode, the address bus is limited to 20 bits to preserve compatibility with the XT computer. So only 1 Meg can be directly addressed.

To access the full 24 (80286, 80386SX) or 32-bit (80386DX/80486) address bus width, the microprocessor must be switched into protected mode, in which all memory can be addressed directly. However, DOS applications cannot run in protected mode because of problems with memory management. Only a few special programs can access the microprocessor in protected mode.

The start address for extended memory lies beyond 1 Meg. So extended memory isn't available for DOS. However, there are still a few ways in which extended memory can be used. Simply reconfigure extended memory so it can be used by DOS.

RAM disks

The most frequently used procedure involves setting up a RAM disk in the extended memory region. An appropriate driver, which the computer loads during booting, causes the computer to treat a certain memory region as a logical drive.

It's possible to use the extended memory region as an extremely fast supplementary drive. However, the contents of this drive are lost when the computer is switched off. Temporary files can be stored in a RAM disk if the following line has been added to the AUTOEXEC.BAT file:

```
SET TEMP = drive
```

There are other device drivers that allow the extended memory to be used as an intermediate buffer, either as a cache for the hard drive or as a buffer queue (sometimes referred to as a spooler) for an attached printer. With a buffer, the microprocessor can continue its work while data are still in the buffer waiting to be stored on the hard drive or memory, or waiting to be sent to the printer.

The driver permitting the use of this memory and managing access is usually activated by an entry in the CONFIG.SYS file.

Extended Memory Specification

There are several drivers for configuring extended memory. However, these drivers aren't always compatible with one another. Until recently, different memory utilization procedures were used. A standard for memory utilization has been established for extended memory. This is called the Extended Memory Specification (XMS). It's intended to create a uniform programming environment for using extended memory. However, you may still experience some compatibility problems because developers tend to use short-cuts or interpret the standard differently.

High memory

Normally, under DOS, there are 20 bits available for the direct addressing of the total memory area. This is adequate for addressing the 1 Meg of RAM, but the addresses beyond 640K, for backwards compatibility reasons, cannot be used. The High Memory Manager (HMM), which is part of the XMS standard, is used to make at least an additional 64K available to the user.

An additional 64K

8086/8088 microprocessors control only 20 address lines and are unable to directly address more than 1 Meg. The 80286 and 80386SX microprocessors use 24-bit address lines, while the i486 microprocessors uses 32-bit lines.

Besides the 20 address lines used for high memory access, there is a 21st line, which increases the quantity of addressable memory by 64K. This memory is found beyond the 1 Meg barrier and forms the High Memory Area.

When high memory is used, the A20 address line is active. The only lines available to the 8088/8086 are lines A0 through A19. The Extended Memory specification provides a hardware-independent way to control the "A20" path (A20 gate). So this controls access to the HMA.

The HIMEM.SYS driver

Access to the HMA, according to the XMS process, is made possible by the HIMEM.SYS device driver. This driver is loaded by CONFIG.SYS during the boot process. The HIMEM.SYS driver requires the first 64K of extended memory and must be the first driver in the CONFIG.SYS file. This will enable it to be installed before any of the other drivers using extended memory.

The XMS is a software interface for AT and 386/486 computers. XMS enables these computers to gather extended memory and the regions of conventional memory, which aren't controlled by DOS, into a block that is then used collectively. Three memory groups, in which memory blocks can be reserved, changed, or released with access functions, are defined:

- Upper memory blocks (UMB) between 640K and 1 Meg

- High memory area (HMA) between 1 Meg and 1 Meg plus 64K (see below)

- Extended memory blocks (EMB), which are located above the HMA

A device driver that implements the XMS functions is called an XMM (eXtended Memory Manager). The HIMEM.SYS, mentioned above, is a well-known XMM. Windows needs this driver to make any continuous memory available for its applications. There are other XMM programs available from other developers. For example, Quarterdeck's QEMM.SYS can be used as a replacement for HIMEM.SYS for Windows 3.0/3.1.

Expanded memory

What is EMS?

EMS is an abbreviation for Expanded Memory Specification. The management of supplementary memory as expanded memory is also called LIM-EMS, which is an abbreviation for Lotus-Intel-Microsoft Expanded Memory Specification.

In EMS, memory is accessed by using a process called bank switching. With this process, a switch is made between memory regions. This means that the microprocessor has direct access to only a part of a memory region. The remainder of the memory region is managed by bank switching logic. Several versions of EMS are recognized: Standard EMS, Expanded EMS, and Enhanced EMS (EEMS), which is actually similar to Version 4.0 of the LIM standard.

EMS hardware

A group of memory expansion components corresponding to the Expanded specification is used for EMS. The bank switching logic and possibly the RAM for the bank switching are included in this component group. This hardware element can be either an Intel Above Board, a compatible card, or even corresponding electronics on the motherboard.

EMS drivers

A software driver, which enables the software to take hardware-independent control of the bank switching logic, is part of this component group. This EMM (Expanded Memory Manager) is a driver loaded during booting from the CONFIG.SYS file. Its name can be EMM.SYS, LIMEMS.SYS, or something similar. The memory expansion operations according to the EMS standard are accomplished in the computer and AT by a combination of hardware and software.

EMS functions as they apply to software

The Intel 80386 and the 486 has a special property, which enables them to use the EMS standard through software. These software drivers can use virtual addresses and have the commands needed for bank switching. Details about some software drivers are included below.

Access through a window

To avoid the restrictions placed on the 640K conventional memory (the region controlled by the bank switching logic), the memory "window" is focused into the controller memory region. This area contains enough free regions between 640K and 1 Meg for this purpose. In the standard EMS version, the memory window, which is also called a page frame, occupies 64K. The memory region needed by the application program is focused into the window.

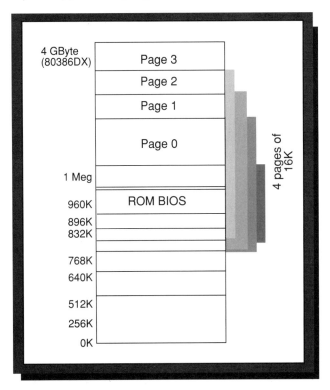

The standard memory window occupies 64K into which four 16K blocks can be switched

The application program doesn't always need to request the entire 64K. The standard EMS window consists of four 16K pages, each representing an independent window to the available expanded memory. Each of these pages is able to represent the same memory region.

Physical and logical pages

The pages actually present within the page frame are called physical pages. The pages in the memory on the card or the board are called logical frames. The size of the memory that can be modeled in the memory window by this procedure depends on the driver version. In the 3.0 or 3.2 LIM version, the size is only 8 Meg. In the current version of LIM (4.0), up to 32 Meg can be used as EMS.

Expanded EMS

The 64K window size has become too small for many programs. So developers have looked at the additional unused memory in the regions between 640K and 1 Meg.

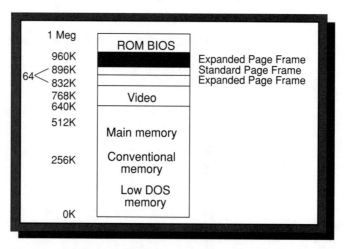

The large-frame module opens additional addresses

The size of a page depends on how much memory is used by other hardware (e.g., graphics cards). In a computer with an EGA controller, this can be as much as 176K. In this case, eleven pages of 16K each are available. The expanded page frame must be managed by the hardware and software. The expanded memory window can also cause problems when other hardware extensions (e.g., network cards) claim areas within the controller memory.

To position the window properly, you must become familiar with the structure of the memory. This is especially true if you're able to create a window in Setup.

Page frame mapping

If a computer has a Hercules or CGA card, the window is subdivided under certain circumstances. This isn't a problem if the individual elements aren't less than the 64K size (four pages of 16K).

Using a Hercules or CGA graphics adapter leaves a few pages of the expanded EMS frame below the image refresh memory, in the region between 640 and 702K. This region is used only by Hercules or VGA cards in the high resolution graphics mode. Not all programs will work with the memory window subdivided in this way.

EEMS and LIM-EMS 4.0

The second E in "EEMS" indicates "Enhanced" and originates from the memory card developed by AST. This standard is part of the most recent version of LIM-EMS, 4.0. Not all memory expansions sold under LIM EMS 4.0 support the complete specification.

Enhanced EMS differences

Enhanced indicates that standard and expanded EMS memory extensions are operating according to the standard and expanded EMS rules. This enables a program to store blocks of data and program parts (overlays) in the expanded memory.

The necessary parts are accessed via the memory window. This also applies to EEMS and it's also possible for the operating system to move entire applications into expanded memory. Several programs can be loaded and run simultaneously in the memory. Each program believes that it's running by itself and is able to use its own EMS window (Standard or Enhanced).

The EEMS standard uses part of conventional memory as a memory window for the management software. Windows uses memory from 256K to 640K as the EEMS page frame. The lower portion (up to 256K) is set aside by Windows for its own use. This area is the "shared memory" (protected memory). Several programs can store data here and exchange the data among themselves.

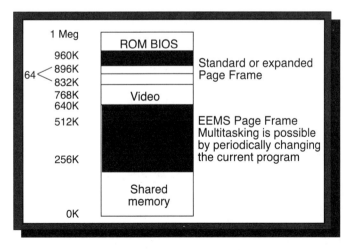

Enhanced-expanded memory configuration

The memory formed by the EEMS memory window of many EEMS memory expansions is located on their own board. When the lower boundary of the EMS page frame is established, as required by the management program, you must adapt the memory to the expansion and then deactivate it on the motherboard.

This may be difficult to do with some computers. Then the unused conventional memory can be used on the EEMS memory card only if the chip banks are of the same type. If conventional memory cannot be reduced, the expansion can be used only as standard or expanded EMS memory.

Multitasking is possible with EMS by periodically changing the current program (the program currently located in the memory window). Because of the frequent memory changes, it appears that all applications are running simultaneously (multitasking). However, this option isn't used under DOS.

If you want to use multitasking under the EEMS standard, you must use an operating system that either makes this possible or runs with a user interface that uses this principle (e.g., Windows).

Because of the expanded addressing capabilities of the 80386 and 80486 microprocessors, software that assumes complete control of EMS management without requiring the corresponding hardware, has been developed. These programs (e.g., 386MAX) are discussed in Chapter 12.

3.3 Memory Expansion

It's important to expand memory correctly and with the proper amount. Most 486es have from 1 to 4 Meg of memory. A minimum of 1 Meg is required to use the computer effectively.

On 386 and 486 computers, we recommend placing the lower limit at 4 Meg. According to the memory type and the number of banks, it's possible to install up to 64 Meg on the motherboard of 486es.

You must use cards for additional memory. 32-bit memory cards or plug-in cards for the AT bus are available. These cards are inserted in the 16-bit slot. Unfortunately, the 486 microprocessor can access these cards only via the narrow 16-bit bus. However, the microprocessor has full 32-bit access to the RAM on either the motherboard or the 32-bit card.

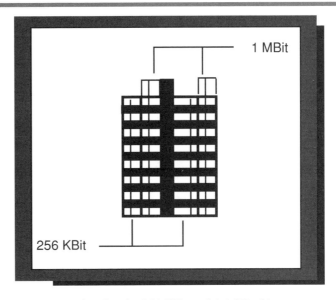

Dual socket for 256 KBit and 1 MBit chips

Inserting a RAM plug-in card is simple. We'll explain this in more detail later. At this point, we'll present the three types of memory chips. Each is handled the same way, whether they're installed on the motherboard or on plug-in cards.

The thumb is used to press the chip into the socket

Sockets for inserting memory chips are available on the motherboard or plug-in card. Usually these are dual sockets that are able to accept both 256 KBit and 1 MBit chips. Two staggered rows of holes are used, one inside the other. The 2 x 8 rows accept the 256 KBit chips, the 1 MBit chips with 2 additional pins, and a slightly different switching arrangement, are inserted into the 2 x 9 holes.

Only chips of the same type can be inserted in each bank. All chips should have the same specification (access type) to prevent problems.

Handling RAM chips

QUICK TIP

RAMs are very sensitive to static electricity. So, for safety reasons, ground yourself by touching something metal, such as a table leg or the computer case, before touching a chip or trying to insert it in the socket. Grounding straps are available at many computer stores.

Position the chip with the ends of the pins in the socket. Inspect the legs of the chip carefully for proper positioning. The legs are quite fragile and can be bent or broken easily. Once all the pins are secure, press the chip down carefully with uniform pressure on all the pins. Use your thumbs or something flat. Push until all the pins are in the socket as far as they will go.

Replacing defective chips

If a chip is defective or if you want to convert your 386 from 256 KBit to 1 MBit chips, you must remove the chips from their sockets.

We recommend purchasing a special tool, called a chip extractor, from an electronics store. Another alternative, if you don't mind risking damage to the chips you extract, is to carefully use a flat screwdriver to pry the chips from their sockets.

Begin at the middle of each chip, and move the blade gently in such a way that all the pins are released uniformly from the socket springs.

Installing and removing SIMMs

SIMMs are small boards containing all the chips of a single bank. They are inserted in special sockets; inserting these small boards is much easier than removing them.

SIMMs are designed so the memory chips are on the same side of the board as the retaining clips.

For installation, simply insert the SIMM in the two guides to the right and to the left, so the two retaining clips snap into the corresponding holes in the module.

To remove the SIMM, first you must spread the guides outward carefully with the ring fingers. Then grasp the module at both sides with the thumbs and middle fingers.

Press it back gently with the thumbs until the retaining clips are no longer engaged in the holes and pull the module upward.

Removing and installing SIPs

SIPs are easier to install than SIMMs. Instead of guides, there are sockets on the board. The corresponding pins of the SIM module are inserted into these sockets.

When inserting the pins, ensure that all the pins are placed in the correct holes. Since there aren't any guides, it's easy to insert SIPs with one pin in the wrong hole.

To remove SIPs, simply pull the board out of the motherboard or memory card. If the plugs are too firmly seated, carefully pry the module out with a small screwdriver.

Be as careful as you are with the memory chips. Pry out each pin gradually, a little at a time, until the board breaks free of the mounting.

Special hint regarding individual 486 boards

Although most everything else is standardized, the memory expansion of a 486 differs depending on the individual computer.

Boards with the ISA bus and special memory expansion

The ISA bus and special memory expansion boards are used primarily in less expensive 486es. The memory on these boards is located on special RAM plug-in boards.

There are various kinds of expansion cards. One that's frequently used contains 2 banks and has 1 MBit chips or 256 KBit chips.

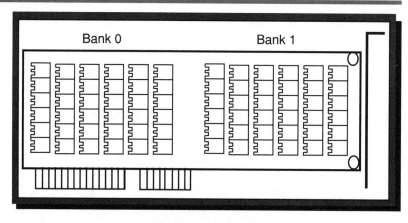

Example of an 8 Meg card for special RAM slots

Remember that both banks must have chips of the same type; a combination of 256 KBit and 1 MBit chips isn't possible. The following memory configuration is possible with such a card:

Memory Configuration of 8 Meg Card			
Bank 0	**Bank 1**	**Total memory**	**Interleave**
256 KBit	-	1 Meg	
256 KBit	256 KBit	2 Meg	Possible
1 MBit	-	4 Meg	
1 MBit	1 MBit	8 Meg	Possible

In many 486 models, you can install two of these expansion cards and in others you can install only one. This card is suitable if you're not planning a large-scale expansion of the computer.

However, this isn't likely, considering the increasing selection of available cards. So, you should select a 4-bank card. This card contains 1 MBit SIMMs and provides twice the expansion capacity while occupying the same amount of space.

Example of a 16-Meg card for special RAM slots

Only one RAM type (256 KBit or 1 MBit SIMMs) can be used. The following table shows the possible memory combinations:

Possible Memory Combinations of 16 Meg Card					
Bank 0	Bank 1	Bank 2	Bank 3	Tot mem	Interleave
256 KBit	-	-	-	1 Meg	-
256 KBit	256 KBit	-	-	2 Meg	Possible
256 KBit	256 KBit	256 KBit	256 KBit	4 Meg	Possible
1 MBit	-	-	-	4 Meg	-
1 MBit	1 MBit	-	-	8 Meg	Possible
1 MBit	1 MBit	1 MBit	1 MBit	16 Meg	Possible

EISA boards

The modern 486 boards with the EISA bus can usually be expanded to as much as 64 Meg on the board.

Since it's possible to use 256 KBit, 1 MBit, and 4 MBit RAMs in various arrangements, you can create almost any combination on these boards.

The modern 486 boards usually contain SIMM banks, which must contain four identical memory modules.

Possible Memory Combinations of EISA Board				
Bank 1	**Bank 2**	**Bank 3**	**Bank 4**	**Total memory**
4 x 256 KBit				1 Meg
4 x 256 KBit	4 x 256 KBit			2 Meg
4 x 1 MBit				4 Meg
4 x 256 KBit	4 x1 MBit			5 Meg
4 x 256 KBit	4 x 256 KBit	4 x 1 MBit		6 Meg
4 x 1 MBit	4 x 1 MBit			8 Meg
4 x 256 KBit	4 x 1 MBit	4 x 1 MBit		9 Meg
4 x 256 KBit	4 x 256 KBit	4 x 1 MBit	4 x 1 MBit	10 Meg
4 x 1 MBit	4 x 1 MBit	4 x 1 MBit		12 Meg
4 x 256 KBit	4 x 1 MBit	4 x 1 MBit	4 x 1 MBit	13 Meg
4 x 1 MBit	4x1 MBit	4 x 1 MBit	4 x 1 MBit	16 Meg
4 x 4 MBit				16 Meg
4 x 1 MBit	4 x 4 MBit			20 Meg
4 x 1 MBit	4 x 1 MBit	4 x 4 MBit		24 Meg
4 x 1 MBit	4 x 1 MBit	4 x 1 MBit	4 x 4 MBit	28 Meg
4 x 4 MBit	4 x 4 MBit			32 Meg
4 x 1 MBit	4 x 4 MBit	4 x 4 MBit		36 Meg
4 x 1 MBit	4 x 1 MBit	4 x 4 MBit	4 x 4 MBit	40 Meg
4 x 4 MBit	4 x 4 MBit	4 x 4 MBit		48 Meg
4 x 1 MBit	4 x 4 MBit	4 x 4 MBit	4 x 4 MBit	52 Meg
4 x 4 MBit	4 x 4 MBit	4 x 4 MBit	4 x 4 MBit	64 Meg

With some EISA boards, only two memory banks can be used. "Two story" SIMMs are inserted in these banks. So, a maximum of 64 Meg can be addressed by using special memory management techniques.

Drivers

You must use drivers to use memory according to the extended or expanded memory process. Drivers are either device (unit) drivers or separate management programs.

CONFIG.SYS calls drivers

Device drivers are loaded before the DOS command processor, COMMAND.COM. Which drivers are loaded is recorded in the CONFIG.SYS file, which must be at the root level of the boot partition.

Other important system settings are also recorded here (e.g., the location of the DOS command processor COMMAND.COM or the amount of conventional memory reserved for DOS). Also, information about other device drivers to be installed is located here.

A device is a hardware expansion

These devices can be an additional disk drive, a special graphics card, or even a scanner. These device drivers inform the operating system about these additional devices and enable addressing them properly. Even additional memory, which for DOS means anything above 640K, must be addressed with a device driver.

Programs from AUTOEXEC.BAT

Separate memory management programs, however, are started from AUTOEXEC.BAT. These programs must also be located at the root level of the boot partition. In Chapter 11 we'll explain how CONFIG.SYS and AUTOEXEC.BAT should be handled.

Several drivers make the present memory available to the 80486 either as EMS memory or XMS memory. MS-DOS 5.0 includes two memory managers that can be used with a 386: HIMEM.SYS and EMM386.SYS.

Both of these must be on the boot partition and called one after the other from the CONFIG.SYS file. The utilization of extended memory is handled by the HIMEM.SYS driver, as well as by the VDISK.SYS and SMARTDRV.SYS drivers.

MS-DOS 6.0 includes HIMEM.SYS and EMM386.EXE which can be used as memory managers with a 386.

Memory drivers from individual manufacturers

Some manufacturers supply their own memory drivers with their computers. These are usually EMM (Expanded Memory Manager) programs.

The Compaq expanded memory manager

One such expanded memory manager included in the package supplied with Compaq computers is called CEMM. This program supports the LIM standard up to and including Version 3.2. The memory manager is available as an EXE file and can also be started from DOS. CEMM must be installed if a Weitek coprocessor is installed.

A special routine, which automatically determines the correct values during installation and saves them as part of the device loader command in the CONFIG.SYS file, is provided.

If you want to install the program manually, perhaps because you're not happy with the suggested allocation of memory (usually the entire expanded memory is used as EMS), first you must transfer the CEMM.EXE file to the hard drive.

The following entry must then be made in the CONFIG.SYS file:

```
DEVICE=path/CEMM.EXE [parameters]
```

The path includes the drive and subdirectory, in which CEMM.EXE is located. For parameters, you can enter the following values:

nnnn	For the EMS process *nnnn*K will be used. 256K are standard. The value can be between 16 and 8192, but should never exceed the memory that's actually present.
M*x*	Address specification for the EMS memory window.

The following parameters can be used either from the CONFIG.SYS file or in a program call from DOS:

/ON	The expanded memory becomes available immediately after the start of the memory manager; and the expanded memory manager is activated.
/OFF	The CEMM is not initially active.
/AUTO	The CEMM is then activated if a program requests EMS memory. (Standard setting if neither of the other two is indicated.) Automatic activation is useful when other programs also require extended memory (e.g., Windows).
W=ON1	A Weitek coprocessor is present and requires support.
W=OFF	A Weitek coprocessor isn't present.

The Dell expanded memory manager

A driver program for expanded memory is included in the Dell Systems package. The program, called MM.SYS, is on the system diskette, which also contains the video driver.

Like all other memory drivers, the MM.SYS file needs to be on the boot partition of your hard drive and is activated with the following entry in the CONFIG.SYS file:

```
DEVICE=MM.SYS
```

The memory manager supervises memory according to the LIM EMS Standard, Version 4.0. It's also possible to modify the driver's operation by using parameters appended to the program call. The parameters are specifically:

/A=*nnn*	Establishes the I/O base address for the EMS port at nnn (hexadecimal number). Any value between 100 and 3FF can be selected; 208 is the default value. This setting shouldn't be changed.
/C=*nnn*	Limits the number of register settings that can be stored, which provides compatibility with earlier versions of the expanded memory manager. The selected value can be between 3 and 255.
/D=*nnn*	Limits the size of an individual register setting that is stored to nn (decimal number)K. A value between 1 and 32 can be selected; 5 is the default.
/F	During installation the present parameters of the memory manager are indicated.
/H=*nnn*	Sets the maximum number of handles a program can use. This parameter is used only by system programmers.
/S=*nnnn*	Sets the address of the page frame to hexadecimal nnnn. This can be located between C4000 and DFFFF; the default is from D0000 to DFFFF.
/X=*xxxx-yyyy*	Excludes the memory region between the two hexadecimal addresses *xxxx* and *yyyy* from the page frame.
/Z	The memory is tested during the boot process.

Parameters that cancel one another (e.g., /S and /X) shouldn't be used together.

3.4 Memory Problems

Since memory is electronic instead of mechanical, technical problems rarely occur. However, when an error does occur, it's difficult to locate. You should always write down the exact memory location (address) at which the error was reported. This is helpful if your computer must be repaired.

Memory chips are among the most sensitive electronic components in the computer. They can (and do) go bad for seemingly inexplicable reasons at any time.

In the worst case, an application crashes and a message similar to the following appears on the screen:

SYSTEM HALTED

Sometimes the computer actually provides the address at which the error occurred. Also write down the messages that appear.

Looking for the cause

You should try to determine what could have caused the problem. This might help if you encounter the problem again later.

Static electricity

Memory chips are sensitive to electrostatic discharge (static electricity). Usually you encounter static electricity everyday.

However, this can be a problem when you open your computer. You can accidentally touch some component after discharging a minute amount of electricity. This amount may be so small that you don't even see or feel the discharge. The current goes through the chips and one chip or another can be destroyed.

Ground yourself

To prevent this from happening, connect yourself to a good ground while working on your computer. As we mentioned earlier, you should purchase a ground strap from an electronics or computer store.

Heat

Heat can also damage memory chips. There isn't much space in the modern compact cases and mini-towers. So, the microprocessor and a few of the other components, such as hard drives, generate heat.

If a component is sensitive to heat and is located too close to a heat source, it can easily be damaged.

Unfortunately, this type of problem appears only when the computer has been in operation over a relatively long period of time. So, when you place your computer in your car, which is cold, and take it to your computer dealer, it operates flawlessly. Then when you get home and run your computer for several hours, it fails again.

Improper installation

Chip or module installed backwards

Another problem can occur when you've recently installed or expanded memory. If the computer won't boot or displays error messages during the memory test, a chip or module may have been installed backwards.

This occasionally occurs with DIPs and SIPs. DIPs have a U-shaped marking on the chip, which matches one on the socket; both of these point in the same direction. However, SIPs don't provide this security and the manuals supplied with the computer aren't always helpful.

Sometimes one of the chips may be installed out of position by one pin. This occurs when your computer contains multi-sockets, which accept both 256 KBit and 1 MBit chips.

Contact problems

Finally, contact problems can also be the cause of memory failure. This usually affects older computers. The contacts oxidize in the sockets. So, good electrical contact is no longer possible. In this case, carefully remove all the chips and squirt a little contact cleaner (available at many electronics stores) into the sockets.

Too little memory?

Even though 4 Meg are installed in your computer, when the MEM command is activated, only 3.6 Meg are indicated. In this case, your upper DOS area can be used only as shadow RAM and is unavailable for use by DOS as extended memory. The only solution to this problem is to activate the shadow RAM in Setup and then use this memory in some way.

HIMEM.SYS cannot be installed

If the HIMEM.SYS driver won't allow itself to be installed, the high memory region is already being used for some other purpose. Rearrange the sequence in which drivers are loaded in CONFIG.SYS so HIMEM.SYS is loaded first.

Chapter 4 — Bus

When the first PC was introduced in 1981, one of IBM's main goals was to create a computer that represented an open system. So, plug-in slots containing all the electrical signals of the computer were installed in the computer. This enabled third-parties to develop peripheral cards.

The open system

Since extensive technical documentation was available, it wasn't difficult for third-party developers to build cards for the computer. Unfortunately for IBM, the open system also produced some negative side effects. Clones were produced and standards were developed in various areas (e.g., graphics).

Utilization via the bus

At first, the computer's system was accessible to others via the bus. The bus consists of a few contacts (plug-in slots) that transfer electrical signals between the individual components and the electronics on the motherboard. It also contains a part that supervises and controls bus operations.

Bus types

There are three different bus types:

- System bus
- Memory bus
- Input/output bus

The system bus forms the basis for the development of a computer system. The CPU, memory, and rapid input/output devices are attached to it.

Very large computers have an I/O bus in addition to the system bus. The computer is equipped only with a system bus, while the CPU and memory are connected without a bus.

Although the computer bus has been successful, this success cannot be attributed to its properties. Unlike industrial buses, where bus control is affected by logic components, the computer bus is controlled by the CPU.

Also, industry buses have multimaster functions, which assign a priority to each peripheral within the system.

4.1 Bus Standards

Four different bus standards are currently used in computers:

- 8-bit ISA
- 16-bit ISA bus
- MCA bus developed by IBM
- EISA bus

In 386/486 computers only the 16-bit ISA bus, the EISA bus, and the MCA bus are used. The following table provides an overview of the various bus systems:

Overview of Various Bus Systems				
Bus type	PC bus ISA-bus	AT-bus ISA-bus	EISA-bus	MCA-bus
Data width	8-bit	8/16-bit	8/1 6/32-bit	16/32-bit
Address space	1 Meg	16 Meg	4 Gb	16 Meg/4 Gb
Maximum data transfer rate	6.5 Meg/s	20 Meg/s	32 Meg/s	160 Meg/s
Multimaster capability	no	registered	yes	yes
Microprocessor dependency	yes	yes	yes	no

With the introduction of the AT model by IBM, the computer bus was adapted to the new capabilities of the microprocessor. Besides the eight lines already present in the computer bus, eight additional lines were added to the ISA/AT bus (Industrial Standard Architecture). This resulted in a data width of 16 bits. The number of address lines was also increased from 20 to 24, making it possible to address 16 Meg.

The 80286 microprocessor used in the AT has a data width of 16 bits and 24 address lines. With these simple changes, the ISA bus was adapted to the capabilities of the microprocessor used in the AT.

The ISA/AT bus is also downwardly compatible with the computer bus. It can be controlled even with 8-bit computer expansion cards. Both 8-bit and 16-bit expansion cards can be used.

However, the microprocessor has problems identifying which card type is being used.

Additional control lines were added

Additional control lines, which signal to the microprocessor whether the next data transfer should be made in 8-bit or 16-bit mode, were added. Before the data transfer begins, the card reports that it's a 16-bit card.

Otherwise, the microprocessor transfers the data in the 8-bit mode, which naturally results in loss of speed.

Although the downward compatibility of the ISA/AT bus sounds practical, it does have a disadvantage. The 16-bit expansion card must first produce a signal before the transfer begins.

To enable the card to know that it's immediately required, special switching is needed. Four address lines are duplicated, but in a rapidly decoded form, which enables the card to recognize that it's being used.

Another problem is that IBM never published the ISA bus specification. So, standardization and improvement was very difficult. Because of this, the 8 MHz clock speed at which the ISA bus is driven was retained. When microprocessors with a higher clock frequency are used, the bus is driven by another clock. This type of bus control is probably the most widely used principle in 386/AT and 486/AT computers.

Additional interrupt and DMA control lines were also added with the introduction of the ISA/AT bus. The bus was also expanded to include a bus-master control line which enabled an expansion card to assume control of the entire computer. However, since this bus-master arrangement is sluggish, it takes over control of the computer very slowly. It can be used only for a second microprocessor, but not for a graphics controller, which would assume system control for a few milliseconds.

Problems with the ISA bus

The introduction of the 386/486 microprocessors also led to a re-evaluation of the ISA bus. However, it's obvious that the performance of the ISA bus is usually adequate for a computer with these microprocessors and that, in most cases, expansion cards don't fully use the ISA bus.

However, the bus speed has become less important because the functions that previously required expansion cards are now integrated directly on the motherboard.

The ISA bus isn't suitable for memory expansion in 386/486 computers because, unlike these microprocessors, it has a data width of only 16 bits and is unable to address more than 16 Meg of memory. In practice, however, this problem is offset by the fact that more computers accommodate 16 Meg and more of memory on the motherboard.

If the memory present on the system board isn't sufficient, many manufacturers have solved the problem by using their own proprietary 32-bit memory bus. These proprietary bus expansions don't usually deserve the name "bus" because in most cases they represent a physical expansion of the main board, which permits the installation of additional memory chips.

MCA bus

Along with the new PS/2 computer family, a new bus type called the micro-channel was introduced by IBM in 1987. The most important characteristic of the MCA bus (Micro-Channel Architecture) is the fact that it's completely incompatible with the ISA bus.

This characteristic is both an advantage and a disadvantage. A completely new beginning was made, making it possible to develop a simpler and faster bus. Unfortunately, however, the existing ISA cards can no longer be used in an MCA bus computer.

Types of MCA buses

The MCA bus was implemented as a 16-bit bus and as a separate 32-bit bus. There are two types of MCA buses:

- 16-bit bus for the 286 and 386SX

- 32-bit bus for the 386DX and 486

Therefore, there are also 16-bit and 32-bit expansion cards for the MCA bus. It's useless to place 32-bit expansion cards onto a 16-bit MCA bus. There is also a 16-bit plug-in card with video expansion.

An MCA computer permits up to three different types of plug-in slots for expansion cards.

The MCA bus and the EISA bus represent the two modern bus technologies. The 32-bit MCA bus is similar to the EISA bus. It's a complete 32-bit data bus with 32 address lines. The 16-bit version closely resembles the ISA bus. Technically, the main difference between MCA and EISA is that the MCA bus is an asynchronous bus, and the EISA bus is a synchronous bus.

Unalterable clock frequency

Synchronous buses operate with an unalterable clock frequency; it's not affected by how quickly a component group can transfer data. A synchronous bus gets its clock frequency from the units participating in the data transfer. The receiving unit reports the receipt of data to the transmitting unit over the bus lines and requests new data from the sending unit.

This data transfer mode leads to a more complicated bus structure of the asynchronous bus. Although the asynchronous bus is more complicated, it has higher performance potential.

The MCA bus originally permitted (according to the specification published by IBM) a maximum data transfer rate of 20 Meg/s. Recently a new data transfer procedure was introduced by IBM. This procedure allows up to 160 Meg/s of data to be transferred with the MCA bus in a sort of burst mode.

Compared to the ISA bus, even interrupt control was improved in the MCA bus. The interrupts are flank-controlled with the ISA bus, but the MCA bus operates with marker-controlled interrupts. Effectiveness and reliability can be significantly increased in systems with numerous interrupts.

Programmable Option Select

MCA systems and cards also no longer need to be configured with jumpers and DIP switches. They have an unchangeable identification number, called the POS (Programmable Option Select).

The POS makes installation easier because it uses a file called ADF (Adapter Definition File), in which all the configurations for the card are stored.

The EISA bus

Although the EISA (Extended Industrial Standard Architecture) bus was developed as a rival of the MCA bus, it's based on the ISA bus and is downwardly-compatible with this bus. So, an EISA bus system must be able to accept ISA expansion cards easily.

This problem is solved via the two-story structure of the EISA expansion slot. The first level contains the ISA connections, which gives the EISA slot the outward appearance of an ISA slot.

The lower level contains the EISA connections. Stops in the plug-in slot prevent the ISA card from being inserted all the way, which prevents it from receiving inappropriate signals.

So the signals reserved only for EISA cards are available between the second-story ISA connectors.

Since ISA bus compatibility was retained, the EISA bus is driven at a clock frequency of 8 MHz. It's a complete 32-bit bus with 32 address lines, being completely adapted to the capabilities offered by 386/486 microprocessors.

With the EISA bus it would be possible to transfer a maximum of 32 Meg/s (i.e., 32 bits or 4 bytes) at a frequency of 8 MHz.

Improved interrupt control

As in the case of the MCA bus, interrupt control was improved in the EISA bus. The EISA has interrupt lines that can be used in common, because they are no longer flank-controlled as in the ISA bus, but marker-controlled as in the case of the MCA bus.

The bus-mastering capabilities were also improved. A bus master can gain control over the bus very quickly and then directly transfer data between the units. The EISA chip set eliminates the problems that occur whenever a 32-bit bus master attempts to communicate with a 16-bit unit.

Each EISA expansion card has an unchangeable product code, which is assigned by the EISA society. This code can be read by the microprocessor to determine where the cards are located. This simplifies configuring the EISA hardware and software.

The companies that participated in the development of the EISA bus precisely defined the EISA standard and the bus timing.

Intel's EISA chip set

With the development of the 82350 chip family, Intel created the first set of chips designed according to the EISA specification. These chips support the CPU, i386, or i486 of the 82385 cache controller and of the 80387 numeric coprocessor. Two of these chips are essential; the other two are useful additions.

82357 ISP chip

The 82357 ISP (Integrated System Peripheral) chip handles the DMA (Direct Memory Access) functions of the system and is completely compatible with the ISA system. It also refreshes address generation and monitors it when the bus is unavailable.

The ISP chip also supports multiple bus masters, using clever algorithms for the allocation of bus-master rights. The ISP chip has seven 32-bit DMA channels, five 16-bit timer/counters for the clock frequency of the EISA bus or the CPU, for example, and two 8-channel interrupt controllers.

EBC chip

The EBC (EISA Bus Controller) chip, which is designated as 82385, is the actual EISA manager. It can control several 8/16/32-bit bus masters and bus slaves. It regulates the connections between the host and the EISA/ISA bus.

The EBC chip represents the interface between the main microprocessor and the EISA bus and also handles any data incompatibilities between ISA and EISA systems. It also controls cache operation between the host and the EISA/ISA bus.

Although the 82353 chip (EISA Bus Buffer) isn't absolutely necessary for EISA bus operation, using this chip has many advantages. The EBB chip combines the various modes available in the EISA system for data transfer between the separate bus systems.

It serves to buffer data and provides the various transfer modes with their special control logic and their buffering properties. So it replaces up to 20 other separate ICs.

82355 BMIC chip

The 82355 BMIC (Busmaster Interface Controller) chip, which is integrated on an EISA expansion card, represents the counterpart in the EISA bus system. It permits the utilization of the improved capabilities of the EISA bus system by using expansion cards. The BMIC chip is specifically used for data transfer in burst mode.

It's also responsible for assuming the busmaster capabilities of the expansion card and controls the bus system in asynchronous operation.

So, the BMIC is a highly specialized independent microprocessor that supervises the communication between the host system and external system. Its functions and capabilities are for that reason as diverse as those of a complete computer.

Bus selection

Usually the bus isn't important to the user because:

> - Many powerful extensions have been integrated onto the motherboard so a bus isn't required.
>
> - System performance depends on the bus only when very demanding applications are being used.

If you're using a 386/486 system in the usual way, the ISA bus should be adequate. The MCA bus offered by IBM isn't compatible with the ISA bus and ISA plug-in cards cannot be used.

The EISA bus is compatible with the ISA bus and represents an expansion opportunity. However, you should determine whether using this bus is justified. The EISA bus is generally used in the following situations:

> - Network cards in the server with very high data transfer rates.
>
> - Hard drive controller cards with high data throughput and disk cache systems.
>
> - Extremely high resolution graphics cards with 2 K x 2 K pixels.

4.2 Types of Cards

An entire series of computer expansion cards is available for the AT bus, which we'll discuss in the following section. To build a computer system, you must allocate the available expansion slots wisely and ensure that the power supply has the capacity for all the system components.

A 200-watt power supply is adequate for most 486 computers. However, if your computer has a smaller power supply and is equipped with many cards and other internal peripherals, your power supply could be stretched to its limits and may eventually fail.

Although it's possible to change the power supply, a new power supply may not fit into the old location because of its size and the position of the connectors and fan.

On the following page is an overview of some cards you can install in your computer. The listed cards represent only a small segment of the card selection that's available for computers using the ISA or the MCA bus.

Approximately 70 percent of all computers use the ISA bus. Therefore, ISA cards are cheap, even if they cannot deliver the performance of the MCA or EISA cards.

Interface cards

You can easily add interfaces to your computer by using interface cards. These cards are also called "multi-I/O" cards and usually cost about 50 dollars. They usually contain one parallel and two serial interfaces, a gameport, and a realtime clock. (You can deactivate the realtime clock because there's already one on the motherboard.) These types of cards should be installed in an 8-bit slot.

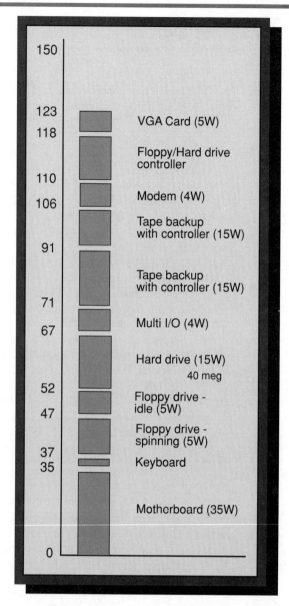

Power use by computer components

There are also special interface cards with more than the usual two serial and one parallel interfaces. These cards are used in multi-user operating systems like UNIX or the multi-user DOS from Digital Research.

Game cards

The computer also supports joysticks. These joysticks aren't the digital joysticks found in most home computers and game consoles, such as the Nintendo or Sega game systems. Instead, they are analog units addressed by a special interface.

A maximum of two joystick ports can be used in the computer. One is usually located on the multi-I/O card, though this often leads to problems regarding the correct interrupt. A better solution is to install an extra plug-in card containing the two gameports. The gameports are recognized and used independently by game programs.

Bus mouse interface card

If you don't want to attach your mouse to the serial interface, you can assign it to a separate interface with its own interrupt. This contains the electronics needed to tie in the rolling-ball mouse system.

Generally, you'll find that a bus mouse has many advantages. The most obvious advantage is that your serial port can be left open for other devices. You'll also notice that the mouse operates more smoothly and quickly in many applications.

Graphics cards

The card controlling the data display is also usually installed in a computer slot, although the video circuitry is usually included on the motherboard in some computers. We'll discuss video cards and graphics in Chapter 7.

Memory expansion

If all the space available for memory on the motherboard is occupied, the only option is to add a plug-in card for additional memory. You can use either a 32-bit slot available in some 386es, which provides the benefits of 32-bit memory transfer that's possible with the 386, or you can install a plug-in card in a 16-bit slot. The latter option should be used only for 80386SX computers or if there isn't a 32-bit slot available on the motherboard. For more information on memory, refer to Chapter 3.

Modems

You need a modem card if your computer is extensively used for data transfer or for communicating with people in various locations. The advantage of this card is that the serial data transfer "bottleneck" begins only downstream of the modem. An internal modem is usually much less expensive than an external modem.

Fax cards

Transferring documents using the telefax process is very popular. Although currently there are more stand-alone units, more computers contain cards that allow teledocuments to be sent and received directly with a computer. You may also want to add a scanner and a printer for use with a Fax card. Transmitting the document is handled entirely by the computer.

Voice control for the computer

With voice control cards, a computer can respond to the spoken word. A microphone is attached to the card and it's possible to program the computer to perform a specific action in response to a limited number of spoken commands. The computer will respond to a command, regardless of the word that's used. For example, if you teach the computer to display the directory in response to the command "Bologna", it will do exactly that whenever it hears this word.

Sound cards

One limitation of computer hardware is its sound capabilities. The tone generator and the speaker in computers were originally designed only for emitting simple signal tones. So several companies have developed expansion boards. These boards contain a sound chip with several tone generators as well as output connectors, which enable you to attach headphones or an amplifier. These plug-in cards are inserted into a computer slot.

Sound cards are mainly used for computer games. However, by adding a MIDI plug-in card or box, it's also possible to attach them to keyboards and produce some impressive audio results.

Many sound cards are available. Among these cards are Ad-Lib from AdLib, Inc. ($299), Sound Blaster v1.5 from Creative Labs, Inc. ($239), and Sound Commander from MediaSonic, Inc. ($239). The musical capabilities of the cards vary. The cheaper cards usually offer sound capabilities similar to an electric organ. They may have 11 or 12 voices.

The LAPC-1 (from Roland for about $600) is a synthesizer installed in a computer. It has 32 voices that can be programmed in eight different sound colorations.

The sound cards are controlled by a special driver. If a game doesn't support the installed sound card, it cannot produce any sounds.

The AdLib sound card brings music to your computer

MIDI cards

MIDI is an acronym for Musical Instrument Digital Interface. This is an interface that allows you to add musical instruments to the sounds on your computer. These sounds are then controlled by digital signals. Several MIDI devices can be switched in succession and mutually controlled.

IBM-compatible computers haven't concentrated on the music market as much as other computers. So MIDI cards are currently available from only a few manufacturers. The best known manufacturer is Roland, which produces the LAPC-1 plug-in sound card (see above).

Roland's MIDI card is called the MPU IPC-T and consists of a plug-in card and a connector box. This connector box can also be attached directly to the LAPC-1 sound card. Besides the MIDI connector sockets, this box also contains outlets for synchronization with a multi-track tape recorder.

This hardware is useless without the associated software. Other companies can supply these programs.

Radio

For about $150, you can add a card to your computer to interface to a shortwave radio and receive Radioteletype (RTTY), Morse Code, and various other types of telemetery, including television signals from satellites.

MCA cards

Currently, the microchannel architecture is in only a relatively small number of computers (about 20 percent). However, an entire series of expansion cards is available for the PS/2 system. The range of offerings exceeds even that in the ISA field because microchannel is a more powerful system.

EISA cards

The EISA standard is the most recent enhancement of the three dominant computer bus systems. The first computers with the EISA bus were available during late 1989. There isn't a large selection of cards yet. EISA cards are usually developed by companies that produce EISA computers.

For example, Olivetti has built an EISA-SCSI hard drive controller into its new flagship computer, the CP486, which is equipped with a 486 microprocessor and i860 coprocessor socket.

Utilization of full data transfer on the EISA bus enables the controller to achieve a data throughput of 4 Meg/s, which is four times that currently obtainable with the fastest controller standard (ESDI). The controller also contains an ST-506 and ESDI emulator for the attachment of hard drives operating according to those standards.

The Olivetti EISA video controller (EVC) is a 32-bit graphics card offering a maximal resolution of 1024 x 768 pixels. In new operating modes, the memory organization of the VGA standard has been changed so the 32-bit data width is possible. The original VGA standard, which is also supported by the card, prevents 32-bit access due to its EGA compatibility.

Other companies use the EISA bus even more cautiously. In its new high-end computers, Systempro and the Deskpro 486/25, which have an EISA bus, Compaq uses 16-bit VGA graphics electronics and an "advanced graphics" card for the 16-bit ISA bus, which offers a resolution of 1024 x 768.

EISA is successful when the specifications of this bus are needed instead of in standard peripheral devices. For example, EISA is useful for rapidly transferring large amounts of data within, and outside of, a network. Some network cards use optoelectronic methods to achieve data transfer rates of 100 Meg/s.

The EISA bus is useful in all operations, in which the CPU cannot be queried again. For example, the direct transfer of data from the expansion card into memory and controlling the bus system with the expansion card (bus mastering).

Hard drive controllers

SCSI controllers

In the few 486es with the EISA bus that are currently being sold with an installed EISA card, this card is usually a SCSI controller for the hard drive. An American company, Mylex, was one of the first manufacturers to make such a controller available.

There are also similar cards from other firms (e.g., the 1740 from Adaptec whose AT-bus SCSI controller 1542 is used in many computers). Unlike the 1542, the 1740 doesn't have an accompanying floppy controller on the motherboard.

Besides the EISA bus system, the manufacturers are increasingly giving their computers their own cache memory. The standard version of the Mylex controller comes with 4 Meg of cache memory.

Obviously, the hard drives achieve exceptionally high marks in the various benchmark tests. This occurs because benchmarks frequently transmit large amounts of identical data. In these instances, a cache displays its strength, driving the perceived data transfer rate upward, although it's actually much lower.

TAKE NOTE

> It's better to buy a hard drive that's capable of a higher data transfer rate because of physical capabilities (rate of rotation, sector density) than to try to increase this rate by using a cache.

Interfaces

The interfaces are responsible for data transfer from and to the computer. You should use EISA cards when their special properties (intelligence and rapid transfer) are needed.

The DigiCHANNEL EISA C/X from DigiBOARD, contains two RS422/RS485 synchronous interfaces and can be attached to the external C/X interface system, which offers up to 64 asynchronous (serial) interfaces.

In the ALC system from Computone, the user can determine the properties by selecting a module. The available selections include an asynchronous, a synchronous/asynchronous, an Ethernet (network) and a fax-scanner module.

User areas: UNIX

EISA cards are especially effective in UNIX computers. Since some of these cards contain their own CPU, the main microprocessor of the actual computer isn't bothered by overhead processes.

Graphics cards

True-color graphics cards

The creation of graphics data doesn't require high data transfer rates. Because of this, there aren't many graphics cards available for the EISA bus. EISA graphics cards are useful only if the memory on the card is used by auxiliary microprocessors and rapid image manipulations are being performed (e.g., with animation in 3-D).

One EISA graphics card is the Mylex GXE020A, which is based on the Texas Instruments TMS34020 that runs on this card at a clock speed of 40 MHz. The card operates according to the TIGA standard and offers a maximal resolution of 1600 x 1280 pixels in 256 of 16.7 million colors (True Color).

EISA network cards

The following properties make the EISA bus particularly suitable for network applications:

- 32-bit data width permitting data transfer rates of 33 Meg per second.

- 32-bit address width, enabling up to 4 gigabytes to be addressed on the bus.

- Up to 15 busmasters are possible, which execute input/output operations independently of the CPU.

ARCNET cards

Computers can be linked together in a network in several ways. About one fifth of the networks work according to the ARCNET system, in which the networked computers are arranged around the server in the shape of a star. The net itself is constructed from 93 ohm cables.

An ARCNET card for a 486 can have four or eight connectors. An example of such a card is the SMC ARCNET EISA 3200, which permits cabling with coaxial cable (Version C) or with "twisted pair" (two wires, similar to telephone cable).

Ethernet cards

The other large network standard is called Ethernet. The net is built up on the bus principle (i.e., all the computers are linked sequentially). EISA cards for this network standard are available from Novell, TORUS, and Codenoll.

Token Ring

The Token Ring standard is currently only supported by one EISA card, the DualSpeed Token Ring Controller from Compaq.

Analog-digital converters

The EISA A2000 is a card that converts analog measurements into digital signals. Rapid data transfer and the possibility of controlling the bus or the memory nullify the need for large memory on the plug-in card, which is still necessary with the AT bus for temporarily storing analog values.

Also available with this card is a program that converts the computer into a digital oscilloscope.

4.3 Installing Expansion Cards

Anyone can upgrade a computer with a plug-in card. Since everything in the computer is usually attached with screws or plugs, all you need is a few tools.

For most installations, you'll need a Phillips screwdriver and flat nose pliers.

Before working on your 486, disconnect the power cord and remove all cables connecting the unit to the peripherals (keyboard, monitor, printer, mouse, etc.).

ISA 8-, 16-, and 32-bit slots

There are several types of slots for ISA cards. The 8-bit slot has 8 data lines and 20 address lines. The 16-bit AT slot has 16 data lines and 24 address lines.

The 32-bit slot in the ISA bus system (the special variants from individual manufacturers) is provided only for memory expansion cards. Most motherboards still have one or two 8-bit slots available in addition to the 16-bit AT slots.

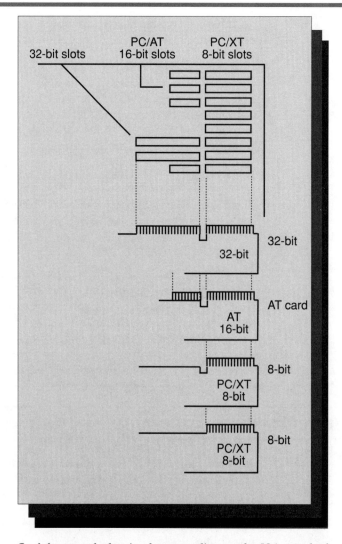

Card forms and plug-in slots according to the ISA standard

Expansion cards that are designed to fit an 8-bit slot can also be driven electrically in a 16-bit slot. Many 8-bit cards have a shape that prevents them from being inserted in a 16-bit slot.

To use these cards, a few of the slots in ATs and 386s were equipped with only the 8-bit portion of the card edge connector. If all slots must be 16-bit, with many computers, you can simply install the missing part of the card edge connector. The electrical wiring is already present.

Many 16-bit cards can also be operated in 8-bit slots with the loss of the AT data and address bus. The bus width is particularly important if the cards are addressed in protected mode or are expected to deliver a relatively high data throughput.

TAKE NOTE

> The general procedure for installing a plug-in card is essentially the same for all types. It doesn't matter whether the card is an ISA, EISA, or MCA card. It's important that the EISA and MCA cards are plugged into the correct slot because they use geographic addressing. This means that the address, from which the card accesses the system, depends on the slot in which it's installed.

The first step: Configure the card

To configure a card, first you must set any required DIP switches or jumpers. Which switches and jumpers and where they are located always depends on the purpose of the card. Consult the documentation included with the specific card.

The second step: Remove the slot cover or any card already installed

Next look for a free slot for the card. The expansion slot cover, which covers the opening in the case adjacent to this slot, is removed. The new card is inserted in the slot and the appropriate screw is tightened.

If you're installing the new card as a replacement for one already present (e.g., a graphics card), the existing card must be removed. To remove a card, loosen the screw attaching the card to the case and carefully pull the card vertically out of the slot.

The third step: Install the card

Insert the expansion card in the slot that is now free and push it vertically into the socket(s) with uniform pressure. Be sure that the card is straight. Once the board is securely in the slot as far as it will go, fasten it to the case with the screw you removed.

The fourth step: Check it out and close the case

Finally, ensure that everything is operating properly. Attach the keyboard, monitor, and any peripheral needed and test whether the card is operating as it should. If it is, close the computer case again; you're now finished.

Peculiarities with microchannel computers

Beginning with Model 50, the IBM PS/2 models are equipped with the MCA bus. For the 386 computers (Model 70 and Model 80), there is no variant with the old ISA bus, as with the 8086 and 80286 computers. The Model 70 contains three MCA slots which, in the basic version, are all free because the system components are either on the motherboard (VGA graphics electronics) or in internal slots.

IBM designed the PS/2 computers so maintenance would be simple. For this reason, there are no connecting cables inside the case. Everything is either plugged in or attached with screws. So inserting or removing an MCA card is very easy.

User friendly

Microchannel cards, like AT cards, have edge connectors that are inserted in the corresponding slot. The attachment screw is located on the back of the case for the PS/2 main unit. Unlike ISA cards, it's important which MCA cards are mounted at which location.

This determines the address at which the card will be accessed. You should remember the slot when you interchange one or more MCA cards. No tools are needed to loosen or tighten the edge screws that attach the MCA cards; these screws can be turned with your fingers.

Automatic configuration

IBM discovered that approximately 60 percent of all technical problems that occur with adapter cards are caused by incorrectly setting the small configuration switches and jumpers. For this reason, the cards are configured by using the Programmable Option Select (POS) system.

An adapter definition file, which contains all possible configurations, is associated with each adapter. This file, which is read in by a configuration program after a card is installed, allows settings to be stored in a CMOS-RAM. The configuration is completed with a reference diskette that's supplied with each PS/2 computer.

4.4 Networks

Communicating with others

As we described earlier, internal communication within a computer is handled by the bus systems. However, for external communication, two or more computers are simply joined together to form a network. Networking offers many advantages:

> • Expensive peripheral devices can be shared by all network participants.
>
> • Databases, which are continually updated and used by the entire network, can be maintained and managed by one computer (e.g., the server).
>
> • Data security is simplified.
>
> • The individual workstation computers are unburdened because the programs that aren't needed by all network users have to be installed only on the main computer (e.g., the server).
>
> • Communication among network participants is simplified.

Setting up the network requires hardware and software. There are several options which can be combined in various ways.

Serial nets

Dual linkage

The simplest networking option involves connecting computers via the serial interface. This interface has an inlet and an outlet, which enables only two computers to be linked with one interface by joining the outlet of one to the inlet of the other and vice versa.

Suitable software

Once you've decided what you want to do with this network, you should select the software. For transferring files, programs like Laplink from Traveling Software, are suitable. The program is started on both of the computers, the files are transferred, and then the connection is broken.

Norton Commander

You can also do this by using Norton Commander 3.0. The *Connect* function is found in *File* menu. Use the dialog box that's displayed when you select this option to declare one computer as "master" and the other as "slave" (subordinate). The master always has priority in case of simultaneous access.

If the connection is established in this way, you'll then be able to access the hard drive of the attached computer as auxiliary mass storage. If one of the two starts its programs from the Norton Commander, it's possible to access the hard drive of the other.

UNIX

With UNIX and a main computer, to which other computers are attached as terminals, more complex network operation is possible. The UNIX operating system provides everything you need to do this (see Section 9.4).

Advantages and disadvantages

The advantages of a serial network is that you don't have to purchase a lot of expensive hardware and even the software, depending on the type, isn't very expensive.

The disadvantage of this approach is that only two computers can be linked. You can attach additional computers with extra serial interfaces, but the connection remains dual.

Large and small networks

The linkage goes one step further if a small network is constructed from separate plug-in cards. These networks are connected to the everyday operation of the operating system by using a supplementary program for DOS.

The large networks are founded on one of the many operating systems. There are three standard card types: ArcNet, Ethernet, and Token Ring.

Arcnet

The Arcnet network standard uses a star-like structure. For control, the net uses a token passing protocol. A token moves within the net from one station to the next. Any station that wants to transmit data then attaches the data to the token; then the token carries the data to the location where they are accessed by the appropriate computer.

4.5 Problems with Expansion Cards

If your computer has expansion cards, eventually they may not work. This can be the result of a problem with the card itself or a conflict between two cards.

Coexistence

Each component of a computer can be tied to the system in three ways. First, there is the memory address in the low memory region. This is used by each expansion.

Next is the interrupt level. There are 16 interrupt levels by which the computer controls its periphery. This is the only way to use many cards. Unfortunately, there are only 16 levels and of these only 3 or 4 are available to an expansion card.

Finally, there is also DMA access. Only a few cards use this method. One example is the SCSI controller. An expansion card usually has either DIP switches or jumpers for setting this parameter. If this isn't the case, it's possible that the setting is preset and cannot be changed, which is common among the older manufacturers.

Memory

The computer uses the lower memory region for data exchange and addressing. The registers, in which the computer deposits and obtains its data, are located here.

Many cards use additional memory in the upper memory region with their own BIOS (i.e., their own mini-operating system). Both the lower and upper memory regions can be allocated only once per card. If two cards are set to the same address, this can create memory conflicts and then neither card will work. In this case, you must reconfigure one of the cards.

Interrupts

The interfaces and other cards in the computer are also addressed by the computer via the interrupt component. Sixteen interrupt levels are established for this. An expansion can report "on command".

Two cards cannot use the same interrupt (at least not with the ISA bus). However, there is one exception to this rule. Since the interrupt is used only when the card is active, it's possible to set two cards to the same interrupt, as long as they aren't used together.

For example, since you probably won't be playing a computer game and printing simultaneously, you can configure the sound card and the parallel printer to the same interrupt.

DMA

Computer cards use Direct Memory Access (i.e., immediate access to memory) only for rapidly transferring data on the AT bus. DMA also provides several channels, to which the corresponding cards can be set.

Again, two cards shouldn't use the same channel. DMA also usually requires that two jumpers be set: One for the actual channel and the other for access to this channel, called DACK (DMA Acknowledge).

Mechanical problems

Besides problems with the settings, mechanical problems can also cause a card not to operate. It's possible that the card isn't properly seated in its slot although it was positioned with the slot cover.

Chapter 5 Setup

Various types of peripheral equipment can be included with IBM-compatible computers. How memory, graphics, disk drives, and hard drives are configured depends on your preferences and budget.

What is the purpose of Setup?

The computer's operating system must be able to recognize these components to use them. The required information is located in a special area of memory called CMOS. The Setup program allows you to access the CMOS and change the values stored there.

From DIP Switch to CMOS

The first computer generation (the XT computer) had such a limited choice of equipment that all the information could be set up, on the main board, with a series of small switches (DIP switches). With the AT, the range of peripherals had expanded so much that coding with DIP switches was no longer sufficient.

Manufacturers came up with the idea to store the information in a special type of memory. So AT systems, along with the subsequent generations of computers (386, 486), have a variable memory (RAM) that isn't related to the actual conventional memory. This system information memory is continuously supplied with power from a battery. So, a realtime clock, which is included with every AT, is possible.

Interaction of CMOS and BIOS

The CMOS has a series of registers that are given information, from the Setup program, about the various system components. The BIOS needs this information to ensure that the components work together smoothly. BIOS is an abbreviation for Basic Input Output System; it is a mini operating system that controls the lowest level of communication between individual components of the computer.

During input and output, all operating systems will access the BIOS, which in turn operates according to the information stored in the CMOS. For example, if an incorrect hard drive is stored here, the BIOS may try to respond to areas that don't exist on the hard drive, which may damage the system.

Controlling internal system processes

With the newer AT's you can not only control the interaction of the computer system (main board) with its external components, but also influence some of the mechanisms within the system itself, such as memory access. The internal information is also stored in the CMOS and can be changed via the Setup program.

POST - system check of CMOS-RAM information

It's very important that the CMOS information is accurate. To verify this, the computer checks the individual components each time you start the computer. This test is known as the Power On Self Test (POST); it tests the following components in sequence.

Main microprocessor

- ROM (Read-Only-Memory) with BIOS

- RAM (memory)

- Main board circuits (e.g., timer)

- Keyboard

- Hard drive

- Floppy disk drives

Then POST searches the system bus for enhancements with a BIOS of their own. This includes EGA and VGA cards.

Following the test

The POST test provides an inside look of the computer, depending on the BIOS. Check the screen display for any strange entries. If something doesn't look right, reset and perform the test again. It's possible that an enhancement wasn't recognized. For example, if you've installed an interface card, the new interfaces may not be displayed.

Error messages

If the Power On Self Test detects an error or fails to correctly identify a particular component, the BIOS sends an error message. This can be a detailed description of the error, a numeric code, or a warning beep.

TAKE NOTE

> A two to four digit code identifies a component that the POST has identified as defective. A beep also specifies a particular device. However, the device varies depending on the BIOS manufacturer. The definitions of some of the individual codes are listed in the Appendix.

An incorrectly stored component in the CMOS usually leads to an error message similar to the following:

> Configuration error - please run Setup

If the Setup program is located within the ROM-BIOS, you'll be given the option of activating it with F1:

> Press F1 to run Setup, F2 to continue

This error message will most likely appear when you start operating a self-assembled system or after you make additions to a particular component (e.g., if you expand the memory). With 486es that have been purchased assembled, everything should already be set up correctly. Unfortunately, this isn't always the case.

Which parameters are set up?

The Setup program determines the date, time, memory partitioning, and type of floppy disk drives and hard drive. This applies to virtually all 486 computers.

Some BIOS routines in 486es are so intelligent that they can identify the components by themselves. The AMI-BIOS automatically determines memory size and which RAM chips are in use.

Expanded system control

Also, the user can influence certain internal system processes with some 486es. With chips made by the Chips & Technologies Co., you can adjust memory access yourself.

Since adjusting parameters in this area may create a system setup that no longer runs, these registers aren't accessible in all 486es. In this case, you need a separate program for the adjustments.

Types of available Setup programs

The Setup programs of various computers differ according to whether they are stored in the ROM-BIOS or whether they need to be started from diskettes. They also differ according to manufacturer.

Not all Setup programs provide the same settings. Instead, the settings vary depending on how much influence the user has over the internal processes. In 486es with an EISA bus, multiple setups are included within the Setup program.

Normal and extended Setup

Let's look at the most important Setup programs and explain their settings individually. First, we'll describe the settings common to all 486es. Later we'll discuss extended options that are available only with some of the Setup programs.

Write down the Setup settings

QUICK TIP

Your computer may no longer function properly if there are incorrect entries in Setup. It's also possible for poorly written software to destroy the CMOS settings. So you should write down all the settings, both normal and extended, that your system uses and keep them with the technical data in your 486 manual.

It's especially important that you record the hard drive type, or its parameters, for a user-defined hard drive.

5.1 Normal Setup

Settings for routine work

A normal Setup program sets up the components that a 486 computer uses everyday. This includes the date and time and also the number and types of diskette drives and hard drives.

Then the memory size and partitioning are determined. Finally, the system must know the type of graphics card and whether a coprocessor is installed.

Auto-recognition

Many modern 486es require entries only for the date, time, and type of hard drive. All other components are automatically recognized by the gate arrays. With the diskette drives, only 360K drives are correctly identified; other types must be set up.

Date and time

The computer accepts the date and time entered in Setup as the system time and transfers it to its realtime clock. This is a quartz clock that is fairly accurate.

Each time a file is written to, the date and time are saved along with the file. (This doesn't occur when you copy a file.)

QUICK TIP

Set the date and time correctly

Always set the date and time correctly. This can be very helpful when you must determine the more current version of two almost identical text files.

You should check the time at least once a month. Even with the quartz clock, many computer clocks aren't completely accurate.

TAKE NOTE

MS-DOS counts time starting with 01/01/1980. You'll never find a file dated before then. If, during Setup or within a program, you enter a two-digit number for the year between 0 and 79, the computer automatically assumes you mean the years 2000 to 2079.

Daylight Savings Time

Some of the newer Setup programs even include daylight savings time. When this is activated (enabled), the computer moves the clock one hour ahead in the spring.

Diskette formats

Setup presets the format and capacity of two possible connecting drives. These values are automatically used by the FORMAT command if the user doesn't provide any other instructions.

Only the standard formats supported by MS-DOS can be used. For more information, see the following table:

Typical Diskette Formats		
Format	**Capacity**	**Diskette type**
5.25-inch	360K	DS SD (double-sided, double-density)
5.25-inch	1.2 Meg	DS HD (double-sided, high-density)
3.5-inch	720K	DS DD (double-sided, double-density)
3.5-inch	1.44 Meg	DS HD (double-sided, high-density)
3.5-inch	2.88 Meg	DS ED (double-sided extra high-density)

QUICK TIP

Additional diskette formats with DRIVER.SYS

If you need to use a special diskette format, first select the format that most closely matches the one you need. Then use DRIVER.SYS, which is an optional device driver, to set up your special format. Drives that have their own BIOS, such as the new 2.88 Meg disk drives, normally use their own drivers. These drivers are activated via CONFIG.SYS.

Hard drives

To set up your hard drive, the system asks you to select the appropriate type from a list. You must enter the correct type. The controller will try to address the hard drive sectors based on this setting.

If it addresses values that are too high, it may damage the disk. However, as long as you know the parameters of the disk, most Setup programs provide a list, from which you can choose the correct type.

QUICK TIP

Identifying hard drive types

If you're not familiar with your hard drive, you have three options:

1.   Ask your computer dealer or the manufacturer of the disk.

2.   Answer with "not available" during the Setup routine. So the hard drive Help program will try to determine the type. Another good program for this is the Seagate Disk Manager.

> 3. SCSI hard drives and some RLL and MFM disks have an intelligent controller. So a Setup setting is unnecessary and may even create a problem. You should enter "not available" during Setup. The computer BIOS will receive its information from the controller's BIOS.

A second hard drive

Hard drive controllers now available allow you to manage two hard drives. The same general principles apply for specifying the second drive as for the first one.

TAKE NOTE

> In Setup, the designation "Drive C" for the first hard drive and "Drive D" for the second is needed only for internal management. These designations don't affect the allocation of the disks themselves. With larger hard drives you may have to divide the disk into several partitions.

Another logical drive designation, which is also considered to be Drive "D", may be in use. So you would partition the "D" hard drive with a letter following the last one used.

New capabilities of modern BIOS versions

In addition to the settings mentioned above, modern BIOS versions provide numerous conveniences depending on the chipset used. These are designed to make life easier for the user as well as to protect system data.

Boot process

For example, the system is able to determine from which storage location the BIOS will load the operating system.

QUICK TIP

> ### Always make the boot drive C:
>
> Set up your boot drive as C:. The boot process should always be set to access drive A: first, then drive C:. If a non-system diskette is inserted in drive A:, it will be read and the boot process will stop. If a diskette isn't present, the boot process will continue by accessing drive C:. In an emergency, the computer can be booted by inserting a system diskette in drive A:.

Hard drive support

In addition to allowing for many user-defined hard drives, the more powerful Setup programs provide the option of checking the hard drive for defective sectors, determining the best interleave, and performing the hard drive formatting process.

Keyboard

Setup specifies whether the keyboard should be tested and how this should be done. The newer Setup programs also allow you to set the repeat and delay rates of the keyboard.

Internal components

Many setup functions for NEAT-ATs and 486es have been integrated into one large Setup program. To use this program's special features, you don't have to go through all the system documentation or fiddle around with bits. All the settings can be entered via menus.

However, even with such a simplified system, it's still possible to enter incorrect values. In this case, refer to the values you recorded before changing the Setup values and re-enter these values.

5.2 Extended Setup

Extended Setup sets up additional registers. ATs and the 386es already provide more system control than previous computers. The Chips & Technologies Co., which is the manufacturer of the NEAT chipset, also supplies gate arrays for several 386 and 486 hard drives. These gate arrays consist of six chips that are mainly responsible for controlling data traffic within the hard drive.

The chips have certain registers that the user can use to determine the system's mode of operation. The registers are set via an extended Setup program. This program is usually stored next to the normal Setup in the ROM-BIOS if the 486 has an AMI-BIOS. In 486es with the OPTI-chipset (HiB/486), a variation of the Award-BIOS sometimes controls the registers.

Options in extended Setup

The extended Setup enables the user to obtain maximum system performance. Each of the following registers can be set individually:

- Memory wait cycle

- Clock frequency for the main microprocessor, bus, and remainder of the system

- Shadow-RAM for video and ROM BIOS as well as other areas of upper memory

- Efficient use of memory with memory interleave

- Mode of cache operation

The last item was first introduced with the OPTI version of extended Setup. Unfortunately, after storing each register's parameters, the system doesn't check whether it's capable of running. If you set a register for a parameter that the system cannot handle, your 486 may crash once you exit the Setup program.

QUICK TIP

Emergency termination for C&T or OPTI 486es

If your system no longer works, then reset the computer while holding down the i key. This sets all registers back to their original values. The system will run, but you may have to start from the beginning to complete the performance optimization.

The OPTI chipset

In many 486es the gate array functions have been taken over by two chips manufactured by OPTI. These constitute the "HiB/486" chipset. In some 486 systems they are combined with gate arrays from other manufacturers, for example Chips & Technologies.

Registers of the OPTI HiB/486 chipset

82C481 CPU/AT Bus Controller		
Register Index	**Description**	**Controls**
00h	REG00	Cache and clock frequency selection
01h	REG01	486 internal signal management

82C482 Memory Controller		
Register Index	**Description**	**Controls**
10h	Remapping Address	Memory movement
11h	Shadow RAM	Type of Shadow-RAM from D0000h to EFFFFh
12h	Memory Enable	Shadow-RAM Memory from D0000h up
13h	Bank Configuration	Storage for RAM banks
14h	DRAM Configuration	Wait cycle for RAMs
15h	Video Adapter	Storage for Shadow RAM from
	Shadow RAM	C0000h to CFFFFh and type of Shadow RAM
16h	Fast Gate A20	
17h	Cache Configuration	Cache type
18h	Non-cacheable Block 1 Size	Area not supported by the cache
19h	Non-cacheable Block 1	
1Ah	Non-cacheable Block 2 Size	
1Bh	Non-cacheable Block 2	
1Ch	Cacheable Area	Supported by the cache

The 82C481 chip sets the clock signal

The proper clock frequency setting is extremely important when considering performance. In 486 computers, this frequency is set in the 82C481 CPU/AT Bus Controller chip. This chip controls connections between the main microprocessor and the various system components as well as the AT bus. The chip produces two times two output signals from two different input signals.

The input consists of the CLK2IN signal oscillating at the nominal CPU frequency, and OSX1 with a frequency of 14.31818 MHz. From these output signals, the 82C481 produces CLK and ATCLK as well as OSC and OSC/12. One of the first two signals is then given to the 82C482 (memory controller) chip and the CPU.

Compatibility is important

To enhance performance without limiting compatibility, the CPU and memory run at low frequencies, while the AT bus uses a high frequency. How high this should be depends on the specific add-on cards being used.

82C482 CPU/AT Bus Controller

Register 10h   Remapping Address Register

The region of memory between 640K and 1 Meg is the area used by the video card and the BIOS. To use the RAM located within this area, you can copy the ROM onto the RAM (Shadow RAM). To use the area as extended memory for EMS or XMS, it must be relocated to a different address (remapped).

QUICK TIP

Remapping depends on memory size

With less than 4 Meg of memory available, always activate the remapping function. From 4 to 8 Meg, the advantages of remapping depend on the types of programs you're running. If you work mainly with Windows, you need every extra kilobyte of extended memory you can get and should activate the function.

However, if you work primarily with DOS applications, which access extended memory via EMS, you can manage without remapping. The extra 384K won't make much of a difference. In this case, you should activate Shadow RAM. Finally, if you have plenty of memory available (8 Meg or more), take advantage of the extra speed of Shadow RAM in favor of the 384K gained by remapping.

Register 10h Bits	
Bit	**Function**
7 - 5	Reserved
4	Remapping activated (1) or deactivated (0, standard)
3 - 0	Address range to which the area from 640K to 1 Meg is relocated

Bit 3	Bit 2	Bit 1	Bit 0	Address	Memory limit
0	0	0	0	No remapping	
0	0	0	1	10000h	1 Meg

Bit 3	Bit 2	Bit 1	Bit 0	Address	Memory limit
0	0	1	0	20000h	2 Meg
0	0	1	1	30000h	3 Meg
0	1	0	0	40000h	4 Meg
0	1	0	1	50000h	5 Meg
0	1	1	0	60000h	6 Meg
0	1	1	1	70000h	7 Meg
1	0	0	0	80000h	8 Meg
1	0	0	1	90000h	9 Meg
1	0	1	0	A0000h	10 Meg
1	0	1	1	B0000h	11 Meg
1	1	0	0	C0000h	12 Meg
1	1	0	1	D0000h	13 Meg
1	1	1	0	E0000h	14 Meg
1	1	1	1	F0000h	15 Meg

QUICK TIP

Set start address for RAM

You should set the start address at the top limit of memory. If you specify an address higher than your RAM has available, the computer may crash or fail to function properly.

Register 11h   Shadow RAM

Since the main microprocessor can access RAM more quickly than ROM, you can use the "double allocation" between 640K and 1 Meg (the area known as "upper memory"), by copying ROM into RAM in this area. Instead of ROM, its "shadow" will overlay RAM at this location. This allows you to manipulate the BIOS functions as well. However, the main advantage of Shadow RAM is its speed.

Register 11h Bits	
Bit	**Function**
7	Shadow RAM in the system BIOS range from F0000h to FFFFFh: Permit read access only to Shadow RAM (0) or permit read access to ROM, write access to RAM (1, standard).

Bit	Function
5	Overlay Shadow RAM in bus-card range from E0000h to EFFFFh (1, standard) or overlay ROM in this region (0). With 1 (Shadow RAM active), you can exclude in Register 12h certain ranges /switch back to ROM access.
4	Shadow RAM from D0000h to DFFFFh can be read-only (1) or write-and-read (0, standard). During bootup this bit must remain at 0; afterwards setting it to 1 write-protects the RAM, so poorly programmed software won't write to this area and thereby disrupt the BIOS routines.
3	Shadow RAM from E0000h to EFFFFh can be read-only (1) or write-and-read (0, standard). During bootup this bit must remain at 0; afterwards setting it to 1 write-protects the RAM, so poorly programmed software won't write to this area and thereby disrupt the BIOS routines.
2	Switch on RAS Timeout Precharge (0, standard) or switch it off (1).

Register 12h   Shadow RAM partitioning

The range from D0000h to EFFFFh contains the ROM addresses where bus card BIOS routines begin. This area can also be copied into RAM by shadowing to speed up access not only to internal routines but also to the 486 bus cards. So you can activate in this register 16K of Shadow RAM (1) or switch to ROM (0, standard).

To use this register, you must know the exact address ranges of each card. For example, a SCSI controller uses jumpers to set the range on the main board; this also applies to network cards.

Register 12h Bits			
Bit	**Range**	**Bit**	**Range**
7	EC000h-EFFFFh	6	E8000h-EBFFFh
5	E4000h-E7FFFh	4	E0000h-E3FFFh
3	DC000h-DFFFFh	2	DC000h-DBFFFh
1	D4000h-D7FFFh	0	D0000h-D3FFFh

Register 13h   Bank configuration

Memory chip types are assigned to two banks with 3 bits each. The OPTI chipset is usually able to determine the type of chips that are present.

Register 13h Bits				
Bit	**Function**			
6 - 4	DRAMS in Bank 0 and 1			
6	5	4	Bank 0	Bank 1
0	0	0	256 KBit	empty
0	0	1	256 KBit	256 KBit
0	1	0	256 KBit	1 MBit
0	1	1	1 MBit	256 KBit
1	0	0	1 MBit	empty
1	0	1	1 MBit	1 Meg
1	1	0	empty	empty
1	1	1	256 KBit	empty
2 - 0	DRAMS in Bank 2 and 3			
0	0	0	256 KBit	empty
0	0	1	256 KBit	256 KBit
0	1	0	256 KBit	1 MBit
0	1	1	1 MBit	256 KBit
1	0	0	1 MBit	empty
1	0	1	1 MBit	1 Meg
1	1	0	empty	empty
1	1	1	256 KBit	empty

Register 14h   DRAM configuration

To use memory chips with longer access times, you may have to insert wait cycles for read and write access to the DRAMs. This register allows you to do this.

Register 14h Bits	
Bit	**Function**
7 + 6	Wait cycles for read accesses to DRAM
	00 0 Wait cycles
	01 1 Wait cycles (standard)
	10 2 Wait cycles
	11 3 Wait cycles
5	Wait cycles for write accesses
	0 no wait cycle
	11 wait cycle (standard)
4 - 0	Reserved

Register 15h   Video adapter Shadow RAM

This register activates or deactivates Shadow RAM. With RAM shadowing, the contents of ROM in upper memory are copied into RAM, which physically has the same address. This is the area that contains the computer BIOS and the various system expansions (graphics card, hard drive controller, etc.). The CPU then accesses RAM instead of ROM, which speeds up the operation.

TAKE NOTE

> ROM shadowing occupies 384K of extended memory. So the decision to activate this function depends on the total amount of memory available. If you own one of the few 486es with less than 4 Meg of RAM, it may be better to do without the Shadow ROM. With 4 Meg or more, you can sacrifice the additional 384K of memory in favor of increased performance.

	Register 15h Bits
Bit	**Function**
7	Reserved
6	Write control for Shadow RAM from C0000h to EFFFFh
0	Write access to AT bus (standard)
1	Write access to Shadow RAM
5	Between C0000h and EFFFFh permit read access only (1) or read/write access (0, standard)
4	Activate Shadow RAM between C0000h and CFFFFh according to-bits 0-3 (1, standard) or deactivate Shadow RAM (0)
3	Shadow RAM from CC000h - CFFFFh
2	Shadow RAM from C8000h - CBFFFh
1	Shadow RAM from C4000h - C7FFFh
0	Shadow RAM from C0000h - C3FFFh activate (1) or deactivate (0, standard)

Register 16h   Fast Gate A20

Fast Gate A20 regulates access to Extended Memory and switching from real to protected mode.

Register 16h Bits	
Bit	**Function**
7 - 4	Reserved
3	Control Fast Gate A20 by Gate A20 (0) or the CPU (1, standard)
2 - 0	Reserved

Register 17h   Cache configuration

This register sets the type of second-level cache (i.e., the cache outside of the 486 microprocessor). Obviously the process also depends on the type of cache chips found on the main board, if any.

Register 17h Bits	
Bit	**Function**
7	NCA Output switches to low (1, standard) or remains unchanged (0)
6 + 5	Reserved
4 + 3	Burst Mode
00	Switched off
01	Reserved
10	Switched on with second-level cache
11	DRAM-Burst-Mode without second cache
2 - 0	Reserved

Register 18h   Size of Non-cacheable Block 1

Up to two blocks of memory may be excluded from caching. This register and Register 1Ah sets the size of the blocks, while Registers 19h and 1Bh contain their start addresses.

TAKE NOTE

If your application crashes or an add-on board doesn't function, you may have to exclude the affected memory areas from the cache. We haven't seen this yet, so it's best to leave these registers alone.

Register 18h Bits	
Bit	**Function**
7 - 5	Size
	000 64K
	001 128K
	010 256K
	011 512K
	100 1 Meg
	101 4 Meg
	110 8 Meg
	111 switched off

Register 19h   **Address of Non-cacheable Block 1**

The bits which determine the address depend on the size set in Register 18h.

Register 19h Bits	
Bit	**Function**
7 - 0	Start address

These are determined by the following table:

Size	Bits
64K	7 - 0
128K	7 - 1
256K	7 - 2
512K	7 - 3
1 Meg	7 - 4
2 Meg	7 - 5
4 Meg	7 - 6
8 Meg	7 only

Register 1Ah   Size of Non-cacheable Block 2

Register 1Ah Bits	
Bit	**Function**
7 - 5	Size
	000 64K
	001 128K
	010 256K
	011 512K
	100 1 Meg
	101 4 Meg
	110 8 Meg
	111 switched off
4-0	Reserved

Register 1Bh   Address of Non-cacheable Block 1

The bits that determine the address depend on the size set in Register 1Ah.

Bit	Function
7 - 0	Start address

Determined by:

Size	Bits	Size	Bits
64K	7 - 0	1 Meg	7 - 4
128K	7 - 1	2 Meg	7 - 5
256K	7 - 2	4 Meg	7 - 6
512K	7 - 3	8 Meg	7 only

Register 1Ch   Cacheable area

Register 1Ch Bits	
Bit	**Function**
7 - 4	Cacheable memory area
	0000 F0000h
	0001 00000h
	0010 10000h
	0011 20000h
	0100 30000h
	0101 40000h
	0110 50000h
	0111 60000h
	1000 70000h
	1001 80000h
	1010 90000h
	1011 A0000h
	1100 B0000h
	1101 C0000h
	1110 D0000h
	1111 E0000h
3	Caching activated (1=standard) or 0=deactivated)
2 - 0	Reserved

Whether the Remap area set in Register 10h should be supported by the cache is determined here.

5.3 Using Setup

BIOS or system-specific

Most 486es have their setups stored in ROM along with the BIOS. Some manufacturers don't rely on these stored setups. So they include their own Setup programs with their computers. In this case, the Setup program is started from a diskette.

QUICK TIP

Emergency termination of Setup

Most Setup programs allow you to exit without rewriting the CMOS parameters. If such an "emergency exit" isn't available, you can always use the [Reset] button.

The registers for setting the date, time, diskette drive type, and hard drive type are identical in almost all 486es. So, the computer is able to use a "foreign" program to adjust them. However, this doesn't apply to other specific registers. When setting up Shadow RAM or any other special feature, avoid using a program that isn't designed for your particular computer.

The following section lists the setups of individual BIOS manufacturers and some common Setup programs included with many 486es.

BIOS Setup programs

Recognizing the type of BIOS Setup

To activate the 486 Setup found with the ROM BIOS, first you must know what BIOS the computer is using and the Setup program that goes with it. If this isn't clearly stated in the documentation supplied with your system, then switch on the computer.

Watch the first message that appears on the screen. If there isn't a VGA BIOS lurking in the foreground, you should be able to read which BIOS your system is using.

AMI-BIOS

Wide-ranging program

Almost half of all 386 and 386SX-based computers are equipped with the American Megatrends BIOS (also called the AMI-BIOS). At first the AMI-BIOS worked only with Chips & Technologies chips, but now it's used in computers with other chipsets as well. Many 486-based computers are equipped with this BIOS.

Access to the AMI-BIOS is slightly unusual. In the past, you would press the [Del] key to access the AMI-BIOS. Now you press [Esc]. Unfortunately, you always land in Setup any time you want to interrupt the memory count. (This process requires the [Esc] key.)

The AMI Setup program's menu is much more extensive. Instead of four or five entries, as with both large and small 386es, there are nine entries in the main menu.

Entries in the AMI Setup Main Menu	
Standard CMOS-Setup	Date, time setup etc. Advanced CMOS-Setup System option configuration.
Advanced Chipset Options	Register for chipset configuration. Auto Configuration with BIOS Defaults. Set up CMOS-RAM values needed by BIOS. Auto Configuration with CMOS Defaults. Reset to previously saved CMOS-RAM data.
Change Password	Activate/deactivate password request.
Hard-Drive Utility	Program section for hard drive formatting.

With the last two items you can exit Setup with or without saving your values. The basic operation is the same for all of AMI-Setup's menus and sub-menus.

Keys used in the AMI Setup	
Key	**Function**
F1	Help
F2	Monochrome display
F3	Color display
F5	Menu setups
F6	BIOS Setup-standard settings
F7	Power On-standard settings
PgUp / PgDn	Change value
↑ ↓ ← →	Change parameters

If nothing runs after the AMI-Setup

Considering the number of adjustments you can make, it's possible to "fix" the computer so it no longer runs.

With ATs and 386SX- and 386DXs with the NEAT chipset and AMI-BIOS, you could press the [Ins] key to reboot the system. However, this no longer works with the new generation of AMI-BIOS. After returning to Setup with [Esc], you must select either "Auto Configuration with BIOS Defaults" or "Auto Configuration with CMOS Defaults."

Advanced Setup

The first part of the Advanced Setup allows you to set parameters for expanded system control. If nothing else pertains to the selection, you can either activate (enable) or deactivate (disable) the corresponding function. Otherwise, values may be retrieved in several steps.

Parameters for Expanded System Control	
Typematic Rate Programming	Set repeat rate via Setup
Typematic Rate Delay	Length of time between repeats
Typematic Rate Repeat Rate	in characters per second
Memory Test Tick Sound	Ticking during memory count
Memory Parity Error Check	Memory chip test for control bit
Hit <Esc> Message Display	Display for [Esc] request following memory test
Hard Disk Type 47 Data Area	Memory area for user-defined hard drive type - at 0000:0300h or within the 1 Meg DOS limit
Wait for <F1> if any Error	[F1] to be pressed after errors
System Boot Up Num Lock	[Num Lock] activated after bootup
Weitek Co-Microprocessor	Present or absent
Floppy Drive Seek At Boot	Test diskette drives during bootup
System Boot Up Sequence	First from A:, then from C: or vice versa

Always boot from drive A: first, then drive C:. This allows for emergency access to the diskette drive at each bootup.

System Boot Up Speed	Clock frequency/system speed after bootup - high or low
External Cache Memory	80486/80486SX cache
Password Checking Option	Password protection

You're able to allocate areas of Upper Memory for Shadow RAM (ROM Shadow) in 16K increments. Enter "enabled" only for the video and system ROM areas, and for those areas that contain a BIOS (e.g., with SCSI controllers or network adapters).

Advanced Chipset Setup

This submenu takes you one level down within the Setup options. Here you can adjust chipset or gate array operations. CLKIN is the quartz crystal that provides the timing signal for the main microprocessor.

Bus Clock Selection	CLKIN/3, CLKIN/4 or CLKIN/5

The following table shows bus timing for various computers:

Bus Timing for Various Computers			
Timing	CLKIN/3	CLKIN/4	CLKIN/5
20 MHz	6.6 MHz	5 MHz	4 MHz
25 MHz	8.3 MHz	6.25 MHz	5 MHz
33 MHz	11 MHz	8.25 MHz	6.6 MHz
50 MHz	16.6 MHz	12.5 MHz	10 MHz

Set these values as high as your system will allow.

Extended I/O Decode	Extended decoding of the I/O-signal.
Concurrent Refresh	CPU stops during RAM-Refresh (disable) or does not stop (enable).
DRAM Read/Write State	Wait cycles during read/write memory access.
Page Mode RAM	Keeps track of the Page and transmits the Column only.

The Advanced Chipset Setup also lets you adjust memory access (refreshing). The menu entries labeled RAS or CAS should be changed carefully. We've never noticed an improvement resulting from changing the CAS signal pulse interval.

Finally you can exclude up to four blocks of memory from caching, in which you designate the start address and size for each block. You may have to do this if an add-on board or program doesn't work with the cache.

AWARD Setup

AWARD-BIOS lets you see entire POST

All 486 computers with the AWARD-BIOS display not only the memory count, but also the entire POST program on the screen. You should take advantage of this and ensure that everything is displayed correctly, even when there aren't any error messages. You can access the AWARD-BIOS Setup program by pressing Ctrl + Alt + Esc immediately after bootup.

Using AWARD Setup

Choose the parameters you want to change with the ↑ and ↓ cursor keys. You can change the values with the ← and → keys, although sometimes an actual number is required. F10 saves the settings after asking you to confirm your settings.

The F1 key interrupts the routine leaving the CMOS parameters unchanged. Once completed, with or without saving the changes, the system reboots itself. The F2 key allows you to switch back and forth between color and monochrome.

POST-STOP

The second option of the AWARD-BIOS is *Error Halt*. Here, you determine what the computer will do if POST detects an error.

AWARD Setup Error Proceedings	
Entry	**Interrupt bootup**
Halt on all errors	With all errors
No halt on any errors	Never
No keyboard error halt	Not with keyboard errors
No disk error halt	Not with hard drive errors
No keyboard or disk error halt	Not with keyboard or hard drive errors

You should enter "No keyboard error." Then you won't have any problems stopping the memory count (press Esc), adjusting the clock frequency (press Ctrl + Alt and − or +), or accessing Setup (Ctrl + Alt + Esc).

Cycle Selection

"Speed select" allows you to determine the 486 clock frequency. This option is available only if it's supported on the main board. You have three possible choices.

Cycle Selection Options	
Setting	**Effect**
No Change	Speed cannot be changed
Low	Low speed
High	High speed

Extended Options	
System Configuration	Memory type and other manufacturer-specific settings.
Shadow RAM	Deactivated, for system, video, or both.
Cache Controller	Internal 486 cache activated or deactivated.

MR-BIOS

The MR-BIOS (MR represents Microid Research) contains a Setup program that supports modern chipsets. To access the MR-BIOS Setup, press the Esc key following the memory count.

A screen appears with a summary of important system information and a menu bar. Move the cursor keys to highlight the menu item to be changed. Then press Enter or PgDn to make the selection.

Enable activates the selection while *Disable* deactivates it.

MR-BIOS Menu Options	
Menu item	**Remarks**
Clock	Time
Time	Time (12-hour format)
Date	Month-Day-Year
Daylight Savings	Daylight Savings Time
Video	Graphic adapter
Primary Video	Monochrome, Color (CGA), EGA, or VGA

Menu item	Remarks
Floppy	Diskette drive type
Floppy Drive 1	Diskette Drive B:
Fixed	Hard drive type
Fixed Disk 80 (C:)	First built-in hard drive
Fixed Disk 81 (D:)	Second built-in hard drive, allocation of partitions independent of designation in parentheses
(Low Level) Format	Utility program for hard-formatting both hard drives

There are 46 predefined drive types and two user-specific drive types (USER TYPE) available for the hard drive.

Other MR-BIOS Options	
Option	**Function**
Boot-Seq	Boot sequence
Screen Prompt	During bootup you are prompted to boot from Drive A: (F1) or Drive B: (F2)
C: 1st A: 2nd	Try system startup first from Drive C: then from Drive A:
A: 1st C: 2nd	Try system startup first from Drive A: then from Drive C:
Keyboard	Keyboard
Powerup Numlock	Numlock on/off during bootup
Typematic Override	Repeat rate adjustable
Delay before Repeat	Amount of time before repeat
Typematic Repeat Rate	Repeat rate in cps (characters per second)

The keyboard repeat feature is from the chip in the keyboard and not the BIOS. The Setup program merely sets the registers in the keyboard chip.

First Aid	Help
Novell Keyboard Management	Setup required only if keyboard Problems occur in Novell networks
Speed	Speed

You can set the speed to high (normal microprocessor frequency) or low (8 MHz). For high use q + a + O and for low use q + a + –.

MR-BIOS Cache Information

Cache	Cache settings
Internal Cache	Internal 486 cache activated / deactivated
External Cache	Second-level cache activated / deactivated (if present on the main board)
SRAM Banks, SRAM Size	Size of second-level cache and type of RAM is automatically recognized by the system
Non-Cacheable Regions	The user can exclude up to four blocks of memory from the cache

QUICK TIP

Areas of memory to be excluded from caching

The first areas to be excluded from the cache should be the memory regions used most often by programs and device drivers (e.g., the EMS Window). Suppose that this is located at c000h and occupies 64K of memory.

The settings would then be as follows:

```
Size:  64K
Base:  c000
```

You can also lock out the entire 256K area between 640K and 1Meg, which can be converted to Extended Memory through remapping.

DMA	DMA chips
DMA-Clock	Clock frequency for DMA chips
8-Bit-Waits	Wait states at 8-bit bus access
16-Bit-Waits	Wait states at 16-bit bus access

| Command Width,
    MEMR#, MEMW# | Command width of read or write DMA signals |
| Shadow RAM | Upper Memory write-protection activated (vacant) or deactivated (R/W) |

TAKE NOTE

> In most cases you should keep write-protection activated in Upper Memory, so poorly programmed software won't write to this area. The only time you shouldn't activate the write-protection is when certain expansion cards need the ROM area for storage.

| Chipset | Access to memory, AT-bus, and keyboard microprocessor. |
| Page-Mode Interleave | Page only (enabled) or deactivated (disabled). |

With interleave, while one memory bank is in-between accesses (refreshed), the other bank is already being given the next memory address. With paging, the RAM remembers the page address and transmits only the column address. Interleaving works only with an even number of memory banks with equal amounts of RAM.

| Refresh | CPU halts during refresh (standard setting) or continues running (concurrent) |
| Read/Write Cycle | Wait cycles in read/write process |

Enter three wait cycles if you have a 33-MHz microprocessor. With 25-MHz, two wait cycles are sufficient.

CAS Width	
Bank X DRAM	Memory type in Bank X (X depending on the computer 0, 1, or also 2 and 3)

AT Bus Parameters	
Bus Speed	16.5, 11, 8.3, or 6.6 MHz

TAKE NOTE

To obtain maximum computing speed, make the AT bus as fast as possible. Since graphics cards, as well as all other peripheral equipment, run on the AT bus, open up this bottleneck as wide as possible.

8042 Enhancement Security	Support for fast reset via A20 Gate Password protection activated/deactivated

TAKE NOTE

Password protection is activated/deactivated by the same jumper that sets up the monitor type on the main board. Only a setting of *Color* makes password protection possible. With *Mono* the Setup settings are ignored.

Under password protection, the user has three chances to enter the correct password. If unsuccessful, the computer emits a warning beep until it's switched off. When the correct entry is made, the computer boots up as usual.

A warm start ([Ctrl] + [Alt] + [Del]) won't take you through the password inquiry again. This is required only with a reset (or cold start).

External Setup programs

To maintain compatibility among Setup programs, some manufacturers place the Setup programs on separate diskettes.

Compaq

The Setup program for Compaq computers comes on a diskette, along with a test program and display utility for all system parameters. You can start the program via a menu, using TEST or by calling it up directly.

A system configuration menu appears with all the parameters that are stored in Setup. To change the values, press [F4]. A pop-up menu, in which you enter the settings, then appears. However, a few settings are determined by the system and cannot be changed.

Help menu

The [F1] key displays a Help menu, which you can print (on LPT1) by pressing the [F7] key. The [F3] key writes the values to the CMOS, while [Esc] allows you to leave the program without making any changes.

```
                    System Configuration Summary

      To change the configuration, press F4 and select an item.  When you are
      satisfied that the configuration is correct, press F3 to exit SETUP.  To
      print the summary, press F7.  For help,  press F1.
      _____

      Date . . . . . . . . . . . . . . . 09-10-1990
      Time . . . . . . . . . . . . . . . 13:40:12

      Numeric Coprocessor. . . . . . . .Not Installed

       Diskette Drive A:               1.44 Megabyte (3.5 inch)
       Diskette Drive B:               1.2 Megabyte (5.25 inch)


      Primary Controller
        Fixed Disk 1 . . . . . . . . .Type  25 (130 Megabyte)
        Fixed Disk 2 . . . . . . . . . Not Installed


      Secondary Controller
        Fixed Disk 1 . . . . . . . . . Not Installed
        Fixed Disk 2 . . . . . . . . . Not Installed
      _____

      Esc=Cancel   F1=Help   F3=Exit   F4=Change Configuration  F7=Print
```

The Compaq Setup Menu

Compaq Setup Options	
Function	**Remarks**
Date	Month-Day-Year
Time	Time (24-hour format)
Primary Controller, Fixed Disk 1 and 2	Hard Drive Controller 1
Secondary Controller, Fixed Disk 1 and 2	Hard Drive Controller 2

Compaq allows you to install two controllers, each of which controls two hard drives. The type of each hard drive is entered in Setup.

Numeric Coprocessor	Determine numeric coprocessor
Diskette Drive A and B	Diskette drive types

Inspection program

In addition to the Setup program, there is another program, called INSPECT, on the diskette that checks an entire list of system parameters.

```
                          INSPECT
The following operating environment information was detected when INSPECT
was loaded. To print the information to either a file or printer, press F7.
To exit INSPECT, press F3.  For help, press F1.
                                                         More: ↓


Product . . . . . . . . . . .UNKNOWN: NON-COMPAQ System Unit

Machine ID
  From Configuration Memory . . 00

Processor . . . . . . . . . . 80486 at 33 MHz

Numeric Coprocessor . . . . . . Not Installed

CPU Mode . . . . . . . . . . Real Mode

System ROM
  Revision . . . . . . . . .   NON-COMPAQ

Video Controller ROM


Esc=Cancel  F1=Help  F3=Exit  F7=Print
```

The Compaq Inspect Program

Running this program is identical to running the Setup program, except that you can reroute the printout to diskette in a file named INSPECT.OUT.

The following parameters are displayed:

Date — Current system date. If set correctly, you can assign the date a printout was made.

Product — If the computer is an original Compaq computer, its type is displayed. Otherwise, Inspect displays the message:

UNKNOWN: NON-COMPAQ System ROM

Machine ID — Every 486 computer has a two-digit ID number that's stored in its Configuration Memory.

Microprocessor — Microprocessor (type only, without SX or DX) and clock frequency.

Numeric Coprocessor — If there is a built-in coprocessor, Inspect notifies you of its existence.

CPU Mode — Main microprocessor mode. Calling Inspect from DOS displays Real Mode while starting from Windows 3.0/3.1 displays Protected Mode.

System ROM   BIOS version. Anything not from Compaq isn't specified more precisely; it's simply designated as "NON-COMPAQ."

Video Controller ROM
                  Version and type (family) of graphics adapter.

Keyboard Controller ROM
                  Version of keyboard chip.

Option ROMs   Areas reserved for ROM expansions.

Keyboard   Keyboard type (MF2 is "enhanced").

LPT Ports   Memory addresses of parallel interface(s).

COM Ports   Memory addresses of serial interface(s).

Diskette Drive A and B
                  Drive types.

Primary or Secondary Controller
                  All hard drives present are reported with their model numbers from the CMOS-ROM.

Video Mode   Number and description of current graphics mode.

Primary Monitor attached to
                  Whether the primary monitor is hooked up to the internal VGA graphics or to an external graphics card, and the type of monitor, is specified here.

Base Memory   System Total and Amount Free.

Extended Memory
                  Amount Free (Extended Standard).

Expanded Memory
                  Size and type of Expanded Memory used after EMS (LIM Driver Support).

Memory Detected at Power-On
                  Base Memory, Extended Memory, as well as Total Memory Counted by ROM.

Operating System
                  Type and version of the operating system in use.

Status of file   Shows whether original system files are present (IBMBIO.COM and IBMDOS.COM as well as COMMAND.COM).

Dump of AUTOEXEC.BAT
          Contents of file.

Environment variables
          Environment variable assignments (e.g. TEMP, PROMPT, APPEND, COMSPEC, PATH, etc.).

Memory Allocation (including INSPECT)
          Allocation of memory, including the following values:

PSP   Start address

SIZE   Program size

NAME   Program name

TRAPPED INTERRUPTS
          Trapped interrupts

System Configuration Memory
          Hexadecimal contents of the system configuration memory from 00h to 3Fh.

BIOS Data Area
          Hexadecimal contents of the BIOS memory from 0040:0000 to 0040:00F0.

Interrupt Vector Table (including INSPECT)
          Interrupt distribution from 00h to FFh.

Dell

Dell systems store their Setup routines in the ROM BIOS. They can be called at anytime with the key combination [Ctrl] + [Alt] + [Enter].

Unlike most computers, you can make changes in Setup while the computer is operating, instead of only immediately after bootup. Dell computers also include a diskette for system analysis and hard drive formatting.

Normal Setup

[Ctrl] + [Alt] + [Enter] accesses the normal Setup. A window, containing the parameters to be changed, appears. Individual parameters are accessed with the cursor keys, which then change the settings from left to right.

The ⌜F1⌟ key provides a short description of the currently selected item. ⌜F10⌟ exits Setup without changing the CMOS, while ⌜Esc⌟ transfers the new data to the CMOS and resets the computer.

The Dell Setup Options	
Item	**Remarks**
Time	Time (24-hour format)
Date	Month-Day-Year, day of week is calculated by the system
Diskette A and Diskette B	Diskette drives
Hard drive C and Hard drive D	Hard drive type

Always enter a value of 1 for ESDI hard drives with 90, 150, or 322 Meg capacities. Types for other hard drive brands can be selected from a list that's activated by pressing ⌜F1⌟.

Base Memory	Conventional memory
Board Memory	Board memory (640K, 512K, or 256K)
Extended and Expanded Memory	Allocation of additional memory
Display	Graphics card mode
Keyboard	Keyboard
CPU Speed	System speed (16, 8, or 6 MHz)
Fast BIOS and Fast Video	Shadow RAM Function
Coprocessor	Message of whether coprocessor was identified

System Support

The System Support program is located on a 5.25-inch diskette. The SHELL command activates a menu that contains the analyzer program and the formatting and park routines.

From the menu bar at the top, highlight your choice and press ⌜Enter⌟. The corresponding program section is then loaded from the diskette. It's very important that you keep this diskette in the drive. Now you can choose from the following items:

- Dell Analyzer

- Hard Disk Drive Setup - formatting program

- Park - for the hard drive

- Restart

Dell System Analyzer

The Dell System Analyzer is loaded from a diskette. This program's main menu contains several tests that are also loaded from the diskette. On the left side you'll see a list of components that the system is able to test.

The top right shows the current system configuration. Below you'll find instructions on running the program. The menu items are at the bottom of the screen and, when selected, a short explanation appears about each one.

Select the item either with the cursor keys or by pressing the capitalized letter in the item. F1 provides a detailed description of the selected item.

Test all	All components are tested in the order they appear on the list.
Select Test	Individual tests can be selected and run by pressing Enter.
Print Results	Results of just-completed tests are output not only to the screen but also to the LPT1 printer. This option may be switched on or off.
Parameters	Allows you to set test parameters. Here you can choose the output device for status and error messages - screen, printer, or diskette (file). Output sent to a file is saved under the name RESULT.

With *Error Limit* you can set the number of errors that will cause the test to stop. This value can be a number between 0 and 9999.

Number of repetitions is the number of times a particular test should run; this can be any number between 1 and 9999.

When Pause is ON, the program stops after each one of the tests and also after any errors that occur. Otherwise if Pause is OFF, the test continues to run and displays an error message only if the *Error Limit* value is exceeded.

Keyboard allows you to enter the type of keyboard found on your computer.

Quit   Exits the System Analyzer and takes you back to the main menu, which is loaded from diskette.

Hard Disk Drive Setup and Park
                              Here you can hard-format and park an internal Dell hard drive.

Tulip

Tulip 486es are set up with the help of the DIAGNOSE program. This program controls additional functions for testing as well as prepares the computer for transport.

You'll find the program on a diskette that's included with the computer. Start the program either by booting from this diskette (place in Drive A: and then reset), or by entering the DIAGNOSE command directly from DOS.

After an input message, the DIAGNOSE menu appears. Use the cursor keys to select one of the items and start the subprogram by pressing (Enter). The (F1) key displays a help menu that explains the keyboard layout.

The DIAGNOSE program has four main components:

• Setup	• System check
• Transport	• System information

Setup

Setup determines the system parameters; additional options are accessed via a pull-down menu.

Absolute timer   System time (24-hour format) and date (Day-Month-Year).

Disk drives   The storage units of the Tulip are set up here. Drives A: and B: can be set to any of the four usual formats as well as the option *None*.

For drives C: and D:, you can select the correct one from a list by using the cursor keys. Here C: and D: represent the third and fourth disk drives instead of hard drive partitions that must be designated as C: and D:.

Memory

Memory size, divided into *Standard* and *Extended* memory.

Configuration

This item contains all the parameters that haven't been mentioned yet, such as the video card where you can choose from the following:

- VGA/EGA

- CGA, 40 characters per line

- CGA, 80 characters per line

- Monochrome/Hercules

Then you learn whether the system has a coprocessor and, if a printer is hooked up, whether it has the standard or extended character set. After an item has been completed, the system asks you whether to save the setting in the CMOS.

System check

Includes several diagnosis programs that you can run individually or as a complete group.

Tulip AT 486/25 components

A pull-down menu lists the Tulip AT 486/25 components that can be tested.

Transport

This option parks the Tulip AT 486/25 hard drive.

Systeminfo

A window, containing important system information, opens in the middle of the screen.

System Control Manager

Besides Setup, the Tulip AT 486/25 has another program, called the System Control Manager (SCM), it can use. This routine is stored in a ROM and is activated by the key combination (Ctrl) + (Alt) + (Esc), regardless of the operating system being used. You can replace the key combination with a different one; we'll discuss this in more detail later.

The SCM communicates with the user not only about the screen but also about the screen's LCD display. The SCM is also available if you've switched the Tulip AT 486/25 to Standby mode (also via the SCM).

A user-defined password can protect the SCM against unauthorized access. Once the SCM is activated, the following options are available to you by pressing the appropriate function key:

F1   Switch system on (Power up)/Switch system to Standby mode (Power down)

F2   Enable/Disable system switch-on via application program (Trigger)

The Tulip AT 486/25 sometimes comes with a Shutdown program that switches the computer to Standby mode (SCMDOWN, see also below). However, this program can accomplish its task only when it's allowed by the SCM through *Enable Trigger*.

F3   Keyboard lock/unlock

              This function is identical to the keylock switch in other programs. You should use this function only if the SCM is password-protected.

F4   Cold start (Reset)

              After the password request (if activated), this option causes the Tulip AT to perform a cold start.

              This is exactly the same as pressing the Reset button or switching the computer off and then back on; Ctrl + Alt + Del performs only a warm start.

F9   Enable/disable password request

              This option allows you to protect the SCM functions from F1 to F4 against unauthorized use. It always asks for a password first, as the F10 function does.

F10   Change Password

Here, the SCM asks you for the old and new passwords. The standard setting, if you want to change the password after buying the computer, is "1234" (but please don't pass this on to anyone).

The password can contain between four and sixteen characters and may consist of anything that can be typed in on the keyboard.

WARNING!

> If you forget the password, the only way to crack the system is with a chip available from Tulip dealers.

Utility programs

Besides the DIAGNOSE program, there is another diskette that contains additional utility programs.

LCD.SYS   Device driver for LCD-display. Here a new device is set up with an LCD-display, to which you can reroute output (with COPY or >).

For example, you could use this program for a time display, though this requires some work. First create the following file:

```
COPY CON RETURN
[Enter]
[F6] [Enter]
```

There will be a file on your hard drive containing only a carriage return. Now enter:

```
TIME < RETURN > LCD
```

Here the TIME command is called; the request for the new time is answered with the RETURN file and rerouted to the LCD-display. You can also execute this procedure with the date.

SWDRIVE   Switch A and B drive allocations

Sometimes a program insists on reading in data from Drive A:, although this data is in a format that's compatible only with Drive B:.

You could use ASSIGN to change the drive letters, but this won't work if drive scans are made through the hardware instead of through DOS. In this case, you don't have to open the computer to switch the connections.

Instead you can simply call the SWDRIVE program. After the switch, the Tulip AT reboots itself. SWDRIVE is extremely useful, especially for installing different operating systems.

SWCOM   Switch serial interface allocations

With this program you can switch serial interfaces 1 and 2, which is useful if you have software that works with only one of them while the device is connected to the other port.

EISA-Setup program

Second Setup

Aside from the ROM Setup, 486es with an EISA bus have a program that allows you to configure the cards and the main board. This program is located on a diskette included with the computer.

First, you should transfer all the files on this diskette to an appropriate subdirectory on your hard drive. The actual configuration utility is started with the command:

CF

A window appears with the main board files that were on the diskette. Here you choose the file for the main board. If only one file exists, the choice is easy. However, if there are many configurations to choose from, you must know the type of main board you have.

If you don't know the type and this information doesn't appear on the documentation, then ask your computer dealer or the computer manufacturer. For proper configuration, it's important that the program sets only parameters that actually exist.

Now you can easily set parameters for the eight slots, such as the interrupt in use, DMA access, etc. You may have to adjust one of the jumpers; the program will inform you in this event.

This setup is needed only for the main board and the EISA boards. However, ISA boards should also be defined here so the program always has an overview of the entire system. EISA boards usually come with a diskette containing their configuration files (in ASCII format) with all the parameters.

CF program

The Configuration program contains five pull-down menus, which are accessed with [Alt], [F10] and the cursor keys or with the key combinations called shortcut keys. The following pages show the most important key combinations.

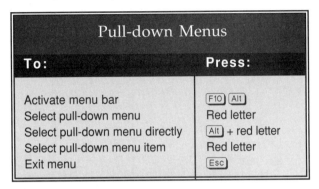

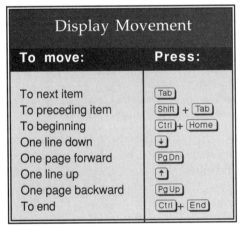

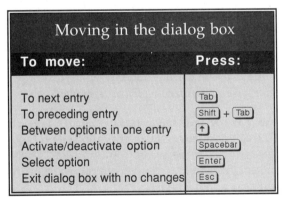

Key Combinations/Shortcuts	
To:	**Press:**
Print	Ctrl + P
Verify	Ctrl + Y
Save as	Ctrl + A
Exit	Ctrl + X
Add	Ins
Remove	Del
Change function	Ctrl + F
Change resource	Ctrl + R
Lock	Ctrl + L
Unlock	Ctrl + U
Overview	Ctrl + O
Detailed by slot	Ctrl + D
Changing connections	Ctrl + C
Help topics	Ctrl + F1
Help	F1
Help on keys	F9
Switch Insert/Overtype	Ins
Switch Help/main screen	Alt + F6

For each add-on board the CF program makes an entry in a configuration list (the CFG file). Now if you install a new EISA board, you must first start the CF Utility and then add the new entry. The CFG file must be loaded from the diskette accompanying the board.

Configuring the computer

First, select *Configure computer* from the main menu. For installing boards and other enhancements, select *Copy CFG files* for each one. Select *Configure computer - basic method* if this is all you are doing. However, if you also want to enter settings, then select *Configure computer - advanced method*.

You'll know that the computer is correctly configured if no error messages appear. Check the jumper or DIP switch settings and then safeguard the entire configuration. The program will tell you which DIP switch or jumper settings must be made and then you can add the enhancements.

Adding boards

Select *Add* from the Edit pull-down menu to determine which board you want to install. A list of CFG files appears with all the possible additions. With the cursor, select one of these files.

To select more than one board, select them with the (Spacebar) and then press (Enter) or click on the (OK) button with the mouse. You'll then be asked to choose a slot for the board. Once this is done, the information is then added to the main file.

Changing functions and resources

Select *Edit-Change Function* to either specify board functions (e.g., *graphics card*) or to change them. Resources are the conditions of a board accessed by an enhancement (e.g., interrupts). Resources are set in the *Edit-Change Resources* menu. Both are possible only in *Detailed by Slot* or *Detailed by Type* mode (View).

Configuration error

Once you're informed of a resource conflict, you can either cancel the configuration or continue with the error by entering "Continue." The board functions that produce the conflict are then marked with a symbol. Then proceed as follows:

> - Ensure that two add-on boards aren't performing the same function. For example, only one serial port can be set to COM1. In this case, you can reconfigure one of the cards with *Edit-Change Function*.
>
> - Two cards shouldn't use the same resources. You can check this in the View pull-down menu. Any changes here should be made in *Edit-Change Resources*.
>
> - If you cannot correct the problems, remove the addition.

Moving boards

To move a board from one slot to another, the configuration must also be changed. Some programs work with the information contained in CFG files. This can lead to problems if data doesn't match exactly.

To relocate the board, select *Edit-Move*. Then don't forget to actually switch the board. Obviously the system board, integrated EISA components, and virtual boards cannot be moved.

Removing boards

To remove a board or enhancement from the configuration, simply select *Edit-Remove*. The system board and integrated EISA components cannot be moved. Prior to deleting the information from the configuration file, the system performs its usual safety check and asks for confirmation.

Special functions

Auto Verify   Activating this option in the Settings menu causes the system to automatically check each entry after it's made. To deactivate this option, select *Settings-Manual Verify*.

Auto-added   An add-on board was automatically recognized by the program and its parameters are added to the configuration file.

Board Specifications
                 Other information about the board (such as manufacturer, Board ID number etc.).

By Slot   Display set up by function slots (*Overview*) or detailed display (*Detailed by Slot*).

By Type   Display set up by menu functions (*Overview*) or detailed display (*Detailed by Function*).

When you display the configuration sorted by function, the following functions in the Edit pull-down menu cannot be used: Reset to Defaults, Revert to Saved, Lock, and Unlock.

TAKE NOTE

Connections   This item in the View pull-down menu contains information about board connections, including external connections.

Deactivated   If a board cannot be installed due to conflicts, it is designated as deactivated.

CFG-Files   These contain all the necessary information for EISA expansion. Every EISA board comes with a diskette that contains standard CFG data, from which you can load the configuration directly. Therefore, you don't have to perform the configuration manually.

Detailed   Detailed configuration display.

5.4 Problems with Setup

Most users are reluctant to run the Setup program because they're afraid of damaging their computers in case of error. However, you don't have to worry about this; the worst thing that can happen with an incorrect setup is that the system or some part of it fails to work or works improperly. You cannot physically damage your computer.

■ **Nothing runs**

After Setup, the computer no longer boots. An extended Setup has probably set the registers working in opposition to each other. With most computers, you can reboot while pressing the ⟨Ins⟩ key. This returns all registers to their original values.

■ **Wrong type**

When the computer can no longer find the hard drive, an incorrect type has been set up. Call Setup again and enter the correct one.

■ **CMOS failure**

The following error message:

indicates the memory size is incorrect. Remember, with EISA-486es you must call the EISA-Setup-Utility.

■ **Wrong type II**

If the computer sends an error message but boots without any problem, then the graphics card type is incorrect. In this case, simply correct the setting.

Chapter 6 Mass Storage

Y have two methods of storing data from your computer. For years diskettes were the most popular method, but they have been replaced by hard drives. Hard drives hold more data and programs than individual diskettes. They also access data by a different process, which makes them much faster than diskettes. Each form of storage has its advantages and disadvantages.

6.1 Disk Drives

Two formats - two recording modes

Two types of diskette formats have evolved for computers; each has a different recording mode. At first all computer disk drives were made for diskettes with a 5.25-inch format. However, eventually 3.5-inch diskettes became more popular. This format features a sturdy outer case and a slide to protect the magnetic surface.

Within these two basic formats are two different recording modes. PC/XTs generally have a 5.25-inch drive that can store 360K of data on a diskette. With the advent of the AT, a second drive type was invented with specially coated diskettes that could store over three times as much data (1.2 Meg).

The PC/XT 3.5-inch diskette drives were equipped with the double recording density, which resulted in a capacity of 720K. The process was once again improved for the AT, where 1.44 Meg of data fits onto the 3.5-inch diskette.

Computer Diskette Formats		
Format	Capacity	Diskette type
5.25-inch	360K	2S 2D (double-sided, double-density)
5.25-inch	1.2 Meg	2S HD (double-sided, high-density)
3.5-inch	720K	2S 2D (double-sided, double-density)
3.5-inch	1.44 Meg	2S HD (double-sided, high-density)
3.5-inch	2.88 Meg	2S ED (double-sided extra high-density)

386 computers use the same higher capacity formats as the AT. Like hard drives, the diskette drives are governed by a controller that shares responsibility for the format.

Ensure that your controller can activate both types of diskette formats. Controllers that can work only with 360K, 720K, and 1.2 Meg, but cannot handle the 1.44 Meg format still exist, especially in older computers.

New diskette type

Now there is a new type of 3.5-inch drive that has double the previous capacity, a 2.88 Meg drive. Unfortunately, conventional diskette controllers are limited to a capacity of 1.44 Meg. So if you install a new 2.88 Meg drive, you'll also need a new diskette controller. This medium is also still quite expensive. However, since MS-DOS 5.0 already supports this format, most likely the 3.5-inch/2.88 Meg drives will be the storage medium of the future.

Two formats - flexible but not neat

Today computer's are usually equipped with both diskette formats to provide the most flexibility. So, theoretically, the disk drives should be able to process smaller capacities. However, this isn't always true. Because the tracks are different for each format, read errors may occur when a high-capacity drive writes to a low-capacity diskette. Even more problems are created by formatting low-capacity diskettes on high density drives, which you should avoid if possible.

Internal or external?

Format question hasn't been decided yet

Currently a conflict exists within the software world. On one side is the modern 3.5-inch format, with its high recording density and sturdy diskette casing, and on the other side is the older 5.25-inch format. Since there is no standard yet, software manufacturers are forced to provide diskettes in both formats. Users also need to have a 5.25-inch drive in their computer along with the modern 3.5-inch one, because less expensive software is usually available in only 5.25-inch versions.

So, we suggest that you have both a 3.5-inch and a 5.25-inch drive for your computer, where one is designated as Drive A: and the other as Drive B:. A computer cannot handle more drives than this. In the past, two identically formatted drives were common. Users would insert the program diskette into one drive and the data diskette into the other. However, this is no longer necessary because all 486es come with a hard drive.

External drives offer flexibility

External disk drives provide an alternative to built-in drives. These drives are useful if, for example, you don't have enough room for a second drive or you would like several diskette drives at the second location.

External drives are plugged into the connector via an adapter

6.2 Hard Drives

It's hard to imagine a modern computer system without a hard drive. Because of the different materials used for the magnetic coating, magnetized hard drives can store larger amounts of data than a diskette.

Also, because of the compact motion of the drive head across the surface, much more information can be written on the disk.

The first PC/XT had a 10 Meg hard drive, which seemed enormous at the time. Today the lower limit for hard drives is 20 Meg. It's very easy to reach this limit even with only a few programs. Even 40 Meg is barely enough for an active user.

Hard drive structure

Unlike diskettes, the inside of a hard drive is hermetically sealed from the outside world. This is important because dust particles and moisture from the surrounding air could damage the hard drive.

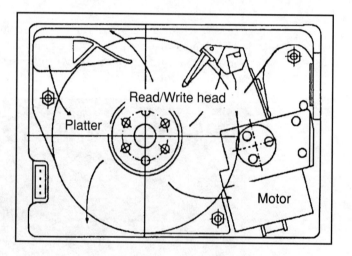

Diagram of a hard drive

The hard drive consists of a number of fixed aluminum platters, arranged one on top of the other. These are covered with a magnetized coating that has a thickness between 0.00005 and 0.0002 mm, depending on the material.

The platters rotate at a speed of about 3600 revolutions per minute around an axis known as the spindle.

Floating heads

On each side of a platter, a read/write head either writes to the magnetized surface or reads the data. The heads never touch the surface; it floats above it at a height of 0.0005 mm.

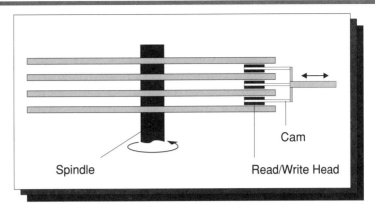

Hard Drive Read/Write Heads

In contrast, diskette read/write heads are constantly touching the surface of the diskette. The hard drive's rapid revolution creates an air cushion that prevents any contact.

Since the read/write heads are mounted on a carriage, it's impossible for the heads to move independently. The carriage, with its heads, reaches between the platters in a comb-like fashion.

Read/write heads in a hard drive

Because read/write heads in a hard drive access a magnetized area much smaller than in a diskette drive, much higher write densities can be achieved.

Dirt is harmful

Note in the following illustration how the heads operate within such a short distance from the magnetic surface.

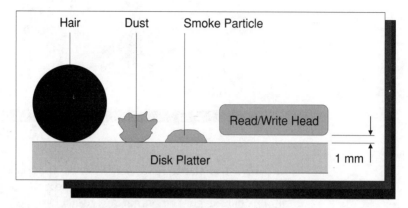

Read/Write Head gap

Since a tiny particle of dust could cause problems, the platters are hermetically sealed so most of the dirt cannot get inside.

However, there is another threat to the hard drive. Vibrations can cause the read/write head to come in contact with the magnetic coating. This is called a "head crash" and will destroy most of the data stored on that cylinder.

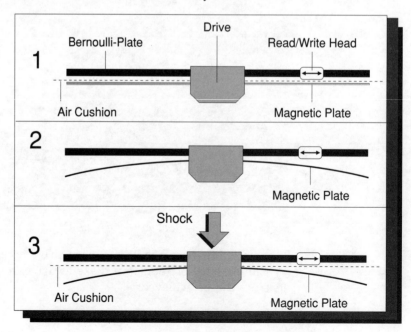

Hard drive head crash

Make certain to "park"

The only way to prevent this is by parking the hard drive after you're finished working with the computer.

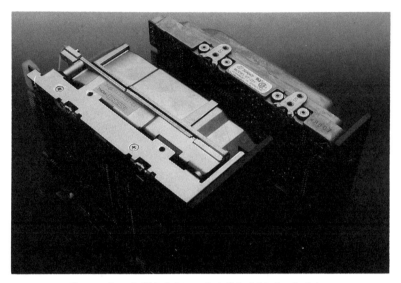

Comparing half-height and full-height hard drives

Access

Before the hard drive controller and the operating system can properly use the hard drive, it must be divided into easily managed sections. This is called formatting the hard drive.

This process divides the disk surface into sides, tracks, and sectors. Sides are the number of magnetized surfaces, tracks are circular sections, and sectors divide the platter surface into equal sections (similar to a pie).

With hard drives, we also refer to cylinders, which represent all tracks that lie on top of one another.

Park for protection

To avoid damaging your hard drive, you should park the read/write heads. You must do this before moving the hard drive or before any action that may disturb the hard drive, such as installing or removing something.

When you park a hard drive, the carriage will move the heads to a region of the disk where a head crash won't cause any damage.

An even better method is head lifting, in which the heads are also lifted slightly from the surface. Only older models need a program to park the hard drive.

Modern hard drives come with an auto-park mechanism, which automatically sets the disk to a resting position after the computer is switched off.

Drive types

Since hard drives are usually built into the same unit that contains the disk drives, they are available in the same formats used for diskettes. So, there are 5.25-inch and 3.5-inch hard drives.

What is half-height?

Hard drives are also available in two different heights. Today the standard height for hard drives is 1.5 inches. This is called half-height. There are also full-height hard drives, which are 3 inches high.

The designation "full" comes from the early days of the IBM computer when this was the standard height for both disk drives and hard drives.

Internal, external, and removable

Hard drives are usually built into the computer. However, they can also be set up externally. This is useful if you use the same data at home and at work and don't want to carry around a lot of diskettes.

An external hard drive can also prevent others from accessing important data.

Economical solution: 3.5-inch hard drive in removable frame

The Vobis Co. makes a removable frame, which is made from a synthetic material and has a carrier the size of a 5.25-inch disk drive. A 3.5-inch drive is mounted in this slot. Kyocera's removable drives are built the same way but are more expensive because they are made out of aluminum.

The Tandon Co. has taken portability one step further. Their computers and 386es have a hard drive, called the Data Pac, that's specifically designed to be transported.

Data Pacs have a mechanism that enables you to automatically release the drive from its mounting. It also parks the read/write head and lifts it up slightly from the surface (head lifting).

Unlike the inexpensive removable drives, Data Pacs have a sturdy housing with rounded edges. Also, Data Pacs can be used with computers from other manufacturers.

The Data Pac removable hard drive systems

The only disadvantage is space. Unlike the economical portable option discussed above, which has a width of 5.25-inches and a height of 3.5-inches, Data Pacs aren't small.

With both of these systems, you must transport the entire hard drive mechanism, including the motor and the read/write heads. However, with some systems only the data medium is transported.

The most well-known of these systems is the Bernoulli disk, which is named after the discoverer of the principle upon which it operates. A Bernoulli Box is about as big as a 5.25-inch diskette and slightly thicker. The magnetic surface is on a flexible disk which hangs loosely in its resting state.

Above this movable disk is a second disk at a fixed location. If the movable disk is accelerated by the drive motor to 2000 RPM, it becomes flat and straight. An air cushion, which is exactly 0.127 mm thick, is created between it and the fixed disk.

The read/write head oscillates at a height of 0.13 microns within this air cushion. Since the rotation automatically carries dust particles to the outside, the disk surface doesn't have to be hermetically sealed.

A similar system is produced by Syquest. Magnetized data is placed directly on the disk. The read/write heads also float within an air cushion in this system.

Technical data

How much space do you need for your data?

Obviously the most important aspect of a hard drive is its capacity. The capacity depends on how many platters the drive contains and also the drive activation process (see Controller). You must determine how many megabytes you need (you may have already determined this amount for your first hard drive).

Generally, you'll need 2 Meg for each standard application program that will be installed. For DTP and CAD programs, increase this value to 5-10 Meg per application. Storage capacity is needed not only for the program itself but also for the working files needed by the program. For example, a DTP program may need fonts or a CAD program may need icon files, etc.

Some working files become more complex as the programs themselves become more complex. A word processing text file will occupy less space than a document created by a DTP application. Also, graphics occupy a lot of storage space. As you can see, it's not easy to predict the capacity you'll need.

However, generally you should have at least 40 Meg; 60 to 100 Meg is even better. If you plan on running disk-intensive applications, such as anything running under Windows, more capacity is definitely better.

In addition to storage capacity, the hard drive's speed is another important factor. The hard drive is an integral part of an application's operation. Applications temporarily store portions of the program or the working file on the hard drive. So, the fastest computer is useless if the hard drive cannot keep up.

Average access time

The speed of a hard drive is primarily determined by the drive's average access time. This is the average time it takes the read/write head to move from one position to the next. The value is represented in milliseconds.

A 20 Meg hard drive, which is found in many XTs, usually works with an average access time of 80 ms. This is much too slow for 486es. A good hard drive works with access times between 40 and 20 ms, while a 486/33 computer should have values under 20 ms.

Controller

Other speed factors depend on which hard drive controller is being used. The controller manages the hard drive and transforms the data sent back and forth between the hard drive and the CPU. Most ATs and 386es also have a combination controller for the diskette drives.

The controller card is usually located in a slot and, depending on the type, can control up to two hard drive drives. Usually this is also the maximum number possible on a computer. Higher numbers of hard drives aren't supported by the BIOS.

Controller manages the hard drive

Four types of hard drive controllers

There are four ways to control hard drives. For disks up to 100 Meg, until recently basically two processes have been used, MFM and RLL. Controllers using one or both of these are connected to hard drives via the ST-506 interface.

For medium to high capacities, ESDI or SCSI interfaces are used. The AT-Bus Standard, which is also known as the IDE hard drive, is relatively new.

Mode of operation

The most economical interface is the ST-506/ST-412, which is found in XTs, ATs, and less expensive 386es. The controller card, installed in one of the expansion slots, controls up to two hard drives through a joint 34-pin control cable and a separate 20-pin data cable for each drive. Often the controllers also have electronic components to run the diskette drives as well.

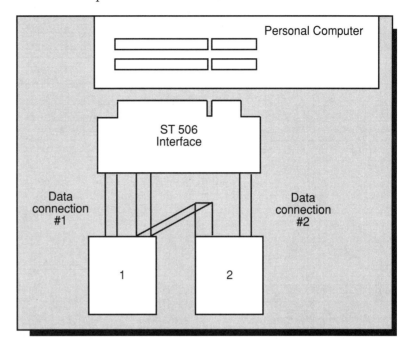

Connection diagram for hard drives with the ST-506 interface

Through these control circuits, the system selects the drive and activates the corresponding read/write head. It also makes a drive status inquiry. Bits and bytes are sent through the separate data cables.

Controllers with the ST-506 interface use two different processes for controlling the hard drive, MFM or RLL.

Track density

MFM stands for Modified Frequency Modulation. MFM hard drives divide the tracks into 17 sectors.

The RLL (Run Length Limited) is more efficient because it uses 26 sectors. Because of greater data density, RLL improves utilization of a hard drive's capacity by 50 percent. Problems occur only with programs that govern the hard drive directly from the controller registers. You must ensure that the drive is capable of accessing the more densely packed sectors. Older hard drives in particular have problems with this. So these drives should be connected only to an MFM controller.

In general, you should attach an ST-506 hard drive only to the controller specifically designed for it. Even greater use is achieved by a new improvement called ARLL (Advanced RLL). This uses 39 tracks per sector and works only with high-quality disk drives.

Fixed transmission speed

Fixed transmission speeds enable ST-506 hard drives and controllers to cooperate in the controlling process. With MFM, this speed is 5 Meg/sec, which transmits approximately 500K per second. RLL has a standard speed of 7.5 Meg/sec, which results in a transmission of 800K/sec. ARLL disks transmit data at 10 Meg/sec. These values are ideal values and can be up to 20% lower due to track switching, interleaving, and other circumstances. Generally, a good MFM disk can attain 400K/sec, while RLL can attain up to 650K/sec.

BIOS is a necessity

Although the ST-506 interface can drive a lot of hardware, this process, with few exceptions, isn't possible without the computer's BIOS. When installing a hard drive, you must place its parameters in the CMOS, which contains the hardware configuration. This is done via the Setup routine, as we explained earlier. The CMOS is where both hardware and software retrieve the data they need to respond to the hard drive.

Intelligence is needed

For a fast computer, the ST-506 standard isn't the best. This interface is too slow and inflexible. Also, it's better if the hard drives are able to tell the computer what type they are, so you don't have to set them up manually. So 486 users have three alternatives.

SCSI - flexible and expandable

SCSI is an acronym for Small Computer System Interface. The SCSI standard has already firmly established itself with certain computer manufacturers (e.g., Apple Macintosh). With this interface, peripheral devices (including hard drives) have their own "intelligence" and the controller communicates between two worlds.

Besides hard drives, other devices can be connected to the SCSI interface: Magnetic tape drives (streamers), printers, scanners, removable disk drives, etc. Up to eight different units can be connected to the interface via one 50-pin cable and each unit can consist of subunits (e.g., several hard drives).

Although data transmission on the SCSI-bus isn't serial, as with ST-506 and the others, it can proceed as 8-bit parallel. Because of data security considerations, the hard drive may also run in asynchronous serial mode. However, this slows things down so much that, in the end, the SCSI hard drive isn't faster than other types of fast controller setups.

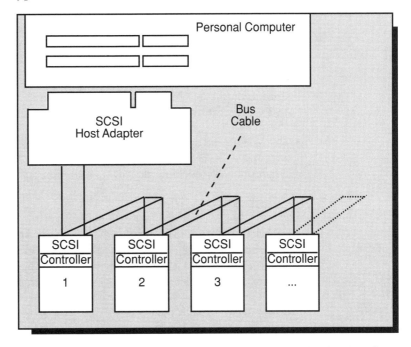

Connections for hard drives and other peripherals with SCSI interfaces

The system must first check if the bus is free for data transmission. Then the responding device must be selected and identified. The data can be transmitted only when the two are united.

More connecting than controlling

The SCSI controller (also called host adapter), as well as the peripherals attached to it, have more "intelligence" than the other types. Data transmission speeds range from 1.5 to 4 Meg/sec. Because SCSI takes over the main work of the computer, data can be stored more effectively and a cache can be used more easily. Even automatic error correction can be provided.

The role of SCSI

SCSI interfaces always played a subordinate role in the computer world because they haven't been supported by IBM. Because of this, there aren't any standards for software-driven control. Each operating system requires a separate hard drive driver.

A host adapter that enables you to attach other devices in addition to the hard drive is still fairly expensive. The Seagate ST01 controller, which costs about $50, can be connected only to hard drives.

Even when a host adapter, which can serve other peripheral devices, is available, the SCSI devices aren't automatically compatible with each other.

SCSI - the most open-ended standard

Despite all this, SCSI is still the most open-ended standard. New storage media, such as removable drives and optical drives, can be easily integrated into a system.

The SCSI/2 standard will be the next development. This standard will offer SCSI-bus expansion from 8 to 16 or 32-bits, a fast synchronous protocol mode, new commands, and much more.

ESDI - fast and efficient

IBM installs the Enhanced Small Device Interface in its large computers. On the outside it's barely distinguishable from the ST-506 interface. Here also, hard drives are connected with one 34-pin control cable and each disk is connected with a 20-pin data cable.

Identical in appearance only

However, the similarities end here. ST-506 hard drives and ESDI drives each need their own specific controllers; otherwise they will be damaged. You can avoid this requirement by obtaining a controller that accommodates both interfaces. However, the controller must be set up according to the drive type.

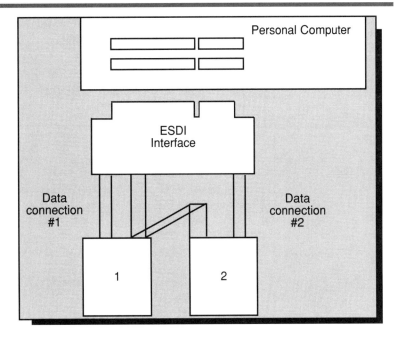

Connections for hard drives with ESDI interfaces

In the ESDI process, hard drive components assume the task of coding and decoding the data. Data are transmitted serially, but synchronization takes place on a separate clock cable. This allows for a variable data transfer rate and integration of hard drive capabilities with those of the controller.

Intelligent hard drives

With ESDI hard drives, theoretically you can reach a speed of 2-3 Meg/sec. In practice, this value is actually closer to 1 Meg/sec. The hard drive possesses its own intelligence. So it's capable of executing simple commands. However, the buffering and controlling processes are left to the controller (with a BIOS of its own).

For this reason, usually you don't have to set up ESDI hard drives with the Setup program. Some controllers have a driver for this purpose, which ensures that all applications function smoothly along with the hard drive.

AT-Bus - integrated and compact

Newest hard drive standard

The AT-Bus controller is the newest hard drive standard. It consists of an ST-506 interface, in which a large portion of the hard drive circuitry has been shifted onto the hard drive. This controller is also known as an IDE (Integrated Device Electronic) controller or an embedded (integrated) controller.

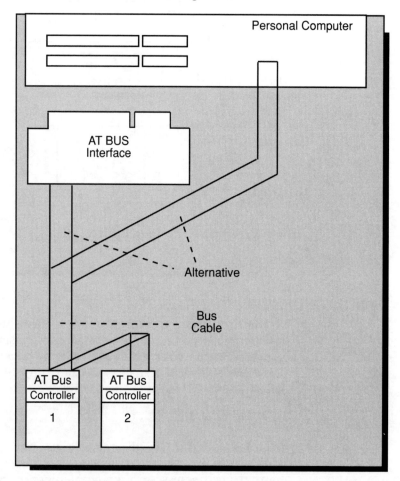

Connection diagram for hard drives with AT-Bus interfaces

The AT-Bus hard drive can be compared to a speaker in a stereo. The hard drive cable no longer connects the controller to the hard drive; instead it connects the controller/hard drive to the computer.

The connection can be made with a single 40-pin data cable either through a simple plug-in card or a separate attachment to the hard drive.

More expensive

However, an AT-Bus hard drive is more expensive than its ST-506 counterpart, which has identical storage capacity. Also, it's difficult to avoid problems with multiple hard drives, especially when a separate controller must be installed with each one.

A direct and fast connection

Eliminating serial circuits speeds up data transmission. Also, only the familiar ISA-AT-Bus standards must be followed.

All this has created an enhanced capacity for optimization. So you can set the data transmission rate as high as possible, and also use Zone Bit Recording on your disks. This increases the number of sectors on the outer tracks of the disk, which eliminates the wasted space that occurs with a constant number of sectors.

Unused capabilities

For compatibility reasons, these capabilities remain unused. So an AT-Bus hard drive is simply a fast ST-506 hard drive. You're limited to a maximum of two drives per computer. Because computer hardware doesn't support systems with two controllers, your computer cannot have an AT-Bus controller and an ST-506 controller.

Interleave

Regardless of the coding process, a hard drive's speed also depends on the interleave attainable by the controller and the hard drive. Interleave refers to a relocation of sectors, and describes the logical numbering of sectors in relation to their actual (physical) position. With an interleave of 1:1 no relocation exists, and all sectors lie directly behind the other. A fast controller can read the contents of a track with a single revolution of the disk.

Many older ST-506 controllers have only one 512K buffer, which can store only a single sector. Since the CPU is unable to read the data out of the buffer fast enough to be free for the next sector, the controller is obliged to do an "extra lap" between each read, which wastes valuable time.

If you arrange the sectors so they aren't located one after the other, the read/write head must always cover a certain distance between two sectors; during this time interval the CPU can empty the buffer. Depending on the microprocessor's speed, a desirable interleave might be 1:1, 1:2, 1:3, or 1:6. With a 486, hard drives with an interleave of 1:1 are used.

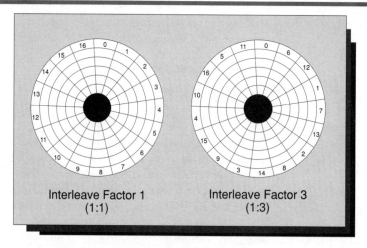

Hard drive interleave

When purchasing a controller, ensure that it will support an interleave of 1:1, that it has a large enough buffer, and can keep up the same pace as the hard drive. With an MFM disk, the differences are as follows:

MFM Disk	
Interleave	**Data output**
1:6	80K/sec
1:2	240K/sec
1:1	480K/sec

Cache

Certain hard drive controllers and/or drives have a hardware cache, in which data are temporarily stored (buffered). In the optimal case, where the computer uses all stored data, a cache can speed up operation four to six times.

SMARTDRIVE

Certain types of software can also establish a cache within the conventional memory of the computer. The best known of these is SMARTDRIVE from Microsoft.

Setup entry - requested type

Computers address data on the hard drive by giving the controller the cylinder, head, and sector numbers. Therefore, it's important for the computer to have stored the hard drive type along with all parameters in the CMOS.

When the computer is switched on, these values are transferred to the controller so, when accessing several sectors in a row, the controller can switch to the next track by itself.

Not all hard drive types can be stored in the CMOS. Many computers have a place in Setup where the parameters can be entered by the user (the *user-defined* entry). This is usually located at the end of the regular CMOS type listing.

If this isn't the case with your Setup, then the only possibility left is to define the hard drive with a driver. Certain utility programs, such as Disk Manager, can be used to do this.

Translation Mode

Hard drives with their own intelligence are able to translate the parameters in Setup to the ones that are actually available. To do this, enter either "No Type" in Setup or any type (1 for instance); the rest is handled by the controller.

The translation mode can also be useful in a different situation. DOS (up to Version 4.0) cannot handle hard drives with more than 1024 cylinders. However, this number of cylinders is quickly reached with the larger capacities.

Formatting a hard drive to just 1024 cylinders when it can hold more is an unnecessary waste of potential capacity. This can be remedied with the help of translation. The controller fools the computer into thinking that the hard drive has fewer than 1024 cylinders by artificially raising a different parameter (e.g., the number of heads).

Precompensation and reduced write current

Because of the circular structure of a hard drive, the outer tracks have a larger circumference than the inner ones. Since each track contains an equal number of sectors, recording densities are higher on the inside, which diminishes the accuracy of data. When many bits lie close to one another, some may cancel each other out because of overlapping. There are two ways to protect the inner sectors from data loss.

Write precompensation

The first method is write precompensation. The data are rearranged so bit flow changes (from 0 to 1 and vice versa) rarely appear. When write precompensation is switched on, as many bits as possible are written next to each other on the disk.

Reduce write current to the inner regions

Another method is to reduce write current to the inner regions. The particles on the inner cylinders are magnetized with less energy to prevent the overlapping. Also, modern hard drives and controllers allow for a variable number of sectors to be written to each track; this is called Zone Bit Recording.

Working with the hard drive

Technical data for drives and controllers aren't the only factors that determine a hard drive's performance. How your daily applications interact with the hard drive is also important.

File management structure (hierarchy)

Hierarchical structure

There are several ways you can avoid losing track of the large amounts of data that accumulate over time. For example, if you want to keep your personal and business documents organized, you'd probably store them in some sort of filing system. By doing this, you could organize your documents according to certain subjects. This type of arrangement is known as a hierarchical structure, because each step provides a higher level of organization.

DOS and other operating systems manage data using the same principle. You can create subdirectories to store files related by subject. You should do this not only to have a good overview of the files, but also because DOS has a limit to the number of entries it can manage in the main directory.

The following table shows the maximum entries in one directory:

Drive	Maximum Entries
360, 720K	112
1.2, 1.44 Meg	224
Hard drive	512

Tree structure

This hierarchical directory technique, which is called a tree structure, prevents chaos on the hard drive. Create at least one file for each major application. This maintains a reasonable limit on what DOS must remember. You should also have a separate directory for your own personal data files.

Use the DOS PATH command to set search paths to other directories. This enables you to call all important programs from within your personal directory. However, don't connect the directories too much. This slows down directory switching even if you have a program that's able to jump around, such as Norton Change Directory.

Making room

At first your hard drive's capacity may seem unlimited. However, you must organize and manage your resources in an optimal manner so your storage capacity will actually be sufficient.

A hard drive also needs a certain amount of room to function well; approximately 10-20% should remain free at all times. With a 20 Meg hard drive, leave at least 2 Meg free.

Also, to use a hard drive properly, install only the programs that you need. Don't install programs that you may be able to use someday. In addition, save files you're finished using on a separate diskette.

By following these principles and regularly eliminating what's no longer needed, your hard drive capacity should remain sufficient for a long time.

DOS and the hard drive

The DOS operating system contains certain commands and drivers that can significantly speed up the operation of a hard drive. Device drivers are placed in the boot partition. Both the commands and the device drivers are called and installed by an entry in the CONFIG.SYS file.

Use the FILES command

DOS has a file handler that manages files by determining their status. Usually DOS cannot open more than eight files unless specifically stated otherwise in the FILES command. The FILES command sets the maximum number of open files, with the following syntax:

```
FILES=(number of open files)
```

This command is crucial to performance only in certain cases, for example, when working with a compiler. You must give the FILES command, otherwise DOS has to close the open files first.

The BUFFERS command

The BUFFERS command has a greater influence on routine performance. This sets the number of buffer units DOS can use to transport data between mass storage (diskette/hard drive) and conventional memory (RAM). One buffer unit equals 528 bytes. You can set buffers from 2 to 99, as follows:

```
BUFFERS=(buffer units)
```

Version 4.0 and up also allows you to enter the number of sectors, separated by a comma, to be read into one unit. If you've expanded memory, you can also specify that buffers shouldn't be branched off from conventional memory but placed into expanded memory instead.

Buffers speed up the read/write process. However if more files are opened than there are files available, the buffer contents must be refreshed more often. So BUFFERS should always be higher than FILES. Usually a value of 20 to 30 is sufficient for both commands.

Cache

We've already discussed the memory cache. It's also useful to have some temporary storage for hard drives. You can use either conventional memory or extended or expanded memory to do this. PC Tools, for example, has cache programs for conventional memory.

SMARTDRV.SYS command

Anyone that has extended memory, which is included in all 386 computers, should use the SMARTDRV.SYS command. The smartdrive driver, which is included with Windows and DOS Versions 4.0 and up, uses extended memory.

This driver is transferred to the boot partition and is called as follows in CONFIG.SYS:

```
DEVICE=SMARTDRV.SYS / (memory size) {/a}
```

Memory size is given in bytes. This cache normally uses extended memory, so if you want to use expanded memory, you must add "/a".

The system uses the previous commands and drivers to support the hard drive via the CONFIG.SYS file. There are also certain DOS commands, which can be started from the AUTOEXEC.BAT file, that also enhance performance.

FASTOPEN

The FASTOPEN command has been part of DOS since Version 3.3, and speeds up file access by considering the hierarchical positions of the directories and files being used. With each new access, DOS first searches the contents of the FASTOPEN memory before it goes to the hard drive. This saves a lot of time when the same files are continually used.

Call this command as follows:

```
FASTOPEN (drive): {= (number of file accesses)} {/x}
```

The number of file accesses can be set anywhere from 10 to 99; if a value isn't given, DOS uses a standard value of 34. The option "/x" tells DOS to store the file structures in expanded memory. Starting with Version 4.0, you can call FASTOPEN from the CONFIG.SYS file, but it must then be preceded by the command INSTALL=.

Indirect influence

Hard drive performance is also influenced by how the search path is defined (through the DOS PATH command). It's important to list only the major directories so DOS doesn't have to look through a long path for each unknown command. Also, it's important to list the most frequently used directories at the beginning.

The longer you work with your hard drive, the more fragmented your files and directories become. This means that the files are stored in disconnected pieces. As fragmentation increases, the read/write head must move around more, which decreases operating speed.

It's a good idea to regularly defragment the hard drive files with a compression program, such as the BeckerTools Disk Optimizer from Abacus or Compress from PC Tools.

6.3 CD-ROM

With more powerful computers, the volumes of data being processed are always increasing. Computers are also increasingly being used as a fast information medium.

This increases the need for larger hard drive capacities and for interchangeable storage. Magnetic technology limits the amount of information that can be recorded to approximately 10 Meg with flexible and 40 Meg with fixed data storage media. Much larger amounts can be attained (up to ten times as much) when the bits are optically scanned and placed on a CD.

The process of putting information on CDs has existed for many years and has dominated the audio market. Music produced in this way is digitally recorded, and almost indistinguishable from the original.

Little available CD software

CDs haven't been as successful in the computer market because of a lack of software. Also, normal CDs can only be read; data cannot be written to them. The amounts of data stored on CDs are enormous for a computer. The maximum CD capacity of 550 Meg can store about 200,000 pages of text.

How CDs work

Data arranged concentrically

As with diskettes and hard drives, information on a CD is arranged concentrically on a disk, which rotates at a certain speed around the center point.

However, the CD doesn't revolve at a constant speed like a record player; instead, the number of revolutions per minute increases as the outer tracks of the CD are read. This is necessary to keep the same amount of data passing by the read head each time around.

The distance to be covered for an equal amount of data is always longer on the outside than on the inside. The process described here is also known as CLV (Constant Linear Velocity).

With CAV (Constant Angular Velocity) systems, tracks are arranged as on a hard drive in concentric circles, and the rotation speed is constant. All tracks, both outer and inner, contain the same number of data blocks. Although CLV disks allow more data to be stored, access times are better for CAV disks. CD-ROMs use the CLV process, with speeds of 215-500 revolutions per minute.

Pits and lands

On a CD the bits used to store information are coded as small depressions on an aluminum surface, which is protected by a transparent synthetic coating. The aluminum layer contains pits alternating with non-pits (lands).

The computer interprets each land-pit and pit-land switch as a logical 1 and each non-changing structure (whether pit or land) as a 0. Tracks of pits and lands are 0.6 μm wide and are spaced approximately 1 μm apart from each other. Without touching the surface, a laser beam scans the pits while an electronic mechanism converts them into bytes and coherent streams of information.

Since the tracks are so narrow, it's no longer possible to detect individual bits. For this reason the pit-land method has been expanded through EFM (Eight to Fourteen) modulation. This sets the following requirements for the CD-ROM code: After two zero values at the earliest but after eleven at the latest, a 1 follows.

Since the usual method of computer byte coding (eight bits) isn't sufficient here, it has expanded to a 14-bit method. By using a conversion table, each 8-bit value is assigned a 14-bit number.

Because data are read in without physical contact, this system is relatively immune to outside influences. A complicated error correction procedure lowers the error rate to 1:0.0000000000001 ($1:10^{-13}$) at a capacity of 540 Meg; with an error rate of $1:10^{-9}$ the CD can even hold 635 Meg. This error correction is necessary, because an incorrect bit in the field of data processing is much more noticeable than it is with an audio or video CD.

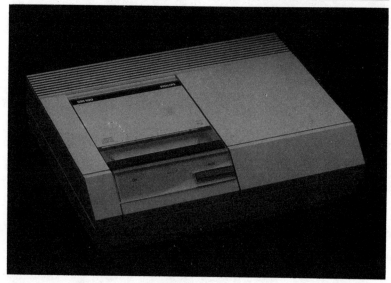

CD-ROM drive

300-500 Meg capacity

The CD's compact structure allows 300-500 Meg of data to be stored on one CD. With high quality drives, access times to the data are similar to those of a fast hard drive (an average of 35 ms). Although the CD isn't the fastest medium available, it's definitely fast enough for finding information.

You need to load a driver to process the information delivered by a CD-ROM drive. The driver ensures that DOS will treat the CD-ROM drive as an additional hard drive.

DOS versions up to 3.3 limit hard drive capacity to 32 Meg but a CD contains over 500 Meg. The driver program leads DOS to believe that the CD-ROM drive is actually the hard drive of a computer connected to a network. This type of hard drive is supported starting with DOS 3.1, and can contain over 32 Meg per partition.

Drives

CD-ROM drives are currently produced by several Japanese manufacturers that are also very active in the audio market, such as Sony and Hitachi. CD drives for the most part are limited to specific purposes. This means that you cannot change your audio CD player to a data storage device.

CD drives are built-in or external

CD drives are either built-in or attached externally. Certain brands use the RS-422.A interface, which reaches a data transmission rate of 1.4 Meg/sec.

A controller card is required and is usually included with the drive. Install this card in the computer as you would any other card (see Chapter 4). Some controller cards come with the SCSI interface. Internal drives are installed like hard drives or diskette drives.

Available programs

At this point the type of information available on CDs is still limited. There aren't any programs on CDs. Instead, there are huge databases that are accessed by search programs.

Question and answer

This inquiry program for CD data is found either on the CD itself or on a separate diskette, from which it must first be started. You start the program like any other DOS program. Several options then become available. The program quickly searches the CD for a particular keyword. The texts can also be selected and stored on the hard drive for further processing.

Outlook

Unfortunately, using CDs for only specific purposes doesn't demonstrate all of its capabilities. Some developments have already combined computer technology with audio-visual information. This system is called CD-I (interactive CD).

ROD (Rewritable Optical Disks)

Optical storage media, which can be rewritten, already exist. For example, the NeXT Cube uses magneto-optical disks for mass storage. Unlike CD-ROM drives, these RODs (Rewritable Optical Disks) can be read and rewritten any number of times.

TMO (Thermo Magneto-Optical Recording)

When writing to the disk, the laser heats up a magnetic surface so strongly that the molecules arrange themselves in one particular direction. Upon cooling, the information is "frozen" in place. Reading requires much less energy by the laser. This process is also known as TMO (Thermo Magneto-Optical Recording).

Such drives are already available for computers (e.g., from CSS). The largest drives cost just under $4,000, while a 600 Meg opto-disk is only $400. The drives are hooked up via SCSI adapter, which, along with the required drivers, is an additional $400.

WORM (Write Once Read Many)

WORM (Write Once Read Many) storage uses a process that's almost identical to the CD. The coating is prepared so initially the laser can write to it and then it can only be read. This process is especially suited for archiving purposes.

6.4 Tape Drives

To protect your data, you should make regular backups. You should also back up the hard drive with diskettes. However, if your drive is larger than 30-40 Meg, this process is too time-consuming and costly. So you may want to find other alternatives.

Tape drives

Magnetic tape drives (tape streamers) are one solution. Magnetic tape is contained in a cassette that's looks like an audio cassette. The tape passes by the tape drive's read/write head, which writes to the tape along several tracks. With this method, you can back up a several hundred megabyte drive on one tape.

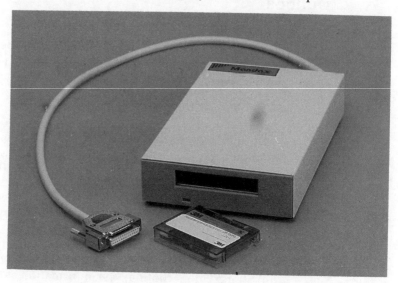

External tape drive is attached to an interface card

Cassettes and cartridges

Cassettes

There are many types of cassettes, depending on the amount of storage required. Small drives work with either cassettes that look like compact audio cassettes or with more durable cartridges.

Even the cassettes are sturdier and come with higher quality tape than the audio cassettes. To avoid accidents, the cassettes have a gap that prevents you from inserting an ordinary audio cassette into the tape drive.

Cartridges

Cartridges also have a better mechanical construction than tapes. They have a stable baseplate, which is made of metal. The motor doesn't directly move the spools, around which the tape is wound.

Instead, a belt with a special surface drives the tape back and forth. The belt is stretched over a drive reel while the tape is wound around the two hubs, which lessens mechanical strain. Since the tape is much thinner than audio or videotape, it can tear very easily.

Drives

Two drive types are available. With the economical DC2000 version, you don't have to expand your system further. Simply connect the drive to any diskette controller that's compatible with high density drives. Its data transmission rate is approximately 60K/sec. Data protection is even easier when, instead of a second diskette drive, you have an external removable device.

Although DC600 drives offer a higher transmission rate (approximately 90K/sec), they need their own controller.

Software

Tape drives are controlled by the same software that handles backing up and restoring data. Good programs have a variety of data security features. It's possible to tell the system to backup only the data that's been added since the previous backup.

An Image Backup backs up the entire drive all at once, which creates a 1:1 copy (image) of the hard drive. With a File Backup, you can back up certain files or subdirectories. This process can be automated so the tape drive automatically begins the backup at a certain time.

6.5 Installing Mass Storage

Installing diskette drives and hard drives along with their controllers is basically the same on all computers. Only the mounting method varies depending on the computer. However, setting up the system is identical on all computers.

First the diskette drives, as well as the hard drive(s), must be entered into the computer's Setup program (this was explained in Chapter 5). Next, install the hard drive.

Usually changes to diskette drives are necessary only if you have one drive and would like to add a second one or if your boot diskettes are a different format than the drive configured as Drive A:.

Second drive

If you have only one diskette drive, you can add a second one inexpensively. The controller that governs the first diskette drive is set up to control two drives. So, simply purchase the second drive, install it, and then hook it up.

When you open the computer, determine whether the cable connecting the controller to the first drive also provides for a second connection and whether this is suitable for the drive you want to install.

5.25-inch drives are attached with a cable connector that's inserted into the end of a card at the diskette drive. 3.5-inch drives have a double-row of solder pins and the controller cable has a jack on top of it.

If the cable for connecting the second diskette drive doesn't have a matching jack or plug, purchase one with the correct connections or get an adapter.

Switching diskette drives

This may be necessary if you want to reverse the roles of your A and B drives. For example, some versions of OS/2 are available only on 3.5-inch diskettes. However, most computers have a 5.25-inch drive as their drive A:.

Whether the controller considers a drive to be either drive A: or drive B: depends on the cable connection. One jack is provided for drive A: and another one is provided for drive B:. Some cables have both a 3.5-inch and a 5.25-inch connection for each drive, so you can switch them very easily. Unplug both drive A: and drive B: and plug in the other cable provided for each.

Installing a second hard drive

Today all 486 computers have at least a 40 Meg hard drive; usually they have a maximum of 80 Meg. At first this capacity seems limitless, especially if you've been using a computer that has only diskette drives. However, programs and data are taking up much more space. So eventually your hard drive may be too small.

There are two ways to add more space for programs and data:

> • Exchange your current hard drive for a larger one
>
> • Install a second hard drive to supplement the first one

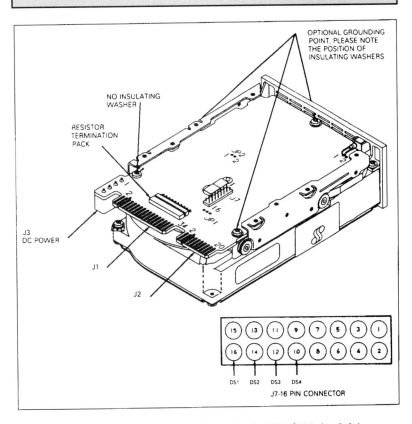

Connectors, jumper and terminators for 3.5-inch MFM/RLL hard drives

You should exchange the hard drive along with its controller if the current setup is too slow. A new hard drive that's both bigger and faster is easier to work with than using the old slow one as a second hard drive. However, a complete exchange can be more expensive than simply adding a second drive.

The cost of installing either a new or an additional hard drive depends entirely on the current equipment. The size of the drive depends on the amount of space available in your computer's case. So before buying anything, inspect your computer.

Unplug all the cables from the computer and open up the case. (If you're familiar with your computer, you don't have to do this.) Large desktop and upright models usually provide enough space for one or two half-height hard drives. With compact cases, often only a 3.5-inch drive will fit; otherwise the drive must be placed to the side.

The controller is on a board that you place into an expansion slot. Often these controllers also control the diskette drives. In modern AT-Bus hard drives, the controller circuitry is located within the hard drive itself. They are attached to the slot only with a board connector plug.

Connection and configuration

The type of cable used to connect hard drives and floppy drives, as well as the setup of logical drive numbers, depends on the interface between the system and the hard drive and on the size of the drive.

The following illustrations show the connector, jumper position, and terminator status for Seagate hard drives. Other brands use a similar procedure.

DIP Switch Settings for Hard Drive Configuration			
No.	Explanation	Drive 1	Drive 2
1	Drive number determination	On	Off
2		Off	On
3, 4		Off	Off
4-9	Terminal resistor	On	Off
10	Reserved	Off	Off

With MFM and RLL controllers using the ST-412 interface, the hard drives are all connected by a wide flat 34-pin ribbon connector.

Over this cable, the controller governs the hard drive(s). There is also a 20-pin data transfer cable for each hard drive. The drive's physical address is set with DIP switches or jumpers.

Also, for all drives, except the last one, attached to the ribbon cable, a terminal resistor must be removed. This Resistor Termination Block is located in different places depending on the hard drive.

The illustrations apply to Seagate hard drive models. With hard drives that are configured via DIP switches, the terminal resistor is activated or deactivated by the switches.

Tandon hard drives are one example of this type.

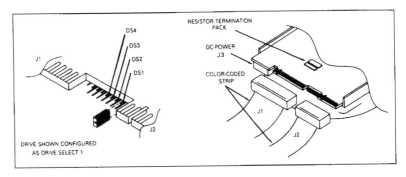

Connectors, jumper and terminal resistor for 5.25-inch MFM/RLL hard drives, half-height

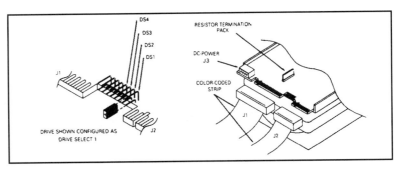

Connectors, jumper and terminal resistor for 5.25-inch MFM/RLL hard drives, full-height

SCSI and AT-Bus disks are all connected, in a row, to the controller (SCSI) or to the AT-Bus by a single ribbon cable.

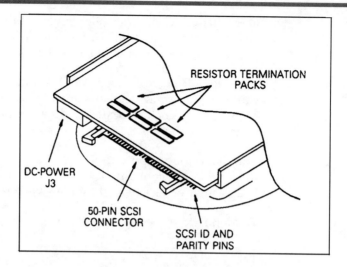

*Connectors, jumper and terminal resistor for 5.25-inch
SCSI hard drives*

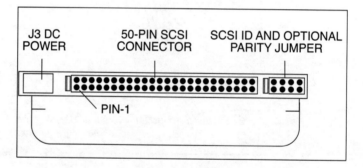

50 Pin SCSI Connector for 5.25-inch SCSI hard drives

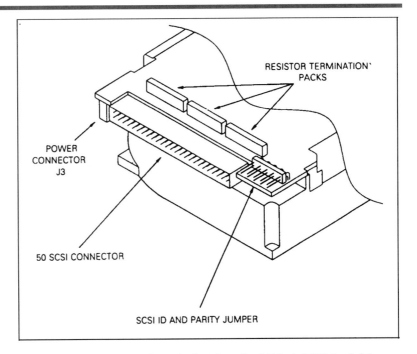

RESISTOR TERMINATION·
PACKS

POWER
CONNECTOR
J3

50 SCSI CONNECTOR

SCSI ID AND PARITY JUMPER

Connectors, jumper and terminal resistor for 3.5-inch SCSI hard drives

SCSI mass storage

Identification by house number

SCSI hard drives, removable hard drives, CD-ROMs, and other mass storage devices hooked up to SCSI interfaces have no physical address.

They are all attached, one behind the other, to a 50-pin ribbon cable. Each device has an identification number set by either jumpers or DIP switches.

In the Seagate hard drives shown here, the SCSI-ID numbers are set by three jumpers. Syquest removable hard drive configurations follow the same principles, with jumpers A, B, and C determining the ID.

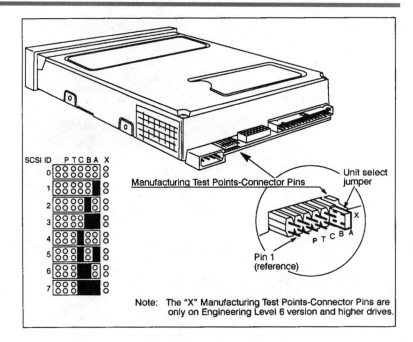

Syquest removable hard drive jumper

The settings are as follows:

	Jumper:		
SCSI-ID No.	4 C	2 B	1 (Seagate) A (Syquest)
0	-	-	-
1	-	-	closed
2	-	closed	-
3	-	closed	closed
4	closed	-	-
5	closed	-	closed
6	closed	closed	-
7	closed	closed	closed

Jumper Settings for Hard Drive SCSI-ID Numbers

QUICK TIP

Setting the SCSI device number

You can set up SCSI device numbers any way you want. However, you should follow some guidelines. The host adapter has the highest SCSI-ID number (7). The number 0 is assigned to the boot hard drive and number 1 to the second hard drive. Then all the others follow.

Terminal resistor

The terminal resistor also plays an important role with SCSI hard drives. SCSI devices are connected to each other via a 50-pin ribbon cable. Both devices at either end of the cable must have a closed terminal resistor. So the terminal resistor must be removed from all devices in the middle.

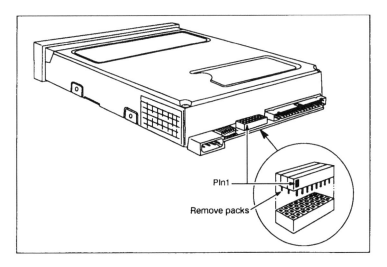

Terminal resistor status of a Syquest SQ555 removable disk drive

This also applies to the host adapter. When you attach internal and external devices to the controller, you must remove the resistors from the controller card because it's no longer the last link in the chain.

Controller

Configuring the host adapter

Along with hard drives and other SCSI storage devices, the host adapter must also be configured. In other words, your computer needs a properly installed controller card. We'll explain this procedure with the Adaptec 1542B, which is a widely-used SCSI controller.

Adaptec 1542B

Usually only limited documentation is included with the Adaptec 1542B, which makes setting parameters rather difficult. For this reason, we'll provide a brief summary of the most important jumper settings.

QUICK TIP

> ### Purchasing the Adaptec Controller
>
> If you want to install the Adaptec 1542B in a 486 computer, you must buy the Master Kit. In addition to a detailed manual, you'll also have the software needed to make the host adapter run smoothly with EMS, Windows 3.1, and other software. Otherwise, you would have to obtain the special software separately.

Hardware settings with jumpers

Hardware settings for the Adaptec 1542B are made with five rows of jumpers. Row J5 controls the following settings:

Pin	Function
1	Synchronous negotiation
2	Diagnosis
3	SCSI parity
4 - 6	SCSI address
7 + 8	DMA channel

Pin pair: 7	8	DMA channel	J9-Jumper
open	open	7	4+8
closed	open	6	3+7
open	closed	5 (standard)	2+6
closed	closed	0	1+5

Pin	Function
9 - 11	Interrupt channel

Note that tabs for Row J9 must also be set accordingly.

Pin pair:			Interrupt channel	J9-Jumper
9	10	11		
open	open	open	9	9
closed	open	open	10	10
open	closed	open	11 (standard)	11
closed	closed	open	12	12
open	open	closed	14	13
open	open	open	15	14

Pin	Function
12 + 13	DMA transfer rate

Pin pair		Speed MB/sec
12	13	
open	open	5.0
closed	open	5.7
open	closed	6.7
closed	closed	8.0

In Jumper-Block 2 only Jumpers 1 and 5 are used, 2 to 4 are reserved. It's best if both jumpers remain in their standard positions.

Pin	Function	Closed	Open
1	BIOS	activated (standard)	deactivated
5	Automatic recognition	activated	deactivated (standard)

Jumper-Row J7 is placed directly next to the external SCSI connector. It's used for the following settings:

Pin	Function	Closed	Open
1	Floppy controller port address	170h-177h	1F0h-1F7h
2 - 4	SCSI adapter port address		(Standard)

Pin:			
2	3	4	Address
open	open	open	334h
closed	open	open	330h (standard)
open	closed	open	234h
closed	closed	open	230h
open	open	closed	134h
closed	open	closed	130h

The two remaining combinations aren't used.

TAKE NOTE

> The integration of a controller depends not only on the interrupt and the DMA channel, but also on the port address. You must match up all three factors for the remaining components of your computer (e.g., network cards) so two devices don't have the same interrupt, DMA channel, or storage address.

Software

Once you've installed the Adaptec 1542B controller and are working with DOS and Windows or a memory manager, you must call ASPI4DOS.SYS as a device driver from your CONFIG.SYS file.

This program is either included with the Master Kit or is available separately from the same dealer that supplied the controller.

Transfer the driver from the diskette to the hard drive and add the following line to your CONFIG.SYS file:

```
DEVICE=(Path)ASPI4DOS.SYS (Parameters)
```

This driver usually runs without parameters, although the following are available:

/D   When installing the driver, this gives you a detailed status report.

/Fnn   Sets Bus-Off-Time to nn µs (1 to 64, default is 4).

/I	The INT13 Manager isn't loaded. This option exists only for debugging purposes and normally shouldn't be used.
/L	SCSI units with a logical number (LUN) other than 0 will be supported.
/Nnn	Sets Bus-On-Time to nn µs (2-15, default is 11).
/NORST	Upon installation, the driver doesn't initiate a reset of all attached devices.
/Pnnn	Port address is located at hexadecimal nnn.
/W	Activates virtual-mode buffering. The driver uses an extra 64K of expanded memory (or conventional memory if expanded memory is unavailable). This option is meant for Windows 3.0. It's unnecessary for Windows 3.1.
/WM	The buffer is always taken from conventional memory. The /WM and /W parameters cannot be used together.
/Xnn	Sets the AT-Bus master transfer rate. nn stands for a number that represents speed as follows:

nn	Transfer rate (MB/sec)
00	5.0
01	6.7
02	8.0
03	10.0
04	5.7

WARNING!

5.7 Meg/sec are possible only with the 1542B.

> Not all systems with the AT-Bus (ISA-Bus) can tolerate a bus master transfer rate higher than 5 Meg/sec. If your system "hangs", then switch to one step lower.

You may want to install several controller systems in your computer. The following table shows which controller systems are compatible and which ones cannot be installed together:

Non/Compatible controller systems				
Controller	MFM	RLL	SCSI	ESDI
MFM	-	-	+	-
RLL	-	-	+	-
SCSI	+	+	-	+
ESDI	-	-	+	-

Installing a second hard drive

All hard drive controllers can manage two hard drives. So installing a second hard drive may be a suitable and less expensive alternative to a complete exchange.

When installing the second hard drive, you don't have to erase the data on the first one; the data can remain in the first partition. If you perform the installation process carefully, your data shouldn't be disturbed.

The procedure with hard cards is slightly different because the controller and hard drive are combined into one unit and inserted into a single slot. Although they are easier to use, hard cards are rarely compatible with other hard drives. Also, in this case, the controller isn't capable of managing a second hard drive.

The basic procedure for installing a second hard drive is identical to the procedure for exchanging hard drives. When purchasing a new hard drive, be sure you have the following components: Drive, controller card (if necessary), one or two flat ribbon cables, the user manual, and a diskette containing the formatting program.

To protect the existing hard drive, first run a disk parking program. Then open the case. If you're removing the hard drive, first you must disconnect the cables connecting it to the controller. Remove the card and then the drive.

If you're connecting the second hard drive to the original controller, first you must determine whether the disk is compatible with the controller and whether they use the same controlling process. Then, at the drive itself, you must identify it as a second hard drive; otherwise conflicts will result with the first hard drive. This is usually done by switching jumpers or setting DIP switches.

The final step in the exchange is to mount the controller in a slot so the connecting cables reach the drive.

Install the hard drive in the place provided for it inside the case. Depending on the device, either attach mounting rails or insert the disk directly into the drive bay.

Connect the controller to the drives with the ribbon cable. All hard drives that are hooked up to a controller use a wide cable that must have two plugs for two drives. Each of the narrow cables is used for connecting one of the hard drives to the controller. Place the side of the ribbon cable marked in red on the solder posts of the card, on the side with the lowest number. AT-Bus hard drives are connected to the multifunction card with only one cable.

Once the hard drive has been successfully installed, you must report its presence in the Setup program. With a new first hard drive, simply replace the existing entry with the new one. Second hard drives are entered as "Disk 2" or "Drive D".

As with the first hard drive, you must enter its type. The remaining steps are the same as the ones used for the original hard drive. You can omit the "/S" parameter only when formatting additional partitions or logical drives because you already have a boot partition.

Setting up the hard drive

Very few 486es are ready to use when they are delivered from the manufacturer. Although all the devices are present, the hard drive setup is usually left to the end user. The reason for this is that each user may have a different operating system or may want to partition the hard drive differently.

Preparing a hard drive for use involves four steps:

- Entering it in Setup

- Low-level formatting ("hard" or physical formatting)

- Partitioning

- Formatting under an operating system ("soft" formatting)

Many manufacturers perform the low-level formatting because it's a difficult process. The end user must partition and format the drive. However, this is easy to do. In DOS versions higher than 4.0 and OS/2, these tasks are controlled by a menu driven installation program.

Entry into CMOS

Although the CMOS entry doesn't affect low-level formatting, DOS uses the values contained there as the basis for its partitioning and formatting. An incorrect entry in Setup could cause problems.

The computer's ROM has approximately 46 different types for identifying the hard drive. You must find the matching drive parameters. However, this doesn't apply to the ESDI and SCSI hard drives. Controllers for these drives are so intelligent that the parameters are transferred to the CMOS automatically.

If there is no place in the Setup menu where you can enter the parameters, you must use a utility program, such as Speedstor.

```
SpeedStor(TM)   Hard Disk Preparation/Diagnostics,  version 5.11
Copyright(C)  Storage Dimensions  1985,  1988. All rights reserved         .
─────────────────────────────────────────────────────────────────

   M A N U A L   D R I V E   P A R A M E T E R   O V E R R I D E

      Go Through the parameters and modify only those that
      need changing.  Press ESC to Abort all changes

Drive   Manufacturer/Model   Cyls   Heads   Secs   Precomp   Lzone  TotalBytes
  1     <Unsupported Type 47> 1024     5      26       0       1024   68.156.928


        Number of Cylinders <305-2048>                    [     1024]
        Number of Heads <2-64>                            [        5]
        Starting Cylinder for Pre-Composition             [        0]
        Control Byte                                      [        0]
        Sectors Per Track                                 [       26]
        Landing Zone Cylinder                             [     1024]
        Starting Cylinder for Reduced Write Current(XT)   [        0]
        ECC Burst Byte(XT)                                [        0]
        Standard Time-out factor (XT)                     [        0]
        Time-out for Format(XT)                           [        0]
        Time-out for Check(XT)                            [        0]
```

Using Speedstor to enter non-matching hard drive types into CMOS-RAM

Low-level formatting

One type of low-level formatting physically divides the hard drive into tracks and sectors. Depending on the controller and the recording process it uses, the disk is divided into 17, 26, or more sectors. Low-level formatting also determines the interleave with which the controller accesses the hard drive.

Low-level formatting occurs independently of the operating system being used. There is a separate program for it, which is stored in either the hard drive or the computer BIOS. In 486es this program is often part of the Setup routine.

You can also perform low-level formatting with an external hard drive utility program. Such utility programs are usually located on a diskette that's included with the computer. These programs are usually preferable to the routines contained in Setup because they provide more options.

For example, these programs allow you to enter defective sectors. Almost all hard drives have defective sectors; otherwise they would be very expensive to produce. Usually the defective sectors are listed on a sticker directly on the hard drive or on an accompanying document. The sectors contained on the "defect list" should be entered prior to hard formatting so they are excluded from the start.

If you don't know which sectors are defective or if you have an error-free hard drive, programs such as Disk Manager can search through the hard drive and find the defective sectors. Even if you have a defect list you should do this to verify the list.

Once the defect list is entered and verified, you can perform the actual formatting. At this point the program usually wants to know the interleave factor. You must determine which interleave is best for your hard drive.

An incorrect interleave hinders optimal performance but a larger interleave is always better than a smaller one. For example, if you aren't sure that your hard drive works with 1:1, it's best to format it to 1:3; otherwise it will always do an extra lap (which in MFM disks would be equivalent to a factor of 1:17).

Partitioning

After low-level formatting, the next step is partitioning the hard drive. This process originated when operating systems couldn't handle large disk capacities all at once. Since then, the maximum size has increased to several gigabytes under DOS 5.0 and DOS 6.0 and OS/2 2.0 and OS/2 2.1.

However, it's still useful to partition the disk if the computer will have more than one operating system. Since different operating systems don't always use the same control structures, each system should have its own area on the hard drive. Each partition is managed independently of the others. Once a partition has been allocated to a particular operating system, it cannot be used by the others.

Normally an operating system isn't allowed to occupy more than one partition. Also, the partitions are usually limited to a size of 32 Meg each. However, this limitation is becoming obsolete.

Extension

Starting with DOS Version 3.3, you can create two partitions for DOS files, but each partition has a different status. The first partition is the primary DOS partition, which under DOS 3.3 is limited to 32 Meg. The system is booted from this primary partition, which also contains all the important files.

The remainder of the hard drive can now be set up as an extended DOS partition. Unlike the primary partition, its size isn't limited to 32 Meg. However, since DOS 3.3 cannot handle capacities larger than 32 Meg, the extended DOS partition must be divided into logical drives, which have the 32 Meg limit.

So a 100 Meg hard drive is divided into a primary partition of 32 Meg and a secondary partition of 68 Meg. The secondary partition is then divided into logical drives of 32, 32, and 4 Meg. The maximum number of logical drives is limited only by the number of letters in the alphabet. Because only letters can be used for drive names and A: and B: are already assigned, there are 24 possible logical drives remaining.

When DOS 4.0 was released, maximum partition size increased to 2 gigabytes, which has carried over to DOS 5.0 and DOS 6.0. However, you can still create two partitions and up to 24 logical drives. The modified DOS Version 3.31, which is found in Compaq computers, also uses this extended structure.

While DOS 3.3 limits hard drive capacity to 768 Meg, under DOS 5.0 the maximum has increased to 48 gigabytes.

The extended hard drive functions of DOS 4.0 are used only when you're working with partitions larger than 32 Meg. With smaller capacities, DOS 4.0 uses the same methods as DOS 3.3. This ensures the downward compatibility of DOS.

The hard drive is partitioned with the FDISK program. The procedure is the same with all DOS versions (3.3, 4.0, and DR DOS 3.41) except that DOS 5.0 and DOS 6.0 provide additional input options. All FDISK versions also use identical procedures.

First you must decide whether you want to partition the disk and then you must determine how to partition the disk. In any case, FDISK must always be run, even with only one partition. First Step 1 sets up and activates the primary partition (i.e., makes it bootable). Then the extended DOS partitions are set up and divided into logical drives (a minimum of 1).

Once the partitioning is complete, the system reboots itself and you can perform the soft formatting. You can either use the installation program or install the system manually. This procedure is described in detail in Chapter 9.

Park for safety

The distance between the read/write head of a hard drive and the magnetic surface it glides over is extremely small. Vibrations can easily cause the head to touch the surface. When this happens, the data at that location may be destroyed.

Parking programs move the read/write head to a location where it can't destroy data. There are various types of parking programs. One of the most common is called SHUTDOWN. This program displays a switch on the screen that changes to the "off" position when all hard drives detected in the system have been parked. Then you can safely switch off the computer.

Otherwise, there should be a parking program on the diskette included with your hard drive. PC-Tools Version 5.5 has a Disk pull-down menu with a Park command that will move the read/write head off to the side.

6.6 Problems With Diskettes

There are many causes for a diskette that is no longer readable or writeable. Either the diskette itself is defective or the hardware is at fault.

Defective diskette

When the diskette is also unreadable in other drives, the cause of a problem can be traced to a defective storage medium. If another computer isn't available, then use the same drive to check other diskettes that you know are in good condition.

However, you cannot do this by simply using DIR because the directory is located on the first track of a diskette and some misadjusted read/write heads may still be able to decipher it. Instead, take a README file from any installation diskette and try to display its contents or try to copy this diskette with DISKCOPY. If you can perform both of these tasks without any problems, then your program diskette is definitely defective.

Not recognized

Not all diskettes are defective just because your computer doesn't accept them. Trying to format a HD diskette in a DD drive leads to the error message:

```
Invalid Medium or Track 0 Bad
```

However, this diskette simply isn't suitable for your drive.

Some drives allow you to format 3.5-inch DD diskettes as HD. These inexpensive drives don't consider the opening that distinguishes the two types of diskettes. So, if you try to read this diskette on a drive that does notice the difference, an error message is displayed although the data is still intact.

Unfortunately there is no way of coaxing the data from the intelligent diskette drive. Your only alternative is to recopy the data onto a properly formatted diskette.

Rescuing techniques

Various utilities, such as the Norton Disk Doctor/NDD and PC-Tools Diskfix, can help you retrieve data that has become unreadable. If you're unable to retrieve the data from your original diskette, try it on a copy made with DISKCOPY. You'll have the option of skipping the defective sectors by selecting *Ignore*.

Incorrect entry

If your problem is the result of a defective drive, there are still ways to retrieve your data. With an AT or a 386/486, the drive settings may have been deleted from the CMOS. To determine whether this has happened, activate the Setup program and check the entries.

You should also check the cables to ensure that they are properly connected, especially after installing new equipment. It's possible that a cable was accidentally loosened or plugged in incorrectly. However, if all the connections are working, the drive must be repaired.

6.7 Problems With The Hard Drive

In this section we'll discuss several reasons for hard drive failure and also provide some tips for solving this problem.

CMOS-RAM entry was deleted

This error is indicated when the computer displays the following (or a similar) error message at bootup:

> No system disk found - Please insert bootable disk

Calling the Setup program, from either the diskette or the BIOS, will indicate whether the hard drive still exists or some program has deleted the entry.

This is possible, especially if other entries, such as the second diskette drive or the memory allocation, have also been deleted. In this case, simply re-enter the original value for the hard drive and correct any other values so your system runs without errors again.

With a new computer, the following error may occur:

> The hard drive is not partitioned and formatted.

In this case, you must partition the disk with FDISK and install DOS. Format the disk with FORMAT C:/S. If the computer doesn't boot from the hard drive, the C: partition hasn't been set to "active". Call FDISK and activate the partition.

If you hear strange noises coming from your computer during bootup and the computer can no longer find the operating system, then an incorrect hard drive type is stored in the CMOS. Call Setup and enter the correct type.

Improperly connected cables

After installing a new hard drive, you may forget to plug in a cable connector or plug one into the wrong location. If a hard drive light doesn't appear, the power cable probably wasn't plugged in. However, if the light is on and remains on or behaves strangely, one of the ribbon cables that lead to the controller is probably incorrectly attached to the cable connector.

The proper connection is usually indicated by the cable marked in red, which is always placed on the side with the lowest number.

Deleted files

You're probably familiar with this error. You insert a diskette to delete all its files. Then you enter the DEL command from the main hard drive directory without specifying the drive and completely skip the prompt asking whether you're sure you want to delete the files. Soon your CONFIG.SYS, AUTOEXEC.BAT, COMMAND.COM, and other important files are gone and your system obviously cannot boot again. Our "Rescue Diskette", described on the next page, should be able to help you.

You should always make a copy of the important system files on a bootable "Rescue Diskette".

> Create a subdirectory with the name LIFE, or something similar, and copy these files to this subdirectory by calling the following statements from your AUTOEXEC.BAT file:

```
COPY AUTOEXEC.BAT LIFE
COPY CONFIG.SYS LIFE
COPY COMMAND.COM LIFE
```

TAKE NOTE

Do this for all your important files, drivers, and programs on the main directory level. This ensures the copies are always current.

Bad FAT

A more difficult error to fix is a disruption of the FAT (File Allocation Table). The computer indicates this error by sending a message stating that it can no longer access a certain sector. To solve this problem, you need a diagnosis program such as Norton Disk Doctor. This error also occurs if, after compressing the hard drive, you try to access the hard drive without booting first.

The best way to avoid data loss is by making regular backups of your most important files. The safest way to do this is by using BACKUP/RESTORE or a similar program. If this is too much trouble, back up only your working files. The programs can be re-installed from their original diskettes or from backup copies.

The Rescue Diskette

TAKE NOTE

Every computer owner should have a diskette that can get the computer "back on its feet" in case of an emergency. Since this is a boot disk, it should be the same format as your drive A:. We also recommend using HD diskettes (high density).

Format this diskette as a system diskette (using the /s option, i.e., FORMAT A: /s) and copy the following files and programs to this diskette:

DOS files

- COMMAND.COM
- FDISK
- FORMAT

External programs

- Norton Disk Doctor or PC-Tools Diskfix
- UNERASE/UNDELETE

If your system files are deleted from the root directory of the hard drive, these programs can help you retrieve them.

Batch files and System files

- AUTOEXEC.BAT
- CONFIG.SYS
- The system files included in the CONFIG.SYS file

Once you have copied the AUTOEXEC.BAT file and the system files listed in your CONFIG.SYS file to the "Rescue Diskette", you will have to edit the AUTOEXEC.BAT file and CONFIG.SYS file so they work with drive A:.

Place a write protect tab on the "Rescue Diskette" (5.25-inch) or open the write protect (3.5-inch). Keep this diskette in a safe place, in case something goes wrong and your hard drive will no longer boot. To boot from the "Rescue Diskette", insert the diskette into drive A: and press Ctrl + Alt + Del to reboot the computer. Make sure to test the "Rescue Diskette" to see that it boots your computer properly.

Chapter 7

Graphics

The computer screen represents the interface between the user and the computer. This is where the user receives information from the computer. Carefully select your screen and graphics card. If you make the wrong selection, you may encounter many problems in the future.

Graphics are independent

Following the "open" principle of system architecture, the graphics card has always been an independent element within the entire system. The electronic circuitry for graphics are usually located on a plug-in card in one of the computer's expansion slots. Only modern computers, with all components on one board, also have integrated graphics.

There are many technical aspects of graphics. The first of these is resolution. The principles governing screen display have remained the same since the first computer was introduced. A computer image consists of many points arranged horizontally and vertically. The number of these points in width and height is known as the resolution. These points are also called pixels.

It all began with monochrome

The first computer screens didn't have color. Characters were displayed on a monochrome picture tube, which was mainly black-green at first and then black-amber instead of black and white. White screens have been used only recently. Color monitors were developed as computers began to be used for entertainment purposes, such as computer games.

Displayable colors

There are two basic concepts for color monitors. The number of simultaneously displayable colors is determined by screen memory organization. The more memory the screen has available, the more information (colors, brightness, etc.) it can hold.

Color palette

The color palette consists of the "pot", from which the displayed colors are "mixed". Each color is composed of the basic elements red, green, and blue.

The proportions of these basic colors at a particular point on the screen determines the color of the point. The color palette determines the range of possible gradations in producing a compound color from the basic three colors.

7.1 Graphics Standards

Graphics electronics and IBM compatible microprocessors continued to develop but followed two different sets of rules.

Monochrome graphics adapter

The IBM computer and its compatibles were originally designed as office computers. The first graphics card could display only alphanumeric characters on the screen. The monitors (all monochrome) could display only the color of their picture tubes.

The first graphics standard was called Monochrome Display Adapter or (MDA). It was able to display 80 characters on 24 lines and had a character matrix of 9 x 16 points.

Monochrome graphics standard

The Hercules Computer Technology company quickly realized that eventually computers would have to be able to display graphics instead of only characters. They also realized that the introduction of the CGA card (see below) didn't solve this problem.

So Hercules developed a graphics system, in which individual pixels could be controlled separately. This system provided a resolution of 720 x 348 pixels. Since the remaining circuitry didn't change, the same monitors that were using MDA began using Hercules.

QUICK TIP

Detecting the flicker

If you have a Hercules monitor, you can easily see the flickering when you look to the left or to the right of the monitor.

Depending on the manufacturer, graphics cards are called either Hercules or Hercules-compatible. Even today Hercules graphics cards are still standard equipment on some computers.

They produce images on the screen with a refresh frequency of 50 Hertz. This causes the picture to flicker slightly, which is especially noticeable over large bright areas.

CGA

First color graphics card

Along with MDA, a new adapter capable of displaying colors was simultaneously introduced. At that time, the Color Graphics Adapter (CGA) was the only card available for both text and graphics. Today many computers still have graphics cards that follow the CGA standard. The CGA card can run in two different modes: Graphics mode and text mode. In graphics mode, you can have either 320 x 200 pixels in four colors or 640 x 200 pixels in two colors (monochrome).

In text mode, the CGA card can display 16 colors at low resolution. This low resolution produces a character matrix of only 8 x 8 pixels, which makes it difficult to work with the CGA card for a long period of time.

EGA

Color with higher resolution

The EGA card was the first to significantly improve quality and comfort. EGA, which stands for Enhanced Graphics Adapter, provides a resolution of 640 x 350 pixels displayed simultaneously with 16 colors that can be chosen from a 64 color palette. The EGA card has a character matrix of 8 x 14 pixels. An 8 x 8 font, which allows for a text resolution of 80 characters x 43 lines, also exists.

EGA monitors

EGA graphics cards can control both monochrome and color monitors. A simple Digital RGB monitor, although it can still be used with CGA cards, is no longer sufficient for EGA. The horizontal deflection frequency of 21.85 KHz requires at least a double-scan monitor.

Downward compatibility

Most EGA graphics cards are able to display the previous standards of CGA and MDA. The Hercules standard, however, is emulated only in text mode. Another capability of EGA is enhanced resolution electronics. A good EGA card can attain the Hercules graphics standard of 720 x 348 pixels, and two higher resolutions: 640 x 480, which is usually compatible with software set to VGA (see below), and 800 x 600. With higher resolutions, you can choose 16 colors from a total of 64.

Memory requirements

Because of its higher resolution and numerous colors, the EGA card requires so much memory that it wouldn't be practical to combine it with the ROM of the operating system. So EGA cards have their own screen memory, which can be 16 to 256K, depending on system configuration.

VGA and MCGA

A new standard

When IBM introduced its PS/2 model, two new graphics adapters were introduced. At first the VGA card was installed only in Models 60, 70, and 80. However, later it was installed in smaller computers, which initially had an MCGA (Multi Color Graphics Array) card. Theoretically this card was an enhanced version of the CGA mode.

Analog instead of digital

Both MCGA and VGA allow you to choose colors from a palette of 262,144 colors. Such a vast array of colors requires a new type of monitor, which is controlled by an analog instead of digital process. This method conserves the memory that would otherwise be needed for the various shades.

VGA (Video Graphics Array) provides a standard resolution of 640 x 480 pixels in 16 of the mentioned 262,144 colors. Graphics in this format are often of photographic quality and can barely be distinguished from real pictures. A straight MCGA card was installed in only first generation PS/2s and can produce the VGA resolution but only in two colors. In contrast, all VGA cards can run in MCGA mode as well as HGC, CGA, and EGA.

A new type of monitor, called the analog RGB monitor, was introduced along with the Graphics Array cards. This monitor runs on a much higher horizontal deflection frequency of 31.5 KHz. So if you purchase a new VGA card, usually you must also purchase a new monitor.

Since it produces very complex graphics, the VGA card has a minimum of 256K of memory of its own.

Enhanced VGA

Today there are many graphics cards whose capabilities surpass the VGA standard. This is possible because the memory on the card isn't completely occupied by the 640 x 480 pixels and the 16 colors. So many graphics cards can bring additional specialized formats to your screen.

Specialized formats

These formats depend on the amount of screen memory the card has. A normal VGA card with 256K of memory can display additional resolutions of 800 x 600 pixels in 16 colors or 640 x 400 pixels in 256 colors. 512K of memory already gives you 256 colors at a resolution of 640 x 480; more memory gives you even higher resolutions.

Unlike VGA, these high resolutions haven't been standardized yet. Programs that use them generally need a special screen driver. There are already two standards, which still haven't established themselves yet.

The VESA standard

One of these is the VESA standard, which was established by a few video card and monitor manufacturers. This standard provides 800 x 600 pixels in 256 colors, as well as 1024 x 768 pixels in 16 colors. This requires a video card with a minimum of 512K of video RAM and also quartz crystals, which will run high resolutions at a horizontal frequency that doesn't flicker.

Many 512K cards offer high resolution only with the interlace process, in which two half pictures are generated. Because the horizontal frequency is cut in half, interlaced displays can flicker.

Additional drivers required

To use the higher resolutions offered by VGA cards, many programs need additional drivers. These drivers are usually included with the graphics cards themselves. But, unfortunately, which cards provide which drivers for which software hasn't been established. The more popular DTP and CAD programs, as well as the user interfaces GEM and Windows, have their own drivers, but drivers for word processing, spreadsheets, and other applications are more difficult to find.

VESA

Several graphics card manufacturers have recognized this driver problem and formed an organization called VESA (Video Electronics Standards Association). VESA has tried to standardize the higher resolutions. Instead of every program using a driver to create its own graphics, VESA cards at high resolutions use the same set of BIOS functions, which future programmers will be able to use.

Although almost all major graphics card manufacturers are members of VESA, not every new Enhanced VGA card automatically follows the standard. If you're unsure, contact your dealer or a manufacturer's representative.

Advanced intelligence

The practical limit for conventional graphics cards is a resolution of 1024 x 768 pixels and 256 colors. These cards display a screen image produced by identically organized RAM areas within the graphics card. Each pixel is assigned one or more bits that determines the pixel's existence and its appearance.

The main microprocessor controls all these bits, which, depending on image size and complexity, involves a lot of work and results in a corresponding loss of speed.

Also, the screen memory isn't directly accessible by the CPU; instead (like Expanded Memory) it can be addressed only within a 64K window between 640K and 1 Meg.

Graphics memory must be separate

To make any further progress, the graphics memory must be separated from the system and governed by a processor of its own. Such graphics processors are available from Intel (i82786), Hitachi, and Texas Instruments (TMS 34010 and TMS 34020). They take over the "legwork" necessary for graphics output.

The main processor still must give a command for a particular image (such as a line); the graphics processor, along with the other video card components, does the rest. Because the graphics processor has only one function to perform, it's optimized for this task and can complete it much faster than the CPU.

Drivers not required

A graphics processor also offers other advantages. Since it has its own operating system, it doesn't need drivers. So, even if cards offer greater resolutions and more colors, the commands to activate them will only be enhanced instead of changed. With this upward compatibility, you can avoid the kinds of problems that Enhanced-Hyper-VGA cards users experience; their cards don't work with all programs.

The three types of graphics processor cards which we'll discuss include the following:

- 8514/A from IBM
- DGIS cards
- TIGA cards

Unfortunately, these cards also contain three different operating systems.

8514/A

The 8514/A graphics standard has been available for some time. It uses a microchannel graphics card that processes commands with a graphics microprocessor developed by IBM. Western Digital makes a compatible chipset; it's also installed on ISA-Bus cards. However, this isn't a very popular standard.

The 8514/A is the successor to an adapter called PGA (Professional Graphics Adapter). This adapter could display 640 x 480 pixels in 256 colors long before VGA but because it was expensive, it wasn't successful. The PGA's tasks were performed by an externally programmable Intel 8080 chip, while the 8514/A has a "custom" chip that produces graphics with fixed programmed routines.

Similar to VGA, the 8514/A establishes contact with the current application through several registers. The program has access to several graphics routines, which are stored in the Adapter Interface (AI).

TIGA

Texas Instruments was also considering ways to develop the VGA standard. It came up with its own graphics microprocessor, called the TMS 34010. This microprocessor is equipped with registers like a conventional CPU, and also has many graphics commands and monitor control options.

Texas Instruments Graphic Adapter

Cards with this microprocessor adhere to a standard known as TIGA (Texas Instruments Graphic Adapter). Because the graphics microprocessors carry the designation TMS 340xx, this standard is also known as "TIGA-340".

The TIGA-standard offers a maximum of 16.7 million colors at a resolution of 512 x 480. This is the same palette from which you can choose 33,768 colors at 640 x 480 or 256 at 1024 x 768. As with Enhanced VGA cards, programs that want to use these colors must have TIGA drivers, which provide the necessary commands. Drivers for Windows 3.1 are usually included with the TIGA cards.

DGIS

Direct Graphics Interface Standard

Besides 8514/A and TIGA, some graphics chips follow another standard, called Direct Graphics Interface Standard (DGIS). DGIS exists for many microprocessors and works independently of the hardware.

Graphics cards with their own microprocessors work with many of the above standards and with a few VGA modes, but not simultaneously. Cards with such high resolutions require high quality multi-frequency monitors.

7.2 Electronics

The clock frequency and speed of the computer determine the ultimate speed of a graphics card. So they are important factors in determining access time to the graphics card's screen memory. Accesses to the Video RAM (another name for the screen memory) are performed via the card's data and address bus.

The bus width determines the number of bits that can travel simultaneously from the CPU (main computer microprocessor, e.g., 80486) to the graphics card, via the address and data bus of the main board (motherboard).

Bus width limited to 8 bits

With PC/XT systems, the bus width of graphics cards is limited to 8 bits. In AT, 386, and 486 systems you can also install cards with a 16-bit bus. Usually a larger bus width provides faster access to the graphics card. It's important that the bus frequency of the main board matches the bus frequency of the graphics card.

If the frequencies don't match, for example if the graphics card has a much higher bus frequency, the graphics card might retrieve data from the CPU only every second or even third bus cycle. Because of this, the microprocessor must wait for the graphics card. These microprocessor cycles are called wait states. The microprocessor operates at its maximum output rate only if there are no wait states.

The output rate of a graphics card depends not only on bus width but also on the coordination of bus frequencies between the main board and the graphics card. Speed is also influenced by the operating system as well as the driver software included with some cards. A part of the operating system, known as the Video BIOS (Basic Input Output System), is responsible for monitor access.

The Video BIOS has been a part of the operating system since the first personal computers were introduced. Since it's based on the microprocessor technology of that time, it doesn't match the capabilities of today's new graphics cards.

To obtain optimal performance from the new graphics cards, the cards themselves contain extensions to the operating system. These Video BIOS extensions are located on a ROM (Read Only Memory) chip, which, since it can only be read, protects the extensions from being accidentally deleted.

When the system boots up and loads the operating system into conventional memory or RAM, the extended functions are tied into the Video BIOS. Programs can then call them like the original Video BIOS functions and use the advanced capabilities of modern graphics cards.

The Video BIOS handles most of the accesses to the graphics card. So it's important to the operating speed that the extended BIOS functions are executed very quickly. However, because of their design, the ROM chips containing these functions take longer to access than an ordinary RAM chip.

Shadow ROM

So many graphics cards give you the option of transferring their Video BIOS from the slow ROM chips to the faster RAM chips in conventional memory. This technique is known as Shadow ROM because a shadow of the original Video ROM will exist in the computer's conventional memory.

No need to copy ROM contents

Instead of placing the Video BIOS enhancements on a ROM chip, some video cards now include a diskette whose programs are loaded into memory at system bootup. The more extensive Video BIOS enhancements almost always do this. Otherwise, they would require more ROM chips on the graphics card and occupy more space. With this process, you don't have to copy the ROM contents into conventional memory.

Usually these diskettes also contain a brief set of instructions and an installation program, so that you can install the BIOS enhancements optimally with a minimum of technical knowledge.

With the more extensive programs it's possible to concentrate on the structure of the graphics card and its built-in chips. Minimizing the data that needs to be transferred to the card leads to a higher output rate, which is one of the most important factors for optimal use.

By optimally setting up and installing the BIOS enhancement software, a graphics card with an 8-bit bus width can attain a higher output rate than one with a 16-bit bus.

Graphics cards developed especially for large screens are included with numerous software programs. These programs, which are also called software drivers, are specially designed to support the application program's video functions.

These types of screen and graphics cards are mainly found in CAD and DTP programs. When you purchase this type of graphics card, software drivers for the majority of applications currently on the market are included.

These cards have their own Video RAM of at least 256K and may have up to 4 Meg. The microprocessors on the cards have their own command set, so that, depending on the configuration level of the graphics card, increasingly high-level video functions can be executed independently of the main microprocessor or main board.

For example, in CAD applications it's possible to zoom in or out of certain windows (make a section larger or smaller) and shift images by using only the microprocessor installed on the video card.

All of this lead to unbelievable growth in the capabilities of computer systems used as CAD workstations. For example, a high resolution, moving graphic image requires a data transfer of 30 Meg/sec, or 30,000,000 bytes per second. This is rapidly approaching the limits of current computer bus systems.

VGA cards and chipsets

In 1987 IBM began installing the VGA adapter as standard equipment, beginning with Model 50 of its PS/2 series. VGA (Video Graphics Array) is actually the designation for a highly integrated graphics chip. However, the term VGA has been used mainly to describe the entire graphics system. In PS/2 models the graphics system is installed completely on the main board and in most other computers is found on an 8-bit or 16-bit plug-in card.

The most important components of the plug-in card or the graphics system are the VGA graphics chip, the VGA BIOS with its accompanying ROM chips, and the Video RAM (screen memory), which consists of either 256 or 512K, depending on the card's resolution.

The VGA card produces an analog signal for each of the three RGB (red, green and blue) outputs. Since an analog signal, unlike a digital one, can have an endless number of intermediate states, the VGA card has significantly increased the number of colors that can be displayed.

Digital output

Digital color graphics cards, such as EGA, that are already on the market have a digital output. This means that for each color state or each pixel, one memory location is used. With increasing resolution of graphics cards and more colors, this process causes both memory and transmission problems.

262,144 different shades

While CGA can display a maximum of 4 colors and EGA has a maximum of 16, with VGA you can choose from a palette of 262,144 different shades. This figure is derived from the fact that each shade is composed of the three basic elements (red, green and blue); each one of these elements internally has 6-bits available. So the maximum number of possible combinations is calculated as follows: 3 primary colors x 6-bits = 18. The possible combinations are then $2^{18} = 262,144$ different shades.

In addition to its improved resolution and extensive array of colors, the VGA standard also has another advantage. One pixel at a VGA resolution of 640 x 480 is square shaped, so that the ratio of horizontal to vertical resolution matches the ratio of screen width to screen height. This is extremely useful for creating circles, which can be displayed as round without requiring any corrections.

As you can see, analog graphics systems have an overwhelming advantage over the once common digital graphics cards. Because of this, analog systems dominate the graphics card market so much that by 1992 the production of digital cards had been virtually eliminated.

Compatibility problems

IBM, the developer of VGA, wasn't very helpful in defining the VGA standard. So compatibility problems eventually occurred with the IBM original.

There are two levels of compatibility: BIOS compatibility and register compatibility. BIOS compatibility is guaranteed if application programs don't directly control the graphics card, but instead use the low-level graphics routines already on the card.

Any hardware differences between the VGA standard and the respective adapter being used are reconciled through the BIOS routines. Register compatibility means that the VGA graphics card matches the original IBM hardware. This strict requirement is met by very few graphics cards that aren't made by IBM.

Since the VGA chip was easily copied, numerous VGA cards are available today. You should determine whether these "clones" are actually better than the original. BIOS compatibility was quickly reached by the various manufacturers, even when only small differences existed among the BIOS versions. However, these differences didn't affect most of the applications.

Many applications bypass the relatively slow BIOS and directly access the VGA hardware. Obviously, this required register compatibility because the VGA adapter performs most of its functions by reading and writing to one of the 64 (or more) internal VGA registers.

VGA cards must emulate registers

To be compatible, a VGA card must emulate all these registers through its hardware. This register-compatibility pertains not only to the VGA chip but also to all input and output ports, as well as the Video RAM organization and VGA BIOS region of the computer RAM. As you may have guessed, 100% compatibility isn't always possible. However, for standard applications, this isn't a big problem.

Extended VGA or Super VGA

Many graphics cards now offer higher performance than the VGA standard. For example, it's possible to display up to 1024 x 768 pixels in 16 colors, while the 800 x 600 mode gives you a choice of 256 colors. Usually these cards have a Video RAM with 512K. Both of these display types match the VESA standard, which is used by some video card and monitor manufacturers. This agreement was both necessary and practical. Unlike VGA, the higher resolutions hadn't been standardized. So programs that wanted to use them needed special software drivers.

IBM XGA-standard

For its PS/2 Model 90 XP 486, IBM developed its own 32-bit graphics card, called XGA (eXtended Graphics Array). This graphics card can be installed on the MCA bus of the PS/2 computer. It's compatible with VGA, but offers significant improvements in performance as well as additional modes of resolution. A maximum of 1024 x 786 pixels can be displayed in 256 colors. The VGA mode gives you a choice of 65,536 colors at a resolution of 640 x 480.

TIGA

A graphics card that contains a graphics subsystem/microprocessor specially designed to perform graphics operations and has quick access to Video-RAM, which is also located on the graphics card, is characterized as an intelligent graphics adapter. Programs and data can be loaded without using the main microprocessor, such as extensive vector graphic lists or display lists. There are two standards for these intelligent graphics adapters: the IBM 8514/A and TIGA from Texas Instruments.

TIGA is a software standard

Unlike IBM's 8514/A-standard, which represents a hardware standard, TIGA (Texas Instruments Graphic Adapter) refers to a software standard. This standard was developed by Texas Instruments and can be used by any manufacturer of intelligent graphics cards. It's an open standard, but since it was developed for the TMS 34010 and TMS 34020 graphics microprocessors, it can be viewed as the graphics programming language for these microprocessors.

Both chips are actually complete and efficient microprocessors; the TMS 34010 is the 16-bit version and the TMS 34020 is the 32-bit version. The TMS 34020, with a clock frequency of 60 MHz, has a 32-bit data bus with 30 general registers, which creates up to 512

Meg of addressable video memory. It also has an additional 512-byte on-chip instruction cache.

So, the TMS 34020 attains a maximum performance level of 10 MIPS for interactive instruction loops. Its graphics coprocessor, TMS 34082, performs up to 80 million floating-point operations per second. So it's 100 times faster than the usual math coprocessors, such as the Intel 80X87-series.

Theoretically, all software containing a TIGA driver can work with any TIGA graphics card. Also, TIGA works independently of resolution. When resolution capacity of graphics hardware improves, the higher resolution can be implemented through the existing software. The reason for this is the universal interface between computer and graphics card (i.e., the TIGA standard).

Requires only one driver

According to this interface, only one driver is needed for all graphics resolutions. This is possible because of the nature of TIGA instructions (e.g., "Draw a circle with radius r and center x,y"), which don't provide specifics on how this should be done.

The already implemented graphics language can be expanded even further with special software tools for the Assembler and C programming languages. Programmers can then develop their own graphics routines, compile them, and insert them into their applications. These routines are loaded into the TIGA card memory, which further enhances its already extensive standard function set.

Other graphics cards

The Intel 82786 graphics microprocessor directly supports window modes. So it's especially suitable for today's graphic operating systems, such as Windows and Presentation Manager. Other graphics cards are based on the NEC-722.0 microprocessor or the 8 MHz Hitachi ACRTC 63484.

The QPDM microprocessor developed by Advanced Micro Devices has a clock frequency of 20 MHz. On the surface it looks like a 16-bit microprocessor, but hidden underneath are four parallel running central microprocessors that enable the simultaneous processing of 4 x 16-bits of data. So 16 pixels on four bit levels can be processed simultaneously.

7.3 Monitors

VGA monitors are standard

As long as a computer isn't being used as a file server (central unit of a computer network), VGA monitors are almost always standard for 486es. VGA stands for Video Graphics Array and is an analog graphics standard, which in 16-color-mode has a resolution of 640 x 480 pixels. Here the matrix for displaying a character consists of 9 x 16 pixels.

Types of monitor screens

Monitors have either fixed frequency screens and or multifrequency screens.

Fixed frequency monitors are adapted for a particular graphics standard, while the multifrequency monitors can either be adjusted to different graphics modes or can adjust themselves automatically. VGA paperwhite monitors are an exception. These monitors are mainly used for high quality graphics word processing or in DTP workstations.

Applications, such as DTP and CAD, are placing more demands on monitors because they require larger, better-quality monitors.

Structure and technical data

Similar to color TV

A computer monitor, like a color TV, consists of a cathode ray tube (CRT). The CRT in turn consists of an electron gun where a beam of electrons is deflected so that when the electrons hit the flat glass surface of the screen, they cause this surface to glow.

To generate a color picture, three electron guns are needed. By mixing the three primary colors red, green, and blue, every color is produced. The inside of the screen contains a fluorescent phosphor layer consisting of many individual phosphor points or lines in primary colors. Here the electron guns, depending on how directly they hit a certain point, produce either one of the primary colors RGB, or, depending on intensity, one of the individual components of a mixed color.

Shortly before the electrons hit the phosphor layer, they pass through a mask (a perforated metal plate which lies just in front of the layer), which enhances the accuracy of the electron beam. The perforated mask comes in two versions like the phosphor layer, a circular-hole mask or a slit-hole mask. The shortest distance on the screen between two points of the same color is designated as either a dot pitch or a pitch. High resolution monitors have a dot pitch of .012 to .011 inches (0.31 to 0.28 mm).

Basic types of CRT tubes

The two different types of masks and phosphor layers correspond to two basic types of CRT tubes.

- First there is the Trinitron tube with the slit-hole mask. It has only one electron gun, whose beam of electrons is still divided into three individual horizontal beams. Focusing the beams requires only one deflecting coil, which functions as an electron lens.

- The second design is characterized by its circular-hole mask as well as three separate electron guns. This design differs from the first design. The inline tube or precision inline tube consists of three adjacent horizontal beam guns, each with its own deflecting coil. In the Delta Gun tube, the electron guns are arranged along an equilateral triangle.

Vertical frequency

The vertical frequency refers to the refresh frequency in Hertz (i.e., the number of individual images displayed on the screen per second). Here there are two distinct processes.

In the non-interlaced mode, the images are written line by line without skipping any lines. A steady picture requires a minimum of 50 Hz but, for health reasons, a minimum of 70 Hz is recommended. With line skipping or the half picture process (also called the interlaced mode), the odd and even lines are alternately displayed. So, the picture is composed of two partial images interlaced with one another. Thus, a vertical frequency of 60 Hz in interlaced mode corresponds to an actual frequency of only 30 Hz.

On a monitor with 1280 x 1024 pixels and a refresh rate of 60 Hz in interlaced mode, a horizontal or line frequency of 64 kHz is necessary. This can be explained as follows: 1024 pixels x 60 Hz = 61,440 Hz. To write one line, the electron beam needs time not only for the image contents but also for a black compensation impulse and a synchronization impulse.

As a monitor's dot pitch decreases, good convergence becomes more important so better and larger images can be maintained on the screen. Experimental studies show that expert observers can readily detect a misconvergence of 0.2 mm.

Today there are three well-known methods of correcting convergence:

- Autoconvergent
- Analog
- Analog/digital correction

Inline tubes use autoconvergence; the effect is produced by a special deflecting unit. In the analog method, the convergence is corrected manually by potentiometers or trimmers. With analog/digital correction, deflection of the electron beam going through the tube is governed by certain stored values. All three methods are considered to be static convergence corrections, as the corrections proceed according to previously fixed values.

Dynamic convergence correction

Temperature fluctuations can create continual changes in convergence. Controlling this requires a dynamic convergence correction, which can be accomplished by the autoconvergence method. Autoconvergence continuously detects fluctuations within the tube and corrects them through software in the computer.

The back side of the perforated mask has special markings that are scanned one after the other by the individual electron beams, thereby creating light impulses which are then registered in the tube. From this data the computer is able to determine the exact position of the individual beams.

LCD and plasma displays

Another development in monitors is flat screens, such as LCD displays. At first these displays weren't considered a viable alternative to conventional picture tubes. Their screen sizes, character sizes, and sharpness of images weren't considered improvements. Currently, LCD's are used mainly for laptops because of their size and low power requirements.

The plasma display screen, which was introduced in 1985, was the first alternative to CRT monitors. This screen operates according to a gas emission, or fluorescent tube. Individual points on the screen are lit up by an electrical discharge in the gas filled interior, which requires a voltage of approximately 120 V. The screens are made up of a plasma cathode, a control panel with line and column circuits, and a fluorescent screen. Currently they have a resolution of 512 x 512 pixels, with a pixel size of 0.25 mm.

Plasma displays cannot produce color images; the only color available is neon red. However, they have unlimited image storage potential.

In addition to a circuit for brightness, the electrical wiring allows for the display of certain gray shades as well. The depth of the screen, including its housing, is approximately 2.4 inches (60 mm), or 8 inches (200 mm) with built-in drivers and interface circuits.

LCD graphics

LCD (Liquid Crystal Display) graphics are a more recent development and can contain up to eight colors. The three primary colors are selected by line filters.

Liquid Crystal Displays are made up of two glass plates, between which there is a liquid crystal layer 10 μm thick. Each glass plate is covered by a metal film that functions as an electrode. In the absence of an electrical current, the liquid crystal element is twisted so light falling on the cell's polarity plane is rotated 90°.

Behind the cell a second parallel polarizer absorbs the light, thus making the liquid crystal cell appear dark. When a current is applied to the metal film electrode, the crystals orient themselves parallel to the electrical field, the polarization plane is untwisted, and the screen appears light.

A half-silvered mirror behind the cell enables you to work with even in darkness. Colors are produced by built-in color filters.

Multifrequency monitors

VGA multifrequency monitors can also be driven by other graphics standards, such as EGA, CGA, and 8514/A. Most monitors automatically adjust themselves to the correct standard; only a few must be switched manually to match the existing graphics card.

This type of monitor generally comes with a 14 inch diagonal screen, a maximum resolution of 800 x 600 pixels, and a non-interlaced screen layout. A steady picture requires a frequency of at least 50 Hz, which means that the screen contents are reconstructed 50 times per second.

With higher resolutions, such as 1024 x 768, on a 14-inch screen, the interlaced (half picture) mode is used. On screens with a higher line frequency, it's possible, with a refresh rate of 90 Hz and a resolution of 1024 x 768, to work in the non-interlaced (full picture) mode.

The non-interlaced technique is used with all screens 16 inch or larger because the flicker effect is more noticeable over large surfaces.

VGA-paperwhite monitors with overscan

As its name indicates, this monitor has a paperwhite background display. It's a VGA compatible monochrome black and white monitor with high resolution and is capable of displaying many shades of gray, which is an important requirement in many text-oriented applications.

Some models allow you to change the background display with an inversion circuit. Because of their high resolutions and very subtle gray shades, these monitors are especially suited for high quality word processing as well as DTP applications.

With these screens, you can use WYSIWYG (What You See Is What You Get). This means that what you see on the screen is identical to what will be printed.

Requires flicker free high-res monitor

However, to use WYSIWYG, you must have a flicker free high resolution monitor that produces an exact image even in the screen's margin areas. This is done by using a very flat picture tube. These screens also have an overscan mechanism that allows the background color to cover the entire surface.

*VGA-paperwhite monitor with OVERSCAN Philips 4
BM 2797*

Low radiation monitors

After the keyboard, the part of a computer that receives most of the user's attention is the monitor. Because of increased environmental awareness, some computer users have concerns about the potential health hazards of their workstations. Dust must be wiped off the monitor's surface every few days. If you wear glasses while working, they must also be cleaned more often.

Most monitors operate according to the cathode ray tube (CRT) principle, which results in the formation of various fields and types of radiation.

In the electric field between the cathode and anode of the picture tube, a high voltage (20,000-30,000 V) is used to accelerate an electron beam. The free, accelerated electrons pick up a very high energy of motion, which upon coming in contact with the screen surface, is passed on to the electrons of the fluorescent layer. The fluorescent layer electrons give off most of the energy they receive in a very short span of time, in the form of electromagnetic radiation. This radiation encompasses a wide range of frequencies.

A large portion of the radiational energy lies in the range of visible light. However, there are also some ultraviolet (UV) and X-ray emissions.

As opposed to an X-ray computer, the radiation here has much less energy and is significantly lower in intensity. Instead, we're concerned with "soft X-rays", which are absorbed by the uppermost layers of human skin.

The impact of the negatively charged electron beam upon the inside surface of the screen creates a negative charge on the screen. This leads to polarization of particles floating nearby, whose positive poles then attach themselves to the outer screen surface.

All of this generates a constant electrostatic field originating from the screen surface and spreading to all parts of the surrounding environment, including the keyboard, hands, and face. Approximately 6000 V are produced between the screen and the ground. This is what causes the crackling when you put your hand on the screen.

While using a conventional monitor, this process is almost invisible. Charged or lightly polarized particles are pulled from both ends of the electrical field based on their charge or polarity, similar to a plate condenser.

These air particles include ions, dust, cigarette smoke, and mold spores, fungi and bacteria.

Similar to the buildup of the electrical field, especially high numbers of particles will attach themselves to crooked surfaces or corners, such as chin, nose, eyelids, or perhaps even eyeglasses.

It is known from physics that current moving through a conductor creates or induces a magnetic field; this also applies to monitors.

The power supply unit creates a magnetic field with an alternating frequency of 60 Hertz. Depending on the type of monitor, the deflecting coils for image refresh frequency produce an alternating field between 60 and 110 Hertz.

The electrostatic field produced by the electron beam can almost be eliminated by an electricity-conducting surface coating. This can lower a screen's surface voltage from 6000 Volts to under 500 Volts.

Large screens

Large screens are used mainly for graphics applications, such as CAD (Computer Aided Design), computer animation, or digital image processing. In DTP, they are used as full-page screens so that it's possible to display a complete page on the screen without shifting windows.

As their name implies, these screens have especially large surface areas with diagonal lengths of 19 inches, 20 inches, or even 21 inches. Almost all these screens are controlled by special screen driver cards. Their extremely flat surfaces help minimize distortion.

Large screens produce brilliantly-colored displays by using a completely black background, against which even weak low-contrast colors show up.

This type of monitor offers the highest resolutions, up to 1280 x 1024 pixels. The latest models even reach resolutions as high as 1664 x 1200. For example, the L-View monitor from Sigma Designs displays this resolution in non-interlaced mode at a frequency of 60 Hertz.

Even newer screens of this type offer a frequency of at least 70 Hz in non-interlaced mode. This type of screen is often placed with small 12-inch or 14-inch screens. The large screen is used for displaying graphics while the VGA or monochrome small screen is used for entering commands and displaying text messages.

Some CAD systems even allow you to run two large screens and one small text screen. One of the large screens provides a complete overview of your work and the other displays an enlarged section. Both screens display the character commands being executed.

7.4 Installing/Configuring Graphics Cards

With and without VGA

The type of graphics installed on a computer varies depending on the computer. Many manufacturers have been using the VGA standard for their computers. With a few integrated computers (Amstrad, Dell, IBM), the VGA circuitry is located on the hard drive. With other 486es, VGA cards are usually inserted into a slot.

However, some manufacturers still use monochrome graphics cards and monochrome monitors as standard equipment. But they do offer the option of replacing the Hercules equipment with VGA.

Monochrome displays are usually offered by manufacturers that want to keep prices as low as possible. Depending on quality, VGA color graphics cost approximately $300 more than Hercules monochrome. A monochrome VGA monitor costs half as much.

Hercules

Like all other plug-in cards, monochrome Hercules cards are plugged in into an 8-bit expansion slot. Many Hercules compatible graphics cards have an additional parallel interface on the board. When exchanging one of these cards for a VGA card, make sure that you're still able to print.

Don't buy just any brand of VGA card if you want optimum compatibility with your 486 computer. To distinguish one card from another, we must first see how they work.

Components of a VGA card

A VGA card consists of several components, which determine its mode of operation and its capabilities.

Central element

Obviously, the most important component is the graphics chip. This chip functions as the "CPU" of the graphics card and determines which commands are needed to produce specific resolutions.

Although there are various kinds of VGA cards, only seven manufacturers produce the chips. In some cases, a manufacturer will offer several generations of graphics chips. All graphics cards with the same type of chip use the same commands. So they can function with the same drivers.

You must know the chip type to activate the higher resolutions because these aren't standardized above VGA. The resolutions available with individual chip types are listed in the Appendix. Only cards that follow the VESA standard understand the same commands for higher resolutions, regardless of the graphics chip.

The chip type also provides information about the capabilities and speed of the graphics card. For example, a Tseng ET-4000 card is much faster than an ET-3000 card from the same manufacturer.

BIOS

The graphics card's operating system

After the chip type, the BIOS is responsible for the specialized functions of the graphics card. Many cards offer capabilities, such as an integrated screen protector or a hardware zoom, which allows you to magnify certain areas of the screen.

Since these options aren't governed by a standard, they aren't supported by the operating system. So they need special drivers.

Memory

Graphics occupy a lot of memory. This amount increases with higher resolutions and the number of colors simultaneously displayed. To determine the amount of memory needed, multiply the resolution by the color planes.

Color planes are given in bits and determines the number of colors that can be displayed simultaneously. The number of colors is calculated as two to the power of the color-depth.

Four values are normally used for color-depth: Four, eight, sixteen, and twenty-four bits. The following table shows how many colors are possible with each:

Color-depth	Simultaneously displayable colors
4	16
8	256
16	65,536
24	16,777,216

Most VGA cards usually have only 4 or 8 bit color planes. Color planes of 16 and 24 bits are supported only by special graphics cards. To calculate the memory required for a particular resolution in bytes, simply multiply the resolution by the color plane and then divide by 8 (1 byte contains 8 bits).

Level by level

Since graphics run in certain resolution levels, you cannot choose just any resolution; you must begin with the standard resolutions. The following table shows memory size and possible resolutions of VGA cards. These are the resolutions you can display at each level of memory with the maximum number of colors.

VGA cards Size/Resolution		
Memory	**Possible resolutions**	**Colors**
256K	320 x 200	256
	640 x 480	16
	800 x 600	16
512K	640 x 480	256
	800 x 600	256
	1024 x 768	16
1 Meg	1024 x 768	256

As we mentioned, programs need special graphics drivers to obtain these resolutions from the VGA card.

Bank switching for VGA memory

Similar to the EMS process, the memory address space for a VGA card is incorporated into the computer memory through bank switching in a window. This window is located in the Controller memory between 640K and 1 Meg and is the place to which individual memory pages of the VGA card are transferred.

Chipsets for VGA Cards	
Manufacturer	**Chipset**
ATI	452
	453
Genoa	VGA
Orchid	Prodesigner
Paradise	VGA
Trident	8900
Tseng	ET3000/4000
Video Seven/Headland	VEGA
	VGA

Installing VGA cards

Why a new VGA card?

If your 486 computer doesn't have a VGA card, then you should install a 512K VGA card. If you do have a VGA card but it has only 256K of memory, then exchange it for one with 512K or, if possible, upgrade the existing one to 512K.

Your computer hardware must be set to color graphics. A DIP switch or a jumper is located on the main board for this purpose. Its position is normally shown in the computer manual. On 386es that until now had their graphics circuitry on the main board, you must also deactivate it with a DIP switch or a jumper.

DIP switch settings on a VGA card

Unplug all the connections from your computer and open up the case. Use your manual to find the DIP switches, then switch the one for graphics type to "Color/Graphics" or switch the one that deactivates the internal graphics to Off.

If you've been using a Hercules graphics card, you must remove it because many VGA cards cannot work next to a second graphics card.

To install a VGA card in your computer as original equipment, or if you have your graphics electronics on the main board, simply remove the front panel from a free slot. Your card can be plugged in like any other card and then fastened to the case with the panel.

If your VGA card is configured with DIP switches, it's much easier to enter the settings now instead of waiting until later to squeeze through the narrow opening provided by the card. Close the computer case and reattach all the peripherals along with the new card and the new monitor. They should now be integrated with your system as described in this book.

After the installation, a few additional steps are needed to ensure that your computer fully uses all its colors. On ATs you must enter the new graphics card type in Setup. If you've been using a monochrome Hercules monitor, then a few programs (Windows, Word 5.0, and GEM, among others) require you to install the VGA card driver.

Utility and driver diskettes are usually included with graphics cards. These diskettes normally contain a new standardized driver, which you must enter in the CONFIG.SYS file. Using an editor, type the following line:

```
DEVICE=(Driver name)
```

Typical driver names are ANSI.SYS, RAMBIOS.SYS, etc. Some cards include an additional driver program that must be entered in the AUTOEXEC.BAT file.

Drivers for the non-standardized high resolutions are found in installation programs on the diskettes accompanying the graphics card. You may want to install the standard driver and then enhance them with other programs, such as a zoom window or a screen protector.

Upgrading with CEG

Adding a CEG chip is an inexpensive way to get your VGA card to produce more colors and to minimize slanted lines while drawing.

This package includes the chip, instructions, AutoCAD driver, Windows 3.1, Lotus 1-2-3, and test and demo programs. The CEG chip enables a conventional VGA card to display 792,096 colors simultaneously. It accomplishes this not by changing the screen memory but through another analog/digital transformation of the video signal. Also, this chip can control the aliasing of lines.

Mixture

A computer can never display a line exactly like the original because the graphics card has only a limited grid made up of pixels. So, a line that's not exactly horizontal or vertical deviates slightly from the grid pattern and is represented by steps.

The antialiasing process is used to minimize this stepwise formation. A certain point (pixel), where the line is only partially located within the grid, is assigned a color mixture consisting of the foreground and background colors. This color contains the same proportion of line color as the proportion of the point that's included within the line.

You can add the CEG chip to almost any VGA card. This chip has the following requirements:

- Tseng (ET3000/4000), Video Seven, Paradise, Trident (8800 or 8900), or Genoa (6000) chipset

- 256K screen memory

- Socketed analog/digital transducer

The first two requirements are fairly easy to check, but where is the analog/digital transducer? Usually this is the chip found closest to the output jack. Depending on the VGA card, this may be marked as follows:

```
ADV476
BT476
TR171
GS0276
AV3676
IMS171
IMS176
```

Once you've found the chip, if it isn't socketed you should unsolder it and exchange it for a CEG chip socket. If you don't trust yourself with this, then have it done by your computer dealer, a repair shop, or the supplier of the CEG chip.

Procedure

Electronic components are very sensitive to static electricity. So before you handle the card you should touch a grounded surface first (such as a heater, metal table leg, etc.).

Remove your VGA card and place in on the table. Use a flat screwdriver to lift the analog/digital transducer out of its socket, pin by pin. Now put the CEG chip in its place, so that the round marking points are in the same direction as the socket. Move the chip to its final position by putting equal pressure on all its pins. This is done easily with the help of a flat object such as a screwdriver handle.

The most useful feature of a CEG chip is its program drivers. Use the accompanying installation program to install the drivers into your system.

7.5 Graphics Cards and Monitor Problems

The largest source of problems in matching graphics cards and monitors usually involved making the connection between the two pieces of hardware. These problems have been eliminated by manufacturers who devised different connectors for analog video equipment (VGA) and digital video equipment (EGA and Hercules). However, some problems can still occur when working with graphics cards.

What is the cause?

If the screen remains dark when you switch on your computer, first you must determine whether the computer, the graphics card, or the monitor is at fault. This is relatively easy to do.

When you first switch on the computer, the keyboard LEDs light up briefly, various devices display their memory counts, the diskette drives are briefly accessed, and finally the system boots from the hard drive, which is indicated by its flickering LEDs. If this process occurs without any problems, you can eliminate the computer as the source of the problem. To verify this, type DIR to determine whether the computer accessed the hard drive.

Graphics card or monitor?

Now you must locate the source of the error among the output devices. There are two indications that it's the graphics card. If the computer emits unusual beeps, the Power-On-Self-Test that's always performed at the beginning has determined that the graphics card is defective. The computer isn't concerned with the type of monitor that's hooked up to it. If you pull the connector cable from the monitor and it lights up, it's also working.

Is the cable plugged in correctly?

First you should check the connector cable. Ensure that both ends are plugged into the jacks correctly. The VGA jack is especially sensitive because there are 15 pins arranged in three rows. So these pins may break off.

This is noticeable if certain colors are missing in the image or the image runs together. It's possible that the plug fits perfectly but the monitor remains dark because it has a non-standard layout and requires a special cable. This applies, for example, to Sony monitors.

Setup

Configuration of DIP switches or jumpers

With some VGA cards, you must set the monitor type with DIP switches. An incorrect setting causes the card to activate the incorrect output jack (e.g., if there is a VGA monitor hooked up but the setting is for a digital monitor). DIP switches also set other parameters, which influence the monitor's functioning, such as whether or not interlaced mode is used for high resolutions.

Correct conditions

Now we can discuss resolutions. Ensure that your graphics card runs only at the resolution that your monitor can display. The maximum resolution is usually provided in the user's manual. If you see the word "interlaced", you'll know that your graphics card can produce the resolution only from two half-pictures.

Most 14 inch monitors use this technique to manage high resolutions. So you should obtain the right size monitor for the resolutions you're using. An incorrect monitor size may cause headaches and eye strain.

Memory

Memory isn't always recognized

With VGA cards that have 512K or 1 Meg of memory, some test programs have problems recognizing the memory (i.e., the resolutions and colors that are produced there). This is because the internal system commands for calling these resolutions are non-standardized and vary depending on the chipset. In this case, you obtain additional pixels and colors only with a driver.

Colors

Monochrome VGA not always recognized as VGA

Some programs have problems adapting themselves to a VGA monochrome monitor. One example of this is when the monitor goes blank after exiting Word. Usually typing in the word MODE will bring it back to life.

Chapter 8 Interfaces

In this chapter we'll discuss the various interfaces of a computer. These are input/output devices, such as the keyboard, the mouse, and the interfaces that connect printers, modems, and other devices.

8.1 Keyboards

Similar to the monitor, the keyboard is considered a direct interface between the user and the computer. So, the keyboard is as important as the other components.

The keyboards that were used with the first computers had 83 keys. These keys, which are similar to those of a typewriter, were responsible for the major input functions. On the right side of the keyboard was a numeric keypad, which also could be used to control the cursor. Function keys were located to the left.

The IBM-AT slightly improved this keyboard arrangement. Most importantly, the Enter and Shift keys were enlarged and the Help key or "SysRq" (System Request) key was added, although it usually doesn't have a function. This key was intended to call either a Help screen or other system functions. However, programs don't use it because then they would be incompatible with older keyboards. Some laptops use this key to call the Setup program.

The ideal input device wasn't available until 1986, when IBM introduced the MF2 keyboard with its AT03 computer. The function keys were moved to the top of the keyboard and two function keys were added, F11 and F12. The cursor control keys were placed in between the main alphanumeric keyboard and the numeric keypad so the numeric keypad could be used for its intended purpose. However, it's still possible to control the cursor from the numeric keypad, which is helpful if you're used to the AT keyboard. The Esc key was placed in the upper-left corner and the Backspace key was enlarged.

A new key was also added to the right of the spacebar. This key allows you to use certain triple key combinations easily.

Illustration of the MF2 keyboard

The MF2 keyboard has conformed to industry standards, which are used in the majority of computers. Only a few manufacturers use non-standard designs.

Using the keyboard

Similar to a typewriter

Normal keyboard operation is very similar to using a typewriter. Each letter key produces a lowercase letter; if the (Shift) key is pressed, an uppercase letter is created. This also applies to the number keys and the symbols located above the numbers. However, some keys on the computer keyboard don't appear on a typewriter.

Control keys

The control keys (Ctrl) and (Alt) only appear on a computer keyboard. The (Ctrl) key lets you send control characters directly to the system or to attached peripheral devices. For example, (Ctrl) (M) produces a carriage return, which is equivalent to pressing (Enter). Or, with the printer switch on, enter the following at the DOS level:

ECHO (Esc) (L) > PRN

The printer feeds one page since you've sent it a Form-Feed command. Some programs use the (Ctrl) key to directly execute commands. This key is often designated in user manuals and in programs as "^". So if you see ^X, you would press (Ctrl) + (X).

Direct input

The (Alt) key enters special characters that aren't found on the keyboard. The (Alt) key allows you to enter any ASCII character between 0 and 255. Press and hold the (Alt) key. Then, from the numeric keypad, enter the number of the ASCII character you want to produce. When you release the ⟨Alt⟩ key, the character appears on the screen, unless your program suppresses this type of input.

Menu control

Many of the newer software programs have given the ⟨Alt⟩ key another function. In all programs that conform to the SAA standard, the ⟨Alt⟩ key directly calls a menu item or a function. For example, ⟨Alt⟩ + ⟨F⟩ activates the File menu, ⟨Alt⟩ + ⟨E⟩ activates the Edit menu, and ⟨Alt⟩ + ⟨X⟩ exits the program.

The most important key

In addition to input keys, there are also keys that govern system functions. The most important of these is the ⟨Enter⟩ key. On the DOS level, this key lets the computer know that the command you've entered should now be executed. In word processing, ⟨Enter⟩ is used to indicate the end of a paragraph.

TAKE NOTE

> Unlike a typewriter, in word processing you don't have to press ⟨Enter⟩ after each line.

Emergency brake

Most programs use the ⟨Esc⟩ key as their emergency brake. If the program allows it, the ⟨Esc⟩ key will cancel the function you just entered. However, some programs use the ⟨Esc⟩ key for other purposes. For example, up to Version 5.0 Word uses ⟨Esc⟩ to activate the menu on the bottom of the screen.

On the MF2 keyboard cursor control keys are located between the main keyboard and the numeric keypad. The arrow keys move the cursor one field in the direction of the arrow on the key. The six keys above the arrow keys are divided into two rows. These six keys are used to toggle insert mode on or off (⟨Ins⟩), delete characters (⟨Del⟩) or move in a document (⟨Home⟩, ⟨End⟩, ⟨PgUp⟩, ⟨PgDn⟩).

Direct effects

Many keys have direct or immediate effects. ⟨Prt Sc⟩ sends a hard copy of the screen to the printer in text format. With ⟨Ctrl⟩ + ⟨Pause⟩ you can terminate output to the screen as well as end certain programs, such as batch files. The same effect is also produced by ⟨Ctrl⟩ + ⟨C⟩. The ⟨Pause⟩ key, which was introduced on the MF2 keyboard, interrupts the output of the current program until you press another key. To some degree, ⟨Ctrl⟩ + ⟨S⟩ has the same function.

Toggle keys

Three keys are set up as toggle switches; an LED indicates their status as on or off. Depending on the keyboard, the light is either within the key or in the upper-right corner of the keyboard. The [Caps Lock] key is above the left [Shift] key and activates the Shift function. This is similar to using Shift on a typewriter.

The [Scroll Lock] key makes the cursor keys move the screen instead of the cursor, although this doesn't work in all programs. The [Num Lock] key activates the numeric keypad. When [Num Lock] is switched off, the keys on the numeric keypad control the cursor.

Scan codes

A computer keyboard contains more than just keys. The keyboard is connected to a microprocessor that converts the keypunches into codes the computer can understand. These are called scan codes. When you press a key, the microprocessor generates the corresponding code. The scan codes for AT keyboards are listed in the Appendix.

8.2 The Mouse

The mouse as part of a computer

The mouse is an input device that has become very popular among computer users. By using a mouse, you can move a pointer, a crosshair, or an arrow across the screen. When you press the mouse button, you can select items from a menu, mark text in a word processing program, or paint in a drawing program.

In user interfaces such as GEM, Windows, or the DOS 5.0 and 6.0 Shell, you can click on the appropriate symbols to display diskette contents, start programs, and move, display, or delete files and subdirectories.

Using a mouse simplifies many tasks that would otherwise require you to enter several commands. For example, deleting subdirectories that have subdirectories of their own can be done with three mouse clicks under GEM. The same task with DOS commands is much more complicated.

How the mouse works

The internal workings of a mouse are very complicated. The central element of practically all mice is a rubberized control ball. This ball, using two rollers and a scanning unit, transmits the distance traveled by the mouse to electronic components that evaluate the impulses and then transmit the information to the computer. A driver program translates the various mouse movements into actions that should be performed by the current application program.

Serial or bus

The mouse can be connected to the computer in two ways. The serial mouse (hooked up to the serial port) is the most widely used and works with most programs. If you want to connect an additional serial device, either you need a second serial interface on your computer or you must use a bus mouse.

The bus mouse comes with a card that's plugged into a slot and contains a special jack for attaching the mouse. Since both of these mice function identically, it's difficult to determine which mouse is better.

Two or three buttons

The control buttons of the mouse are located on top. Some mice have two buttons, while others have three. Current software supports only two buttons; the third (middle) button is rarely used. If you have a two button mouse, you can activate the functions of the third button by pressing both buttons simultaneously.

Resolution

Because of the recent advancements in mouse technology, resolution is another way to differentiate between mice. The normal unit of resolution is dpi (dots per inch). This indicates how many pixels the mouse travels when it's moved one inch.

For example, a 400-dpi mouse would cover about two-thirds the width of a VGA screen. The higher the resolution, the less you must move the mouse to reach your destination.

The correct resolution

QUICK TIP

A tip on older mouse models

Older mouse models usually have a resolution of 200 dpi. However, it's better to have a mouse with 300 or 400 dpi so you can traverse the entire screen without lifting the ball.

Standard mice

Certain devices have established themselves as standards in the mouse industry. One of these is the Microsoft mouse; other well-known models are made by Logitech and Mouse Systems. However, the Microsoft mouse is the most popular.

As a result, all computer programs allow for Microsoft mouse installation and other manufacturers ensure that their mouse is compatible with it. This means that you can install or configure software for the Microsoft mouse, but a compatible mouse will also be able to use it.

Reserve enough space

Even though the mouse itself is quite small, you must have enough space on your desk to move it around. The size of a sheet of paper (8 1/2 x 11 inches) is usually sufficient. Higher resolutions require less space. For instance, a 400 dpi mouse needs a space the size of only about a half a sheet of paper.

To ensure that you have enough space on your desk, use a mouse pad. The surface of these pads is specifically designed for rolling the mouse ball. You can use either a woven or smooth surface. Optical mice need a special pad because they need printed lines to transmit their coordinates.

Software

For all programs recognize the mouse as an additional input device, you must integrate it into your system at the start of the program. This is done with drivers loaded either from the CONFIG.SYS or AUTOEXEC.BAT files. These drivers are included with the mouse. Usually there is also an installation program on the diskette.

Although every mouse comes with a driver that makes it Microsoft-compatible, problems can occur. Some programs won't recognize a third party mouse as a Microsoft mouse. This is particularly frustrating when programs won't run without a Microsoft mouse driver at all, which is the case with Deluxe Paint.

Microsoft compatibility with the Microsoft driver

QUICK TIP

There is a way to avoid this problem. However, you must have the rights to an original mouse driver from Microsoft. After the driver for your mouse is installed by AUTOEXEC.BAT or CONFIG.SYS, simply install the Microsoft Mouse driver program. The driver will announce its successful installation with the message "Existing driver disabled." You must always install your driver first; otherwise the Microsoft installation may fail because a Microsoft mouse doesn't exist.

Customizing the mouse driver

If the driver is Microsoft-compatible, the mouse cursor or arrow will appear at the start of your program, as long as the software supports a mouse. However, some programs don't provide mouse support.

Some manufacturers provide an option for reprogramming functions and keypresses for the mouse. In a word processing program, for example, the mouse could control cursor movement, activate the main menu with its left button, and cancel the previous command with its right button.

An example of mouse programming

The following is the procedure for these menu programs. Using a word microprocessor, first create an ASCII file that will contain the mouse control program. Each command appears on its own line. On the first line, after the word BEGIN, enter the mouse actions that you want to program.

LeftB represents the left mouse button, MidB represents the middle button, and RightB represents the right button. LeftM, RightM, UpM, and DownM indicate the directions for mouse movement. You can also enter a step width in 1/200, above which the mouse movement should be recognized as a keypress.

Now the mouse actions are assigned a particular keyboard action. To do this, simply enter the command TYPE, followed by the scan codes of the keys. For example, to assign an upward movement of the mouse enter the following:

```
LeftM: TYPE 0,75
```

In the Appendix you'll find a table that lists all the scan codes for AT keyboards.

8.3 Parallel Interfaces

As the name suggests, parallel interfaces involve parallel data transmission (i.e., alongside each other or simultaneously). Data are transmitted in packets of 8-bits each or 1 byte. Compared with serial interfaces, in which data are transmitted one after the other, parallel interfaces attain much higher transmission speeds.

In most cases, parallel interfaces are used for data output. Because of their high data transmission speeds, they are used as printer ports. However, one disadvantage is that they cannot transmit data over distances longer than approximately 20 feet. This doesn't cause a problem for printers because they are usually located next to the computer.

Centronics or IBM format

There are two types of parallel interfaces, the Centronics interface and the IBM format interface. The Centronics interface has a 36-pin plug, while the IBM-compatible version has a 25-pin "Sub-D" plug. This is the type used on most 486 computers.

If you compare the pin layouts of the two types, you can see that the individual pin functions either match each other or lack the corresponding function. So, by using an adapter, you can easily hook up a printer with a Centronics plug to a computer with an IBM interface.

How parallel interfaces work

The computer transmits information on the eight data circuits by using TTL (Transistor Transistor Logic) levels. The control circuits STROBE and ACKNLG or STROBE and BUSY monitor the eight data channels during data transmission. The STROBE signal indicates to the computer that the eight channels contain data for the printer.

The printer sends acknowledgments to the computer over the ACKNLG and BUSY circuits. If the printer sends the BUSY signal, this tells the computer that it's presently receiving data and is busy processing it. The printer's ACKNLG signal confirms that the data were received. While this signal stays on, the interface for data transmission is blocked. This process is known as the Handshaking Method of data transmission.

Number of interfaces

386 and 486-class computers generally have at least one parallel interface. On standard AT Bus models the parallel interface is usually located on the main board. You can easily install another parallel interface (e.g., for a second printer) by adding an interface card. However, then you must assign a specific channel to the card. To do this, reset one of the jumpers.

The MS-DOS operating system allows up to three parallel interfaces, designated as LPT1, LPT2, and LPT3. The parallel interface on the main board has a device code of LPT1. The second and third interfaces, installed on cards, are coded as LPT2 and LPT3 respectively by resetting the jumpers. The BIOS then configures the port addresses LPT1, LPT2, and LPT3.

The following table lists the address assignments that are possible in computer systems. Here the BIOS determines which port address to use in response to a particular device code. In computer systems the parallel interface was assigned an interrupt address of 17h, which is also accessible by programs.

Port Address Ranges for Parallel Interfaces	
Port address range	**BIOS-configured device code**
278 to 27F	LPT1, LPT2 or LPT3
378 to 37F	LPT1, LPT2 or LPT3
3BC to 2BF	LPT1

If you have a computer with a monochrome graphics card, you should determine whether this card contains an additional parallel interface. Most monochrome graphics cards have this extra interface.

Even if you exchange the monochrome card for a VGA color graphics card, you should still keep the monochrome card inside the computer. Most color graphics cards allow for the parallel operation of a monochrome card.

Preventing conflicts

You should take advantage of this when installing the color card because the extra parallel interface on the monochrome card will still be available for future use. Since the monochrome card's graphics routines and interrupt addresses aren't used by the EGA or VGA card, conflicts between the two won't occur.

Interface expansion cards are available for serial, parallel, or combined interfaces. The cards can be plugged into the ISA/EISA Bus, the IBM Micro-Channel, or the MCA Bus. However, because both the serial and the parallel interfaces have a lower data transmission speed than either the EISA or MCA Bus, it's usually not worth using these costly bus interfaces as parallel interfaces. Most serial and parallel ISA or AT interface cards can use the more economical 8-bit bus interface without sacrificing performance.

When installing serial and parallel cards into an ISA Bus computer, simply set a few DIP switches or jumpers on the main board and/or the interface card. This initializes the corresponding interface addresses for the BIOS.

Obviously by installing an additional interface card you lose one of the valuable slots on your computer. This is especially significant if you use your computer for various applications, such as data communications via modem, text and image input via scanner, or control, measuring and monitoring via control and measuring cards.

Installing an extra interface card

Another alternative to installing an extra interface card and thereby occupying a slot, is a T-switch or printer switch that can be used to control two or more printers. Since the fewest number of computers in the workplace are used for multitasking operations, they each need only one parallel device. A multi-pin switch allows two users (printers) to be hooked up to one interface. Before sending a print job you must manually switch over to the desired printer. Printer switches are also available for multiple outlets.

Special parallel interfaces

Special parallel interfaces are also being used for high-performance plotters, such as thermal plotters and laser plotters. These plotters run at such high speeds that transmission and conversion of image data over serial interfaces takes much longer than the output time for the drawing.

To counteract this imbalance, plotter manufacturers have abandoned the serial interfaces used for pin plotters and developed an enhanced parallel interface that adheres to the Centronics format for data transmission. Transmission rates are thereby increased significantly.

8.4 Serial Interfaces

Every computer has at least one built-in serial interface, which conforms to the RS-232-C standard of the Electronic Industries Association (EIA). This interface is also known as a V.24 or a DIN 66020 interface. Here the connector is either a 9-pin or 25-pin Sub-D plug.

Parallel to serial data conversion

The bus system on the main board oversees a parallel transfer of data. Since the serial interface sends data bit by bit, any data to be transmitted there must first be converted from its parallel structure to the serial mode.

Various methods of conversion are used; each type is implemented on a different integrated chip. Some conversion types/chips are as follows:

- USART (Universal Synchronous Asynchronous Receiver Transmitter)

- ACIA (Asynchronous Communications Interface Adapter)

- PCI (Programmable Communications Interface)

We'll focus on the most common types. We'll also discuss the Intel MUART (Multifunction Universal Asynchronous Receiver/Transmitter) 8256 chip, a programmable multifunction unit that contains an asynchronous serial interface with a programmable baud rate, parallel interface, timer, and an interrupt control.

The main interface used in computers is the USART chip. This is generally an Intel 8251 chip that functions as sender and receiver as well as data converter.

When the interface chip functions as sender (transmitting data from the computer outward), it receives a parallel data stream from the CPU via the bus system and converts it to a serial signal stream.

When acting as a receiver, it receives the serial data stream and converts it to a parallel signal via a shift register. So only one data circuit exists for both sending and receiving.

Serial data format

Two standards have been adopted for constructing serial data words. One is the ASCII (American Standard Code for Information Interchange) format, which is 7-bits long and the other is the 8-bit IBM code.

Data transfer begins with a start bit, which initiates the transition from H-Level (High Level), associated with the idle state, to L-Level (Low Level). This voltage drop is known as "mark space" and serves to synchronize the receiver.

After the start bit, seven or eight data bits are transferred. Then a parity bit is sent. The parity bit detects simple transmission errors. The parity bit can also be set to odd or even.

Following the parity bit, 1 or 1.5 stop bits are sent. These bits signify the end of the data word transfer and complete the data format.

The baud rate is always specified when discussing serial data transmission. This is a measure of serial data transfer speed and is the reciprocal value of the shortest pulse duration in one data word, including the start, stop, and parity bits. One baud is equivalent to a data transmission rate of one bit per second.

With a bit length of 5 ms (milliseconds), where all bits are of equal length, a baud rate of 200 baud is reached according to the following formula:

$$\text{Baud rate} = \frac{1}{\text{Bit timing}} = \frac{1}{5 \text{ ms}} = 200 \text{ baud}$$

A transfer in ASCII format with two stop bits results in a total data word transmission time of 5 ms x 11 = 55 ms. So in one second more than 18 data words can be transmitted.

In the above example with a transmission rate of 200 baud, the USART chip needs a steady clock pulse frequency of 200 Hz to be available to both sender and receiver, thus maintaining a synchronous transfer of data.

Adjusting the interface

The 8251 interface chip can be set to different data transmission rates, with values from 0 to 19.2 kbaud. You can set the chip, and thereby the serial interface, through hardware by using DIP switches on the main board or through software by using the DOS command MODE.

As its name indicates, the USART 8251 chip can operate in both synchronous and asynchronous modes. In synchronous operation, the ratio of clock frequency and baud rate is always 1.

In asynchronous mode, this ratio is fixed at 1, 32, or 64. The operational mode selection is relayed to the chip via the system's data bus (Lines D0 to D7). These circuits also convey the commands and the synchronization values.

Construction of the transfer format involves setting the character length in bits, as well as determining the existence of parity bits and their type (odd or even). Asynchronous operation also requires notification of stop pulse and stop bit lengths.

In synchronous operation, the type of synchronous idle character, which is abbreviated as SYNC, must be indicated. Whether this is a single or a double character must also be indicated.

The following table illustrates possible settings for a serial interface DIP switch:

1	2	3	4	5	6	7	8	
								Baud rate:
					0	0	0	75
					0	0	1	150
					0	1	0	300
					0	1	1	600
					1	0	0	1200
					1	0	1	2400
					1	1	0	4800
					1	1	1	9600
								Baud rate:
			0	0				2
			0	1				1.5
			1	0				1
			1	1				0
								Parity:
		0						even
		1						odd
	0							no parity
	1							with parity
								Data length:
0								7 bit
1								8 bit

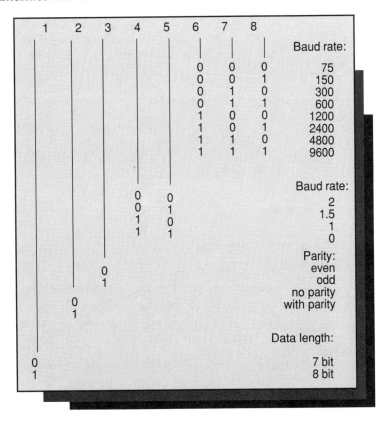

DIP switch settings for a serial interface

The DOS operating system uses the device code COM for serial interfaces; the first such interface is called COM1. Four serial interfaces have been established for computer systems.

The following lists the port addresses assigned to each interface (COM1 to COM4). The interrupt address 14hex can be used to directly access the serial interface through to the chips.

Serial Interface Port Addresses	
Interface designation	**Port address hexadecimal**
COM1	3F8 to 3FF
COM2	2F8 to 2FF
COM3	3E8 to 3EF
COM4	2E8 to 2EF

When using a serial interface to control certain devices (e.g., a pin plotter), you must adapt the computer's serial interface to the plotter's input interface by using the MODE command along with the appropriate parameters. The MODE command is set up as follows:

```
MODE COM#:baudrate,parity,data-bits,stop-bits,parameters
```

The following command sets a data transmission rate of 9600 baud for the COM1 interface:

```
MODE COM1:96
```

The other settings use the default values: Even parity, seven data bits, 1 stop bit.

Plug layout

The data stream originating from a USART chip is fixed somewhere between 0 and 5 Volts. A special circuit driver chip converts this to ranges of -25V to -3V and +3V to +25V. The circuit driver chip runs on a voltage of +12V to -12V, which results in a voltage differential of 24V.

The ground wire at Pin 5 represents the most crucial connection between sender and receiver because it delivers a common reference potential for signal transmission.

The V.24 and RS232C serial interfaces have a limit of approximately 30 m (100 ft.) on data transmission distances. For this reason and also because of the limited transmission rate of 19.2 kbaud, additional serial interfaces have been developed with longer transmission distances and faster rates, along with matching conversion chips.

Comparing Serial Interface Specifications			
RS232C	**RS423** V.24,V.28	**RS422** V.10,X.26	V.11,X.27
Max. transmission dist.	30 m	600 m	1200 m
Max. transmission rate	20 kBaud	200 kBaud	10 MBaud
Operation	One-wire	One-wire	Differential
Max. voltage	+25 V	+6 V	6 V
Norm. voltage	+5 to +15 V	+3.6 V	2 V
Max. current	+500 mA	+150 mA	+150 mA
Input hysteresis	-3 to +3 V	-0.2 to +0.2 V	-0.2 to +0.2 V

Modems

Even longer transmission distances can be achieved by using the telephone system, which enables you to transmit data between two computers. The sender must have a modulator while the receiver must have a demodulator. (MODEM is an acronym for MOdulator/DEModulator.)

The modulator transforms the computer's digital data so they generate AC voltages in the frequency range of human speech (from 200 Hz to a maximum of 3 kHz).

Multiplex interfaces

As we mentioned earlier, the Intel 8256 MUART (Multifunction Universal Asynchronous Receiver/Transmitter) chip contains a serial and a parallel interface, as well as a counter (timer) and an interrupt control. The serial interface operates asynchronously in full-duplex mode, where data bit length can be programmed to 5 to 8-bits. This also applies to the other optional settings for a serial interface (e.g., baud rate and the number of stop-bits).

The 8256 parallel interface, which conforms to the Centronics specifications, consists of two 8-bit wide ports and is also programmable. With this chip you can create highly adaptable serial and parallel interfaces in your computer with few components and a minimum of wiring.

The printer multiplexer circuit provides a more interesting use for the MUART chip. It enables you to construct an LPM (Line Printer Multiplexer) interface, with which you can attach up to eight computers to one printer. Data from the computer travels to the LPM module through V.24 interfaces, which are completely programmable.

8.5 Gameport

The gameport is an interface for special input devices used by computer games. However, the 486 computer doesn't have any special connections just for games. The joystick, which is an important computer game device, is hooked up to the gameport. To use a joystick, the computer must be equipped with a special interface called a gameport adapter.

Gameport adapter, special or multi-I/O card

Two types of gameport adapters are available for computers. First there is a special gameport card, which is designed exclusively for connecting joysticks. These cards have two 15-pin plugs for two separate joysticks. Unfortunately on AT computers (80286, 80386, or i486 microprocessors) these cards occupy a valuable expansion slot and can also create problems.

The addresses 0200hex to 020Fhex within the port address range are reserved for the gameport adapter. Obviously the card needs only one of these addresses. Normally PC-XTs use the address 0200hex while ATs use 0201hex. Test programs and games sometimes don't recognize a gameport adapter because of the variable address. As a result, the joystick won't work.

In most cases, the computer's BIOS is responsible for this. Often, by changing or expanding the BIOS inquiry routine, you can prevent the non-recognition of a gameport adapter. The interrupt address for gameports is 15hex. Originally this interrupt was intended to control a cassette recorder but is used today for other tasks (e.g., controlling the gameport adapter interrupt).

Using a multi-I/O card as a gameport adapter

For AT computers, we recommend using a multi-I/O card as a gameport adapter. This card, which is only slightly more expensive than a gameport card, offers distinct advantages. This card contains several interfaces, usually one parallel and two serial interfaces, as well as a 15-pin gameport adapter interface where two joysticks can be attached. However, to do this you must install a Y-cable between the slot jack and the joystick.

Pin	Type	Signal
\multicolumn{3}{c}{Multi-I/O card Gameport Adapter Pin Layout}
1	Output	+5 Volts
2	Input	Button 1 Joystick A
3	Input	x-value Joystick A
4	Output	Ground
5	Output	Ground
6	Input	y-value Joystick A
7	Input	Button 2 Joystick A
8	Output	+5 Volts
9	Output	+5 Volts
10	Input	Button 1 Joystick B
11	Input	x-value Joystick B
12	Output	Ground
13	Input	y-value Joystick B
14	Input	Button 2 Joystick B
15	Output	+5 Volts

Joystick, digital or analog

There are two types of joysticks. One is a cheaper digital type for home computers and the other is an analog joystick, which is made especially for computers.

The digital joystick has one microcircuit for each of the four directions (up, down, left, and right), which you close by moving the lever. The resulting closed circuit creates a movement on the screen in the corresponding direction.

The joystick can produce only two states for each of the directions: On or off. This is the biggest disadvantage of digital joysticks. Individual movements aren't graduated and therefore cannot be executed exactly.

Moving the joystick diagonally activates two microcircuits, which the computer identifies as a slanted motion. You can recognize a digital joystick by its 9-pin connector plug.

Instead of microcircuits, analog joysticks use two potentiometers (i.e., variable resistances). One potentiometer represents movement in the x-direction (left and right), while the second one represents the y-direction (up and down). This involves variable resistances in the range of 0 to 100 kOhm.

Moving the joystick lever sets up a variable resistance within the potentiometer and a variable current flows through the different cables to the gameport connection. Instead of only logical 1 or 0, which is the case with digital joysticks, the computer evaluates a much larger range of in-between states.

Usually 64 different values can be distinguished for the x- and y-directions. At the center position, both the x-direction and the y-direction have a value of 31.

Adjust analog joysticks to center

To guarantee the full range of motion in all directions, analog joysticks must be adjusted to center. This means that the game program must be informed that the joystick has reached the zero position. This process is also called centering.

Today's joysticks also have one or two fire buttons, which can be used to close menus or shoot invaders from space. To save wear and tear on the fire button, there is another switch called "constant fire", which produces an automatic fire signal.

Better quality joysticks have sturdy microcircuits, but cheaper or older models often have foil switches. So these joysticks are sensitive to rough handling, and, therefore, don't last very long.

Flight Simulator and Leisure Suit Larry

Two of the most popular computer games are the Microsoft Flight Simulator and the adventure game Leisure Suit Larry.

The Flight Simulator offers a realistic flight simulation, with software additions, such as extra airports and airplane designs, and hardware additions in the form of an airplane control joystick.

In addition to improved graphics, modern computer games are providing better representations of noises and musical notes, which often surpass the capabilities of an AT computer. To enjoy the full range of background noises provided by the software, you can purchase special sound cards that feature greatly enhanced sound reproduction.

8.6 Configuring and Installing Interfaces

Keyboard

Connecting a keyboard is very easy. Keyboards on almost all 486es are plugged in with a 5-pin connector, similar to one used in audio systems. Some 486 computers, as well as IBM PS/2 models, have the new Micro-DIN keyboard plug. Otherwise, the keyboards are identical to those with the large plugs.

When plugging in the keyboard, pay attention to where the notch(es) are located on the plug. The Micro-DIN plugs have extremely thin pins, which can be damaged if they are inserted incorrectly.

Using a Micro-DIN plug for all keyboards

QUICK TIP

If you have a Micro-DIN plug on your 486 but want to use a keyboard with the normal 5-pin plug, you can find an inexpensive adapter in most computer stores.

With a keyboard designed for PC/XTs and ATs, before switching on the computer, be sure that it's set up for the correct type of computer. Usually there is a sliding switch or a DIP switch located underneath the keyboard.

Serial and bus mouse

You can connect a mouse either to a serial interface (serial mouse) or to a special port located on a card (bus mouse). This port is either installed in a slot with a bus mouse card or, in some computers, is already on the main board.

A bus mouse card is installed the same way as an expansion card. Simply plug in the mouse in the back.

TAKE NOTE

Some computers have a mouse connection on the main board, but there isn't a jack leading to the outside. In this case, you must buy a jack, then connect it to the main board with a ribbon cable. This type of mouse port is found, for example, on the Elitegroup motherboard.

If your computer already has a jack for a bus mouse, you don't have to buy a Microsoft bus mouse and pay extra for the card that goes with it. The serial Microsoft mouse already has a Micro-DIN plug, which is also used for the bus mouse connection.

The only other mouse that fits into a built-in mouse port with this type of jack is the Logitech bus mouse. However, you would have to buy the card along with it.

Connecting serial and other mice

Mice from other manufacturers are generally designed for the serial port. So, they have only a 9 or 25-pin plug. Some computers offer a system-specific mouse that's plugged into a special jack. These types of mouse ports allow you to connect only their own brand of mouse; others won't be accepted.

Interfaces

Fortunately, there are various types of interfaces for 486 computers. However, for some applications, you may not have enough.

When installing additional cards with serial or parallel ports, ensure these cards are configured ahead of time to avoid conflicts with the existing interfaces.

Interface cards with AT-Bus hard drive connection

Many 486es have an AT-Bus hard drive connected to a multifunction card, which also contains the standard interfaces for that particular computer. This usually includes the diskette controller.

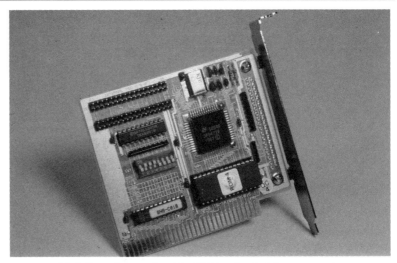

Multifunction card with AT-Bus hard drive connection

These cards have two serial interfaces (one parallel interface and one gameport). They also contain a diskette drive controller as well as a connection for AT-Bus hard drives. The card has several jumpers that help with configuration.

Now we'll present the procedure for configuring the type of card shown in the above photograph.

Jumper Settings for an I/O-card Serial Interface On Multifunction Cards With AT-Bus interfaces					
No.	**Function**	**1 + 2**	**2 + 3**	**4 + 5**	**5 + 6**
JP4 below	Serial 1	COM3	COM1	-	-
JP4 above	Serial 2	-	-	COM4	COM2
JP10 below	COM2	IRQ4	IRQ3	-	-
JP10 above	COM1	-	-	IRQ4	IRQ3

Parallel Interface Jumper Settings		
Parallel Interface	**JP9**	**JP11**
LPT1, IRQ 5	2+3	1+2
LPT1, IRQ 7	2+3	2+3
LPT2, IRQ 5	1+2	1+2
LPT2, IRQ 7	1+2	2+3

The following jumpers activate or deactivate additional components on the card:

No.	Function	Open	Closed
Jumper Settings to Activate Components			
JP1, JP2	Diskette drive controller	deactivated	activated
JP3	Hard drive adapter for AT-Bus disk	deactivated	activated
JP7	Gameport	deactivated	activated

No.	Function	1+2	2+3
Jumpers to Set the Controller's Mode of Operation			
JP6	Precompensation at 250K/sec data output	125 ns	250 ns
JP6	Precompensation at 300K/sec data output	125 ns	208 ns
JP6	Precompensation at 500K/sec data output	125 ns	125 ns
JP6	Precompensation at 1000K/sec data output	83 ns	83 ns
JP8	Hard drive type	normal	older models

Interface cards without AT-Bus hard drive connection

On most 486 computers, the interfaces leading to the outside are usually part of a multi-I/O card, which contains one parallel and two serial interfaces as well as a gameport.

The parallel interface and the gameport are located directly on the card, while the two serial interfaces are connected by a flat ribbon cable and are mounted in the connections on the back.

Several jumpers can be used to set parameters for the card's operation. Jumper Row S1 determines the interface designations.

COM3, IRQ 3	COM4, IRQ 4	closed	closed	open	closed	closed	open
COM3, IRQ 4	COM4, IRQ 3	closed	closed	closed	open	open	closed
COM3, IRQ 3	-	open	closed	open	closed	-	-
COM3, IRQ 4	-	open	closed	closed	open	-	-

Parallel Interface Jumper Settings of an I/O-card			
Parallel interface	**S1-3**	**S2-1**	**S3-1**
LPT1, IRQ 5	open	open	closed
LPT1, IRQ 7	open	closed	open
LPT2, IRQ 5	closed	open	closed
LPT2, IRQ 7	closed	closed	open

Interfaces on the graphics card

If the first parallel interface is on a monochrome graphics card, it can be configured via the jumpers as LPT1 or LPT2. However, the LPT2 setting is useful only if additional interface cards, which permit only the LPT1 configuration, exist.

8.7 Keyboard Problems

When problems occur with a keyboard, the cause is related to either improper connections or wear and tear.

Startup difficulties

Although hooking up a keyboard to a computer is simple, be careful if your computer has a PS/2 keyboard connection. Its tiny plug is much more sensitive than the normal 5 pin connector.

If an error message appears when you switch on your computer, the keyboard is either incorrectly attached or defective. If the Power On Self Test runs without problems and the keyboard doesn't respond or produces the wrong characters, there are two possible causes for this.

If a different character than the one that appears on the key is output, the keyboard is set to the wrong computer type. There are keyboards for PC/XTs and for AT/386/486s. Usually there's a switch beneath the keyboard for entering the proper setting. If your keyboard doesn't have this switch, exchange it for a model that's suited to your computer.

Defective controller

When a keyboard doesn't produce any characters, this may be caused by an incorrect setting or a defective keyboard controller on the main board. This frequently happens if a keyboard is plugged in while the computer is running and the keyboard cable isn't buffered. You should use a different keyboard in order to check for a defective controller.

Keeping the keyboard clean

Clean thoroughly every three months

No other part of a computer is exposed to as much wear and tear as the keyboard. So, eventually some keys may no longer work. This can be caused by dirt that has accumulated on the keyboard.

To prevent this from happening, you should clean your keyboard every few months by using rubbing alcohol and cotton swabs.

However, if many of your keys won't work, you may want to try cleaning the keys. Carefully pull out all the keys. Then place them in a cloth and tie the cloth very tightly. Place the bundle in a washing machine and wash at 100° without spinning.

While the keys are being washed, remove the dust from the keyboard slots with a vacuum cleaner. Spray a small amount of contact spray onto the contact of any key that is no longer functioning. Use the spray sparingly because it's harmful to the environment and only a small amount is needed to restore the contact.

If this doesn't work or you don't want to try this, you could simply purchase a new keyboard. Most keyboards cost approximately $30 to $40.

8.8 Interface Problems

Serial and parallel interfaces are the computer's connection to the outside world; the keyboard and monitor should actually be considered part of the system. The parallel interface is usually hooked up to a printer, while serial interfaces are used for mice, modems, and other external peripherals.

Looking for bugs

When one of these devices doesn't work, the most important task is determining whether the device or the interface is at fault. With printers, this is easy to do because a self-test is usually performed.

When a mouse refuses to work, observe the installation message for the driver carefully. You may need to install another driver. With a modem, the acknowledgment message should indicate whether a proper connection has been made with the computer. If you enter the AT MO command and the terminal program responds with OK but the modem still doesn't work, then you should check the telephone cable connection.

The easiest thing to do is run a diagnostic program, such as CheckIt. This program quickly indicates which interfaces, if any, aren't functioning. When the cause is found, eliminate it.

Conflicts

An interface must meet two requirements in order to function. First, it must use a hardware interrupt and must have a memory area reserved for it. The interrupt and, in many cases, also the memory area are set up with jumpers.

Other computer expansion cards can also use a hardware interrupt. If another card is on the same interrupt as the non-functioning interface, problems can occur. In this case you must reconfigure either the interface card or the other card.

Excessive demands

The interrupts and memory areas may all be evenly distributed, but you may have made excessive demands on your interface. For example, if you've connected your printer to a very long cable or the printer has overloaded the interface, it may no longer function or may be damaged. It's also possible that some interfaces don't deliver the required signal levels. Inexpensive cards in particular don't always meet the standards. Unfortunately, the only solution is to exchange the card for a new one.

Chapter 9 — Operating Systems

Since a computer is a complex machine, a program must be used to coordinate the work of the various components on the lowest level.

What is an operating system?

The operating system handles this task. It represents the interface between the user and the technology. Operating systems control the operation of the microprocessor, the working memory, input/output components, and the memory.

Available operating systems

The operating systems used most widely with IBM compatible computers can be divided into three groups: DOS, OS/2, and UNIX.

DOS stands for Disk Operating System and is also called PC-(Personal Computer) or MS-DOS. (MS is the abbreviation for the software developer Microsoft, which developed DOS.)

DR-DOS is a variation of DOS that was developed by Digital Research Corporation. It's very similar to MS- and PC-DOS. We'll discuss these systems in more detail later.

DOS was the first operating system for the IBM compatible computer and is still the most widely used. Although MS-DOS has continually improved and has been upgraded to Version 6.0, it still has some weaknesses. For example, DOS supports only a maximum of 640K of memory directly. Under DOS, only one application at a time can be used; it lacks multitasking capabilities.

OS/2

OS/2 is an alternative to DOS. This system eliminates the memory limitation of 640K and allows you to use several programs simultaneously (multitasking). Also, OS/2 is delivered with an integrated user interface, called the Presentation Manager, that makes the system extremely user-friendly.

UNIX is used in professional applications

The UNIX operating system is used when several applications must be used simultaneously and several users must be able to access the system. UNIX, which is available in several variations for the PC, has both multitasking and multi-user capabilities.

Using operating systems

Before we discuss the individual operating systems in more detail, we'll examine the concept behind operating systems.

Operating systems aren't actually purchased. Instead, the user obtains a license for the use of the program on a computer. This is the same procedure that's used for all types of software.

The operating system usually isn't sold directly; you can obtain it from your computer manufacturer. This means that the program's package must include a notice, either in print or through a sticker, authorizing the use of the operating system for this type of computer. Before upgrading to a higher version of the operating system or changing to another operating system, consult your computer dealer.

Some operating systems, especially the special DR-DOS, Multi-user DOS 386, and Windows, are exempt from these regulations and can be purchased in computer stores.

9.1 MS-DOS

Microsoft developed the actual IBM PC-DOS, which is based on CP/M. PC-DOS ran on the first computers of this type. Today DOS is the most widely used operating system for IBM and compatible personal computers.

The operating system for the original IBM PC was called PC-DOS and the operating system for IBM compatible computers was called MS-DOS. Both DOS versions had the same commands and structure.

Eventually MS-DOS was upgraded to the current version, MS-DOS 6.0.

DOS is an abbreviation for Disk Operating System. However, an operating system does more than simply control diskettes or the hard drive. It also manages data.

MS-DOS had to be improved to keep up with the technological advancements that occurred. The first DOS couldn't control hard drives, which at that time wasn't important. Slowly DOS "learned" to not only control hard drives, but also handle the various diskette formats. The newest version (MS-DOS 6.0) is also able to use larger memory areas productively.

Unfortunately, MS-DOS still has some limitations. For example, it's still not possible to address more than 1 Meg of memory without using special procedures. Memory is limited to 640K.

Different versions

Currently several versions of MS-DOS are being used: DOS 3.3, DOS 4.0 or DOS 4.01, DOS 5.0, and DOS 6.0.

The earlier versions are still being used because often the improvements of the later versions aren't always worth upgrading to them. So, users continue to use the earlier versions.

However, earlier versions, including Version 3.2, aren't suitable for AT computers, including the 486. These versions support only a hard drive with partitions no larger than 32 Meg. Most 486 systems, even in their basic configuration, exceed this limit. So only DOS 3.3, 4.0, 5.0 or 6.0 can be used with 486 systems.

Which operating system should you use

Which operating system you should use depends on personal preference and available resources. Most application programs work with any later versions of DOS (Versions 3.3 to 6.0). However, we suggest purchasing the latest version because it doesn't contain many of the problems found in the earlier versions.

Similarities

Versions 3.3, 4.0, and 5.0 operate and use files the same way. The commands have the same syntax, but in some instances the results appear differently. Also, the individual utility programs haven't changed much between DOS 3.3 and 4.0. However, in some cases they are more user-friendly.

Differences

The main difference between DOS 3.3 and 4.0 is the way memory is used. This applies to conventional (RAM) and mass storage devices (diskette, hard drive).

Under DOS 3.3, expanded memory (more than 640K) can be used only for a virtual disk (a RAM Disk). Access to the expanded memory is possible only with programs operating with EMS.

DOS 4.0 provides the option of moving some system buffers to the area beyond 640K. However, sometimes this can cause problems.

The operating system also provides an Expanded Memory Manager, which enables you to use expanded memory on PCs with a 80386/486 processor, without an additional driver program.

Up to and including DOS 3.3, the size of a hard drive partition was limited to 32 Meg. With some versions of DOS 3.3 from individual manufacturers (especially Compaq), larger partitions can be created on the hard drive.

With a new FAT structure, the maximum partition size could be increased to two gigabytes with DOS 4.0. Hard drives of this size aren't available yet. So, for practical purposes, the partition size can be considered unlimited.

User-friendliness

DOS 4.0 is more user-friendly than DOS 3.3. DOS 5.0, when compared to DOS 4.0, has almost no faults and doesn't require as much memory.

MS-DOS 6.0 improves on MS-DOS 5.0 by adding a few utilities. An installation program, called Select, configures the system to the user's requirements. Prior to Version 4.0, the user had to do this manually. We'll explain how to use the Select program and how to install DOS 3.3 later.

DOS is a command-oriented language. This means that for every action the computer executes, the user must enter a command. With early versions of DOS, users had to memorize these commands and their effects. This process intimidated many users.

So, IBM and Microsoft developed a user interface for DOS, called the DOS Shell. This was added to DOS starting with Version 4.0 and simplifies using the operating system.

The DOS Shell operates in graphic mode and can be used with the mouse or the keyboard. The most important part of the DOS Shell is the File Manager, which controls disk and file operations. The file operations can be performed by simply selecting the file and choosing the action from the menu bar.

It's also possible to assign program items to areas separate from the directory listings so they can be easily accessed. You can also add multiple program items to a group (e.g., text editors and word processors in a WP group). Also, you can add password protection to a preassigned program item.

The DOS Shell provides on-line help for all commands so you're always able to obtain help.

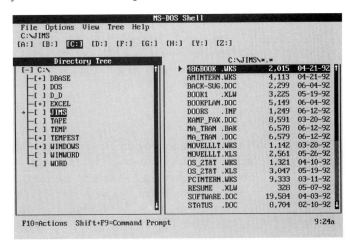

The DOS Shell makes using the PC easier

Even the individual DOS commands have become more user-friendly. For example, the TREE command sequentially lists the directories and enhances the display with graphic characters.

The CHKDSK command provides more information about the hard drive and memory in DOS 4.0 than in DOS 3.3. When the FORMAT command is used, the diskette size can be indicated in kilobytes or megabytes. Also, when FDISK is used to partition a hard drive, sectors don't have to be converted. The size can be indicated in megabytes or percentages.

Advantages and disadvantages

These enhancements increased the memory requirements by about 40K. Although this may not seem like a large increase, this amount could cause complicated applications to crash. After rebooting with DOS 3.3 or switching to DOS 5.0 or 6.0, which is a better solution, the program performs again.

You should use DOS 3.3 if only limited resources, which must be used optimally, are available. This version is recommended if only 640K or 1 Meg of memory are available and if a 32 Meg limitation in the capacity of the individual hard drive partitions is acceptable.

Another reason why you should use DOS 3.3 is if individual programs cannot work together under DOS 4.0. For example, if the programs were written according to the old DOS standards, they might not function properly with DOS 4.0.

DOS 4.0 has a new FAT structure for the hard drive, which permits larger partitions. This often confuses programs that access the hard drive directly. Also some programs request the version number during the installation. If the number isn't 3.2 or 3.3, the installation is terminated. (In DOS 5.0 and 6.0 this problem is avoided with SETVER.)

DOS 5.0

We recommend using DOS 6.0 because it allows you to use extended memory. This enables you to use large applications easily. Other advantages of this version are the improved commands and the user-friendly environment of the DOS Shell. It's also possible to use the entire memory efficiently if you have an 80386 or an 80486 microprocessor. This isn't possible with 80286/8088 microprocessors.

DR DOS

Digital Research offered its own operating system, called DR DOS. This version of DOS is found on many IBM compatible PC, AT, and 386 systems.

DR DOS is fully compatible with MS-DOS. All the commands have the same syntax; in some cases the results of some commands may differ.

The PASSWORD command can protect individual files from being read, written to, or deleted. XDIR improves the file display and the XDEL command allows you to delete entire subdirectories.

A history buffer, which can be various sizes, allows you to store previously entered commands for further use. Before MS-DOS 5.0, MS-/PC-DOS stored only one line.

The maximum size of a hard drive partition in DR-DOS is 512 Meg. If the hard drive is partitioned with FDISK, it's also formatted simultaneously.

Entering"/H" after almost any command activates a user-friendly help page containing information about the command.

Similar to DOS 4.0, DR-DOS provides a user-friendly environment. The installation is as easy to use as the SELECT routine from DOS 4.0. If changes must be made later to the CONFIG.SYS or the AUTOEXEC.BAT files, the SETUP program can be used again so you don't have to worry about the syntax of the configuration files.

Since DR DOS 6.0 is inexpensive (about $75), it's a good choice if you're looking for a powerful operating system but don't want to spend a lot of money.

Installation

The only difference between the installation procedures of MS-DOS 3.3, 4.0, and DR-DOS is the user-friendliness of the operation. The basic procedure is the same for all versions.

After the hard drive is formatted, it must be prepared for the operating system. After the low-level formatting with the FDISK program, the hard drive must be divided into partitions. Then it is soft-formatted and given the operating system files. Always use the FDISK program of the current operating system to install a partition. Versions from other operating systems use different methods to control the hard drive.

Some hard drive utilities already contain the routines for partitioning the hard drive. This capability should be used only if the size can be varied and if the partitioning is later recognized by the operating system. Some DOS versions cannot recognize the extended partitions that were created as DOS types by some programs.

MS-DOS 3.3

This version of DOS is delivered on two diskettes and doesn't contain an installation program. So the user must perform the installation manually. We'll describe this process in the following sections. This procedure would also be used if Version 4.0 is installed without using the SELECT program.

The FDISK program is loaded when the low-level formatting of the hard drive has been completed. The main procedure for the program is almost identical for all three DOS versions. If there are any differences, we'll discuss them. Start FDISK by entering:

```
FDISK  Enter
```

A menu appears, displaying all the possible capabilities of the program.

When the hard drive is partitioned, the following steps are performed:

- Create primary DOS partition

- Activate primary DOS partition

- Create extended partition

- Create logical drives

If more than one partition is created, the number of cylinders for the first partition must be entered. If you don't understand the cylinder numbers, the following formula should help:

```
Number of cylinders to be defined=
partial capacity / total capacity * number of cylinders
```

Starting with DOS 4.0 the partition size can be indicated in megabytes or percentages. The first partition is always designated as drive C:. Additional partitions are designated with the letters D:, E:, etc. Externally, the primary partition doesn't differ from the extended partition and all partitions are treated equally.

The FDISK program automatically jumps from installing the extended partition to the menu for creating the logical drives. The reverse procedure is used to delete the partitions. First the logical drives are deleted and then the extended partition and, finally, the primary partition.

Formatting

After the partitions are created, the system is booted again. Now the hard drive must be formatted with the operating system. The following DOS command is used:

```
FORMAT C: /s
```

The "/S" ensures that the hard drive can boot and that the system is stored on the disk. If you want to give the hard drive a name, add a "/V". Starting with DOS 4.0, a prompt asking for the volume name will automatically appear.

When the formatting is complete, several files are located on the hard drive, but only one is visible. The other files are marked as hidden and aren't displayed with the DIR command. It's difficult to delete these hidden files.

All the DOS commands must be transferred to the hard drive. A subdirectory for DOS must be created so all the files aren't stored in the root directory.

```
MD DOS
```

Change to the subdirectory by entering:

```
CD DOS
```

Then copy the contents of all system diskettes (DOS 3.3: 2 diskettes, DOS 4.0: 6 diskettes) to this directory. For every diskette, enter the command:

```
COPY A:\*.*
```

Once you've copied the first diskette, simply press F3 to display the command on the screen again. Then press the Enter key to execute the command again.

Your system is almost ready. Now create the CONFIG.SYS and AUTOEXEC.BAT files. These files store important information for initializing your system. These files must be in the root directory of your boot partition.

To create the CONFIG.SYS file use a word processor, which reformats the text and stores it in pure ASCII, or use EDLIN. Creating the files can also be simplified as follows. Enter:

```
COPY CON CONFIG.SYS
```

The cursor will move to the next line. Enter the following lines and the CONFIG.SYS file should contain the information shown below:

```
FILES=25
BUFFERS=20
DEVICE=C:\DOS\ANSI.SYS
```

To return to the normal DOS prompt, enter:

Ctrl Z

ANSI.SYS is a driver that makes enhanced functions for the screen available to the user. CONFIG.SYS enables you to add various drivers to the system. For example, since DOS 4.0 was released, certain programs can be loaded with CONFIG.SYS by using the INSTALL= command.

The AUTOEXEC.BAT is a batch file that calls a series of DOS commands after the system is started and the CONFIG.SYS executes. The file is created like CONFIG.SYS. The AUTOEXEC.BAT file should contain the following commands:

@ECHO OFF   The AUTOEXEC.BAT file is executed but the commands that were called aren't displayed.

PATH C:\;C:\DOS

DOS searches for a command in the indicated directories; this permits all commands to be called at any time.

PROMPT PG

The currently active subdirectory is displayed behind the drive letter (prompt).

Refer to the DOS documentation for more information.

MS-DOS 4.0, 5.0, and 6.0

DOS 4.0 can also be installed manually, as described above. However, it's easier to let DOS handle the installation for DOS 4.0 and DOS 5.0. The installation program analyzes the available hardware and automatically installs suitable drivers with the proper parameters.

To install DOS 4.0 or DOS 5.0 automatically, simply insert diskette 1 in drive A:, press Ctrl + Alt + Del, and follow the prompts displayed by the installation program.

A prompt appears asking whether the installation should be continued or terminated. Since the system is being installed, insert diskette 2 and press Enter. Continue to answer the questions about your system.

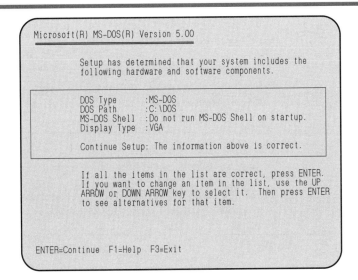

SETUP for DOS 5.0

Some of these questions affect only user-friendliness instead of system operation.

To install the system, you need a blank diskette. The system creates a backup boot diskette, which contains all the important system files. This diskette can be used if the hard drive ever becomes defective. The status of the installation when the hard drive must be partitioned and formatted before the system files are transferred is also stored on the diskette. Prepare a suitable diskette and insert it into the drive when requested.

The installation program takes over the partitioning and formatting. It also automatically creates, according to the settings you select, the CONFIG.SYS and the AUTOEXEC.BAT files. If one of these files was already on the hard drive, it's given a new extension and replaced with the new file.

After the installation is complete, boot the computer again. The new operating system is loaded and the DOS Shell is called, if it should be loaded automatically during booting.

As we mentioned, it's also possible to install the DOS 4.0 system manually. To do this, terminate the installation program by pressing ⌷Esc⌷ when you're prompted for diskette 2. The remaining steps are the same as those used for installing DOS 3.3. However, six diskettes, instead of two, must be copied into the DOS directory.

This procedure becomes more complicated if you want to use the DOS Shell. For the manual installation, you must write the batch file to call the DOS Shell yourself. Before doing this, refer to the DOS 4.0 documentation.

The DOS 5.0 and 6.0 files are stored on diskette in compressed format. A program named EXPAND.EXE is used to manually uncompress these files. The EXPAND.EXE program can be used to manually install DOS 5.0 and 6.0 but the SETUP program is much easier. The EXPAND.EXE program is usually used to copy a single compressed file from the DOS 5.0 and 6.0 diskettes to the DOS directory. This is very useful if you accidentally delete a file.

See the DOS 5.0 or 6.0 manual for more information on how to uncompress the DOS 5.0 files or 6.0 files.

9.2 DR DOS

DR DOS includes a setup program for installation. This program starts automatically when the system is booted from the diskette. This installation program is similar to the program used for PC/MS-DOS 4.0. If you haven't partitioned your hard drive yet, you must exit the setup program and run FDISK.

If you partition the hard drive, the "Create DOS Partition" option not only stores the partition information, but also formats the hard drive.

When the hard drive has been partitioned and formatted, all additional steps can be performed by the DR DOS installation program. This program automatically transfers the required files and creates the configuration files CONFIG.SYS and AUTOEXEC.BAT.

9.3 OS/2

In 1987 a new IBM PC generation, called the PS/2, was announced. About a year later, an operating system specifically designed for these systems was presented. This system is called OS/2.

Compared to DOS, OS/2 has two advantages. First, memory can be addressed consecutively and doesn't have to be made available for the operating system through other procedures. Under OS/2 the user has consecutive access to the entire memory of the 386. This can be the maximum amount addressable by the 386 processor (16 Meg for the 386SX and 4 gigabytes for the 386DX/i486). Through the virtual memory technology, this capacity can increase even more, to a total of 64 terabytes for the DX and 1 gigabyte for the

SX. During virtual memory utilization, portions of memory are relocated to the hard drive.

Another advantage of OS/2 is multitasking. This means that the user can execute several (multi) applications (tasks) in the computer simultaneously. For example, you can work on a long document while the computer prints certain pages of the document in the background and formats diskettes.

These processes are executed simultaneously. Depending on the speed of the processor and the time required by each task, the number of simultaneously executing tasks depends only on the amount of memory available.

9.4 UNIX

While OS/2 can still be compared with DOS, it's more difficult to compare UNIX with DOS.

UNIX was conceived and developed in 1969 by Dennis Ritchie and K. Thompson at the Bell Laboratories of AT&T. Dennis Ritchie first wrote UNIX in assembler language for the PDP-7. Unfortunately, this meant that it couldn't be transferred to other computers easily. To solve this problem, Ritchie developed the C programming language, which is now a standard language in microcomputers. About 90% of UNIX was written in C.

One of the biggest advantages of UNIX is that the operating system and programs that were written for a UNIX machine can be run, with only minor changes, on other computers running UNIX.

UNIX is available for ATs and 386 computers. The versions available for the PC have different names, depending on the manufacturer.

The UNIX version developed by Microsoft is called XENIX and the IBM version is called AIX. Other UNIX versions are SINIX from Siemens and UX from Hewlett-Packard. Perhaps the most widely distributed version of UNIX is SCO-XENIX System V from the Santa Cruz Operation (SCO). There is even a special 386 version called XENIX 386.

Since UNIX is a multi-user system, its internal structure is designed to allow multiple users to access the operating system. Therefore, there are working files for every user and a password query. UNIX controls several connected computers and provides for a regulated interchange of data. A network program isn't needed for the connections. A 386 system with several serial interfaces is sufficient.

A UNIX network usually consists of three or a maximum of five (using the third and fourth serial interface) computers, of which the most powerful has control.

Every UNIX user must log on the system with a password. Each user has a different status, which means that each one can access only certain files.

Multitasking

Besides managing several users, UNIX can also execute several processes simultaneously (multitasking). So you can work on several tasks simultaneously. Simply switch between the tasks by pressing a key.

Because UNIX is so powerful, it's more complicated than DOS. For example, the boot procedure can last several minutes longer than DOS. Also, since many users may be using UNIX, the system cannot simply be shut down when one user is finished. Another user may still be working at a different computer.

Also, the computer cannot simply be switched off. To increase throughput speed, UNIX retains some parts of the hard drive structure in memory. So, before switching off the computer, this data must be written on the hard drive.

Construction

UNIX consists of several shells that surround the kernel. The first shell forms the interfaces to the hardware components, which affect the communication between the hardware and the software (operating system). Next is the system kernel, which is also called the kernel. The kernel manages the system and coordinates several users or processes that are executing simultaneously.

The system calls with the current standard programs, also called binary files, are located one level above the kernel. The kernel and the binary files are independent of the processor and can be used on several computers (i.e., they are portable).

The next level is the shell. This is the command processor, through which the user tells the system what he/she wants to do. Another level is formed by the application programs.

File system

UNIX operates with the same hierarchical file system used by DOS. However, there are some differences between DOS and UNIX.

The root directory in UNIX is called "ROOT." Several subdirectories are reserved for system files: BIN, DEV, USR, ETC, LIB, and TMP, for example. Subdirectories are called catalogs in UNIX. The ROOT directory corresponds to the DOS root directory and is indicated by a slash (/). Also, all lower level catalogs are separated from the higher ones with a slash.

The UNIX utility programs are stored in the BIN directory (binary files). Depending on the UNIX version, this library can be very large. UNIX device drivers are stored in the DEV directory. The USR directory contains the files created and edited by the users (USeR). The USR directory may contain additional catalogs with the names or abbreviations for the users. These catalogs are also called working catalogs.

The ETC catalog holds the files for system control and password administration. The C compiler for UNIX, with its LIBraries, is stored in the LIB directory. The TMP directory is used by user programs for storing temporary files.

The file handling commands are similar to DOS. There is also a user-friendly standard user interface, which is similar to the Presentation Manager for Windows, X/Windows. However, unlike the Presentation Manager, it isn't an intregal part of the system.

Under UNIX a filename always includes the complete pathname. For example, the complete filename of the "demotext" file in the working catalog "tj" is "/usr/tj/demotext." The name of a catalog (between the two slashes) can consist of a maximum of 14 characters.

Except for different names, UNIX handles files like other operating systems. UNIX also contains something similar to AUTOEXEC.BAT and CONFIG.SYS. They are called profile and inittab and are stored in the ETC catalog.

Software

UNIX isn't an outdated command-oriented operating system, on which only a couple of C compilers and a Shell can execute. Instead, there are numerous programs from all applications. There's an unlimited amount of quality software in UNIX.

DOS and/or UNIX

There are several ways DOS and UNIX can coexist on the same hard drive. For example, it's possible to declare the desired (boot) partition as active by using FDISK. However, this process is inconvenient. If you're a UNIX user who only occasionally uses DOS, you should create a DOS environment for your computer with a suitable program, which is then treated like any other task in the operating system.

To install XENIX, first check your system resources. XENIX is a memory-intensive operating system. The minimum configuration is 512K RAM and 20 Meg of hard drive. As an optimum configuration, 2 to 3 Meg of RAM and a hard drive of at least 100 Meg are recommended.

Before installing UNIX on your system, you should backup your DOS partitions so you don't lose any data if an error occurs during installation.

Even after installing UNIX, mostly likely you'll still use DOS applications. This is possible by using special programs that emulate a DOS environment. Users who prefer to use DOS exclusively may use a type of manual "double boot."

Both operating systems can coexist on the hard drive because each has been assigned its own partition. The partition from which booting should occur can be activated with FDISK, which is a program that's included in DOS and UNIX/XENIX.

After the computer has been switched on, the system in the currently active partition is booted. If you're working with XENIX, define the XENIX partition as active; if you want to use DOS applications, make the active partition the DOS partition. When using FDISK, be sure when that XENIX has at least 16 Meg available; otherwise installation isn't possible.

Installation

To install XENIX, you must boot XENIX from the diskette, after you've activated the UNIX partition. Insert the start diskette from the XENIX package into drive A: and switch on the computer.

The start diskette first calls an automatic installation program, which installs the XENIX kernel. You can skip the hard drive parameter query that follows if the drive was already formatted under DOS.

Next a table, listing the partitions of the hard drive, appears. A portion of the hard drive can be assigned to the XENIX system. Also, the routine contains a complete Bad Track manager, in which defective sectors can be entered manually or searched for automatically.

The installation routine determines the swap space required for storing the operating system on the hard drive. This space requirement increases as RAM decreases.

Next the file system is created. As a safety precaution, you're asked to enter the XENIX serial number. Finally, the actual installation is completed and you can boot the computer again with UNIX/XENIX to set the system.

The UNIX operating system is configured with the environment variables. With the "env" command the values that are already set can be output. Starting values for certain programs are provided in the environment variables. Also the hardware configuration is specified. In TERM, the type of terminals is defined and the driver for them is located in TERMCAP. Alternatives for both settings are in the TERMINFO variable.

UNIX contains something similar to a CONFIG.SYS file, which activates the personal values of each user when he/she logs onto the system. The designation differs for every shell and can be either PROFILE or CSHRC.

The AUTOEXEC of UNIX is called RC. It's started globally at the beginning when the system boots. Global settings, such as search paths or a shell for all users, are indicated here.

After every boot process with UNIX, you must log into the system, which includes answering a password query.

When you've installed the system, you automatically own the highest user status, called the Superuser privilege. You have write, read, and delete access to all files. You can admit other users and regulate their access to files. The new user contains its own catalog, a mailbox, and a password. This process is usually handled by a program.

9.5 Other 386 Operating Systems

Besides the DOS, OS/2, and UNIX operating systems, there are also variations of DOS, which enhance the capabilities of DOS.

Multi-user DOS/386

Multi-user DOS 386, from Digital Research, uses all the capabilities of the 80386/486 microprocessor while retaining DOS compatibility. Multi-user DOS provides both multitasking and multi-user operations.

Other solutions, such as DESQview (see Chapter 12), enhance the capabilities of a DOS version.

Multi-user DOS can execute up to four applications simultaneously. Each of these applications has its own screen display area (a window); the user is able to switch between them using [Ctrl] and a number representing the window. One of these applications can be moved into the foreground to fill the entire screen.

The system is also capable of simultaneous multi-user operations. With a simple serial cable, two PCs can be interfaced as external terminals and simultaneously share the system.

Multi-user DOS supports programs that access memory according to EMS. A supplemental Expanded Memory Manager program isn't needed with Multi-user DOS.

Besides the DOS commands, which correspond to the syntax of DR-DOS commands, Multi-user DOS offers some useful utility programs, including a file manager, an editor, a print manager, and a utility for creating of user-defined menus.

Multi-user DOS uses the real mode of the 80386/486 microprocessor. Since each program uses only part of the memory, sufficient memory must be provided for Multi-user DOS. Since full compatibility with DOS exists, problems won't occur with normal applications.

We recommend using Multi-user DOS if you need both multitasking and multi-user capabilities on your system and don't want to change to another operating system.

Chapter 10 — User Interfaces

For many computer users, the command-oriented structure of the operating systems is too complicated and awkward. Because of this, software companies developed user interfaces that use graphics, special menu technology, and the mouse. These interfaces simplify using a computer.

What is WIMP?

During the 1980s, researchers from Xerox first presented the idea of an easy-to-use graphical user interface.

Their ideas resulted in the acronym WIMP, which stands for Windows, Icons, Mouse, and Pull-down menus. This concept involves several windows on the screen, icons (graphic representations of computer elements), mouse operation, and pull-down menus containing functions.

These researchers produced a type of programming language, which was later called Smalltalk. Apple was the first company to adapt this concept to a computer. The "Lisa" model was the first mass produced computer that had a mouse and a screen that operated in graphics mode. Also, the user communicated with the system only through icons and pull-down menus.

In 1984, the first PC (GEM) with a user interface designed according to the WIMP standard was introduced.

Communicating with the machine

The user interface is an intermediary between users and the operating system. This also applies to the command processor. However, the command processor interface considers the needs of the computer, while the user interface designed according to the WIMP standard considers the needs of users.

With some computers (e.g., NeXT, the Commodore Amiga, the Atari ST, and the Apple Macintosh), the user interface is the main interface between the users and the machine. With the PC, a command interface is still used for communication between the user and the machine.

Graphics or Text

Graphic oriented interfaces

The differences of the individual user interfaces are based on how much the user encounters the command line. For example, Windows 3.1 and GEM are extremely icon-oriented. This makes using the system as easy as possible.

To copy files using this type of interface, the files are selected with a mouse click and dragged to the destination icon while the mouse button is pressed.

Interface to programming

The Windows and GEM user interfaces not only provide a way to control the operating system, but also offer interfaces for programming applications. This type of interface is called an API (Application Programming Interface). APIs ensure that all programs use the same principles and operate the same way.

Whether you use a command line interface or a user interface depends on personal preference. An experienced user can probably enter a command faster than performing the corresponding actions with the mouse. However, for inexperienced computer users, working with a mouse and a graphical user interface is much easier.

System Application Architecture

For Windows and many other applications, a unified architecture is becoming more popular. This uniform structure for the software is called System Application Architecture (SAA). SAA programs address the input/output devices (keyboard, mouse, graphics card/monitor, printer, etc.) through the same general program interface.

The SAA should also ensure that the same menu buttons are used in the same way in all programs. This includes the arrangement of pull-down menus. In SAA programs, the first pull-down menu on the left is always used for file functions. Also, keyboard operation is standardized. In all SAA compliant programs, the file menu is always activated by pressing the Alt + F key combination.

Windows goes even further in implementing the SAA concept. During input or output, programs can use resources that are provided by the user interface. This means that they use the keyboard and mouse routines of Windows during input. Output occurs through the Windows display screen driver or printer routines. Windows also makes the character sets available.

10.1 Simple Shells

If you don't want to use a graphical user interface, you could use a shell instead. Shells are programs that simplify using the PC. Although they are user-friendly, shells provide fewer resources than GEM and Windows; they don't provide the Application Programming Interface (API).

Command processor

The command processor is simply the normal DOS interface, as it appears if a DOS Shell or other such utility program isn't loaded.

To communicate with the computer, you must enter commands from the keyboard following a prompt on a command line. With simple commands this isn't difficult, but with commands that have a complicated syntax, mistakes can easily occur.

In these instances, it would be helpful if the last line could be repeated. Normally, the MS-DOS command processor retains only the last command that was entered. But, DR DOS, MS-DOS 5.0, and MS-DOS 6.0 contain a type of DOS Editor, which stores several command lines. Under DR DOS 6.0 this is called "HISTORY". With MS-DOS 5.0, this function is a separate TSR (Terminate and Stay Resident) program called DOSKEY.

DOS Shell

The DOS Shell, which has been part of MS-DOS since Version 4.0, has two main tasks. It performs file operations (copying, deleting, renaming, etc.) and controls programs (starting, passing parameters, etc.). With the Shells supplied with MS-DOS 4.0 and 5.0 and 6.0, the user is in the Program Manager part, similar to Windows 3.0. From here, the utility programs or the File Manager can be activated.

After the Shell is activated in MS-DOS 5.0 or MS-DOS 6.0, the Program Manager and the File Manager are displayed on the screen. Besides the DOS Shell, several programs may be in memory simultaneously.

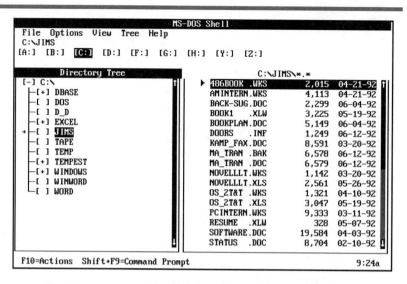

After the start of the DOS Shell, you're in the Program Manager

The basic principle of the Program Manager portion of the DOS 5.0 or DOS 6.0 Shell is the same as that of Windows. Several programs can be collected into a group. The Main group, which is activated after the start, contains three programs: DOS command editor (this is the "normal" DOS interface), File Manager, and the program to set the screen colors. You can place additional programs in the Main group.

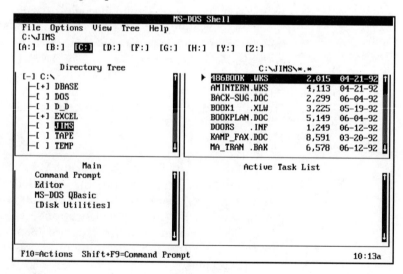

The DOS 5.0 Shell

Unlike Windows, you can create sub-groups within the Main group. These sub-groups can contain programs and additional sub-groups.

To distinguish between programs and sub-groups, the sub-groups contain a special icon in the Group list. Every group can be assigned a password and a Help message.

Although subdirectories in DOS can have a name with a maximum of 8 characters, the designation of groups and sub-groups may be up to 74 characters in length.

Norton Commander

One of the most popular utility programs is Norton Utilities. Its most famous feature is the Undelete program, which can restore deleted programs. Peter Norton, its creator, also developed the shell called Norton Commander.

Norton Commander is a simple but user-friendly way to avoid many of the unpleasant aspects of DOS. Unlike the DOS Shell, file operation is the most important aspect of the Norton Commander. After starting, two windows, in which files or directories can be displayed, occupy the largest part of the display.

The program launcher option is accessed by pressing the F2 key. Several programs can be called with the mouse or by pressing a key. Of course, these keys and mouse actions must be predefined. The Norton Commander obtains the information about hot keys, program designations, and actual calls from a file called NC.MNU.

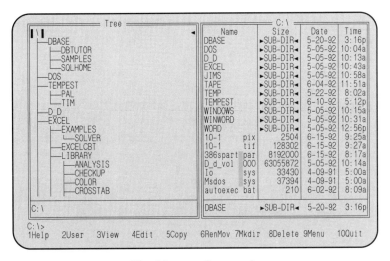

The Norton Commander

A proprietary shell

The easiest way to operate a computer without DOS is to start the various applications from a proprietary interface. This interface allows you to start programs by pressing a single key. To do this you must either:

> • Rename the programs so the program name (the part of the name before the extension) contains only one character (e.g., WORD.EXE to W.EXE)

or

> • Write a batch file that starts the program (e.g., W.BAT)

You'll also need a text page in which these characters are listed and described. This page is easily created with a word processor and then stored as unformatted ASCII text. The line length shouldn't be longer than 80 characters. This text could be named MENU.TXT and could contain the following entries:

```
W - Word
D - dBase
L - Lotus 1-2-3
T - Document directory
X - Turn computer off
```

The batch program needed to display the text is called MENU.BAT and consists of the following lines:

```
@ECHO OFF
CLS
TYPE MENU.TXT
```

The following are the batch files:

Word:

```
REM W.BAT
@ECHO OFF
CLS
ECHO Start Word...
WORD
MENU
```

Displaying the document directory:

```
REM T.BAT
@ECHO OFF
CLS
DIR C:\TEXT
```

```
PAUSE
MENU
```

Switching off the computer:

```
REM X.BAT
@ECHO OFF
ECHO Switch computer off?
PAUSE
PARK
```

As you can see, after calling a program, the Menu batch file is called again. The batch file has an "Emergency Brake". If you respond to the PAUSE command by pressing <kbd>Ctrl</kbd> + <kbd>C</kbd>, the batch program can be terminated. Then you must activate MENU.BAT by entering:

```
MENU
```

10.2 MS-Windows

Today, Windows is the user interface for many 386 and 486 systems. Windows makes the PC more user-friendly by visually representing tasks and utilizing the mouse. For example, programs are no longer started by entering commands on a command line or by double-clicking filenames. Instead they are activated through an icon.

In this section we'll provide an overview of Windows. For more information on using Windows, refer to *Windows 3.1 Complete* from Abacus. If you need complete, in-depth information about Windows, *Windows 31 Intern*, which is also published by Abacus, provides comprehensive information.

The Program Manager is the foundation of Windows.

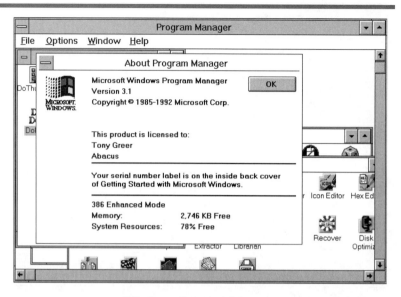

Windows Program Manager

All applications and utility programs can be started with icons from the Program Manager. Windows applications, such as Excel, Word for Windows, or the BeckerTools Shell, use the SAA programming interface.

Common DOS applications can be run in two ways. They are executed in either full screen mode or a separate window. In full screen mode, Windows switches to DOS before starting the application. After completing the application, the user is again switched to Windows. Windows applications are executed in a window.

Every program is assigned its own environment, which can have a maximum size of 640K. To run numerous programs simultaneously, a large amount of memory is needed. The programs can work in parallel and even exchange data with each other. Every DOS application doesn't claim the entire memory area for itself; an application can use only the area that Windows assigned to it.

Besides the advantages of using virtual memory, operating in an environment like Windows also offers other advantages.

By using the SAA concept, Windows ensures that the hardware is used optimally. By providing the driver and the character sets for the output centrally, even small programs can benefit from the numerous drivers and character sets provided by Windows.

Not only the standard devices are supported. Windows also provides various drivers for diverse graphics cards, 9 and 24 pin printers, ink jet and laser printers, and plotters. Since many rare printers and graphics cards are usually delivered with drivers, they can easily be used with Windows.

Windows also offers sufficient memory for large application programs or files. It does this by dumping the unneeded parts onto the hard drive. If several applications are being used simultaneously, Windows simulates multitasking, although DOS doesn't have this capability.

The number of programs that can be started and executed simultaneously depends on the amount of memory available. Extended memory can be defined as a virtual (RAM) disk, instead of the hard drive, to reduce the time needed for storing temporary files. Expanded memory is addressed and used directly.

True multitasking was introduced in Windows 3.0. A menu is used to determine how the individual tasks should be executed, what process should run in the foreground, and what applications should remain in the background.

Windows components

Besides the actual user interface, Windows also contains an entire series of useful utilities and auxiliary programs:

- Write
- Notepad (simple editor)
- Print Manager
- Cardfile
- Clock
- Two games: Minesweeper and Solitaire
- Macro recorder for all Windows applications that don't offer this feature
- Paintbrush
- Terminal program
- Calculator
- Calendar

Several Windows applications can exchange data through a clipboard. To use this feature, cut the data in one application and copy it to the clipboard. Then paste the data from the clipboard into the proper application. This option can be used by all programs under Windows.

The clipboard can handle both graphics and text. However, ensure that the destination application can actually use the data. Non-

Windows programs can also use the clipboard. For example, in MS-Word the clipboard can be used for importing text.

Dynamic Data Exchange

The real secret of Windows is Dynamic Data Exchange (DDE). Two files from two completely different programs can be connected so they exchange data automatically. Data changed in one file is automatically updated in the other file.

For example, Excel and AutoCAD can be connected so when you change a blueprint in AutoCAD, the calculations in Excel are automatically updated.

Installation

Before Windows is installed, the installation program checks the existing hardware. Windows runs on all computers that have at least 640K of memory. However, it runs better on some computers than others. Your computer should be at least an 80286 with at least 2 Meg of memory and a fast hard drive for better performance. For Windows, more is definitely better. An 80486 with 8 Meg of RAM and a 100 Meg hard drive is a definite advantage in this environment.

Windows can simulate memory with the hard drive. If insufficient memory is available, files are stored temporarily on the hard drive.

Windows operates with all the graphic standards for the PC. We recommend using an EGA or VGA card because these graphics cards display the buttons and fields three dimensionally. If the buttons are clicked with the mouse, they appear to move down, as if they were pressed.

The first part of the INSTALL program runs under DOS in text mode. Windows installs itself first as a basic version and then begins the actual installation by transmitting the programs, data, and drivers.

```
Windows Setup

      If your computer or network appears on the Hardware Compatibility List
   with an asterisk next to it, press F1 before continuing.

   System Information
      Computer:          MS-DOS System
      Display:           VGA
      Mouse:             Microsoft, or IBM PS/2
      Keyboard:          Enhanced 101 or 102 key US and Non US keyboards
      Keyboard Layout:   US
      Language:          English (American)
      Codepage:          English (437)
      Network:           Novell NetWare (shell versions 3.26 and above)

   Complete Changes: Accept the configuration shown above.

   To change a system setting, press the UP or DOWN ARROW key to
   move the highlight to the setting you want to change. Then press
   ENTER to see alternatives for that item. When you have finished
   changing your settings, select the "Complete Changes" option
   to quit Setup.

ENTER=Continue  F1=Help  F3=Exit
```

Windows 3.1 installation program

During the printer driver installation you can select your printer from a list. If your printer isn't on the list, use the printer driver, that is compatible with your equipment.

Usually these are:

- 9 pin printer: Epson FX

- 24 pin printer: NEC P6 or Epson LQ

- Laser printer: HP Laserjet II

- Ink jet printer: HP DeskJet or Epson SQ

- Daisywheel printer: Diablo

Once the printer has been selected, some additional parameters can be set. Selecting the port to which your output device has been connected is very important.

Two entries are added to the designations of LPT for the parallel serial interface and COM for the serial interface: FILE and EPT. The FILE designation tells the driver to redirect the output to a print file, which can be sent directly to the printer, and automatically makes the necessary settings by entering:

```
COPY Filename PRN
```

EPT is actually a special printer interface for an IBM laser printer. If this printer interface isn't available, Windows prints to a file called EPT, which is in the same subdirectory as the program from which printing should occur.

The printer setting menu can be called at any time because it belongs to the permanent Desktop Utilities of Windows.

One of the Setup program's tasks is to search the hard drive for executable files. These are then sorted into two groups: Windows applications and non-Windows applications. The user can then select which of these files should be displayed as icons in each group. Later the settings can be changed as desired and the programs regrouped.

After the installation, Windows can be set up according to your own needs.

The nationality setting can be changed at any time. To do this, click on the Main icon and then activate the Control Panel. In the window that appears you'll see an icon shaped like a globe. This is the International icon. Click on this icon; a dialog box, in which you can specify country-specific characteristics, appears. The following settings can be made:

- Country setting general

- Language

- Keyboard Layout

- Measurements (inch or cm)

- Date format: month-day-year or day-month-year

- Currency

- Time calculations: 12 or 24 hours

- Decimal point or comma

You can also change the background design of the Windows screen. For example, it's possible to add a graphic. The Control Panel contains the Desktop option. Wallpaper and a Pattern can be used to customize your desktop.

An image displayed as wallpaper doesn't need to be as large as the screen and can contain several colors. The Center option places the image in the center of the screen. With the Tile option, a smaller version of the graphic is continuously displayed until the entire screen is filled.

Windows 3.1 operating modes

Windows 3.1 operates in two modes:

> • Standard mode, in which all memory is addressable
>
> • 386 Enhanced mode, in which every application can obtain its own virtual environment

Windows 3.1 usually starts automatically in the mode that's best suited to the available processor and memory. Sometimes Windows can be switched to another mode by attaching a parameter to the call.

Standard mode

Standard mode requires at least an 80286 processor. To start Windows in Standard mode, the following command must be entered on the DOS command line:

```
WIN /S
```

In Standard mode, Windows can use all the memory sequentially. Separating memory into conventional and extended is only important for DOS applications (and older Windows programs). All applications written for the newer Windows versions can use memory without limitations.

DOS applications, which are started under Windows, receive complete support but can only use Expanded memory if the necessary hardware (Above Board, memory expansion, or NEAT-SX Chipset) is available.

Memory managers, such as 386MAX.SYS, can be loaded to use EMS outside of Windows. DOS applications started in Standard mode under Windows cannot use expanded memory with these software drivers. The software drivers are deactivated by Windows.

Windows directly addresses memory in Standard mode. It adds conventional and extended memory and uses it for its own purposes only.

Windows uses the XMS driver HIMEM.SYS, which must be installed by CONFIG.SYS. DOS applications that use extended memory according to the XMS standard can also access it under Windows in the Standard mode. Under Windows in Standard mode, Protected mode programs, which have a DOS Extender patterned after the VCPI or the Microsoft DPMI Standard, can be executed.

386 Enhanced mode

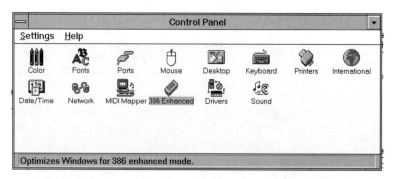

386 Enhanced mode is represented by an Icon in the Control Panel

In the 386 Enhanced mode you can access virtual memory. To run Windows in 386 Enhanced mode, the PC must have a 80386/486 microprocessor and sufficient memory (at least 2 Meg). To activate the 386 Enhanced mode, add the following parameter to the program call:

```
WIN /3
```

In 386 Enhanced mode, Windows manages memory without dividing it into conventional and extended memory, as in Standard mode. When this mode is active, an icon that looks like a circuit chip is displayed in the Control Panel. This is the 386 Enhanced icon.

The 386 Enhanced mode assigns a virtual PC to DOS applications. Every virtual DOS machine has the same environment, which was present when Windows was started from DOS. This means that every driver and every TSR program can be accessed and requires memory. However, the memory size of a virtual DOS machine under Windows is only slightly less than the memory that would be available under DOS without Windows.

Windows used high DOS memory to store four pages of 16K each for a memory buffer used by EMS. Windows, in 386 Enhanced mode, stores this translation buffer for the Protected mode applications, which use the API of Windows. This is important because input and output operations still require DOS, under which Windows runs. This only works below the 1 Meg limit. The translation buffer in the high DOS memory is the window through which DOS communicates with the Protected mode application.

In the best situation, enough free high DOS memory is available for both the buffer and the page frame. If this isn't the case and both require too much space, either expanded memory cannot be used or parts of the buffer are stored in conventional memory (up to 640K).

```
ReservePageFrame=nn
```

If the ReservePageFrame variable is true (nn=-1), first the page frame is created and then the translation buffer. This forces them to be in conventional memory.

If the value is false (n=0), the buffer is created first and then the remaining space is used for the page frame. This setting provides the most memory in the virtual machine, but EMS cannot be used in DOS applications.

QUICK TIP

> If you use an external driver for EMS (e.g., EMS386.SYS), the buffer is always installed in conventional memory.

DOS applications executed in 386 Enhanced mode can access expanded memory only if a consecutive 64KB block of memory is available in high DOS memory.

The LIM 4.0 standard isn't valid here. The EMS support of Windows can be determined with the line:

```
NoEMMDriver=yes
```

In Version 2.11 of Windows, the position of the EMS memory window could be determined with the entries EMMExclude and EMMInclude. In Windows Version 3.0 this function was enhanced to control the API translation buffer.

The current versions of Windows don't use the memory as EMS in 386 Enhanced mode. However, EMS can be made available to DOS applications. Windows applications don't need to use EMS because they can be stored in extended memory.

Windows uses extended memory, which is addressed directly, in both the 386 Enhanced mode and Standard mode. DOS applications that use XMS memory can access this memory under a virtual machine in Windows. Protected mode software, which has a DOS Extender, developed by Microsoft and other companies (the DPMI-Extender) can also be used.

The best feature of the 386 Enhanced mode is virtual memory support. Windows Versions 3.0 and above communicate with the outside world by themselves and the applications receive the necessary resources.

INI files

As you know, DOS has the CONFIG.SYS and AUTOEXEC.BAT files, which contain important system settings. In the same way, Windows and its applications have INI files. Two of these files are important for determining how Windows operates: WIN.INI and SYSTEM.INI.

In the previous section, we referred to some entries found in these files. Now we'll explain the entries that are important for operating Windows on a 386/i486 system. INI files are also created for other programs, but their entries don't affect how Windows operates.

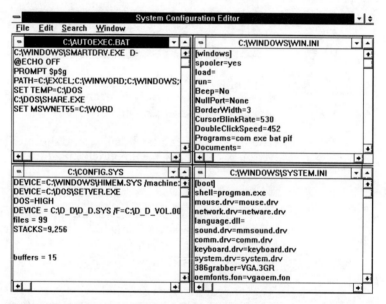

The SYSEDIT program loads the important system files automatically

These entries usually don't have to be changed. The Windows Setup and system control programs make all the basic settings. If you change one of these values, do so carefully. A mistake in an INI file can make the system unusable. Under certain circumstances, you may have to reinstall Windows. So always make a backup copy of the INI files before making any changes.

The entries in the INI files are stored in the ANSI format. To edit these files, use a Windows Editor, such as the Notepad. Also, the SYSEDIT.EXE program is used only for editing WIN.INI, SYSTEM.INI, AUTOEXEC.BAT, and CONFIG.SYS files. This program is located in the SYSTEM subdirectory of your Windows directory.

However, remember that this program doesn't make backup copies. Also, SYSEDIT.EXE isn't automatically installed by Setup; you must add it to a program group yourself.

We recommend using another Editor only if it can load and store unformatted text.

Every INI file contains several sections. The section designations are in the square brackets. Next are the variables that contain an equal sign and an assignment to the variables. These can be one or more numbers or text.

The INI files can also contain comments. A semicolon must be placed in front of any comments. This is useful when changes must be documented.

WIN.INI

The WIN.INI file contains the parameters for the software settings of the interface and the programs. Other Windows applications also store information in the WIN.INI. So, occasionally this file must be cleaned up. Sometimes applications misuse WIN.INI and simply erase existing and important entries. Because of this, it's very important that you have a backup copy of an INI file.

The following are some of the important information that's stored in WIN.INI:

- Programs, that mainly perform their function as icons, for example the Clock

- Programs that remain in the background and don't have to be completely activated to be used, for example screen savers

- Programs that should be loaded, but not executed, when Windows is first run

Program names that appear after run= are executed immediately after Windows is started. This only makes sense for programs that perform their functions in the background, such as network drivers.

Other important entries in the WIN.INI are located in the following sections:

```
[printer]
Spooler=yes or no
```

Usually the printer output should be controlled by the Print Manager. So this value is normally set to "Yes".

```
[ports]
```

This group lists the serial and parallel interfaces. The printer output can also be redirected to a file, which is then named.

```
LPT1:=
```

Serial interfaces appear like the parallel ones. The baud rate, parity, word length, stop bits and, if desired, quit option are indicated after the equal sign. The parameters are separated by a comma.

```
COM1:=9600,n,8,1
```

COM1 to COM4 is supported.

```
[files]
```

Printer output can also be directed to a file. Either Windows requests the filename before the output is sent or the output is automatically sent to an existing file. In the first case, the following line is needed:

```
FILE:=
```

A specific file can also be specified. For example, the filename shown below with the .PRN extension will appear in the Control Panel Configuration dialog box. A printer connected to this filename will direct its output to this file.

```
OUTPUT.PRN=
```

In the statement FILE:=, the colon and the equal sign must be provided. If a filename is specified, the colon must be omitted.

The filenames can be selected in the system control under Printer configuration.

```
[PrinterPorts]
```

This group lists all printers, their connections, and the error waiting period, which access a printer driver. The parameters, which can be configured through the system printer control, appear as follows:

```
Device name=Driver name, Interface name, Error waiting time,
Error repetition time
```

```
[devices]
```

This group lists all active printers with the same settings as the [PrinterPorts] group. These parameters occur without the error waiting and repetition times. Changes can be made through the system printer control.

SYSTEM.INI

The SYSTEM.INI file contains the hardware settings of Windows 3.1. Without this file, a 486 and Windows cannot cooperate.

The general hardware settings are usually made through the Setup program. If the Windows Setup cannot start or crashes, enter:

```
setup/i
```

This command, entered from the DOS command line, bypasses the hardware test.

The groups in SYSTEM.INI are named and surrounded by brackets.

```
[boot]
```

This section contains all the drivers and modules that Windows needs for its own configuration when started. The entries are:

```
386grabber=vga.3gr
286grabber=vgacolor.2gr
```

Both parameters specify the filenames of the device driver used by the Standard mode (286grabber) and the 386 Enhanced mode (386grabber) if an MS-DOS application appears. When installing another device driver, the Setup program for the MS-DOS level must be used.

```
shell=progman.exe
```

This entry determines which program should be started when Windows starts. The default setting is PROGMAN.EXE.

If you're working with only one application and don't need the other features of Windows, place the name and path of your application after :"shell=".

```
network.drv=
```

You can name the network driver in this entry. To include another driver, the Setup program must be started from MS-DOS.

`language.dll=`

This entry indicates the name of the dynamic link library for the country-specific language (DLL). If an entry isn't given, Windows uses the internally stored library for American English.

`fixedfon.fon=vgafix.fon`

This is the name of the font driver. While another device driver is being installed, the Setup program must be executed from the MS-DOS level.

`comm.drv=comm.drv`

The driver name for the serial data transmission is indicated here.

`sound.drv=mmsound.drv`

Name of the sound driver (the default is MMSOUND.DRV), which produces a warning beep. Other sound drivers are available; Windows 3.1 supports most of the popular audio cards.

`oemfonts.fon=`

Font-file for the OEM character set.

`fonts.fon=`

This driver is for proportional fonts.

`mouse.drv=mouse.drv`

Filename of the mouse driver.

`keyboard.drv=keyboard.drv`

Driver name for the keyboard.

With these two drivers, Windows really doesn't need an additional driver. If you work exclusively with Windows applications, you can save a few bytes by not calling the DOS keyboard driver and the mouse driver from the CONFIG.SYS/AUTOEXEC.BAT.

`display.drv=`

Name of the display screen driver used. With a VGA, use VGA.DRV.

`system.drv=`

Filename of the system hardware driver.

QUICK TIP

> Entries that affect the hardware configuration must be copied to the hard drive and partially installed. It's not enough to indicate the new drivers in the SYSTEM.INI file. So, the driver can be changed only with the Setup program, which can be called from DOS.

10.3 Other User Interfaces

Since Windows 3.1 was introduced, competing operating systems have had difficulty establishing an alternative to the standard set by Microsoft. Two operating systems that offer more than the shells discussed in Section 10.1 are GEM and GeoWorks.

GEM was available before Windows. GeoWorks Ensemble, however, is a PC adaptation of GEOS, which was developed for the Commodore 64 home computer.

GEM

GEM is a user interface for the PC introduced by Digital Research in 1984. One year later, Digital Research implemented the interface on the Atari ST series of computers, where it remains today, almost unchanged from when first introduced.

Mouse and Icon

The heart of GEM is the user interface consisting of two windows. The user can display the contents of two of the available mass storage devices (hard drive and diskette). The disk drive, hard drive, subdirectory, executable files, and other files are represented by various symbols (icons). If an icon is selected with the mouse, it's displayed in inverse video and operations, such as copying and deleting, can be performed.

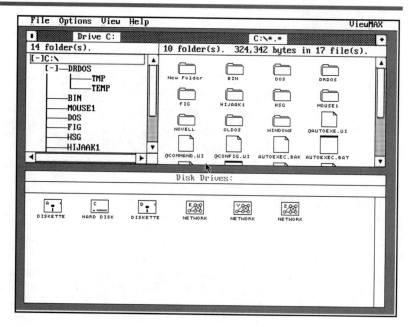

GEM operates with icons and pull-down menus

If a drive icon or subdirectory is clicked on twice (double-clicked), it's opened. An executable file is also started with a double-click.

Besides the normal DOS applications, which can be started from GEM, there are many programs that use the API provided by GEM. Two well-known examples of GEM applications are Ventura Publisher and 1st Word Plus. You can purchase GEM if you need to use a GEM application. Also, GEM may be included with the application software.

Flexible interface

GEM is constructed on several levels, which are located between the user and the hardware as well as the operating system. The Virtual Device Interface (VDI) ensures that GEM operates properly, independent of the hardware used.

Every device is controlled by a special driver program. The user doesn't notice this interface because it operates with a virtual computer and virtual devices. These are made available from the Virtual Device Interface.

The second shell, located between the user and the machine, is the AES (Application Environment System). The AES translates the mouse movements and other input, which the user supplies to the interface, into a form that the operating system can understand.

The quality of GEM depends on the quality of the device drivers that are used. These drivers are so well programmed that even on a 4.77 MHz PC, GEM works fast enough to be useful. This user interface is even better on a 386/i486 computer although multitasking isn't supported.

Memory requirements can also cause problems for the user interface. If GEM and DOS 4.0 share memory, larger applications won't execute or they will terminate unexpectedly with an error message. GEM doesn't support expanded memory so the user must boot with DOS 3.3 and then start GEM.

GeoWorks Ensemble

GeoWorks introduced a graphical user interface called GEOS on the Commodore 64 home computer. This interface was the basis for GeoWorks Ensemble for the PC.

The startup screen of GeoWorks Ensemble displays three main groups. These groups are represented by large icons, which can be selected with the mouse. The EXIT and HELP buttons also appear on the screen. Similar to Windows, an icon or a selection button is displayed three-dimensionally and looks like it's being pressed when it's selected.

The applications (Appliances) icon appears as a desk with a notebook, pencil, telephone, and steaming coffee cup. Other appliances are small utility programs (calculator, a card file, a calendar, and a notepad). These are also represented by icons. This program group can be selected by moving the mouse to an icon and clicking on it. To start a program, click on the icon with the mouse.

The Professional option provides advanced features. When this icon is selected, the GeoManager is activated.

All the programs delivered with GeoWorks Ensemble can be run in a window. The size of the window can be changed and the window can also be reduced to an icon. The GeoManager uses graphics to represent the functions of the applications.

All file and diskette operations can be selected in a menu bar at the top of the GeoManager, similar to Windows. When a menu is opened, a pin appears beside the first menu item. This pin can place the menu at any location on the screen and is available at any time, regardless of any other open menus.

All menus can also be selected with the keyboard by using the Alt key combinations.

The way GeoWorks Ensemble operates is very similar to Windows; even the key combinations are identical (e.g., [Alt] + [F4] will terminate an application). This doesn't mean that GeoWorks is an imitation of Windows. Instead, the programs are similar because of the SAA standard, which promotes identical operation of all programs adhering to this standard.

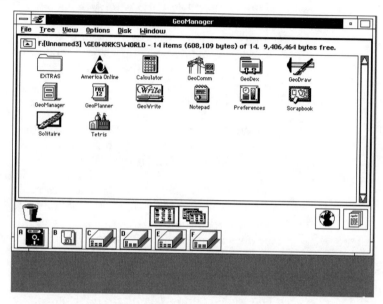

GEOS Professional: GeoManager window of GeoWorks Ensemble

The button used to close the GeoManager is located in the upper-left corner of the screen. In the upper-right corner are two additional selection buttons, which reduce the window to an icon (a dot) or bring it to full screen size (a rectangle).

The Task Manager of GeoManager is the Express Button. This button, marked with a blue "E", is in the active window. When the menus are selected, all active applications are displayed. By clicking on the desired application, you can change to it.

The icons displayed at the bottom of the screen represent the most frequently used functions. The waste paper basket is the Delete function.

When you exit a program, Ensemble remembers the location. So the next time you active the application, you'll be in exactly the same place as when you stopped working. To switch to another drive, click on the corresponding icon at the bottom of the screen.

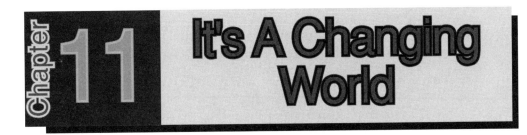

Chapter 11 — It's A Changing World

As you'd expect, things in the computer world have a habit of changing quickly. In rapid succession, Intel has introduced several new 486-class processors. These processors fall into two categories: Feature oriented processors and performance oriented processors.

Better, faster, cheaper

The new feature oriented processors are designed to be used in computer systems that use less electrical power. Not too long ago, these types of processosrs were the notebook, subnotebook, and handheld computers.

But now these computer systems include a new emerging generation of environmentally friendly desktop computers that consume less electrical power. The new performance oriented processors are designed to deliver more computing power to the user at far less cost.

We'll talk about these categories separately. First, we'll discuss the new feature oriented 486 processors.

11.1 Feature Oriented Processors - Saving Power

The SL processors were originally designed to be used in mobile computers - laptops, notebooks and subnotebooks. These processors operate at 3.3 volts instead of the 5 volts required by their predecessors. Since they use less power they extend the life of the batteries which run them.

In addition, an SL processor has a special System Management Mode (SMM) which can control the functions of a computer. For example, SMM can dim the LCD screen, turn off a hard drive, or reduce the speed of the processor, which also extends the life of the batteries. The main function of SMM is power management.

The key to SMM is a new interrupt called the SMI (System Management Interrupt) and a new address space in which the SMM routines are executed. This separate address space is independent of the 486's main address space so it doesn't interfere with operating system routines or application programs.

When the computer system requires a power management service from the SMM program, it issues an SMI to the 486 processor. The processor begins running the SMM program in its own address space, performs the requested service, and then exits the SMM program using a new RSM (Resume) instruction. The computer system is right back where it left off and isn't even aware the system may have been suspended for a few minutes, hours or days by the SMM.

In mid-June 1993, Intel announced that all of the 486 processors will incorporate the SL power management features at no additional cost. Except for operating at 5 volts, the 486SX, 486DX and 486DX2 processors will now contain the SL features. These new chips are known as the SL Enhanced 486 processors. In fact, some of the newer processors will even operate at 3.3 volts.

Using these new features, computer manufacturers will be able to build computers that use less energy. The same processor that is used in a mobile computer can also be used in a desktop computer. This makes it easier for manufactuers to standarize their computer systems and design "green" computers with an additional goal of helping to save the environment.

11.2 Performance Oriented Processors

If you've used a personal computer for at least a few years, then you've witnessed very dramatic jumps in performance and likewise very drastic drops in the price that you pay for that performance. These tremendous price/performance gains have been spurred by Intel, which has been rapidly developing and introducing new microprocessors at a frenzied pace ever since the first IBM/PC was launched more than ten years ago.

Three relatively new, but related, Intel introductions have slightly changed the definition of the original 486 chip. These new technologies are derived from the 486 chip and are aimed at extending the life of 486 computers and ensuring a smooth transition for both users and computer builders to the next generation of post-486 computers.

The first two of these technologies are called the Speed Doubling and OverDrive processors. For marketing reasons, Intel has given them different names, but the technology is identical. The third of these technologies is the Pentium processor which is the successor to the 486 processor.

Speed Doubling Processors

The 486es are part of a family of processors. The different members of the 486 family are designated by a suffix and a clock speed.

Suffix	486 Family Member
DX	486 with math coprocessor
SX	486 without math coprocessor
SL	486 with math coprocessor operating at 3.3 volts

Clock speed:

16MHz, 20MHz, 25MHz, 33MHz, 50MHz

As you know, the performance of a computer depends mainly on how fast the processor can execute instructions. The rate at which a processor can execute those instructions is determined by the processor's clock speed.

Remember the processor communicates with the external components of the computer system - main memory, hard drives, modems, and printer ports for example - at this same clock speed. Each computer manufacturer such as IBM, Compaq, AST or Dell designs its computer systems so all of these components can communicate reliably at that clock speed.

From it's name, you can probably guess how Speed Doubling technology works. A 486 processor with Speed Doubling technology executes at double the normal clock speed.

A Speed Doubling processor is designated by the suffix DX2. A standard 486DX-25 processor operates at a clock speed of 25 MHz. This means that both internal and external operations are performed at 25 MHz.

The Speed Doubling version of this chip is the 486DX2-50 processor. When the 486DX2-50 is performing integer or floating point operations, it performs them at 50 MHz. When it has to go to main memory for data or instructions, it does so at the normal 25 MHz clock speed.

From the above description, you can see that the performance gain is double only for internal CPU operations, in which it accesses only components internal to the processor. The speed of external operations, those where the processor has to access components external to the processor, isn't increased. Intel claims that the overall advantage of a DX2 processor over a DX processor is that it's from 50% to 70% faster.

It may not be obvious, but Speed Doubling technology is a great invention. Because the DX2 processor communicates with the rest of the computer system at the normal speed, a computer manufacturer does not have to redesign his computer system to achieve a higher level of performance. By merely substituting a DX2 processor in a system designed for a DX processor, the manufacturer can offer a new model with 50% to 70% increase in performance.

What do you get when you combine Speed Doubling technology with the new SL Enhanced 486 processor technology? You get a new Intel 486DX2/40 processor. This chip runs internally at 40 MHz and externally at 20 MHz. Since it consumes only 3.3 watts of power and has a built-in SMM, it will be perfect for notebook and subnotebook systems.

OverDrive processors

A companion to a Speed Doubling processor is the Intel OverDrive processor. Speed Doubling processors and OverDrive processors operate the same way. They are different only in how they are sold and packaged.

You can only buy a DX2 Speed Doubling processor in a complete computer system. Intel does not sell the DX2 processors to end users. Instead, Intel sells them only to computer manufacturers, who build the computer system, who in turn sell them to end users.

An OverDrive processor however is user-installable. This means that you can go to a computer dealer, purchase the OverDrive processor, and install it into your 486 computer system yourself. Think of the possibilities of immediately supercharging your computer system by popping one of these onto your motherboard.

For 486 SX systems, you can plug the OverDrive processor into the 169-pin PGA socket. This is the same socket used for the original 487SX math coprocessor. When you upgrade an SX system with the OverDrive processor, you also get a built-in math coprocessor. So for 486 SX systems, you benefit from the Speed Doubling technology and faster execution of floating point operations.

For 486 DX systems, there are two variations of OverDrive processors. The first type is for computer systems that have a dedicated 169-pin PGA OverDrive socket on the motherboard. To upgrade these systems, simply install the OverDrive processor into the dedicated motherboard socket.

The second type is for computer systems that do not have a dedicated OverDrive socket. To upgrade these systems, you must remove the original 486DX processor from its 168-pin socket and replace it with the OverDrive processor. Because the OverDrive processor runs internally at a faster clock speed, it generates more heat. Therefore, older computer systems may require additional cooling for the new OverDrive processor. You may also have to upgrade the BIOS.

If you're thinking about upgrading your system with an OverDrive, you can get additional information about compatibility by contacting Intel:

Voice:

Toll free	1-800-538-3373	Local	1-503-629-7354

Fax: 1-503-629-7580

Automated Fax Back Line:

Toll free	1-800-525-3019	Local	1-503-629-7576

Bulletin Board Service:

503-645-6275 (8-N-1 to 14.4KBPS)

CompuServe: GO INTELFORUM

An OverDrive processor generates a lot of heat. It runs at a temperature of about 180-190° Fahrenheit (80° Celsius). Some of the computer systems are not designed to run with components at such high temperatures. Therefore special fans, customized heat sinks, or other cooling devices are required to keep the heat from damaging other system components.

If you're planning to upgrade your 486 system with an OverDrive processor, contact Intel using one of the above methods to find out more about compatibility and cooling requirements for your particualar computer system.

The first OverDrive processors were available in April 1993. The suggested retail prices (June 1993) for the OverDrive processors were as follows:

Type	Speed	SRP	Type	Speed	SRP
SX	16MHz/20MHz	$399	SX	25MHz	$549
SX	33MHz	$699	DX	25MHz	$549
DX	33MHz	$699			

Remember, these are only suggested prices. Many computer retailers offer the OverDrive processors at discounted prices. Also keep in mind that you may also have to add additional cooling devices to keep the operating temperature down, which will add to the cost of an upgrade. But all in all, the OverDrive processor is a very attractive way to extend your investment in your existing 486 computer system.

You may have noticed that the above price list excludes an OverDrive processor for the DX 50 MHz processor. An OverDrive processor for a 50 MHz chip would have to operate internally at 100 MHz. To do this is no small feat. Intel has not been able to profitably manufacture an OverDrive processor that works at that speed, so at least for the time being, we'll have to be satisfied with the top speed of the 66 MHz OverDrive processor.

However, as of June 1993, there are reports that Intel is working on Speed Tripling technology. If this is true, then we'll see a 33 MHz/99 MHz DX3 processor in January 1994. The processor will run at an amazing 99 MHz internally, while retaining the 33 MHz speed when communicating with the outside world.

Advanced Micro Devices (AMD) a manufacturer of 386 "look alike" chips, is said to be developing two Speed Tripling processors: A 25 MHz/75 MHz and a 33 MHz/100 MHz chip that should be ready in September 1993.

How about a 40 MHz/120 MHz Speed Tripling processor? If it sounds too far fetched, then consider this model is supposedly being developed by the technical giant IBM. IBM is the only authorized second source manufacturer of the 486 processor. Since IBM is not authorized to sell the processor alone, you might expect IBM to sell a complete motherboard to other computer manufacturers so they can build their own superfast computer system.

The march towards faster and better performing computer systems never stops. In early 1994, Intel will deliver an OverDrive processor for computers that are now using DX2 processors. If these computer systems are designed with the Intel-specified 238-pin socket, in early 1994 you'll be able to upgrade such a DX2 system to use one of the new OverDrive processors.

This suggests that Intel has a new Speed Quadrupling technology. Actually, this new OverDrive processor for DX2 systems is part of a family of the next generation chip, the new Pentium processor.

11.3 The Next Generation

Pentium processors

History would lead us to believe that Intel's fifth generation processor would be called the 80586 chip. But the next generation chip is here and it's called the Pentium.

Does the name change mean that this new processor represents a revolutionary departure from the performance and compatibility standpoint from the 486's? Not at all. In fact, one of Intel's prime design criteria was to maintain full software compatibility to the earlier generation processors. The name change to Pentium is Intel's way of protecting the name of the processor.

The Pentium is not just a souped-up 486 processor

This is obvious by looking at a single statistic. The 486 chip contains the equivalent of 1.2 million transistors. A Pentium has more than 3 million transistors on board. This statistic tells us that many more functions have been integrated into the Pentium processor. A computing rule of thumb holds that the more integrated a chip, the faster it runs because the access time is reduced. Putting more functions on one chip means less time spent communicating with outside specialized chips, which would otherwise have to perform those functions.

Intel points to five major areas that account for the Pentium's performance improvements.

Superscalar architecture

A 486 processor executes integer instructions through a single instruction pipeline in five discrete steps: prefetch, decode, address generate, execute and write back When the 486 is executing an instruction, the pipeline is unavailable until that instruction passes to the decode step. Only at that time is the pipeline free to begin another operation on the next instruction.

The Pentium has two independent pipelines called the U-pipeline and the V-pipeline. This means that while one instruction is being operated on through one pipeline, the subsequent instruction can be handled by the second pipeline. Certain classes of instructions cannot be performed in parallel since a subsequent instruction may depend on the outcome of the first instruction's execution. Special circuitry on the Pentium insures that these kind of dependent instructions are properly executed.

A processor having multiple instruction pipelines is termed superscaler architecture. For integer instructions, it's possible to execute two instructions in a single clock cycle. This is responsible for most of the performance gain of the Pentium processor.

Processor Cache

The time to access main memory is multiple clock cycles longer than to access on-chip memory. To increase speed, the 486 processors all contain 8K of this on-chip cache memory. By keeping a copy of the data and instructions the processor needs in the cache memory, less cycles are used to access the much slower main memory.

The Pentium processor doubles the amount of on-chip memory by providing a separate 8K for data cache and 8K for instruction (sometimes called code) cache. Intel claims that the data and instructions can be accessed immediately from the cache memory 95% of the time, speeding up performance enormously.

64-bit Data Bus

A 486 processor communicates with the outside world by using a 32-bit wide data bus. This means that 32-bits of information can be transferred from main memory to the processor with each clock cycle. The Pentium has a 64-bit wide data bus. This effectively doubles the amount of information the processor can transfer at once.

The Pentium also has a new burst transfer mode with built-in data integrity checking so information moves faster and more reliably over the data bus. These new features are capable of increasing the data transfer performance by 3 to 4 times over 486 systems.

Branch Prediction

Any processor spends a large number of clock cycles performing branches. The Pentium uses a Branch Target Buffer (BTB) to speed up branch performance. Here's how it works:

The BTB is a actually another small, high speed cache. When a branch instruction is encountered, the instruction and its branch address (the target) are saved in the BTB. In anticipation of a branch, the instruction code at the target address is preloaded into the instruction cache. If the prediction is right, the branch can be made immediately without having to wait for the instruction code at the target address to be loaded.

Intel claims that the BTB can be used to predict the correct branch in more than 90% of the cases.

Floating Point Processing

Many of today's business applications are designed to use the built-in math coprocessor found in 486DX and 486SL systems and the 487SX coprocessor for 486SX systems. Spreadsheets, database managers, computer aided design, numerical analysis, and almost all graphic-intensive applications are speeded up by the floating point processing performed by a math coprocessor.

Here's a simplified block diagram of the Pentium processor:

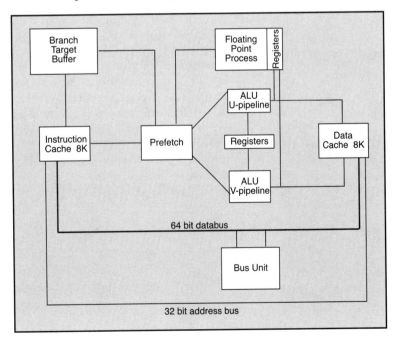

Simplified Pentium block diagram

In the Pentium, the floating point unit has been redesigned to give much better performance. Many of the floating point operations can be performed in a single clock cycle. Overall floating point operations are improved by a factor of 3 to 5 times.

Pentium computers

To date, Intel has announced two versions of the Pentium processor - a 60 MHz version and a 66 MHz version. The clock speeds are so close to each other for economic reasons.

Stuffing 3.1 million transistors onto a cracker-size chip isn't easy. Rather than discarding chips, which cannot pass the rigid quality control standards at 66 MHz, these chips become the 60 MHz versions. The 60 MHz version is fully functional, but not at the 66 MHz clock speed.

The first Pentium computers were delivered in June 1993. These computers are using the 60 MHz processor and have extensive cooling features. Some have mini-cooling fans that mount directly to the processor. Others have oversize heat sinks mounted onto the processor. All use oversize cooling fans to exhaust the hot air, by the Pentium processor from the computer case that generated .

One notable characteristic of these new computer systems is that they all use secondary caches. Many have 256K or 512K of secondary cache memory. Using a large, fast cache significantly reduces the time the Pentium must wait for external data thereby taking advantage of the Pentium's amazing processing speed.

Most of these earlier Pentium computers are being designed as file servers. As such, they are equipped to accomodate huge amounts of main memory, fast secondary storage - mostly SCSI class hard drives and a high performance EISA or Micro Channel bus. Intel has projected that it will deliver between 200,000 - 250,000 Pentium processors during 1993. With this limited supply, computer manufacturers will focus on producing high value, high priced Pentium computer systems.

Chapter 12 80486 Programs

The 80386/486 are not only more powerful than their predecessors, the 8088/8086 and 80286, but also provide new possibilities for programmers. The 80486 even has an integrated coprocessor and an 8K processor cache.

However, instead of being used for normal DOS applications, this coprocessor is used only during extremely complicated calculations (CAD and mathematical programs). In these applications, it produces a noticeable increase in computer speed.

32 -it address and a data bus

The 80386 (DX and SX) and the 80486 have an address and a data bus for 32 bits. Because of this, they can transmit 32-bit data at one time and execute corresponding commands. When a true 32-bit data transport doesn't occur over a bus (see Chapter 4), the 32-bit software produces only a partial increase in speed.

This fact is irrelevant when using DOS because DOS software uses almost no 32-bit commands. (Such programs couldn't be executed on the majority of PCs anyway.)

So, an 80386SX with its 16-bit data bus can be used by almost any user. Also, its price is equivalent to its performance. The SX variant of the 80386 is also capable of executing 32-bit commands.

Data transfer over the 16-bit data bus occurs in the multiplex method. Here every 32-bit number is transmitted in two packages of 16 bits each. As in the 80286, the address bus has 24 bits, which reduces the addressable memory to a maximum of 16 Meg. Since this limitation is barely noticeable, motherboards can be produced more easily and less expensively.

Requires more logic components

But even with the 80386 currently available, larger amounts of memory cannot be used because the gate arrays aren't capable of controlling more memory. For additional memory, more logic components must be placed on the circuit board or the 32-bit connectors of the bus system.

Multitasking capability

The 80386 is capable of multitasking. This means that it can execute several applications simultaneously. This feature is also used in the OS/2 and UNIX operating systems. There are also alternative DOS versions, for example Multi-user DOS/386 from Digital Research, that provide multitasking for DOS applications.

In Real mode, several DOS applications can execute simultaneously. A higher level program or a user interface has assigned them their own "world". Windows 3.0 and above also operate according to this principle.

The processor also has commands that enable you to move address space. Because of this, a program can operate with the Expanded Memory Standard (EMS) under software control.

12.1 DOS Driver and Programs

Easy to manage memory

Another advantage of the 80386/486 is its ability to translate between physical and logical addresses. During this "paging", any memory locations can obtain a logical address, which differs from the real physical address. So, it's possible to manage memory according to EMS, without using bank switching hardware or a complicated way of copying memory.

An entire series of software uses this capability, including MS-/PC-DOS and also special memory managers. These programs not only make an Expanded Memory Manager available, but also provide more memory for DOS applications.

Using memory under DOS 5.0 and DOS 6.0

Using extended memory

With the combination of HIMEM.SYS and EMM386.EXE, for the first time extended memory can be used efficiently. XMS, almost an extended memory with regulated access methods, up to 32 Meg, EMS according to LIM/EMS 4.0, a High Memory Area (HMA, directly above the 1 Meg limit), as well as Upper Memory Blocks (UMB, between 640K and 1 Meg) are available.

DOS Extended Memory Manager

The extended memory area beyond 1 Meg, which can only be addressed indirectly, could also be used by the 80286 computer for certain purposes. In most cases, this involved applications where the addresses aren't switched, but areas are copied, such as cache and buffer programs and virtual disk drives (RAM Disks).

Using high memory

There are also programs, which allow DOS to use the high memory area from 64K, at the lower limit, to the lower limit of the extended memory.

Extended Memory Manager HIMEM.SYS

Using HIMEM.SYS

HIMEM.SYS is an Extended Memory Manager that uses memory above the 640K limit. It also makes 64K of HMA available. DOS 5.0 and 6.0 can be loaded here by using the following entry in CONFIG.SYS:

```
DOS = High
```

This will provide more than 600K of conventional memory.

The HIMEM.SYS driver is loaded by the following entry in the CONFIG.SYS:

```
DEVICE=(Path)HIMEM.SYS (Option)
```

(Path) indicates the drive and the subdirectory in which HIMEM.SYS can be found. The following options are available:

/HMAMIN=xxxx

> A program must request at least xxxxK in the High Memory Area, or no HMA will be made available to it. The default value is 0K. The valid range of values is 0 through 63K.

/NUMHANDLES=xxx

> A maximum of xxx memory blocks can be used by the programs simultaneously in the High Memory Area. The valid range is between 0 and 128; the default setting is 32.

/INT15=xxxx

> Reserves xxxxK of extended memory for programs that address extended memory through the INT15 call.

/A20CONTROL:ON

HIMEM.SYS takes control of the a20 line.

/A20CONTROL:OFF

HIMEM.SYS does not take control of the a20 line.

The version of HIMEM.SYS included with Windows permits additional parameters.

QUICK TIP

Windows 3.0 operates only with its own HIMEM.SYS driver. If CONFIG.SYS already contains the driver call for the DOS 4.0 version of HIMEM, replace it with the one from Windows 3.0. The HIMEM.SYS from MS-DOS 5.0 can be used by Windows 3.0.

The additional parameters for HIMEM.SYS are:

/SHADOW:ON or OFF

HIMEM should activate Shadow RAM (ON) or not (OFF). If PCs with Shadow RAM don't have enough extended memory and have the capability to switch between Shadow RAM and extended memory, Windows normally deactivates it to make as much extended memory as possible available for itself.

By using this option, the user can determine the use of Shadow RAM in advance.

/MACHINE=(Type)

Informs HIMEM.SYS of the computer type, if it couldn't identify it by itself. At the moment, the Acer 1100 is the only machine that needs this parameter. It's placed behind the parameter, as in this example.

/MACHINE=ACER 1100

The following information is possible (and required):

A T	IBM AT
PS2	IBM model PS/2
PT1CASCADE	Phoenix Cascade BIOS
HPVECTRA	HP Vectra (classic)
ATT6300PLUS	AT&T 6300 plus

ACER1100	Acer 1100
TOSHIBA	Toshiba 1600 or 1200XE
WYSE	Wyse 286 m/c (12.5 MHz)

Hard drive cache

Cache memory is intermediate memory for the hard drive. MS-DOS 4.0 and 5.0 contain the Smartdrive cache driver, which creates and manages the cache memory in the extended memory area. This driver is installed from CONFIG.SYS:

```
DEVICE=SMARTDRV.SYS {size} {/A}
```

The following parameters are available:

size: Size of the cache-memory in K. If Smartdrive is called without an indication of size, 256K are reserved.

/A: The cache is created in the expanded memory instead of the extended memory. In this case, the expanded memory must have been previously prepared with a management program.

QUICK TIP

If you're using SMARTDRV.SYS with a software EMS manager, such as EMS386.SYS or 386MAX, the speed won't be increased. The Expanded Memory Manager is mainly used for making the expanded memory more usable for DOS programs.

RAM disk

A RAM disk is a memory area that's managed the same way as a diskette drive or a hard drive. The various DOS versions have RAM disk drivers with different names. All are similar in principle.

The RAM disk driver of PC-DOS 4.0 is called VDISK.SYS. MS-DOS has RAMDRIVE.SYS. VDISK stands for "virtual disk". The driver is loaded from the CONFIG.SYS file. Its syntax is as follows:

```
DEVICE=(Path)VDISK.SYS (parameter) or DEVICE=RAM {size}
{Sectors} {entries} {/E:Sectors} {/X:Sectors}
```

The parameters are:

size:	Capacity of the virtual drive in K. Minimum size is 1 K. If a size isn't indicated, 64K is reserved.
Sectors:	Size of the blocks, in which the data is stored. Transmission speed increases with the size of these sectors. However, more space is wasted, if a sector isn't filled completely.
entries:	Maximum number of file entries in the RAM disk. This permits the limitation of entries in the directory of this "diskette". Default setting is 64 entries, but the number can vary between 2 and 512.
/E:	The memory area for the virtual disk isn't reserved in the main memory, but in extended memory. Optionally, the maximum number of sectors to be read at one time can be between 1 and 8.
/A:	The memory area for the virtual disk isn't reserved in the main memory, but in the expanded memory. Optionally, the maximum number of sectors to be read at one time can be between 1 and 8. The move only works if EMM386.SYS or another memory manager was used to activate an expanded memory driver. The VDISK driver cannot be installed in EMS.

DOS Expanded Memory Manager

The DOS operating system, in Versions 4.0, 5.0, and 6.0, contain two device drivers for the expanded memory area. They use paging made available by the 80386/80486 microprocessors and can be used only with 386/486 systems.

According to the EMS procedure, first a driver, which emulates the required hardware on the PC, must be loaded. Then the actual software, which controls the bank switching, can be loaded.

Expanded Memory Manager

The EMM386.SYS driver is used on 386 systems to permit using extended memory according to the expanded memory procedure. The driver is installed from CONFIG.SYS:

```
DEVICE=(Path)EMM386.SYS(parameter)
```

Path	is the drive and subdirectory, in which the driver is located.
parameter	can indicate additional options that influence the operations of EMM386.SYS.
nnnn	is the size of the extended memory, in k, that's reserved for expanded memory. If parameters aren't provided, all of extended memory is automatically obtained.
X:mmmm-nnnn	is the memory area of hexadecimal mmmm to nnnn not to be used as expanded memory.
RAM	permits the use of EMS and Upper Memory.
NOEMS	means that Upper Memory is used, but EMS isn't available.
Mx	is the start address of the page frame for EMS that should be at the location indicated by x. In this case, x means the following address (hexadecimal value):

1	c400h	2	c800h
3	cc00h	4	d000h
5	d400h	6	d800h
7	dc00h	8	e000h

L=nnnn	determines how much XMS should be made available.
W=ON/OFF	determines whether the Weitek coprocessor should be used.
Y:Path	determines where the EMM386.EXE should be after the boot (e.g., with terminals that don't have a disk drive and boot from a network).

Expanded Memory Emulator

The XMAEMS.SYS driver emulates an IBM Personal System/2 80286 Expanded Memory Adapter/A on the PC with a 386 processor.

Install before XMA2EMS.SYS

This driver must be installed before the XMA2EMS.SYS driver. Besides XMAEM, additional drivers, which use paging, cannot be loaded. This driver doesn't work with other memory management programs. The driver is installed from CONFIG.SYS as follows:

```
DEVICE=XMAEM.SYS {pages}
```

The number of pages from extended memory, which are used for the expanded memory, can be limited to the value indicated. The rest remains available as extended memory for other drivers (Cache, RAM disk). If a value isn't indicated, the complete extended memory area is used for EMS.

XMA2EMS.SYS driver

The actual EMS management is performed by the XMA2EMS.SYS driver. It executes on all PCs that provide bank switching logic for the expanded memory.

This includes:

> •   386SX with NEAT chips
>
> •   Intel Above Board or compatible memory expansions
>
> •   software expansions (e.g., with XMAEM.SYS)

The driver is installed from CONFIG.SYS with the following call:

```
DEVICE=XMA2EMS.SYS (parameter)
```

The following parameters are possible:

FRAME=nnnn: Hexadecimal start address of the memory window for EMS. If parameters aren't provided, the page frame is at D000. 64K of consecutive memory must be usable starting at the address indicated.

Px=nnnn: If no consecutive memory area is available in the High Memory area, a separate area may be specified (*address nnnn*) for every memory page *x* of 16K. *n n n n* must be indicated in hexadecimal. The parameter FRAME cannot be used with P.

Expanded Memory Manager EMM386.EXE

EMM386.EXE is an expanded memory manager, which makes using memory above the 1 Meg border possible. It also makes Upper

Memory available. With DOS 5.0 and 6.0, this driver can be installed from CONFIG.SYS as follows:

```
DOS = High,UMB
```

This area can be used for storing drivers and TSR programs, which makes more of conventional memory available for applications.

The HIMEM.SYS driver must be installed before EMM386.EXE.

```
DEVICE = (Path)HIMEM.SYS (Options)
DEVICE = (Path)EMM386.EXE (Options)
```

(Path) contains the drive and the subdirectory, in which HIMEM.SYS and EMM386.EXE are located.

The following parameters may be used when installing from CONFIG.SYS:

xxxx	A simple value describes the size of the extended memory.
X:xxxx-yyyy	With this you reserve an area of the Upper Memory for use as an EMS page frame.
RAM	Makes the use of Upper Memory possible.
NOEMS	EMS is not made available. This saves 64K of Upper Memory.
FRAME=xxxx	You can indicate the address of the EMS page frame here.
Pn=xxxx	With this parameter you can assign separate addresses to the individual page frames (n=0...3).
B=xxxx	This parameter permits setting a lower limit for the position of the page frames.
L=minXMS	Sets a minimum value for XMS memory.
A=xxx	Determines the number of Alternate Register Map Sets. They accelerate multitasking environments, such as Windows 3.0. Every entry requires 4K of extended memory.
H=xxx	Every EMS memory request reserves a handle (ID-number). The default value is 64, which is usually sufficient.

W=ON/OFF   Switches the Weitek coprocessor support on and off.

Y:(Path)   Sets the path where EMM386.EXE can be found after booting (for diskless workstations).

An example of a useful CONFIG.SYS file

To obtain as much free memory for applications as possible, the CONFIG.SYS could be structured as follows:

```
DEVICE      = \DOS\HIMEM.SYS
DEVICE      = \DOS\EMM386.EXE RAM FRAME=E000
DOS         = High,UMB
DEVICEHIGH  = \DOS\MOUSE.SYS
```

DR DOS 6.0

The DR DOS 6.0 memory management utilities are located under MemoryMAX, which consists of three device drivers and five commands.

HIDOS.SYS

The HIDOS driver is used to make the High Memory area (HMA) of 64K beyond the 1 Meg limit available for DOS applications.

Installing

Install the driver either manually or by using the Setup program. If you do this manually, you'll know exactly what DR DOS does with your memory. The driver is started, like all device drivers, from the CONFIG.SYS. Add the following line in the file:

```
DEVICE=(Path)HIDOS.SYS(parameter)
```

(Path) contains the drive and subdirectory, in which HIDOS.SYS is located. The following options are available as parameters:

/AUTOSCAN   Search certain memory area.

/BDOS   Move the DR DOS operating system kernel.

/CHIPSET=designation
                   To use the capabilities of modern gate array chipsets in the computer, use this option to inform HIDOS.SYS about the type of chipset. The following possibilities are available with this option:

AUTO	HIDOS.SYS automatically identifies the chipset (standard).
NEAT	Chips & Technologies NEAT, NEAT SX, LEAPSet, LEAPSetsx.
SCAT	Chips & Technologies SCAT.
ENSUMB	EMS 4.0 or Enhanced EMS blocks of the Upper Memory area should be used for Shadow RAM.
EMSALL	The complete Upper Memory area of the EMS, including the page frames, should be used for Shadow RAM.
RAM	Shadow RAM should be used as normal RAM.
NONE	Shadow RAM isn't available or shouldn't be used.
/EXCLUDE	Don't use a certain memory area.
/INCLUDE	Use a certain memory area.
/ROM	Create Shadow RAM.
/USE	Use memory area without preceding tests.
/VIDEO	Use memory areas of certain graphics cards.
/XBDA	Normally HIDOS.SYS moves every data area of the extended BIOS from the upper to the lower portion of the main memory. With this parameter, you can suppress the move. For example, you can do this when certain programs expect the BIOS information at the top location in memory and cannot function if HIDOS.SYS moves it.

EMM386.SYS

Upper Memory

Besides managing the expanded memory, the Expanded Memory Manager of DR DOS 6.0 also manages the Upper Memory area between 640K and 1 Meg.

The EMM386.SYS driver cannot be used with memory management programs from other sources. The memory driver is installed from CONFIG.SYS as follows:

```
DEVICE=(Path)EMM386.SYS (parameter)
```

For (Path), enter the drive and the subdirectory, in which the driver can be found.

/AUTOSCAN	Search certain memory area.
/BDOS	Move DR DOS operating system kernel.
/COMPAQ	386 and 486 computers with more than 1 Meg of RAM from Compaq have an additional 256K of extended memory, which EMM386.SYS uses after setting this parameter.
/EXCLUDE	Certain memory areas aren't used.
/FRAME	Determine page frame.
/INCLUDE	Use certain memory areas.
/KB	Determine memory for EMS.
/LOWEMM	Instead of being moved to Upper Memory, EMM386 should remain in main memory.

This option can be used if you're using other expansion cards, which have their own BIOS. For example, network cards, SCSI controllers, or controllers, such as the new 2.88 Meg drives, can limit memory space.

QUICK TIP

/ROM	Create Shadow RAM.
/USE	Use memory area without previous tests.
/VIDEO	Use memory areas of certain graphics cards.
/WINSTD	Windows 3.0 can also operate with EMM386.SYS of DR-DOS 6.0 in Standard mode. Usually this isn't possible.
/XBDA	Normally HIDOS.SYS moves every data area of the extended BIOS from the upper to the lower portion of the main memory. With this parameter you can suppress the move. For example, you can do this when certain programs expect the BIOS information at the upper portion of the memory and cannot function if HIDOS.SYS moves it.

EMMXMA.SYS

The XMA memory driver for PS 2 models has only one option.

/FRAME=xxxx   The page frame should start at the
hexadecimal address xxxx.

Other commands

DR DOS 6.0 also contains several commands allowing you to use
the Upper or High Memory area for internal data. These
commands, which we'll describe in the following sections, can be
used only if HIDOS.SYS was already loaded.

HIBUFFERS

Using HIBUFFERS instead of BUFFERS

If the command HIBUFFERS is used instead of BUFFERS, DR DOS
6.0 can also create the buffers in extended memory. If the HIDOS
switch is set to ON, the buffers are created in High DOS or in the
Upper Memory area. If the switch is set to OFF, they are created
in normal memory.

HIDEVICE

HIDEVICE loads device drivers into high memory. The syntax is
as follows:

```
HIDEVICE=(Option) file description
```

Possible options are:

SIZE=nnn   The application is loaded into the Upper/High
memory only if nnnK of memory is available.
nnn must be indicated in hexadecimal.

The following drivers can be moved in this way:

• ANSI.SYS	• DISPLAY.SYS
• PRINTER.SYS	• VDISK.SYS

HIDOS

HIDOS moves the operating system kernel to the Upper Memory
area.

HIINSTALL

HIINSTALL loads memory resident programs into the Upper Memory from CONFIG.SYS.

HILOAD

HILOAD loads memory resident programs from the DOS level or a batch file into the Upper Memory.

12.2 Memory Management Programs

QUICK TIP

Before DR DOS 6.0 and MS-DOS 5.0 and 6.0 existed, some programs tried to solve the memory situation in IBM compatible PCs. One of the best known of these is 386MAX.

> Although this section describes 386MAX, it's completely suitable for the 80486 and the PCs discussed in this book. A newer version of 386MAX, called BLUEMAX, is also available for 486 computers.

Remember, the i486 is simply a 386, a cache, and a math coprocessor integrated on one chip.

Currently the next best solution for memory management problems is to use QEMM from Quarterdeck. This enables you to make the various memory types available in a flexible and stable way.

MS-DOS 6.0 users can take advantage of the enhanced memory optimization provided by the MEMMAKER utility. This utility examines your CONFIG.SYS and AUTOEXEC.BAT files and makes any changes necessary to provide the maximum amount of free conventional memory.

Use the following DOS 5.0 and 6.0 setting together with the DOS 5.0 or 6.0 function DEVICEHIGH to move drivers and LH to load TSRs into high memory:

```
DOS = High,UMB
```

The DOS 5.0 functions reject QEMM and replace it with EMM386.EXE and HIMEM.SYS.

386MAX 6.0

386 is an EMS-Manager

386MAX is a memory manager for computers with an 80386 or 80486 microprocessor. It makes full memory utilization under DOS possible. The available memory can be used selectively in the extended and/or the expanded memory process.

386MAX operates in the expanded mode according to the EMS specification 4.0, which not only uses a small window between 640K and 1 Meg for the switching segments, but also includes the complete memory area.

Memory juggler

Memory resident programs are automatically placed above the 640K limit in the Upper Memory Block (UMB). This makes conventional memory available even when Sidekick and other background programs are waiting. 386MAX provides a software-based Shadow RAM option, where the ROM content of the system BIOS, the Video electronic, and the hard drive controller are copied into the faster RAM.

The program determines in which bank the fastest RAM is located and automatically stores the main memory area there to increase performance. It uses all memory between 640K and 1 Meg, which isn't occupied by ROM, and supplements it with conventional memory areas.

386MAX supports the Weitek coprocessor and requires only 3K of conventional memory. The current version of 386MAX (6.01) is compatible with the HIMEM.SYS driver of Windows (and MS-DOS 5.0).

12.3 Multitasking

On the PC multitasking is accomplished by having several applications share the memory and the processor. This means that a program or operating system that makes multitasking possible must manage these two resources differently than an application that runs alone.

The original PC operating system, DOS, isn't capable of managing several tasks simultaneously by itself. It cannot recognize when two programs access the same memory or use the same file. There are two ways to make multitasking possible on the PC:

> • An additional program, which takes over managing the different tasks, is loaded
>
> • DOS is completely replaced by another operating system, which offers the multitasking capability

DOS can load programs, which are activated by pressing certain keys, into memory. These programs are Terminate and Stay Resident (TSR) programs.

Although these programs can be called at any time from other applications, this isn't true multitasking because the other applications don't continue to execute. The TSR program simply diverts the attention of the microprocessor to itself, as long as it's active.

Multitasking vs emulated multitasking

True multitasking shouldn't be confused with emulated multitasking. While the idea of the multitasking assumes that all applications execute simultaneously, emulated multitasking only switches temporarily between several applications, which are in memory. While one application is active, the others are stopped. Programs that execute according to this principle were available on the XT computer.

Even true multitasking applications differ in the amount of protection available for applications. For example, if one application crashes, how much are the other tasks and the manager (program or operating system) affected? Only the 80386 processor provides a mode which is able to protect the system in these instances.

How multitasking works

To make multitasking possible, the management program or operating system must be able to assign the memory and the processor time among the applications. The Real mode of the 80386 and 80486 is also important to multitasking.

The most important function is the division of processor time. To actually work simultaneously, the PC would have to use several processors executing in parallel.

This is possible with the Compaq Systempro. Almost simultaneous operation is achieved when the computer switches very rapidly between the various applications. This method uses the time slicing principle.

"Time sharing"

This method was used in large computers, in which it was called time sharing. Every program is allocated a certain amount of processor time, in which it can be active. As soon as this time has elapsed, its status is stored and the next application is activated. When it reaches its turn again, it can continue to work exactly where it was stopped.

There are also additional priorities, which can be assigned to a task. This is important if time critical applications run in a task. A PC used for process control must assign a higher priority to this task than the other tasks. The priority also plays an important part in the division of the hardware resources. An application with higher priority can access the hard drive and other interfaced peripheral devices (printer, etc.) before the other applications.

One way to control the memory and the processor time is through a management program which is started from DOS. This program arranges all programs into a waiting queue. By pressing a key, clicking the mouse, or entering a command, one of the other applications is activated and moved to the foreground.

If another task is activated, the management program stores the registers and system variables so the user can continue working exactly at the same point where the task was stopped.

Preemptive context switching

Used mainly by DOS auxiliary programs

This process is called preemptive context switching and is used mainly by the DOS auxiliary programs that provide multitasking capabilities (DESQview, VM/386). The term "preemptive" indicates that the multitasking manager protects the applications from each other.

However, with cooperative context switching, the application takes over control and when its time has expired, gives it to the next task. This method is used mainly by operating systems that make multitasking possible (OS/2, UNIX, Multi-user DOS, and PC-MOS).

DESQview 386

With DESQview, multitasking was possible on the XT and the AT under DOS although these PCs didn't offer any support for these applications. Only the 80386 microprocessor, using a program or operating system, could execute several applications without drastically slowing each one.

To use these capabilities, DESQview was combined with the QEMM 386 memory manager. This combination is called DESQview 386.

Unlike VM/386, DESQview allows you to run applications in windows. So, you can actually see the applications running simultaneously.

DESQview 386 uses the following capabilities of the 80386 microprocessor:

- Real Mode

- High DOS memory

- Virtual screen display

- Protection against badly written programs, which directly address memory instead of adhering to DOS standards

- Protected mode software

DESQview functions with all Protected mode programs, whose DOS Extender operates according to the VCPI standard.

DESQview 386 also supports:

- Automatic installation of programs, such as Quattro Pro, DOS-5.0-Shell, Aldus PageMaker, Word 5.0, Microsoft Excel, and DataEase.

- Various text sizes and resolutions with VGA, EGA, MCGA, or Hercules.

- Full page monitors.

Installation

To install DESQview 386, you must have an 80386 processor and 640K of RAM. The installation consists of two steps:

- Installing QEMM 386.

> • Installing DESQview. The DESQview diskette must be inserted in drive A: and the installation routine started with:

```
INSTALL
```

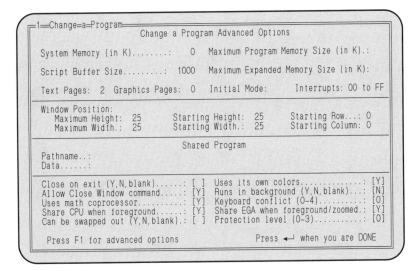

```
┌1═Change═a═Program═════════════════════════════════════════════
                        Change a Program Advanced Options

  System Memory (in K)........:   0   Maximum Program Memory Size (in K).:

  Script Buffer Size.........:  1000  Maximum Expanded Memory Size (in K):

  Text Pages: 2  Graphics Pages: 0   Initial Mode:      Interrupts: 00 to FF

  Window Position:
     Maximum Height:  25     Starting Height:  25     Starting Row...:  0
     Maximum Width.:  25     Starting Width.:  25     Starting Column:  0

                               Shared Program
  Pathname..:
  Data......:

  Close on exit (Y,N,blank)......: [ ]  Uses its own colors.............: [Y]
  Allow Close Window command.....: [Y]  Runs in background (Y,N,blank)...: [N]
  Uses math coprocessor..........: [Y]  Keyboard conflict (0-4).........: [0]
  Share CPU when foreground......: [Y]  Share EGA when foreground/zoomed.: [Y]
  Can be swapped out (Y,N,blank).: [ ]  Protection level (0-3)..........: [0]

    Press F1 for advanced options              Press ↵ when you are DONE
```

DESQview mask for "Change A Program"

During the installation, DESQview automatically searches the hard drive for executable programs and installs them. The user can also do this later at any time.

After the installation, the DESQview systems must be set up. The installation routine starts the Setup program automatically. You can use either the simple or advanced version. The simple setup requires only two entries:

> • Color or monochrome screen
>
> • Type of mouse (Microsoft or Mouse Systems)

The advanced setup requires more information from the user:

> • Serial port, where the Auto Dialer Modem is interfaced (default setting is COM1, if serial mouse COM2 is used)
>
> • Type and extent of colors
>
> • Logical drives, which DESQview uses for switching
>
> • Type and connection of the mouse, if available

- Performance

- Window positions of the individual virtual computers which DESQview creates

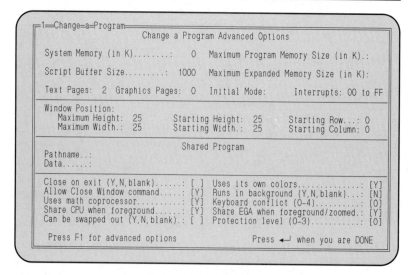

```
┌─1══Change═a═Program═════════════════════════════════════════
│                    Change a Program Advanced Options
│  System Memory (in K)........:    0  Maximum Program Memory Size (in K).:
│  Script Buffer Size.........:  1000  Maximum Expanded Memory Size (in K):
│  Text Pages: 2  Graphics Pages: 0   Initial Mode:      Interrupts: 00 to FF
│  Window Position:
│     Maximum Height:  25      Starting Height:  25      Starting Row...: 0
│     Maximum Width.:  25      Starting Width.:  25      Starting Column: 0
│                              Shared Program
│  Pathname..:
│  Data......:
│  Close on exit (Y,N,blank).......: [ ]  Uses its own colors..............: [Y]
│  Allow Close Window command.....: [Y]  Runs in background (Y,N,blank)...: [N]
│  Uses math coprocessor..........: [Y]  Keyboard conflict (0-4)..........: [0]
│  Share CPU when foreground......: [Y]  Share EGA when foreground/zoomed.: [Y]
│  Can be swapped out (Y,N,blank).: [ ]  Protection level (0-3)...........: [0]
│  Press F1 for advanced options          Press ◄┘ when you are DONE
```

The advanced options in DESQview

After the program installation, DESQview executes the AUTOINST program. The entire hard drive is searched for executable program files. AUTOINST first searches only the partition, in which DESQview was installed. To include software from other logical drives, the program must be started with the input of the letter, for example:

```
AUTOINST D:
```

The programs can also be included manually with the proper menu item. DESQview itself can be stored in expanded memory, if it was started with XDV instead of DV. The QEXT.SYS device driver must have already been started from CONFIG.SYS.

Using DESQview

The Change A Program menu is used to call and modify the information about a program. Press F1 to activate the menu for advanced options, in which system settings can also be changed.

The following settings of the two menus influence the performance of the system. These settings are activated if a "Y" (for Yes) is entered.

Writes text directly to the screen

For the display, the program writes directly to the screen memory (default setting is Yes).

DESQview programs should be permitted to execute as full display applications. If you can't learn what you need to know from the documentation or the manufacturer, select No and experiment with various settings.

Virtualize text/graphics

The program should execute in the window (default setting is Yes).

Here the user can determine if the program always uses the window (default setting is Yes), operates in the window only in the text mode (T), or never functions in a window.

Run in Background

The program should execute only in the background.

If DESQview isn't compatible with your hardware, you can start the program with the following parameters:

/OK	The keyboard test, which DESQview usually performs at the start, is skipped.
/EET	DESQview manipulates expanded memory directly. This is important if you're using expanded memory and have loaded a disk cache driver before the start.

Share CPU when in foreground

All other applications are stopped when the program in the foreground executes. This accelerates the program because the CPU is concerned about only the active program (default setting is "Yes").

VM/386

The VM/386 (Virtual Manager for 386) was developed for the Real mode of the 80386 microprocessor. It differs from DESQview 386, since there's a different version for PCs with the 80286 processor and without the QEMM 386. With this mode, a multitasking system can execute the applications independently of each other. So if a system crash occurs in the application, the other applications aren't affected.

VM/386 divides the 386 into several virtual machines, which act independently of each other. Each one of these parts is assigned a certain amount of processor time and a priority. If a task is active, it occupies the entire screen. The applications cannot execute in a window, as, for example, with DESQview.

The user divides the computer into several virtual machines in the installation menu. Each machine has its own DOS with its own system environment (command processor, AUTOEXEC.BAT, and CONFIG.SYS). The size of the memory assigned to a virtual machine can be, depending on the desired application, 128, 256, 384, 512 or 640K. Beyond that, another application can use additional extended memory according to the expanded memory procedure, with the help of the VMEMM memory manager.

The Switcher has control, which is activated by the otherwise seldom used system query key. The Manager presents the virtual PCs in a selection box and the user can easily select them. It's possible to switch the virtual computers without calling the Manager. Simply double-click the [SysRq] key, while holding down the [Alt] key.

Installation

VM/386 makes some demands on your hardware. The program needs at least 2 Meg of RAM to configure the minimum configuration of two virtual computers. VM/386 works only on the Inboard 386/AT; it doesn't work on the Inboard 386/PC. It also doesn't work with the Toshiba Laptop T5100.

Problems can occur with some hardware components, including SCSI hard drives, hard drives formatted with Golden Bow, or Priam utilities. Certain graphics cards (ATI VGA Wonder, ATI Professional VGA, Wyse 700) can also cause problems. The Zenith graphics cards 449 and 386 can be used only in the EGA mode. You should ensure that the VM/386 operates correctly with your hardware.

Before the actual installation begins, you must remove all entries, from the original CONFIG.SYS and the AUTOEXEC.BAT files, which:

- Call a device driver or a program that operates in Protected mode

- Calls a device driver which makes the memory usable

- Installs a TSR program

TSR programs and drivers for RAM disks, cache, and other memory utilizations can be installed later in the AUTOEXEC.BAT for the individual virtual machines. Also a mouse driver can be installed locally. Programs for the memory management (e.g., 386MAX) cannot be used. So VM/386 also includes VMEMM. VM/386 also includes a RAM disk, to which all virtual machines can have access, and a disk cache.

You must make a working copy of the program diskette and boot the computer again with this diskette in drive A:. This is important, because VM/386 needs the information in the ROM BIOS. It copies this information into a file called VMINTS.

You should boot again from your hard drive and start the installation routine with SETUP. This automatically selects the correct drivers for the video card and the hard drive.

If you change your hardware (e.g., install a new graphics card), you must execute the installation procedure again with an updated version of the VMINTS file. Copy the file to the hard drive in the VM/386 directory.

After the Virtual Manager has been installed, the single virtual computers are created. Select the Create Virtual Machine menu in the program. Here you can specify the following settings for your machine:

- Number of the virtual machine

- Designation of the machine

- Memory requirement (between 128 and 640K)

- Requirement for expanded memory

- Size of the time slice that is assigned to the virtual machine

- Whether the program should be active only in the foreground and after a move into the background, if the program execution should stop

- Priority of the tasks

Also, some internal data can be changed in an Advanced menu. All these parameters are stored in a profile and can be changed at any time. Profiles can be created and stored for use at a later time. The machine number Null (VM0) is always the VM Manager; the other

PCs are designated as VM and a consecutive number. Their name usually indicates the memory size, but this isn't mandatory.

With Terminate VM, the virtual machine is removed from the memory again. With Update VM, changes can be made to a virtual computer while it's operating. Reboot VM resets the virtual machine. This is important if the imaginary PC crashes.

As we mentioned, each machine can operate independently of the others. Each one can be operated with its own command processor and its own configuration file. This file is named CONFIG.VM instead of CONFIG.SYS.

Besides the VMEMM memory manager, VM/386 also has a driver for a RAM disk, which can be accessed by all virtual machines. This driver is called from a CONFIG.VM file. Also the AUTOEXEC.BAT file receives the new extension VM. Besides the usual calls (PROMPT, PATH, etc.), the utilities required for VM/386 are also called.

Expanded Memory driver

The VMEMM driver makes it possible for a virtual machine to address the memory according to the EMS procedure. The driver is included by adding the following to CONFIG.SYS:

```
DEVICE=VMEMM.SYS (parameter)
```

The following parameters are possible:

/QUIET	The start message of the VMEMM driver is suppressed during its call.
/FRAME=nnnn	Sets the start address of the 64K page frame to the hexadecimal value nnnn (default setting D000).
/FRAME=LOW	Places the 64K window into the low DOS memory area directly after the VMEMM.SYS driver.

The VM/386 also includes additional utilities:

SLEEP	Deactivates a virtual machine to a "standby" mode to make more computer time available for other virtual machines.
VMDB	Displays the current register content. The VM/386 Debugger is activated when a terminal is attached to the serial interface.

VMDEVS	Shows the current connections of the peripherals.
VMEGA128	Sets the size of the video memory to 128K.
VMEGA256	Sets the size of the video memory to 256K.
VMEGABGG	Activates the refresh of a screen content of a high resolution video card.
VMEGACLR	Clears the content of the EGA/VGA register.
VMEGAFGG	Deactivates the refresh of a screen content of a video card that operates in the graphics mode and is active in the background. This increases the speed but the display must be restored again with the VMEGABGG command when the task is moved to the foreground again.
VMEGAFST	Terminates tracking of the register contents started by VMEGATRP.
VMEGASTA	Displays the current EGA or VGA video status and the register content.
VMEGATRP	All video refresh procedures are correctly executed when a virtual machine is switched from the foreground to the background and vice versa. The registers are tracked and stored separately. This slows down the execution of the applications in the foreground.
VMFG	Moves a designated virtual machine to the foreground.
VMFSS	Starts the file share subsystem. This program must execute on a virtual machine before it can access the hard drive.
VMID	Displays the ID number of the active virtual machine.
VMLINK	Links a peripheral device with the current virtual machine.
VMMSEMOD	Changes the IRQ number used by a bus mouse.
VMTDDMOD	Program for creating a new device driver, in which an existing one is modified.

12.4 Other Programs

Many memory management and multitasking programs are available for the 386/486 microprocessors. There are also some other areas in which interesting software can be found.

4DOS

This program could almost be considered an operating system. 4DOS is a command interpreter (a shell), which is used instead of the COMMAND.COM.

4DOS adds about 40 new commands to DOS, regardless of the version, and significantly enhances its user-friendliness. This program is compatible with MS-/PC-DOS from Version 2.0 to 5.0. 4DOS needs only about 4K of the conventional memory and only 1K of extended memory.

In addition to the executable file types COM, EXE, and BAT, there is a fast batch type, called the BTM (Batch To Memory) and others that can be defined by the user. For all commands, there is an on-line Help option, which explains how to use the command.

The first improvement to the current COMMAND.COM can be seen when using the new Interpreter. It has an editing function that allows you to place the last command that was entered in the input line. Simply use the ⬆ and ⬇ cursor keys to do this. Unlike DOS, the input buffer isn't limited to one line. Use the HISTORY command to display a complete list of the commands. You can set the command buffer to a size ranging from 512 to 8192 characters.

4DOS also features enhanced wildcards, file descriptions, an ALIAS list, and an enhanced DIR command.

This program can be used with the 80286 and higher processors. The program consists of 4DOS.COM, the program loader, a switching program, as well as 4DOS286. 4DOS also has additional files, such as the help file, which belong to some commands and options.

Installation

To install 4DOS, you'll need at least 70K of free memory; with expanded memory 4K is sufficient. Also, an MS or PC-DOS version should be available as the "foundation". The easiest method is to start the INSTALL routine, which is included with 4DOS. This routine copies the files automatically, creates the paths, and enhances the CONFIG.SYS and AUTOEXEC.BAT system files. If you want to use all the capabilities, install 4DOS manually.

After the KEYSTACK.SYS, 4DOS.COM, and 4DOS286.EXE files have been decompressed, they must be copied to the root directory of the hard drive. When the decompression is complete, copy the HELP.EXE and DOS.HLP files into a subdirectory.

Then determine whether you want to want to operate 4DOS in memory resident mode or in swapping mode. In the memory resident mode, the complete command interpreter remains in main memory and requires about 70K. This mode only makes sense, if extended or expanded memory isn't available. In the swapping mode, only a 4K portion remains in the main memory. The rest is loaded into the extended or expanded memory and placed in main memory when needed.

After copying the files and determining the operating mode of 4DOS, the CONFIG.SYS and the AUTOEXEC.BAT are modified to work with the new command interpreter. Add the following command:

```
SHELL=C:\4DOS.COM (Options)
```

The options can be attached to the SHELL call of 4DOS. Remember that the SHELL line cannot be longer than 33 characters.

/P	Indicates that 4DOS is the primary command interpreter.
@	Stops the input and passes control to the file, which is indicated after the @.
/A:n	The Alias list is nK long (default setting is 1,024K).
/C (command)	Loads 4DOS only to execute a command and then removes it again from the memory. Instead of being used with the SHELL command, this option is used when 4DOS is called externally.
/E:n	Sets the size of the environment memory to nK (default setting is 512 bytes). If an addition sign precedes n, the current environment memory is increased by n bytes. If a U is placed after the memory indication, 4DOS moves the environment memory into the extended memory.

/H:n	Sets the size of the HISTORY memory to n bytes (default setting is 1024 bytes).
/L:(Path)	Indicates the path, in which the 4DOS286.EXE portion of 4DOS is located, unless this file isn't in the root directory.
/P	Allows AUTOEXEC.BAT to execute and 4DOS is permanently loaded. The AUTOEXEC.BAT isn't executed if 4DOS is started without this parameter. This parameter shouldn't be used if 4DOS is loaded as a second shell or the user cannot return with EXIT.
/S:B(Path)	4DOS runs in the swapping mode and an attempt is made to use extended memory, then expanded memory, and finally to store parts on the hard drive, if there is no more space in memory. If a path is indicated after the parameter, it will be used for the swapping to the hard drive.
/S:D(Path)	4DOS runs in the swapping mode and the files are stored on the hard drive. If a path is indicated after the parameter, it will be used for the swapping to the hard drive. The swap file, created by 4DOS, is named 4DOSSWAP.xxx, where xxx is a sequential number.
/S:E	4DOS runs in the swapping mode and the files are stored in expanded memory.
/S:N	4DOS runs in memory resident mode (no swapping).
/S:X	4DOS runs in the swapping mode and the files are stored in extended memory.
/U	The resident part of 4DOS is loaded into an Upper Memory block in extended memory. This reduces the memory requirement to 256 bytes, plus the environment memory. This option can be used only on 286 and 386 systems with XMS drivers (e.g., HIMEM. SYS).

12.5 Protected Mode Software

All the 80386/486 microprocessor's capabilities are demonstrated only through software, which uses the full 32-bit address bus. Besides the memory, which can be addressed through the 32-bit data bus, the bytes can be transmitted almost twice as fast than with the 80286. Currently, there aren't any programs that use these capabilities with 32-bit commands.

Version 2.0 of OS/2 and some of the operating systems, such as the UNIX System V/386 from Santa Cruz Operation (SCO), fully use the 386 capabilities.

Entry through DOS

Besides the 32-bit wide bus, other features also make the 386 software special. For example, it's possible to switch between the various operating modes. With the 80286, switching from Protected to Real mode was only possible through a Reset.

DOS extenders

DOS applications cannot execute in Protected mode and pure Protected mode software can execute only in Real mode. To start this software under DOS, DOS extenders must be used when this software is programmed. DOS extenders install a "platform", under DOS, called the kernel.

From there the program starts in Real mode. The kernel then switches to Protected mode. It also ensures cooperation between the input/output operations, which must be performed with DOS in Real mode, and the application that's operating in Protected mode.

Currently only a few programs use this principle. Many of these programs were already being used on large mainframes and were simply translated to the PC environment.

The following are some examples of this software:

- Inforec, an organizational system for data of various types (e.g., literature).

- 386 Mathlab, a mathematic application that, among other things, permits calculations in 64-bit format.

- PC-MACsyma, another mathematics program, which contains more than 1500 mathematical functions.

Programming for 32 bits

The proper development kit is needed for developing 32-bit software. One solution is to buy a package containing an operating system and a Software Development Kit (SDK).

Such packages are already available for UNIX (MTOS-UX-386) and for OS/2 Version 2.0/2.1. You could also purchase a 32-bit compiler for one of the common programming languages.

The DOS Protected mode interface

As we described, the applications that operate in Protected mode are protected from each other by access rights and priorities that are assigned to them. Working with a user interface, such as Windows 3.1, or a multitasking system, such as DESQview 386, may require that several Protected mode applications execute simultaneously.

Virtual Control Program Interface

However, these applications shouldn't destroy each other's data or crash the system. The Virtual Control Program Interface (VCPI) can be used for programming Protected mode software.

The VCPI consists of a series of conventions that permit the execution of the Protected mode programs in a multitasking environment. However, the VCPI cannot protect programs from being destroyed by other applications.

An application that uses VCPI executes on the highest privilege level, called the ring zero. It has access to all resources of the computer and can access everything. Unfortunately, this increases the chances of data loss.

DOS Protected Mode Interface

Therefore, Microsoft developed the DOS Protected Mode Interface with extensive specifications for Extended DOS programs. According to this interface, Extended DOS applications should execute on the lowest level (ring three) if they are executing with other applications in a multitasking environment. Also, these applications should request system resources instead of simply receiving them.

DPMI 0.9

Not all developers of DOS extenders agree with this convention because they fear Microsoft could use it to suppress competition for

Windows. So, many developers, such as Borland, Eclipse, IGC, Intel, Lotus, Phar Lap, Phoenix, and Quarterdeck, support the DPMI. They use a standard, called DPMI 0.9, that was first published in 1990.

DPMI 0.9 specifies a series of commands, which start the program, switch to the Protected mode, and manage the memory and the systems routines. This standard doesn't contain uniform DOS and BIOS calls yet. All DOS extender manufacturers use their own. However, the DPMI convention 1.0 complies with the recommendations of Microsoft, because these have already been implemented in Windows and OS/2.

Support

The amount of support a Protected mode program receives depends on the environment in which the program is started. If the program is started from DOS, it must perform all mode switches and memory management procedures itself. If an extended memory driver (e.g., HIMEM.SYS) is available, the Protected mode program lets it perform the memory management, but still must manage the switches and the input/output itself.

The application doesn't have to perform these tasks only when it's equipped with a VCPI. In this case, the application must only watch for the orderly protection, the use of system routines (interrupts), and the call of DOS and BIOS functions. For this, a switch to the 8086 /virtual 8086 mode is needed.

If the DPMI is available, it can also take over these tasks and perform a mode switch only when it's required. If, for example, the program calls the DOS function to open a file and the program was started by OS/2, then it remains in the Protected mode and passes the function to the OS/2 file system, which is also executing.

No DOS extender

With DPMI, Protected mode software can be started without a DOS extender and work directly with the DPMI.

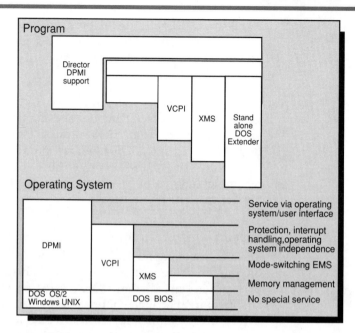

Stepwise support of Protected mode software thro ugh the available operating system

The DPMI offers an entire package of service utilities for the Protected mode application. Currently some of these consists of only a single function.

Chapter 13 The Companion Diskette

The companion diskette contains two programs: PCINFO, including source code, and System Sleuth Professional (c) from Dariana, Inc.

Installation:

Insert the companion diskette in a disk drive. Log to that drive, type the following, and press Enter:

```
INSTALL
```

The INSTALL program will ask you for a source drive and a destination drive. Follow the instructions on the screen. The INSTALL program creates an ABACUS\486 directory, then creates subdirectories, into which the programs are inserted.

13.1 PCINFO

The PCINFO program is located on the companion diskette. With this program you can display information about your computer and its configuration. You can start this program from the diskette or copy it to your hard drive and start it from there.

The source code, which is listed in Section 13.2, is on the included companion diskette. The program was developed in Turbo Pascal 6.0 and the Turbo Assembler 2.5, both from Borland. This section provides a general overview of how to use the compiled program.

General information

All the functions can be called through the keyboard and a mouse, if available. At the bottom of the information windows are three switches, which have the following functions:

Next page   Calls the subsequent function of the menu or the
                   subsequent menu

Previous page   Calls the previous function of the menu or the
                   previous menu

Print page   Prints the currently displayed page on the
                   printer

The switches Next Page and Previous Page don't affect the first and
last page.

Hardware Menu

This menu contains functions, through which you can obtain more
details about your hardware. These functions include the processor,
coprocessor, video adapter, and interfaces. The functions are named
accordingly and can be accessed through the Hardware menu.

Processor function

This function provides information about the type of processor in
your system and the type of computer being used (e.g., PC/AT,
PS/2, etc.). Also, the width of the address and data bus of the
microprocessor used in your system is also provided.

The following illustration was created on a 386 PC/AT. The
processor designation is indicated by an arrow to the left and a
different color. If you have only a Hercules card, this would be
indicated only with the arrow. The system type is indicated in the
"Computer:" box.

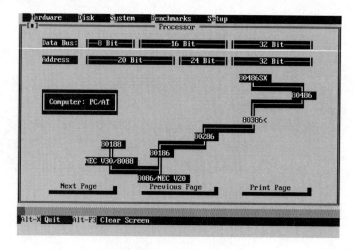

The display of the microprocessor

Two lines appear above the processor designation tree. These lines are labeled as data bus and address bus. The areas marked in these lines correspond to the processors found below. For example, the 80386 represents both the data bus and the address bus under the marking 32 bits and actually has a 32-bit wide data bus and a 32-bit wide address bus.

Coprocessor function

If you call this function with the Hardware menu, you'll receive information about a coprocessor that may be installed in your system.

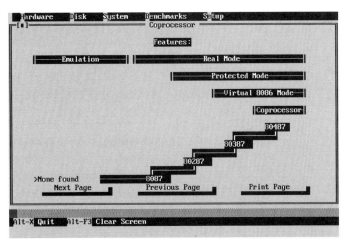

The display of the coprocessors

Similar to the preceding function, lines also appear in the top portion of the window. In this case, the information refers to the current coprocessor.

Video Adapter function

This function indicates which graphics card your system has and what graphic, as well as text resolution, is possible.

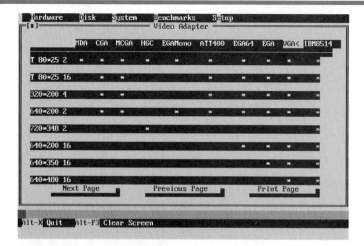

The display of the Video Adapters

The Video Adapters display appears in column format. Each column is assigned to an adapter type. Color and an arrow are also used. If the Video Adapter is capable of one of the resolutions, which are listed in the lines, this is indicated by an asterisk ("*").

Computer function

This function handles the common computer interfaces, such as serial and parallel, and also the gameport, keyboard, and screen. Also, the version of your mouse or the mouse driver is indicated.

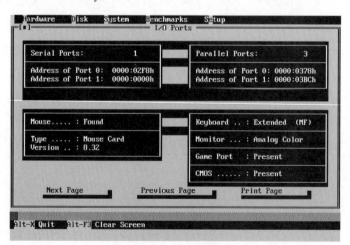

The display of the interfaces

The display is roughly divided into four boxes. There is a box for the serial interface and a box for the parallel interface. The number of the currently recognized interfaces is displayed and the addresses of the first two ports are indicated in these boxes.

There are also boxes that provide information about the currently installed mouse driver, keyboard, monitor, game port, and CMOS.

Disk Menu

This menu contains functions that locate information about the drives.

File Information function

This function displays statistical data about the files currently available on the active drive.

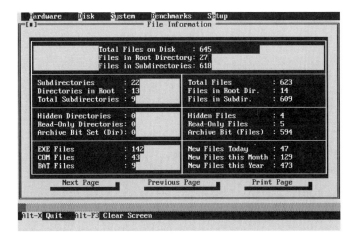

The display of the file information

When this function is activated, the following information is displayed:

Subdirectories   The total number of subdirectories in the current drive.

Directories in Root
                   The number of directories in the root directory.

Total Subdirectories
                   The total number of subdirectories on the drive, minus the ones in the root directory.

Hidden Directories
                   The total number of subdirectories hidden on the drive (hidden bit), including the ones in the root directory.

Read-Only Directory
> The total number of the directories on the drive that are protected from changes (read only bit, which is usually ignored). The subdirectories in the root directory are included.

Archive Bit Set (Dir)
> The total number of changed subdirectories on the drive (archive bit), including the ones in the root directory.

EXE-files
> The total number of files on the drive that have an .EXE extension.

COM-files
> The total number of files on the drive that have a .COM extension.

BAT-files
> The total number of files on the drive that have a .BAT extension.

Total Files
> The total number of files on the drive.

Files in the Root-Dir.
> The total number of files in the root directory.

Files in the Subdir.
> The total number of files in the subdirectories.

Hidden files
> The total number of files hidden on the drive (hidden bit).

Read-Only Files
> The total number of files on the drive that are protected against change (read only bit).

Archive Bit (Files)
> The total number of files on the drive that were changed (archive bit).

New Files Today
> The total number of files whose last change occurred during the current day.

New Files this Month
> The total number of files whose last change occurred during the current month.

New Files this Year
> The total number of files whose last changes occurred during the current year.

Disk Information function

This function specifies the internal parameters of the currently active drive.

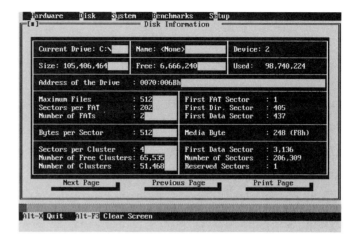

The display of the Disk Information

The following information is provided:

Current Drive	The drive to which the displayed information refers.
Name	The name of the current drive (volume name).
Device	The device number of the current drive.
Size	Size of the maximum available memory on the drive.
Free	Available memory that's free.
Used	Memory that is occupied.
Address of the Drive	The address of the driver for the current drive.
Maximum Files	The maximum number of entries in the root directory of the current drive.
Sectors per FAT	The number of sectors needed for a copy of the FAT of the current drive.
Number of FATs	The number of FAT copies.
Bytes per Sector	The size of a sector in bytes.

Sectors per Cluster
                    The number of sectors per cluster of the current
                    drive.

Number of Free Clusters
                    The number of free clusters.

Number of Clusters
                    The total number of clusters on the current drive.

First FAT Sector   The physical sector, where the first copy of the
                    FAT starts.

First Dir. Sector   The physical sector, where the first directory
                    starts.

First Data Sector   The physical sector, where the first data starts.

Media Byte   The media descriptor byte.

First Data Sector   First sector where the search starts.

Number of Sectors
                    The total number of sectors on the drive.

Reserved Sectors
                    The total number of sectors reserved for system
                    purposes on the drive.

System Menu

The functions from this menu provide system dependent
information.

Operating System function

This function provides information about the DOS version that's
installed. The BIOS used in your system is also indicated.

A display tree, which shows the installed MS-DOS version, appears
on the left side of the window. The DR DOS version is indicated in
the middle of the window. The installed Windows version is
displayed on the right side of the window and the BIOS version is
displayed in a box in the middle of the window.

Memory function

This function indicates the types of memory that are available in
your system and the version of the driver.

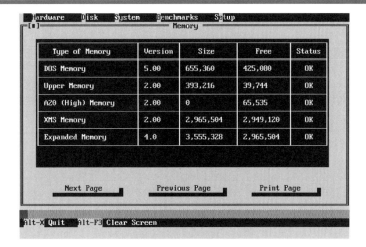

Type of Memory	Version	Size	Free	Status
DOS Memory	5.00	655,360	425,080	OK
Upper Memory	2.00	393,216	39,744	OK
A20 (High) Memory	2.00	0	65,535	OK
XMS Memory	2.00	2,965,504	2,949,120	OK
Expanded Memory	4.0	3,555,328	2,965,504	OK

Display of the memory partition

QUICK TIP

The currently available memory and its maximum size are displayed in column format. If a certain type of memory isn't available, the corresponding line remains blank.

If you use a memory driver such as QEMM386, the total size of the memory displayed may differ from the actual size.

Benchmark Menu

With the functions contained in this menu, you can determine the speed of your individual system components. Both relative and actual values are displayed.

Mainboard function

Your motherboard is tested for speed. The value determined is displayed relative to an IBM XT at 4.77 MHz.

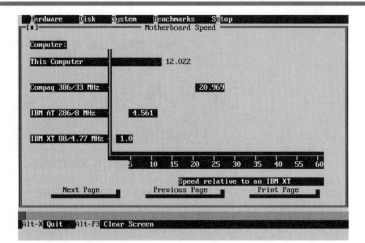

The display of the motherboard speed

The determined value for your system is displayed on the first line; if you have a color monitor, these values are highlighted in white. The values for three other computers are also displayed.

Speed function

With this function you can test the speed of your drive. Various values are provided so you can compare them with other computers and other disk systems (RLL, AT-BUS, SCSI, ESDI, etc.).

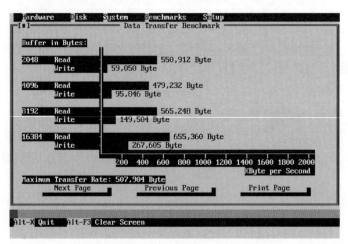

The display of the medium benchmarks

The benchmark evaluates read and write speed. For better comparisons it's written and read with four different buffer sizes.

Video function

This function tests the maximum transfer rate to the video card through direct access and also through the video BIOS.

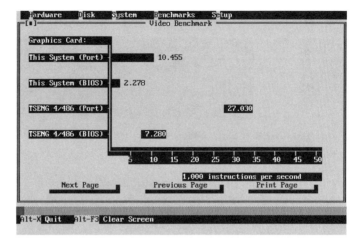

The display of the Video Benchmarks

For comparison, the values for an 80486 with a Tseng ET4000 video card are also displayed. The direct access to the hardware is labeled "Port".

Setup Menu

With the functions in this menu, you can display your CONFIG.SYS and AUTOEXEC.BAT files that set up your system.

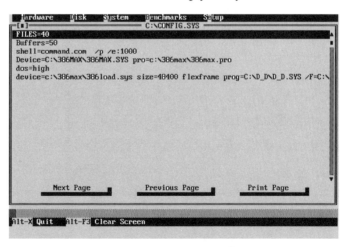

Display of the CONFIG.SYS

To the right of the display window is a scroll bar, which you can use to scroll through the text, if it's longer than one display page. You

can use the ⬆ and ⬇ keys to scroll the text line by line and the
PgUp and PgDn keys to scroll the text page by page.

13.2 Source Code

This section lists the source code of the system information
program, PCINFO, which is located on the companion
diskette. The program was developed in Turbo Pascal 6.0 and
the Turbo Assembler 2.5, both from Borland.

PCINFO.PAS

```pascal
{ PCINFO.PAS -
            Copyright (C) 1991 by Data Becker GmbH
            Copyright (C) 1992 Abacus Software, Inc.
}

{$N+,E+}

{$L getcopz}
PROGRAM SystemInformation;
USES
  Objects,Drivers,Views,Menus,App,Dialogs,Dos,Crt,Graph;

CONST
  EMM_Int         =$67;
  hcHardware      =2000;
  hcDisk          =2001;
  hcBenchmarks    =2002;
  hcView          =2003;
  hcSystem        =2004;
  hcQuit          =2005;

  MinWindow       =1002;
  cmhProcessor    =1002;
  cmhCoprocessor  =1003;
  cmhVideo        =1004;
  cmhPort         =1005;
  cmlFile         =1006;
  cmlDisk         =1007;
  cmsDOS          =1008;
  cmsMemory       =1009;
  cmbCPUBench     =1010;
  cmbDiskBench    =1011;
  cmbVideoBench   =1012;
  cmvConfig       =1013;
  cmvAutoexec     =1014;
  MaxWindow       =1016;
  cmPrint         =10000;
```

```
TYPE

  PFileEntry      = ^TFileEntry;
  TFileEntry      =OBJECT(TObject)
                   Attr            :Byte;
                   Time,Size       :LongInt;
                   Name            :String[12];
                   CONSTRUCTOR
Init(NAttr:Byte;NTime,NSize:LongInt;NName:String);
                   END;

  PStr            = ^TStr;
  TStr            =OBJECT(TObject)
                   St              :String;
                   CONSTRUCTOR Init(NSt:String);
                   END;

  PExtListViewer  = ^TExtListViewer;
  TExtListViewer  =OBJECT(TListViewer)
                   LineCol         :TCollection;
                   CONSTRUCTOR Init(VAR
Bounds:TRect;ANumCols:Integer;AHScrollBar,AVScrollBar:PScrollBar;Path:String
);
                   FUNCTION GetText(Item,MaxLen:Integer):String;VIRTUAL;
                   DESTRUCTOR Done;VIRTUAL;
                   END;

  PExtStaticText  = ^TExtStaticText;
  TExtStaticText  =OBJECT(TStaticText)
                   FUNCTION GetPalette:PPalette;VIRTUAL;
                   END;

  TSysApp         =OBJECT(TApplication)
                   CurrentWindow   :Integer;
                   CONSTRUCTOR Init;
                   PROCEDURE HandleEvent(VAR Event:TEvent);VIRTUAL;
                   PROCEDURE InitMenuBar;VIRTUAL;
                   PROCEDURE InitStatusLine;VIRTUAL;
                   END;

  TDiskBenchArray=ARRAY[1..4]OF RECORD
                                ReadIt,WriteIt:LongInt;
                                END;

VAR
  SysApp          :TSysApp;
  EmsResult       :Integer;
  EmsInstalled    :Boolean;
  XMSInstalled    :Boolean;
  XmsResult       :Integer;
  XmsControl      :Pointer;

  FUNCTION getcopz : Integer; external;

  FUNCTION XmsControlAddr:Pointer;
  INLINE(
  $B8/$10/$43/
```

```
 $CD/$2F/
 $89/$D8/
 $8C/$C2);

FUNCTION CheckForXmm:Boolean;
INLINE(
 $B8/$00/$43/
 $CD/$2F/
 $3C/$80/
 $75/$04/
 $B0/$01/
 $EB/$02/
 $30/$C0);


FUNCTION QueryXmsMemory(VAR TotalFree,LargestBlock:Word):Byte;
VAR
 ErrorCode      :Byte;
BEGIN
 INLINE(
  $B4/$08/
  $FF/$1E/>XmsControl/
  $09/$C0/
  $74/$10/
  $30/$DB/
  $C4/$BE/>TotalFree/
  $26/
  $89/$15/
  $C4/$BE/>LargestBlock/
  $26/
  $89/$05/

  $88/$5E/<ErrorCode);
 QueryXmsMemory:=ErrorCode;
 IF(ErrorCode<>0)THEN BEGIN
  TotalFree:=0;LargestBlock:=0;
 END;
END;

FUNCTION QueryA20Prim:Byte;
INLINE(
 $B4/$07/
 $FF/$1E/>XmsControl/
 $08/$DB/
 $74/$02/
 $88/$D8);

FUNCTION QueryA20:Byte;
BEGIN
 QueryA20:=QueryA20Prim;
END;

FUNCTION AllocUpperMemBlock(SizeInParas:Word;VAR SegmentBase:Word;VAR
Size:Word):Byte;
VAR
 ErrorCode      :Byte;
BEGIN
```

```
  INLINE(
   $B4/$10/
   $8B/$96/>SizeInParas/
   $FF/$1E/>XmsControl/
   $A9/$01/$00/
   $74/$12/
   $C4/$BE/>Size/
   $26/
   $89/$15/
   $C4/$BE/>SegmentBase/
   $26/
   $89/$1D/
   $30/$DB/
   $EB/$07/

   $C4/$BE/>Size/
   $26/
   $89/$15/

   $88/$5E/<ErrorCode);
  AllocUpperMemBlock:=ErrorCode;
END;

PROCEDURE EMM(Call:Word;VAR Regs:Registers);
BEGIN
 IF NOT EmsInstalled THEN
  EmsResult:=$FF
 ELSE BEGIN
  Regs.AX:=Call;
  Intr($67,Regs);
  EmsResult:=Regs.AH;
 END;
END;

FUNCTION GetEmsStatus:Integer;
VAR
 Regs          :Registers;
BEGIN
 EMM($4000,Regs);
 GetEmsStatus:=EmsResult;
END;

PROCEDURE QueryEmsMemory(VAR Total,Avail:LongInt);
VAR
 Regs          :Registers;
BEGIN
 EMM($4200,Regs);
 Total:=Regs.DX*16;
 Avail:=Regs.BX*16;
END;

FUNCTION GetEmsVersion:Byte;
VAR
 Regs          :Registers;
BEGIN
 EMM($4600,Regs);
 GetEmsVersion:=Regs.AL;
```

```
END;

PROCEDURE CheckForEMM(VAR EMM_Found:Boolean);
TYPE
 ID              =ARRAY[1..8]OF Char;
VAR
 Int67            :Pointer;
BEGIN
 GetIntVec(EMM_Int,Int67);
 EMM_Found:=(ID(Ptr(Seg(Int67^),10)^)='EMMXXXX0');
 IF EMM_Found THEN BEGIN
  EmsResult:=GetEmsStatus;
    IF EmsResult=0 THEN EMM_Found:=True ELSE EMM_Found:=False;
 END;
END;


FUNCTION GETVOLUME(drive:String):String;
VAR
 SREC            :SEARCHREC;
BEGIN
 SREC.Name:='';
 FINDFIRST(drive+'*.*',VOLUMEID,SREC);
 IF IoResult=0 THEN ;
 IF Pos('.',SREC.Name)<>0 THEN Delete(SREC.Name,Pos('.',SREC.Name),1);
 GETVOLUME:=SREC.Name;
END;

FUNCTION MakeHexString(Source:LongInt):String;
VAR
 St              :String;
 I               :Word;
 L,HL            :LongInt;
BEGIN
 FillChar(St,SizeOf(St),'0');
 L:=$f0000000;
 FOR I:=1 TO 8 DO BEGIN
  HL:=(Source AND L) SHR((8-I)*4);
    IF HL<10 THEN St[I]:=Chr(HL+48) ELSE St[I]:=Chr(HL+55);
  L:=L SHR 4;
 END;
 St[0]:=#8;
 WHILE(St[1]='0') AND(Length(St)>0)DO Delete(St,1,1);
 MakeHexString:=St;
END;

FUNCTION HiWord(L:LongInt):Word;
INLINE(
 $58/
 $58);

FUNCTION LoWord(L:LongInt):Word;
INLINE(
 $58/
 $5A);
```

```
FUNCTION NicePointer(P:Pointer):String;
VAR
 Segment,Offset :String;
BEGIN
 Segment:=MakeHexString(HiWord(LongInt(P)));
 Offset:=MakeHexString(LoWord(LongInt(P)));
 WHILE Length(Segment)<4 DO Segment:='0'+Segment;
 WHILE Length(Offset)<4 DO Offset:='0'+Offset;
 NicePointer:=Segment+':'+Offset+'h';
END;

FUNCTION FindEntryPath(St:String):String;
VAR
 S               :String;
BEGIN
 GetDir(0,S);
 S:=S+';'+GetEnv('PATH');
 IF S[Length(S)]<>';' THEN S:=S+';';
 S:=S+S[1]+':\';
 St:=FSearch(St,S);
 FindEntryPath:=St;
END;

FUNCTION FindEntry(St:String):LongInt;
VAR
 SREC            :SEARCHREC;
BEGIN
 St:=FindEntryPath(St);
 IF St<>'' THEN BEGIN
  FINDFIRST(St,AnyFile,SREC);
  FindEntry:=SREC.Size;
 END ELSE FindEntry:=0;
END;

FUNCTION GetComputerName:String;
VAR
 TYP             :Byte ABSOLUTE $FFFF:$000E;
 St              :String;
BEGIN
 CASE TYP OF
  $FF:St:='PC';
  $FE:St:='Compaq Deskpro';
  $FD:St:='PC Junior';
  $FC:St:='PC/AT';
  $FB:St:='PC/XT';
  $FA:St:='PS/2 Model 30';
  $F9:St:='PS/2 Convertible';
  $F8:St:='PS/2 Model 80';
  $9A:St:='Compaq Portable Plus';
  $2D:St:='Compaq Portable';
  ELSE St:='Unknown';
 END;
 GetComputerName:=St;
END;

FUNCTION GetDosVersion:Word;
BEGIN
```

```
      GetDosVersion:=(Lo(DosVersion) SHL 8) OR Hi(DosVersion);
    END;

    FUNCTION Compare(VAR Enviorn1,Enviorn2;Length:Word):Boolean;Assembler;
    ASM
      MOV CX,[Length]
      JCXZ @Ende
      LDS SI,[Enviorn1]

      LES DI,[Enviorn2]

      CLD
      REPZ CMPSB
      JZ @Ende
      MOV CL,1
    @Ende:
      MOV AL,CL
      XOR AL,1
    END;

    FUNCTION getprocessor:Byte;
    BEGIN
      ASM
          PUSHF
          PUSH    CX
          PUSH    DX
          PUSH    DI
          PUSH    SI
          PUSH    ES
          XOR     AX,AX
          PUSH    AX
          POPF
          PUSHF
          POP     AX
          AND     AX,0F000h
          CMP     AX,0F000h
          JZ      @small80286

          MOV     DL,006h
          MOV     AX,07000h
          PUSH    AX
          POPF
          PUSHF
          POP     AX
          AND     AX,07000h
          JZ      @pende

          INC     DL

          cli
          db      066h,08bh,0dch
          db      066h,083h,0e4h,0fch
          db      066h,09ch
          db      066h,058h
          db      066h,08bh,0c8h
          db      066h,035h,000h,0h,4h,0h
          db      066h,050h
```

```
        db      066h,09dh
        db      066h,09ch
        db      066h,058h
        db      066h,051h
        db      066h,09dh
        db      066h,033h,0c1h
        db      066h,0c1h,0e8h,012h
        db      066h,083h,0e0h,001h
        db      066h,08bh,0e3h
        sti
        add     dl,al
        JMP     @pende

@small80286:
        MOV     DL,04
        MOV     AL,0FFh
        MOV     CL,021h
        SHR     AL,CL
        JNZ     @t88_86

        MOV     DL,02
        STI
        MOV     SI,0000
        MOV     CX,0FFFFh
        db      0f3h,026h,0ach
        OR      CX,CX
        JZ      @t88_86
        MOV     DL,00
@t88_86:
        PUSH    CS
        POP     ES
        STD
        MOV     AL,0FBh
        MOV     CX,0003
        CALL    @func
@func_ret:
        CLI
        REP     STOSB
        CLD
        NOP
        NOP
        NOP
        INC     DX
        NOP
        STI
@pende:
        MOV     [BP-01],DL
        POP     ES
        POP     SI
        POP     DI
        POP     DX
        POP     CX
        POPF
        JMP     @ende
        NOP
```

```
@func:
      POP     DI
      ADD     DI,0009
      JMP     @func_ret
@ende:
   END;
 END;

 FUNCTION DetectBios:String;
 CONST
  MaxBios          =4;
  BiosKind         :ARRAY[1..MaxBios]OF String=(
    'American Megatrends Inc.',
    'Phoenix',
    'Award',
    'IBM');

 VAR
  P                :Pointer;
  I,K              :Word;
 BEGIN
  FOR K:=1 TO MaxBios DO
   FOR I:=0 TO $1000 DO BEGIN
    P:=Ptr($f000,I);
    IF Compare(BiosKind[K][1],P^,Length(BiosKind[K]))THEN BEGIN
     DetectBios:=BiosKind[K];
      IF K=1 THEN DetectBios:='    AMI' ELSE
        DetectBios:=BiosKind[K];
     Exit;
    END;
   END;
 DetectBios:='Unknown';
 END;

 FUNCTION NiceNumber(L:LongInt):String;
 VAR
  I                :Integer;
  St               :String[20];
 BEGIN
  Str(L,St);I:=Length(St)+1;
  WHILE I>1 DO BEGIN Dec(I,3);Insert(',',St,I);END;
  IF St[1]=',' THEN Delete(St,1,1);
  NiceNumber:=St;
 END;

 FUNCTION DecimalNumber(L:LongInt):String;
 VAR
  I                :Integer;
  St               :String[20];
 BEGIN
  Str(L,St);I:=Length(St)+1;
  WHILE I>1 DO BEGIN Dec(I,3);Insert('.',St,I);END;
  IF St[1]='.' THEN Delete(St,1,1);
  DecimalNumber:=St;
 END;

 FUNCTION MakeBar(Size:LongInt):String;
```

```
VAR
 St              :String;
BEGIN
 St[0]:=Chr(Size);
 FillChar(St[1],Size,#219);
 MakeBar:=St;
END;

FUNCTION MakeLongInt(H,L:Word):LongInt;
INLINE(
 $58/
 $5A
 );

PROCEDURE Wait;
CONST
 X              =30;
 Y              =10;
BEGIN
 TextColor(White);TextBackGround(LightGray);
 GotoXY(X,Y);
 Write('┌───────────────┐');
 GotoXY(X,Y+1);
 Write('║               ║');
 GotoXY(X,Y+2);
 Write('║ Please Wait ... ║');
 GotoXY(X,Y+3);
 Write('║               ║');
 GotoXY(X,Y+4);
 Write('└───────────────┘');
END;

PROCEDURE Not_Found;
VAR
    Dialog      :PDialog;
    R           :TRect;
    Control     :Word;
    B,C         :PView;
    Dlg         :PDialog;

BEGIN
    R.Assign(15,5,60,15);
    Dialog := New(PDialog,Init(R,'Information'));
    with Dialog^Do
    begin
      R.Assign(12,4,29,5);
      Insert(New(PStaticText,Init(R,'File not found...')));
      R.Assign(12,6,29,8);
      Insert(New(PButton,Init(R,'~O~K',cmOK,bfDefault)));
    end;

    Control:=DeskTop^.ExecView(Dialog);
END;

FUNCTION CurrentTime:LongInt;
VAR R           :Registers;
BEGIN
```

```
  R.AH:=0;
  Intr($1A,R);
  CurrentTime:=MakeLongInt(R.CX,R.DX);
END;

CONSTRUCTOR TStr.Init(NSt:String);
BEGIN
 TObject.Init;
 St:=NSt;
END;

CONSTRUCTOR TFileEntry.Init(NAttr:Byte;NTime,NSize:LongInt;NName:String);
BEGIN
 TObject.Init;
 Attr:=NAttr;
 Time:=NTime;
 Size:=NSize;
 Name:=NName;
END;

CONSTRUCTOR TExtListViewer.Init(VAR
Bounds:TRect;ANumCols:Integer;AHScrollBar,AVScrollBar:PScrollBar;Path:String
);
 VAR
  F                 :Text;
  St,S              :String;
 BEGIN
  TListViewer.Init(Bounds,ANumCols,AHScrollBar,AVScrollBar);
  LineCol.Init(1,1);
  Assign(F,Path);
  Reset(F);
  WHILE NOT EoF(F)DO BEGIN
   ReadLn(F,St);
   WHILE Length(St)>77 DO BEGIN
    S:=Copy(St,1,77);
    St:=Copy(St,78,255);
    LineCol.Insert(New(PStr,Init(S)));
   END;
   LineCol.Insert(New(PStr,Init(St)));
  END;
  SetRange(LineCol.Count-1);
END;

FUNCTION TExtListViewer.GetText(Item,MaxLen:Integer):String;
VAR
 St                :String;
BEGIN
 St:=PStr(LineCol.At(Item))^.St;
 IF MaxLen<Length(St)THEN St[0]:=Chr(MaxLen);
 GetText:=St;
END;

DESTRUCTOR TExtListViewer.Done;
BEGIN
 LineCol.Done;
 TListViewer.Done;
END;
```

```
FUNCTION TExtStaticText.GetPalette:PPalette;
CONST
 CCol           =#8;
 CBW            =#8;
 CM             =#8;
 P              :ARRAY[apColor..apMonochrome]OF String[1]=(CCol,CBW,CM);
BEGIN GetPalette:= @P[AppPalette];END;

CONSTRUCTOR TSysApp.Init;
BEGIN
 TApplication.Init;
 CheckForEMM(EmsInstalled);
  IF CheckForXmm THEN XmsControl:=XmsControlAddr ELSE XmsControl:=NIL;
 XMSInstalled:=XmsControl<>NIL;
 CurrentWindow:=cmhProcessor;
END;

PROCEDURE TSysApp.InitMenuBar;
VAR
 R                :TRect;
BEGIN
 GetExtent(R);
 R.B.Y:=R.A.Y+1;
 MenuBar:=New(PMenuBar,Init(R,NewMenu(
  NewSubMenu(' ~H~ardware ',hcHardware,NewMenu(
   NewItem(' ~P~rocessor','',kbNoKey,cmhProcessor,cmhProcessor,
    NewItem(' ~C~oprocessor','',kbNoKey,cmhCoprocessor,cmhCoprocessor,
     NewItem(' ~V~ideo Adapter','',kbNoKey,cmhVideo,cmhVideo,
      NewItem(' ~C~omputer','',kbNoKey,cmhPort,cmhPort,
       NewLine(
        NewItem(' E~x~it','Alt-X ',kbAltX,cmQuit,hcQuit,NIL
        ))))))),
   NewSubMenu(' ~D~isk ',hcDisk,NewMenu(
    NewItem(' ~F~ile Information ','',kbNoKey,cmlFile,cmlFile,
     NewItem(' ~D~isk Information  ','',kbNoKey,cmlDisk,cmlDisk,NIL
     ))),
    NewSubMenu(' ~S~ystem ',hcSystem,NewMenu(
     NewItem(' ~O~perating System ','',kbNoKey,cmsDOS,cmsDOS,
      NewItem(' ~M~emory','',kbNoKey,cmsMemory,cmsMemory,NIL
      ))),
     NewSubMenu(' ~B~enchmarks ',hcBenchmarks,NewMenu(
      NewItem(' ~M~ainboard','',kbNoKey,cmbCPUBench,cmbCPUBench,
       NewItem(' ~S~peed','',kbNoKey,cmbDiskBench,cmbDiskBench,
        NewItem(' ~V~ideo','',kbNoKey,cmbVideoBench,cmbVideoBench,NIL
        )))
      ),
      NewSubMenu(' S~e~tup ',hcView,NewMenu(
       NewItem(' ~C~ONFIG.SYS','',kbNoKey,cmvConfig,cmvConfig,
        NewItem(' ~A~UTOEXEC.BAT ','',kbNoKey,cmvAutoexec,cmvAutoexec, NIL
        ))
       ),NIL))
      ))))));
 END;


PROCEDURE TSysApp.InitStatusLine;
```

```
VAR
 R                 :TRect;
BEGIN
 GetExtent(R);
 R.A.Y:=R.B.Y-1;
 StatusLine:=New(PStatusLine,Init(R,
  NewStatusDef(0,$ffff,
   NewStatusKey('~Alt-X~ Quit ',kbAltX,cmQuit,
    NewStatusKey('~Alt-F3~ Clear Screen',kbAltF3,cmClose,NIL)
    ),NIL)
  ));
END;


FUNCTION WaitDialog:PDialog;
VAR
 Dlg               :PDialog;
 R                 :TRect;
 Control,Labl,Histry:PView;
BEGIN
 R.Assign(25,7,50,14);
 New(Dlg,Init(R,'Info'));

 R.Assign(5,3,21,4);
 Control:=New(PStaticText,Init(R,'Please Wait ...'));
 Dlg^.Insert(Control);

 Dlg^.SelectNext(False);
 WaitDialog:=Dlg;
END;

FUNCTION ProcessorDialog:PDialog;
VAR
 Dlg               :PDialog;
 R                 :TRect;
 Control,Labl,Histry:PView;
 Processor         :Byte;
 St,S              :String;
BEGIN
 Processor:=getprocessor;
 IF (Processor = 8) AND (getcopz = 0) THEN Processor := 9;

 R.Assign(0,1,80,23);
 New(Dlg,Init(R,'Processor'));

 R.Assign(25,16,30,17);
 St:='8088';
 IF Processor=0 THEN Control:=New(PExtStaticText,Init(R,St+'<'))
 ELSE Control:=New(PStaticText,Init(R,St));
 Dlg^.Insert(Control);

 R.Assign(30,18,35,19);
 St:='8086';
 IF Processor=1 THEN Control:=New(PExtStaticText,Init(R,St+'<'))
 ELSE Control:=New(PStaticText,Init(R,St));
 Dlg^.Insert(Control);
```

```
R.Assign(35,18,43,19);
St:='NEC V20';
IF Processor=2 THEN Control:=New(PExtStaticText,Init(R,St+'<'))
ELSE Control:=New(PStaticText,Init(R,St));
Dlg^.Insert(Control);

R.Assign(17,16,25,17);
St:='NEC V30';
IF Processor=3 THEN Control:=New(PExtStaticText,Init(R,St+'<'))
ELSE Control:=New(PStaticText,Init(R,St));
Dlg^.Insert(Control);

R.Assign(21,14,27,15);
St:='80188';
IF Processor=4 THEN Control:=New(PExtStaticText,Init(R,St+'<'))
ELSE Control:=New(PStaticText,Init(R,St));
Dlg^.Insert(Control);

R.Assign(33,15,39,16);
St:='80186';
IF Processor=5 THEN Control:=New(PExtStaticText,Init(R,St+'<'))
ELSE Control:=New(PStaticText,Init(R,St));
Dlg^.Insert(Control);

R.Assign(44,13,50,14);
St:='80286';
IF Processor=6 THEN Control:=New(PExtStaticText,Init(R,St+'<'))
ELSE Control:=New(PStaticText,Init(R,St));
Dlg^.Insert(Control);

R.Assign(56,11,62,12);
St:='80386';
IF Processor=7 THEN Control:=New(PExtStaticText,Init(R,St+'<'))
ELSE Control:=New(PStaticText,Init(R,St));
Dlg^.Insert(Control);

R.Assign(68,8,74,9);
St:='80486';
IF Processor=8 THEN Control:=New(PExtStaticText,Init(R,St+'<'))
ELSE Control:=New(PStaticText,Init(R,St));
Dlg^.Insert(Control);

R.Assign(55,6,63,7);
St:='80486SX';
IF Processor=9 THEN Control:=New(PExtStaticText,Init(R,St+'<'))
ELSE Control:=New(PStaticText,Init(R,St));
Dlg^.Insert(Control);

R.Assign(17,2,29,3);
Control:=New(PStaticText,Init(R,'├─8 Bit──┤'));
Dlg^.Insert(Control);

R.Assign(29,19,50,21);
Control:=New(PButton,Init(R,'~P~revious Page',cmPrev,bfNormal));
Dlg^.Insert(Control);

R.Assign(54,19,73,21);
```

```
Control:=New(PButton,Init(R,'P~r~int Page',cmPrint,bfNormal));
Dlg^.Insert(Control);

R.Assign(6,19,25,21);
Control:=New(PButton,Init(R,'~N~ext Page',cmNext,bfNormal));
Dlg^.Insert(Control);

R.Assign(53,2,73,3);
Control:=New(PStaticText,Init(R,'├──────32 Bit──────┤'));
Dlg^.Insert(Control);

R.Assign(35,16,36,17);
Control:=New(PStaticText,Init(R,'│'));
Dlg^.Insert(Control);

R.Assign(46,12,59,13);
Control:=New(PStaticText,Init(R,'┌──────────┘'));
Dlg^.Insert(Control);

R.Assign(58,9,71,10);
Control:=New(PStaticText,Init(R,'┌──────────┘'));
Dlg^.Insert(Control);

R.Assign(23,17,36,18);
Control:=New(PStaticText,Init(R,'└──────────┤'));
Dlg^.Insert(Control);

R.Assign(23,15,24,16);
Control:=New(PStaticText,Init(R,'│'));
Dlg^.Insert(Control);

R.Assign(34,18,35,19);
Control:=New(PStaticText,Init(R,'/'));
Dlg^.Insert(Control);

R.Assign(24,16,25,17);
Control:=New(PStaticText,Init(R,'/'));
Dlg^.Insert(Control);

R.Assign(58,10,59,11);
Control:=New(PStaticText,Init(R,'│'));
Dlg^.Insert(Control);

R.Assign(58,7,71,8);
Control:=New(PStaticText,Init(R,'└──────────┐'));
Dlg^.Insert(Control);

R.Assign(35,14,47,15);
Control:=New(PStaticText,Init(R,'┌──────────┘'));
Dlg^.Insert(Control);

R.Assign(30,2,52,3);
Control:=New(PStaticText,Init(R,'├──────16 Bit──────┤'));
Dlg^.Insert(Control);

R.Assign(17,4,39,5);
Control:=New(PStaticText,Init(R,'├──────20 Bit──────┤'));
```

```
Dlg^.Insert(Control);

R.Assign(53,4,73,5);
Control:=New(PStaticText,Init(R,'├───32 Bit───┤'));
Dlg^.Insert(Control);

R.Assign(40,4,52,5);
Control:=New(PStaticText,Init(R,'├──24 Bit──┤'));
Dlg^.Insert(Control);

R.Assign(6,4,15,5);
Control:=New(PStaticText,Init(R,'Address Bus:'));
Dlg^.Insert(Control);

R.Assign(6,2,15,3);
Control:=New(PStaticText,Init(R,'Data Bus:'));
Dlg^.Insert(Control);

St:='≥ Computer: ';
St:=St+GetComputerName+' │';
R.Assign(6,9,6+Length(St),10);
Control:=New(PStaticText,Init(R,St));
Dlg^.Insert(Control);

R.Assign(6,8,6+Length(St),9);
FillChar(S,SizeOf(S),#196);
S[1]:='┌';
S[Length(St)]:='┐';
S[0]:=St[0];
Control:=New(PStaticText,Init(R,S));
Dlg^.Insert(Control);

R.Assign(6,10,6+Length(St),11);
FillChar(S,SizeOf(S),#196);
S[1]:='└';
S[Length(St)]:='┘';
S[0]:=St[0];
Control:=New(PStaticText,Init(R,S));
Dlg^.Insert(Control);

 ProcessorDialog:=Dlg;
END;


FUNCTION CoprocessorDialog:PDialog;
VAR
 Dlg            :PDialog;
 R              :TRect;
 Control,Labl,Histry:PView;
 St             :String;
 Coprocessor    :Byte;
BEGIN
 Coprocessor := getcopz;
 IF (getprocessor = 8) AND (Coprocessor = 3) THEN Coprocessor := 4;

 R.Assign(0,1,80,23);
 New(Dlg,Init(R,'Coprocessor'));
```

```
R.Assign(29,19,50,21);
Control:=New(PButton,Init(R,'~P~revious Page',cmPrev,bfNormal));
Dlg^.Insert(Control);

R.Assign(54,19,73,21);
Control:=New(PButton,Init(R,'P~r~int Page',cmPrint,bfNormal));
Dlg^.Insert(Control);

R.Assign(6,19,25,21);
Control:=New(PButton,Init(R,'~N~ext Page',cmNext,bfNormal));
Dlg^.Insert(Control);

R.Assign(6,18,23,19);
St:='None found';
IF Coprocessor=0 THEN Control:=New(PExtStaticText,Init(R,'>'+St))
ELSE Control:=New(PStaticText,Init(R,' '+St));
Dlg^.Insert(Control);

R.Assign(33,18,39,19);
St:='8087';
IF Coprocessor=1 THEN Control:=New(PExtStaticText,Init(R,St+'<'))
ELSE Control:=New(PStaticText,Init(R,St));
Dlg^.Insert(Control);

R.Assign(42,16,49,17);
St:='80287';
IF Coprocessor=2 THEN Control:=New(PExtStaticText,Init(R,St+'<'))
ELSE Control:=New(PStaticText,Init(R,St));
Dlg^.Insert(Control);

R.Assign(52,14,59,15);
St:='80387';
IF Coprocessor=3 THEN Control:=New(PExtStaticText,Init(R,St+'<'))
ELSE Control:=New(PStaticText,Init(R,St));
Dlg^.Insert(Control);

R.Assign(62,12,68,13);
St:='80487';
IF Coprocessor=4 THEN Control:=New(PExtStaticText,Init(R,'80487'+'<'))
ELSE Control:=New(PStaticText,Init(R,St));
Dlg^.Insert(Control);

R.Assign(30,4,72,5);
Control:=New(PStaticText,Init(R,'|─────────────Real
Mode─────────────|'));
Dlg^.Insert(Control);

R.Assign(39,6,72,7);
Control:=New(PStaticText,Init(R,'|─────────Protected Mode─────────|'));
Dlg^.Insert(Control);

R.Assign(49,8,72,9);
Control:=New(PStaticText,Init(R,'|───Virtual 8086 Mode──|'));
Dlg^.Insert(Control);

R.Assign(34,17,45,18);
```

```
Control:=New(PStaticText,Init(R,'┌────────┘'));
Dlg^.Insert(Control);

R.Assign(44,15,55,16);
Control:=New(PStaticText,Init(R,'┌────────┘'));
Dlg^.Insert(Control);

R.Assign(54,13,65,14);
Control:=New(PStaticText,Init(R,'┌────────┘'));
Dlg^.Insert(Control);

R.Assign(59,10,72,11);
Control:=New(PStaticText,Init(R,'┤Coprocessor├'));
Dlg^.Insert(Control);

R.Assign(35,2,44,3);
Control:=New(PStaticText,Init(R,'Features:'));
Dlg^.Insert(Control);

R.Assign(22,18,33,19);
Control:=New(PStaticText,Init(R,'─────────'));
Dlg^.Insert(Control);

R.Assign(6,4,29,5);
Control:=New(PStaticText,Init(R,'├──────Emulation──────┤'));
Dlg^.Insert(Control);

CoprocessorDialog:=Dlg;
END;


FUNCTION VideoDialog:PDialog;
VAR
 Dlg              :PDialog;
 R                :TRect;
 Control,Labl,Histry:PView;
 GraphDriver,GraphMode:Integer;
 St               :String;
BEGIN
 DetectGraph(GraphDriver,GraphMode);
 R.Assign(0,1,80,23);
 New(Dlg,Init(R,'Video Adapter'));

 R.Assign(14,2,19,3);
 St:='MDA';
 IF GraphDriver= -2 THEN Control:=New(PExtStaticText,Init(R,St+'<'))
 ELSE Control:=New(PStaticText,Init(R,St));
 Dlg^.Insert(Control);

 R.Assign(19,2,24,3);
 St:='CGA';
 IF GraphDriver=1 THEN Control:=New(PExtStaticText,Init(R,St+'<'))
 ELSE Control:=New(PStaticText,Init(R,St));
 Dlg^.Insert(Control);

 R.Assign(24,2,30,3);
 St:='MCGA';
```

```
    IF(GraphDriver=2) OR(GraphDriver=10)THEN
Control:=New(PExtStaticText,Init(R,St+'<'))
  ELSE Control:=New(PStaticText,Init(R,St));
  Dlg^.Insert(Control);

  R.Assign(59,2,64,3);
  St:='EGA';
  IF GraphDriver=3 THEN Control:=New(PExtStaticText,Init(R,St+'<'))
  ELSE Control:=New(PStaticText,Init(R,St));
  Dlg^.Insert(Control);

  R.Assign(52,2,59,3);
  St:='EGA64';
  IF GraphDriver=4 THEN Control:=New(PExtStaticText,Init(R,St+'<'))
  ELSE Control:=New(PStaticText,Init(R,St));
  Dlg^.Insert(Control);

  R.Assign(35,2,44,3);
  St:='EGAMono';
  IF GraphDriver=5 THEN Control:=New(PExtStaticText,Init(R,St+'<'))
  ELSE Control:=New(PStaticText,Init(R,St));
  Dlg^.Insert(Control);

  R.Assign(69,2,78,3);
  St:='IBM8514';
  IF GraphDriver=6 THEN Control:=New(PExtStaticText,Init(R,St+'<'))
  ELSE Control:=New(PStaticText,Init(R,St));
  Dlg^.Insert(Control);

  R.Assign(30,2,35,3);
  St:='HGC';
  IF GraphDriver=7 THEN Control:=New(PExtStaticText,Init(R,St+'<'))
  ELSE Control:=New(PStaticText,Init(R,St));
  Dlg^.Insert(Control);

  R.Assign(44,2,52,3);
  St:='ATT400';
  IF GraphDriver=8 THEN Control:=New(PExtStaticText,Init(R,St+'<'))
  ELSE Control:=New(PStaticText,Init(R,St));
  Dlg^.Insert(Control);

  R.Assign(64,2,69,3);
  St:='VGA';
  IF GraphDriver=9 THEN Control:=New(PExtStaticText,Init(R,St+'<'))
  ELSE Control:=New(PStaticText,Init(R,St));
  Dlg^.Insert(Control);

  R.Assign(29,19,50,21);
  Control:=New(PButton,Init(R,'~P~revious Page',cmPrev,bfNormal));
  Dlg^.Insert(Control);

  R.Assign(54,19,73,21);
  Control:=New(PButton,Init(R,'P~r~int Page',cmPrint,bfNormal));
  Dlg^.Insert(Control);

  R.Assign(6,19,25,21);
  Control:=New(PButton,Init(R,'~N~ext Page',cmNext,bfNormal));
```

```
  Dlg^.Insert(Control);

  R.Assign(3,6,73,7);
  Control:=New(PStaticText,Init(R,'T 80*25 16         *     *
*      *    *    *         *'));
  Dlg^.Insert(Control);

  R.Assign(3,12,73,13);
  Control:=New(PStaticText,Init(R,'720*348 2                       *
*'));
  Dlg^.Insert(Control);

  R.Assign(3,8,73,9);
  Control:=New(PStaticText,Init(R,'320*200 4         *     *
*      *    *    *         *'));
  Dlg^.Insert(Control);

  R.Assign(3,10,73,11);
  Control:=New(PStaticText,Init(R,'640*200 2         *     *           *
*      *    *    *         *'));
  Dlg^.Insert(Control);

  R.Assign(3,18,73,19);
  Control:=New(PStaticText,Init(R,'640*480 16
*      *'));
  Dlg^.Insert(Control);

  R.Assign(3,16,73,17);
  Control:=New(PStaticText,Init(R,'640*350 16
*    *      *'));
  Dlg^.Insert(Control);

  R.Assign(3,14,73,15);
  Control:=New(PStaticText,Init(R,'640*200 16
*    *    *      *'));
  Dlg^.Insert(Control);

  R.Assign(3,4,73,5);
  Control:=New(PStaticText,Init(R,'T 80*25 2   *    *    *    *       *
*      *    *    *         *'));
  Dlg^.Insert(Control);

  R.Assign(3,3,76,4);

Control:=New(PStaticText,Init(R,'─────────────────────────
──────────────────'));
  Dlg^.Insert(Control);

  VideoDialog:=Dlg;
END;


  FUNCTION PortDialog:PDialog;
  VAR
   Dlg              :PDialog;
   R                :TRect;
   Control,Labl,Histry:PView;
```

```
CPU               :Registers;
St,S              :String;
Ser0              :Word ABSOLUTE $0000:$0400;
Ser1              :Word ABSOLUTE $0000:$0402;
Ser2              :Word ABSOLUTE $0000:$0404;
Par0              :Word ABSOLUTE $0000:$0408;
Par1              :Word ABSOLUTE $0000:$040A;
Par2              :Word ABSOLUTE $0000:$040C;
KBD               :Byte ABSOLUTE $40:$96;
GraphDriver,GraphMode:Integer;
BEGIN
R.Assign(0,1,80,23);
New(Dlg,Init(R,'I/O Ports'));

R.Assign(43,3,77,4);
Intr($11,CPU);
St:='≥ Parallel Ports:                  ≥';
Str(Hi(CPU.AX) SHR 6, S);
Insert(S,St,29);
Control:=New(PStaticText,Init(R,St));
Dlg^.Insert(Control);

R.Assign(43,5,77,6);
S:=MakeHexString(Par0);
WHILE Length(S)<4 DO S:='0'+S;
S:=S+'h';
St:='≥ Address of Port 0: 0000:'+S+'   ≥';
Control:=New(PStaticText,Init(R,St));
Dlg^.Insert(Control);

R.Assign(43,6,77,7);
S:=MakeHexString(Par1);
WHILE Length(S)<4 DO S:='0'+S;
S:=S+'h';
St:='≥ Address of Port 1: 0000:'+S+'   ≥';
Control:=New(PStaticText,Init(R,St));
Dlg^.Insert(Control);

R.Assign(3,3,37,4);
St:='≥ Serial Ports:                   ≥';
Str((Hi(CPU.AX) AND $E) SHR 1,S);
Insert(S,St,28);
Control:=New(PStaticText,Init(R,St));
Dlg^.Insert(Control);

R.Assign(3,5,37,6);
S:=MakeHexString(Ser0);
WHILE Length(S)<4 DO S:='0'+S;
S:=S+'h';
Control:=New(PStaticText,Init(R,'≥ Address of Port 0:  0000:'+S+'  ≥'));
Dlg^.Insert(Control);

R.Assign(3,6,37,7);
S:=MakeHexString(Ser1);
WHILE Length(S)<4 DO S:='0'+S;
S:=S+'h';
```

```
Control:=New(PStaticText,Init(R,'≥ Address of Port 1:  0000:'+S+' ≥'));
Dlg^.Insert(Control);

R.Assign(3,11,37,12);
  IF MouseEvents THEN S:='Found      ' ELSE S:='Not found  ';
Control:=New(PStaticText,Init(R,'≥ Mouse..... : '+S+'         ≥'));
Dlg^.Insert(Control);

R.Assign(3,13,37,14);
CPU.AX:=$24;Intr($33,CPU);
CASE CPU.CH OF
 1:S:='Bus Mouse    ';
 2:S:='Serial Mouse ';
 3:S:='Mouse Card   ';
 4:S:='PS/2 Mouse   ';
 5:S:='HP Mouse     ';
 ELSE S:='-------------';
END;

Control:=New(PStaticText,Init(R,'≥ Type ..... : '+S+'     ≥'));
Dlg^.Insert(Control);

R.Assign(3,14,37,15);
FillChar(S,SizeOf(S),#32);
Str(CPU.BH,S);Str(CPU.BL,St);
S:=S+'.'+St;S[0]:=#5;
Control:=New(PStaticText,Init(R,'≥ Version .. : '+S+'           ≥'));
Dlg^.Insert(Control);

R.Assign(43,11,77,12);
  IF KBD AND $10>0 THEN S:='Extended  (MF)' ELSE S:='Normal (PC)   ';
Control:=New(PStaticText,Init(R,'≥ Keyboard .. : '+S+'   ≥'));
Dlg^.Insert(Control);

R.Assign(43,15,77,16);
IF getprocessor>5 THEN BEGIN
 CPU.Flags:=0;
 CPU.AH:=$84;
 CPU.DX:=0;
 Intr($15,CPU);
  IF CPU.Flags AND FCarry=0 THEN S:='Present' ELSE S:='Not Recognized';
END ELSE BEGIN
 Intr($11,CPU);
  IF CPU.AX AND $1000<>0 THEN S:='Present      ' ELSE S:='Not
Recognized';
END;
Control:=New(PStaticText,Init(R,'≥ Game Port   : '+S+'           ≥'));
Dlg^.Insert(Control);

R.Assign(43,13,77,14);
DetectGraph(GraphDriver,GraphMode);
CASE GraphDriver OF
 -2,7,10:S:='HGC Mono';
 5:S:='EGA Mono    ';
 1:S:='CGA Color   ';
 2,8:S:='MCGA Color  ';
 3,4:S:='EGA Color   ';
```

```
    6,9:S:='Analog Color';
  END;
  Control:=New(PStaticText,Init(R,'≥ Monitor ... : '+S+'      ≥'));
  Dlg^.Insert(Control);

  R.Assign(43,17,77,18);
  CPU.AH:=8;
  CPU.DL:=0;
  Intr($13,CPU);
   IF CPU.BL<>0 THEN S:='Present        ' ELSE S:='Not Found     ';
  Control:=New(PStaticText,Init(R,'≥ CMOS ...... : '+S+'    ≥'));
  Dlg^.Insert(Control);

  R.Assign(3,2,77,3);
  Control:=New(PStaticText,Init(R,' ┌────────────────────────────────────┐
┌──────────────────────────┘'));
  Dlg^.Insert(Control);

  R.Assign(3,4,77,5);
  Control:=New(PStaticText,Init(R,' ├────────────────────────────────────┤
├──────────────────────────┤'));
  Dlg^.Insert(Control);

  R.Assign(3,7,77,9);
  Control:=New(PStaticText,Init(R,' └────────────────────────────────────┘
└──────────────────────────┘'));
  Dlg^.Insert(Control);

  R.Assign(3,10,77,11);
  Control:=New(PStaticText,Init(R,' ┌────────────────────────────────────┐
┌──────────────────────────┘'));
  Dlg^.Insert(Control);

  R.Assign(3,12,77,13);
  Control:=New(PStaticText,Init(R,' ├────────────────────────────────────┤
├──────────────────────────┤'));
  Dlg^.Insert(Control);

  R.Assign(3,15,37,16);
  Control:=New(PStaticText,Init(R,' └────────────────────────────────┘'));
  Dlg^.Insert(Control);

  R.Assign(43,14,77,15);
  Control:=New(PStaticText,Init(R,' ├────────────────────────────────┤'));
  Dlg^.Insert(Control);

  R.Assign(43,16,77,17);
  Control:=New(PStaticText,Init(R,' ├────────────────────────────────┤'));
  Dlg^.Insert(Control);

  R.Assign(43,18,77,19);
  Control:=New(PStaticText,Init(R,' └────────────────────────────────┘'));
  Dlg^.Insert(Control);

  R.Assign(29,19,50,21);
  Control:=New(PButton,Init(R,'~P~revious Page  ',cmPrev,bfNormal));
  Dlg^.Insert(Control);
```

```
  R.Assign(54,19,73,21);
  Control:=New(PButton,Init(R,'P~r~int Page     ',cmPrint,bfNormal));
  Dlg^.Insert(Control);

  R.Assign(6,19,25,21);
  Control:=New(PButton,Init(R,'~N~ext Page     ',cmNext,bfNormal));
  Dlg^.Insert(Control);

  PortDialog:=Dlg;
END;

FUNCTION DosDialog:PDialog;
VAR
  B_D              :ARRAY[1..8]OF Char ABSOLUTE $FFFF:$0005;
  Dlg              :PDialog;
  R                :TRect;
  Control,Labl,Histry:PView;
  St,St2           :String;

BEGIN
 R.Assign(0,1,80,23);
 New(Dlg,Init(R,'System'));

 R.Assign(30,19,51,21);
 Control:=New(PButton,Init(R,'~P~revious Page',cmPrev,bfNormal));
 Dlg^.Insert(Control);

 R.Assign(55,19,74,21);
 Control:=New(PButton,Init(R,'P~r~int Page',cmPrint,bfNormal));
 Dlg^.Insert(Control);

 R.Assign(7,19,26,21);
 Control:=New(PButton,Init(R,'~N~ext Page',cmNext,bfNormal));
 Dlg^.Insert(Control);

 R.Assign(35,18,36,19);
 Control:=New(PStaticText,Init(R,'/'));
 Dlg^.Insert(Control);

 R.Assign(19,18,24,19);
 Control:=New(PStaticText,Init(R,'——'));
 Dlg^.Insert(Control);

 R.Assign(13,17,36,18);
 Control:=New(PStaticText,Init(R,'└─────────────────┐'));
 Dlg^.Insert(Control);

 R.Assign(19,6,24,7);
 Control:=New(PStaticText,Init(R,'——'));
 Dlg^.Insert(Control);

 R.Assign(19,14,24,15);
 Control:=New(PStaticText,Init(R,'——'));
 Dlg^.Insert(Control);

 R.Assign(46,16,51,17);
```

```
  Control:=New(PStaticText,Init(R,'————'));
  Dlg^.Insert(Control);

  R.Assign(19,16,24,17);
  Control:=New(PStaticText,Init(R,'————'));
  Dlg^.Insert(Control);

  R.Assign(35,16,36,17);
  Control:=New(PStaticText,Init(R,'/'));
  Dlg^.Insert(Control);

  R.Assign(13,15,56,16);

Control:=New(PStaticText,Init(R,'└————————————————————┤'));
  Dlg^.Insert(Control);

  R.Assign(55,13,56,14);
  Control:=New(PStaticText,Init(R,'|'));
  Dlg^.Insert(Control);

  R.Assign(55,14,56,15);
  Control:=New(PStaticText,Init(R,'|'));
  Dlg^.Insert(Control);

  R.Assign(70,3,71,4);
  Control:=New(PStaticText,Init(R,'|'));
  Dlg^.Insert(Control);

  R.Assign(70,6,71,7);
  Control:=New(PStaticText,Init(R,'|'));
  Dlg^.Insert(Control);

  R.Assign(70,7,71,8);
  Control:=New(PStaticText,Init(R,'|'));
  Dlg^.Insert(Control);

  R.Assign(70,9,71,10);
  Control:=New(PStaticText,Init(R,'|'));
  Dlg^.Insert(Control);

  R.Assign(70,10,71,11);
  Control:=New(PStaticText,Init(R,'|'));
  Dlg^.Insert(Control);

  R.Assign(70,11,71,12);
  Control:=New(PStaticText,Init(R,'|'));
  Dlg^.Insert(Control);

  R.Assign(70,5,71,6);
  Control:=New(PStaticText,Init(R,'|'));
  Dlg^.Insert(Control);

  R.Assign(13,13,29,14);
  Control:=New(PStaticText,Init(R,'└——————————┐'));
  Dlg^.Insert(Control);

  R.Assign(13,11,14,12);
```

```
Control:=New(PStaticText,Init(R,'|'));
Dlg^.Insert(Control);

R.Assign(13,12,14,13);
Control:=New(PStaticText,Init(R,'|'));
Dlg^.Insert(Control);

R.Assign(13,3,14,4);
Control:=New(PStaticText,Init(R,'|'));
Dlg^.Insert(Control);

R.Assign(13,4,14,5);
Control:=New(PStaticText,Init(R,'|'));
Dlg^.Insert(Control);

R.Assign(13,5,29,6);
Control:=New(PStaticText,Init(R,'└───────────┐'));
Dlg^.Insert(Control);

R.Assign(13,7,14,8);
Control:=New(PStaticText,Init(R,'|'));
Dlg^.Insert(Control);

R.Assign(13,9,14,10);
Control:=New(PStaticText,Init(R,'|'));
Dlg^.Insert(Control);

R.Assign(43,5,44,6);
Control:=New(PStaticText,Init(R,'|'));
Dlg^.Insert(Control);

R.Assign(43,3,44,4);
Control:=New(PStaticText,Init(R,'|'));
Dlg^.Insert(Control);

R.Assign(30,9,50,10);
St:='|    BIOS             |';
St2:=DetectBios;
Move(St2[1],St[10],Length(St2));
Control:=New(PStaticText,Init(R,St));
Dlg^.Insert(Control);

R.Assign(30,11,50,12);
Control:=New(PStaticText,Init(R,'└─────────────┘'));
Dlg^.Insert(Control);

R.Assign(30,10,50,11);
St:='| Release            |';
St2:=B_D[1]+B_D[2]+'-'+B_D[4]+B_D[5]+'-'+B_D[7]+B_D[8];
Move(St2[1],St[11],Length(St2));
Control:=New(PStaticText,Init(R,St));
Dlg^.Insert(Control);

R.Assign(30,8,50,9);
Control:=New(PStaticText,Init(R,'┌─────────────┐'));
Dlg^.Insert(Control);
```

```
R.Assign(3,18,7,19);
Control:=New(PStaticText,Init(R,'1981'));
Dlg^.Insert(Control);

R.Assign(3,16,7,17);
Control:=New(PStaticText,Init(R,'1983'));
Dlg^.Insert(Control);

R.Assign(3,14,7,15);
Control:=New(PStaticText,Init(R,'1984'));
Dlg^.Insert(Control);

R.Assign(3,12,7,13);
Control:=New(PStaticText,Init(R,'1985'));
Dlg^.Insert(Control);

R.Assign(3,10,7,11);
Control:=New(PStaticText,Init(R,'1986'));
Dlg^.Insert(Control);

R.Assign(3,8,7,9);
Control:=New(PStaticText,Init(R,'1987'));
Dlg^.Insert(Control);

R.Assign(3,6,7,7);
Control:=New(PStaticText,Init(R,'1988'));
Dlg^.Insert(Control);

R.Assign(3,4,7,5);
Control:=New(PStaticText,Init(R,'1990'));
Dlg^.Insert(Control);

R.Assign(3,2,7,3);
Control:=New(PStaticText,Init(R,'1992'));
Dlg^.Insert(Control);

R.Assign(8,18,19,19);
St:='MS-DOS 1.0';
IF GetDosVersion=$1000 THEN Control:=New(PExtStaticText,Init(R,'>'+St))
ELSE Control:=New(PStaticText,Init(R,' '+St));
Dlg^.Insert(Control);

R.Assign(24,18,36,19);
St:='MS-DOS 1.25';
IF GetDosVersion=$125 THEN Control:=New(PExtStaticText,Init(R,St+'<'))
ELSE Control:=New(PStaticText,Init(R,St));
Dlg^.Insert(Control);

R.Assign(36,18,47,19);
St:='PC-DOS 1.1';
IF GetDosVersion=$101 THEN Control:=New(PExtStaticText,Init(R,St+'<'))
ELSE Control:=New(PStaticText,Init(R,St));
Dlg^.Insert(Control);

R.Assign(8,16,19,17);
St:='MS-DOS 2.0';
IF GetDosVersion=$200 THEN Control:=New(PExtStaticText,Init(R,'>'+St))
```

```
    ELSE Control:=New(PStaticText,Init(R,' '+St));
    Dlg^.Insert(Control);

    R.Assign(24,16,36,17);
    St:='MS-DOS 2.01';
    IF GetDosVersion=$201 THEN Control:=New(PExtStaticText,Init(R,St+'<'))
    ELSE Control:=New(PStaticText,Init(R,St));
    Dlg^.Insert(Control);

    R.Assign(36,16,47,17);
    St:='PC-DOS 2.1';
    IF GetDosVersion=$201 THEN Control:=New(PExtStaticText,Init(R,St+'<'))
    ELSE Control:=New(PStaticText,Init(R,St));
    Dlg^.Insert(Control);

    R.Assign(51,16,63,17);
    St:='MS-DOS 2.11';
    IF GetDosVersion=$211 THEN Control:=New(PExtStaticText,Init(R,St+'<'))
    ELSE Control:=New(PStaticText,Init(R,St));
    Dlg^.Insert(Control);

    R.Assign(51,12,63,13);
    St:='MS-DOS 2.25';
    IF GetDosVersion=$225 THEN Control:=New(PExtStaticText,Init(R,St+'<'))
    ELSE Control:=New(PStaticText,Init(R,St));
    Dlg^.Insert(Control);

    R.Assign(8,14,19,15);
    St:='MS-DOS 3.0';
    IF GetDosVersion=$300 THEN Control:=New(PExtStaticText,Init(R,'>'+St))
    ELSE Control:=New(PStaticText,Init(R,' '+St));
    Dlg^.Insert(Control);

    R.Assign(24,14,35,15);
    St:='MS-DOS 3.1';
    IF GetDosVersion=$301 THEN Control:=New(PExtStaticText,Init(R,St+'<'))
    ELSE Control:=New(PStaticText,Init(R,St));
    Dlg^.Insert(Control);

    R.Assign(9,10,20,11);
    St:='MS-DOS 3.2';
    IF GetDosVersion=$302 THEN Control:=New(PExtStaticText,Init(R,St+'<'))
    ELSE Control:=New(PStaticText,Init(R,St));
    Dlg^.Insert(Control);

    R.Assign(9,8,20,9);
    St:='MS-DOS 3.3';
    IF GetDosVersion=$303 THEN Control:=New(PExtStaticText,Init(R,St+'<'))
    ELSE Control:=New(PStaticText,Init(R,St));
    Dlg^.Insert(Control);

    R.Assign(8,6,19,7);
    St:='MS-DOS 4.0';
    IF GetDosVersion=$400 THEN Control:=New(PExtStaticText,Init(R,'>'+St))
    ELSE Control:=New(PStaticText,Init(R,' '+St));
    Dlg^.Insert(Control);
```

```
  R.Assign(24,6,36,7);
  St:='MS-DOS 4.01';
  IF GetDosVersion=$400 THEN Control:=New(PExtStaticText,Init(R,St+'<'))
  ELSE Control:=New(PStaticText,Init(R,St));
  Dlg^.Insert(Control);

  R.Assign(9,3,20,4);
  St:='MS-DOS 5.0';
  IF(GetDosVersion=$500) AND(FindEntry('DOSSHELL.EXE')>0)THEN
Control:=New(PExtStaticText,Init(R,St+'<'))
  ELSE Control:=New(PStaticText,Init(R,St));
  Dlg^.Insert(Control);

  R.Assign(66,12,78,13);
  Control:=New(PStaticText,Init(R,'Windows 1.0'));
  Dlg^.Insert(Control);

  R.Assign(66,8,78,9);
  Control:=New(PStaticText,Init(R,'Windows 2.0'));
  Dlg^.Insert(Control);

  R.Assign(66,4,78,5);
  St:='Windows 3.0';
  IF FindEntry('WIN.COM')=19614 THEN
Control:=New(PExtStaticText,Init(R,St+'<'))
  ELSE Control:=New(PStaticText,Init(R,St));
  Dlg^.Insert(Control);

  R.Assign(66,2,78,3);
  St:='Windows 3.1';
  IF FindEntry('WIN.COM')=44170 THEN
Control:=New(PExtStaticText,Init(R,St+'<'))
  ELSE Control:=New(PStaticText,Init(R,St));
  Dlg^.Insert(Control);


  R.Assign(39,6,52,7);
  St:='DR-DOS 3.41';
  IF(GetDosVersion=$341) AND(FindEntry('VIEWMAX.EXE')<>14208)THEN
Control:=New(PExtStaticText,Init(R,St+'<'))
  ELSE Control:=New(PStaticText,Init(R,St));
  Dlg^.Insert(Control);

  R.Assign(39,4,51,5);
  St:='DR-DOS 5.0';
  IF(GetDosVersion=$341) AND(FindEntry('VIEWMAX.EXE')=14208)THEN
Control:=New(PExtStaticText,Init(R,St+'<'))
  ELSE Control:=New(PStaticText,Init(R,St));
  Dlg^.Insert(Control);


  R.Assign(39,3,51,4);
  St:='DR-DOS 6.0';
  IF(GetDosVersion=$331) AND(FindEntry('VIEWMAX.EXE')>0)THEN
Control:=New(PExtStaticText,Init(R,St+'<'))
  ELSE Control:=New(PStaticText,Init(R,St));
  Dlg^.Insert(Control);
```

```
  DosDialog:=Dlg;
END;


FUNCTION FileDialog:PDialog;
VAR
 FileCol         :TCollection;
 Dlg             :PDialog;
 R               :TRect;
 Control,Labl,Histry:PView;

 Directories,HiddenDirectories,ReadOnlyDirectories:LongInt;
 Files,HiddenFiles,ReadOnlyFiles:LongInt;
 Entries,RootEntries,SubEntries:LongInt;
 RootDirectories,SubDirectories:LongInt;
 RootFiles,SubFiles:LongInt;
 ExeFiles,ComFiles,BatFiles:LongInt;
 YearFiles,MonthFiles,DayFiles:LongInt;
 ArchiveFiles,ArchiveDirectories:LongInt;
 DT              :DateTime;
 I,Year,Month,Day,DayOfWeek:Word;
 St,S            :String;
 PFE             :PFileEntry;

PROCEDURE Note(VAR PFE:PFileEntry;Path:String);
BEGIN
 Inc(Entries);
 IF Length(Path)=3 THEN Inc(RootEntries) ELSE Inc(SubEntries);
 IF PFE^.Attr AND Directory=0 THEN BEGIN
  Inc(Files);
  IF Length(Path)=3 THEN Inc(RootFiles) ELSE Inc(SubFiles);
  IF Pos('.EXE',PFE^.Name)>0 THEN Inc(ExeFiles);
  IF Pos('.COM',PFE^.Name)>0 THEN Inc(ComFiles);
  IF Pos('.BAT',PFE^.Name)>0 THEN Inc(BatFiles);
  IF PFE^.Attr AND Archive>0 THEN Inc(ArchiveFiles);
  IF PFE^.Attr AND Hidden>0 THEN Inc(HiddenFiles);
  IF PFE^.Attr AND(ReadOnly OR SysFile)>0 THEN Inc(ReadOnlyFiles);
  GetDate(Year,Month,Day,DayOfWeek);
  UnpackTime(PFE^.Time,DT);
  IF DT.Year=Year THEN BEGIN
   Inc(YearFiles);
   IF DT.Month=Month THEN BEGIN
    Inc(MonthFiles);
    IF DT.Day=Day THEN Inc(DayFiles);
   END;
  END;
 END ELSE BEGIN
  Inc(Directories);
  IF Length(Path)=3 THEN Inc(RootDirectories) ELSE Inc(SubDirectories);
  IF PFE^.Attr AND Archive>0 THEN Inc(ArchiveDirectories);
  IF PFE^.Attr AND Hidden>0 THEN Inc(HiddenDirectories);
  IF PFE^.Attr AND(ReadOnly OR SysFile)>0 THEN Inc(ReadOnlyDirectories);
 END;
END;

PROCEDURE RecursDirectories(drive:String;VAR FileCol:TCollection);
```

```
VAR
  DirZ              :Integer;
  SREC              :SEARCHREC;
  PFE               :PFileEntry;

  PROCEDURE TraceDir(St:String;Z:Integer);
  LABEL Fin;
  VAR I,K,T,Q       :Integer;

   PROCEDURE Take;
   BEGIN
    WITH SREC DO
      IF(Name[1]<>'.') OR(Attr AND $10=0)THEN BEGIN
       Inc(Z);
       PFE := New(PFileEntry, Init(Attr, Time, Size, Name));
       FileCol.AtInsert(Z,PFE);
      END;
   END;

  BEGIN
   T:=Z;
   FINDFIRST(St+'*.*',AnyFile,SREC);
   IF(InOutRes<>0) OR(DosError<>0)THEN GOTO Fin;
   REPEAT
    Take;
    FindNext(SREC);
   UNTIL(InOutRes<>0) OR(DosError<>0);
Fin:
    IF Z>T THEN BEGIN
     I:=T;
     WHILE I<Z DO BEGIN
      Inc(I);
      Inc(DirZ);
      PFE:=FileCol.At(DirZ);
      Note(PFE,St);
      IF PFE^.Attr AND Directory>0 THEN TraceDir(St+PFE^.Name+'\',DirZ);
     END;
    END;
   END;

  BEGIN
   DirZ:= -1;
   TraceDir(drive,DirZ);
  END;

 BEGIN
  Directories:=0;
  HiddenDirectories:=0;
  ReadOnlyDirectories:=0;
  Files:=0;
  HiddenFiles:=0;
  ReadOnlyFiles:=0;
  Entries:=0;
  RootEntries:=0;
  SubEntries:=0;
  RootDirectories:=0;
  SubDirectories:=0;
```

```
RootFiles:=0;
SubFiles:=0;
ExeFiles:=0;
ComFiles:=0;
BatFiles:=0;
YearFiles:=0;
MonthFiles:=0;
DayFiles:=0;
ArchiveFiles:=0;
ArchiveDirectories:=0;
GetDir(0,St);
St[0]:=#3;
FileCol.Init(1,1);
RecursDirectories(St,FileCol);
FOR I:=0 TO FileCol.Count-1 DO BEGIN
 PFE:=FileCol.At(I);
 Dispose(PFE);
END;
FileCol.DeleteAll;
FileCol.Done;
R.Assign(0,1,80,23);
New(Dlg,Init(R,'File Information'));

St:='Total Files on Disk    : '+NiceNumber(Entries);
R.Assign(20,3,32+Length(St),4);
Control:=New(PStaticText,Init(R,St));
Dlg^.Insert(Control);

St:='Files in Subdirectories: '+NiceNumber(SubEntries);
R.Assign(20,5,20+Length(St),6);
Control:=New(PStaticText,Init(R,St));
Dlg^.Insert(Control);

St:='Files in Root Directory: '+NiceNumber(RootEntries);
R.Assign(20,4,21+Length(St),5);
Control:=New(PStaticText,Init(R,St));
Dlg^.Insert(Control);

St:='| Subdirectories        : '+NiceNumber(Directories);
R.Assign(3,7,3+Length(St),8);
Control:=New(PStaticText,Init(R,St));
Dlg^.Insert(Control);

St:='| Directories in Root  : '+NiceNumber(RootDirectories);
R.Assign(3,8,3+Length(St),9);
Control:=New(PStaticText,Init(R,St));
Dlg^.Insert(Control);

St:='| Total Subdirectories : '+NiceNumber(SubDirectories);
R.Assign(3,9,3+Length(St),10);
Control:=New(PStaticText,Init(R,St));
Dlg^.Insert(Control);

St:='| Archive Bit Set (Dir): '+NiceNumber(ArchiveDirectories);
R.Assign(3,13,3+Length(St),14);
Control:=New(PStaticText,Init(R,St));
Dlg^.Insert(Control);
```

```
St:='| Hidden Directories    : '+NiceNumber(HiddenDirectories);
R.Assign(3,11,3+Length(St),12);
Control:=New(PStaticText,Init(R,St));
Dlg^.Insert(Control);

St:='| Read-Only Directories: '+NiceNumber(ReadOnlyDirectories);
R.Assign(3,12,3+Length(St),13);
Control:=New(PStaticText,Init(R,St));
Dlg^.Insert(Control);

St:='| EXE Files            : '+NiceNumber(ExeFiles);
R.Assign(3,15,3+Length(St),16);
Control:=New(PStaticText,Init(R,St));
Dlg^.Insert(Control);

St:='| COM Files            : '+NiceNumber(ComFiles);
R.Assign(3,16,3+Length(St),17);
Control:=New(PStaticText,Init(R,St));
Dlg^.Insert(Control);

St:='| BAT Files            : '+NiceNumber(BatFiles);
R.Assign(3,17,3+Length(St),18);
Control:=New(PStaticText,Init(R,St));
Dlg^.Insert(Control);

St:='| Total Files          :              |';
S:=NiceNumber(Files);
Move(S[1],St[26],Length(S));
R.Assign(40,7,77,8);
Control:=New(PStaticText,Init(R,St));
Dlg^.Insert(Control);

St:='| Hidden Files         :              |';
S:=NiceNumber(HiddenFiles);
Move(S[1],St[26],Length(S));
R.Assign(40,11,77,12);
Control:=New(PStaticText,Init(R,St));
Dlg^.Insert(Control);

St:='| Read-Only Files      :              |';
S:=NiceNumber(ReadOnlyFiles);
Move(S[1],St[26],Length(S));
R.Assign(40,12,77,13);
Control:=New(PStaticText,Init(R,St));
Dlg^.Insert(Control);

St:='| Files in Root Dir.   :              |';
S:=NiceNumber(RootFiles);
Move(S[1],St[26],Length(S));
R.Assign(40,8,77,9);
Control:=New(PStaticText,Init(R,St));
Dlg^.Insert(Control);

St:='| Files in Subdir.     :              |';
S:=NiceNumber(SubFiles);
Move(S[1],St[26],Length(S));
```

```
R.Assign(40,9,77,10);
Control:=New(PStaticText,Init(R,St));
Dlg^.Insert(Control);

St:='| New Files this Year   :           |';
S:=NiceNumber(YearFiles);
Move(S[1],St[26],Length(S));
R.Assign(40,17,77,18);
Control:=New(PStaticText,Init(R,St));
Dlg^.Insert(Control);

St:='| New Files this Month :           |';
S:=NiceNumber(MonthFiles);
Move(S[1],St[26],Length(S));
R.Assign(40,16,77,17);
Control:=New(PStaticText,Init(R,St));
Dlg^.Insert(Control);

St:='| New Files Today       :           |';
S:=NiceNumber(DayFiles);
Move(S[1],St[26],Length(S));
R.Assign(40,15,77,16);
Control:=New(PStaticText,Init(R,St));
Dlg^.Insert(Control);

St:='| Archive Bit (Files)   :           |';
S:=NiceNumber(ArchiveFiles);
Move(S[1],St[26],Length(S));
R.Assign(40,13,77,14);
Control:=New(PStaticText,Init(R,St));
Dlg^.Insert(Control);

R.Assign(29,19,50,21);
Control:=New(PButton,Init(R,'~P~revious Page ',cmPrev,bfNormal));
Dlg^.Insert(Control);

R.Assign(54,19,73,21);
Control:=New(PButton,Init(R,'P~r~int Page',cmPrint,bfNormal));
Dlg^.Insert(Control);

R.Assign(6,19,25,21);
Control:=New(PButton,Init(R,'~N~ext Page',cmNext,bfNormal));
Dlg^.Insert(Control);

R.Assign(3,4,4,5);
Control:=New(PStaticText,Init(R,'|'));
Dlg^.Insert(Control);

R.Assign(76,4,77,5);
Control:=New(PStaticText,Init(R,'|'));
Dlg^.Insert(Control);

R.Assign(3,3,4,4);
Control:=New(PStaticText,Init(R,'|'));
Dlg^.Insert(Control);

R.Assign(76,3,77,4);
```

```
  Control:=New(PStaticText,Init(R,'|'));
  Dlg^.Insert(Control);

  R.Assign(3,6,77,7);

Control:=New(PStaticText,Init(R,'|─────────────────────────────────
──────────────────────┤'));
  Dlg^.Insert(Control);

  R.Assign(3,2,77,3);

Control:=New(PStaticText,Init(R,'┌─────────────────────────────────
──────────────────────┐'));
  Dlg^.Insert(Control);

  R.Assign(3,10,77,11);

Control:=New(PStaticText,Init(R,'|─────────────────────────────────
──────────────────────┤'));
  Dlg^.Insert(Control);

  R.Assign(3,14,77,15);

Control:=New(PStaticText,Init(R,'|─────────────────────────────────
──────────────────────┤'));
  Dlg^.Insert(Control);

  R.Assign(3,5,4,6);
  Control:=New(PStaticText,Init(R,'|'));
  Dlg^.Insert(Control);

  R.Assign(76,5,77,6);
  Control:=New(PStaticText,Init(R,'|'));
  Dlg^.Insert(Control);

  R.Assign(3,18,77,19);

Control:=New(PStaticText,Init(R,'└─────────────────────────────────
──────────────────────┘'));
  Dlg^.Insert(Control);

  FileDialog:=Dlg;
END;


FUNCTION DiskDialog:PDialog;
TYPE
  PBiosParameterBlock= ^TBiosParameterBlock;
  TBiosParameterBlock=RECORD
                    DriveNumber,DeviceDriverUnit:Byte;
                    BytesPerSector   :Word;
                    SectorsPerCluster,ShiftFactor:Byte;
                    ReservedSectors:Word;
                    FatCopies        :Byte;
                    RootDirEntries,FirstDataSector,HighestCluster:Word;
                  END;
  PBiosParameterBlock2x= ^TBiosParameterBlock2x;
```

```
TBiosParameterBlock2x=RECORD
                        FatSize         :Byte;
                        RootStart       :Word;
                        DevDriver       :Pointer;
                        Media           :Byte;
                        Dirty           :Byte;
                        Next            :Pointer;
                        CurrDir         :Word;
                        CurrPath        :ARRAY[1..64]OF Char;
                      END;
PBiosParameterBlock3x= ^TBiosParameterBlock3x;
TBiosParameterBlock3x=RECORD
                        FatSize         :Byte;
                        RootStart       :Word;
                        DevDriver       :Pointer;
                        Media           :Byte;
                        Dirty           :Byte;
                        Next            :Pointer;
                        ScanStart       :Word;
                        FreeClus        :Word;
                      END;
PBiosParameterBlock4x= ^TBiosParameterBlock4x;
TBiosParameterBlock4x=RECORD
                        FatSize         :Word;
                        RootStart       :Word;
                        DevDriver       :Pointer;
                        Media           :Byte;
                        Dirty           :Byte;
                        Next            :Pointer;
                        ScanStart       :Word;
                        FreeClus        :Word;
                      END;

VAR
 Dlg             :PDialog;
 R               :TRect;
 Control,Labl,Histry:PView;

 CPU             :Registers;
 BPB             :PBiosParameterBlock;
 BPB2x           :PBiosParameterBlock2x;
 BPB3x           :PBiosParameterBlock3x;
 BPB4x           :PBiosParameterBlock4x;
 drive           :String;
 L,DSize,DFree,DUsed:LongInt;
 SREC            :SEARCHREC;
 St,S            :String;
 I,K             :Integer;
BEGIN

 GetDir(0,drive);
 drive[0]:=#3;

 CPU.AH:=$1F;
 MsDos(CPU);
 BPB:=Ptr(CPU.DS,CPU.BX);
 BPB2x:=Ptr(Seg(BPB^),Ofs(BPB^)+$f);
```

```
Pointer(BPB3x):=BPB2x;
Pointer(BPB4x):=BPB3x;

R.Assign(0,1,80,23);
New(Dlg,Init(R,'Disk Information  '));

St:='| Current Drive: '+drive;
R.Assign(3,3,3+Length(St),4);
Control:=New(PStaticText,Init(R,St));
Dlg^.Insert(Control);

St:='| Number of FATs          : '+NiceNumber(BPB^.FatCopies);
R.Assign(3,11,3+Length(St),12);
Control:=New(PStaticText,Init(R,St));
Dlg^.Insert(Control);

St:='| Maximum Files           : '+NiceNumber(BPB^.RootDirEntries);
R.Assign(3,9,3+Length(St),10);
Control:=New(PStaticText,Init(R,St));
Dlg^.Insert(Control);

St:='| Bytes per Sector        : '+NiceNumber(BPB^.BytesPerSector);
R.Assign(3,13,3+Length(St),14);
Control:=New(PStaticText,Init(R,St));
Dlg^.Insert(Control);

St:='| Sectors per Cluster     : '+NiceNumber(BPB^.SectorsPerCluster+1);
R.Assign(3,15,3+Length(St),16);
Control:=New(PStaticText,Init(R,St));
Dlg^.Insert(Control);

CASE DosVersion AND $F OF
 1,2:St:='| Sectors per FAT         : '+NiceNumber(BPB2x^.FatSize);
 3:St:=  '| Sectors per FAT         : '+NiceNumber(BPB3x^.FatSize);
 4,5:St:='| Sectors per FAT         : '+NiceNumber(BPB4x^.FatSize);
END;
R.Assign(3,10,3+Length(St),11);
Control:=New(PStaticText,Init(R,St));
Dlg^.Insert(Control);

CASE DosVersion AND $F OF
 1,2:St:='| Address of the Drive    : '+NicePointer(BPB2x^.DevDriver);
 3:St:=  '| Address of the Drive    : '+NicePointer(BPB3x^.DevDriver);
 4,5:St:='| Address of the Drive    : '+NicePointer(BPB4x^.DevDriver);
END;
R.Assign(3,7,3+Length(St),8);
Control:=New(PStaticText,Init(R,St));
Dlg^.Insert(Control);

St:='| Number of Clusters      : '+NiceNumber(BPB^.HighestCluster-1);
R.Assign(3,17,3+Length(St),18);
Control:=New(PStaticText,Init(R,St));
Dlg^.Insert(Control);

CASE DosVersion AND $F OF
 1,2:St:='| Number of Free Clusters: ?';
 3:St:='| Number of Free Clusters: '+NiceNumber(BPB3x^.FreeClus);
```

```
  4,5:St:='| Number of Free Clusters: '+NiceNumber(BPB4x^.FreeClus);
END;
R.Assign(3,16,3+Length(St),17);
Control:=New(PStaticText,Init(R,St));
Dlg^.Insert(Control);

S:=GETVOLUME(drive);
IF S='' THEN
    S:='<None>';
St:='| Name: '+S;
R.Assign(27,3,27+Length(St),4);
Control:=New(PStaticText,Init(R,St));
Dlg^.Insert(Control);

DSize:=DiskSize(0);
St:='| Size: '+NiceNumber(DSize);
R.Assign(3,5,3+Length(St),6);
Control:=New(PStaticText,Init(R,St));
Dlg^.Insert(Control);

DFree:=DiskFree(0);
St:='| Free: '+NiceNumber(DFree);
R.Assign(27,5,27+Length(St),6);
Control:=New(PStaticText,Init(R,St));
Dlg^.Insert(Control);

DUsed:=DSize-DFree;
St:='| Used:                   |';
S:=NiceNumber(DUsed);
Move(S[1],St[11],Length(S));
R.Assign(51,5,77,6);
Control:=New(PStaticText,Init(R,St));
Dlg^.Insert(Control);

St:='| Device:                 |';
S:=NiceNumber(BPB^.DeviceDriverUnit);
Move(S[1],St[11],Length(S));
R.Assign(51,3,77,4);
Control:=New(PStaticText,Init(R,St));
Dlg^.Insert(Control);

St:='|';
S:='';
Move(S[1],St[25],Length(S));
R.Assign(76,7,77,8);
Control:=New(PStaticText,Init(R,St));
Dlg^.Insert(Control);

St:='| First FAT Sector     :            |';
S:=NiceNumber(BPB^.ReservedSectors);
Move(S[1],St[25],Length(S));
R.Assign(39,9,77,10);
Control:=New(PStaticText,Init(R,St));
Dlg^.Insert(Control);

St:='| First Data Sector    :            |';
S:=NiceNumber(BPB^.FirstDataSector);
```

```
Move(S[1],St[25],Length(S));
R.Assign(39,11,77,12);
Control:=New(PStaticText,Init(R,St));
Dlg^.Insert(Control);

St:='| First Dir. Sector    :                |';
CASE DosVersion AND $F OF
 1,2:S:=NiceNumber(BPB2x^.RootStart);
 3:S:=NiceNumber(BPB3x^.RootStart);
 4,5:S:=NiceNumber(BPB4x^.RootStart);
END;
Move(S[1],St[25],Length(S));
R.Assign(39,10,77,11);
Control:=New(PStaticText,Init(R,St));
Dlg^.Insert(Control);

St:='| Media Byte           :                |';
CASE DosVersion AND $F OF
 1,2:S:=NiceNumber(BPB2x^.Media)+' ('+MakeHexString(BPB2x^.Media)+'h)';
 3:S:=NiceNumber(BPB3x^.Media)+' ('+MakeHexString(BPB3x^.Media)+'h)';
 4,5:S:=NiceNumber(BPB4x^.Media)+' ('+MakeHexString(BPB4x^.Media)+'h)';
END;
Move(S[1],St[25],Length(S));
R.Assign(39,13,77,14);
Control:=New(PStaticText,Init(R,St));
Dlg^.Insert(Control);

St:='| Number of Sectors    :                |';
WITH BPB^ DO BEGIN
 L:=HighestCluster-1;
 L:=L*(SectorsPerCluster+1);
 L:=L+FirstDataSector;
END;
S:=NiceNumber(L);
Move(S[1],St[25],Length(S));
R.Assign(39,16,77,17);
Control:=New(PStaticText,Init(R,St));
Dlg^.Insert(Control);

St:='| Reserved Sectors     :                |';
S:=NiceNumber(BPB^.ReservedSectors);
Move(S[1],St[25],Length(S));
R.Assign(39,17,77,18);
Control:=New(PStaticText,Init(R,St));
Dlg^.Insert(Control);

St:='| First Data Sector    :                |';
CASE DosVersion AND $F OF
 1,2:S:=NiceNumber(BPB^.FirstDataSector);
 3:S:=NiceNumber(BPB3x^.ScanStart);
 4,5:S:=NiceNumber(BPB4x^.ScanStart);
END;
Move(S[1],St[25],Length(S));
R.Assign(39,15,77,16);
Control:=New(PStaticText,Init(R,St));
Dlg^.Insert(Control);
```

```
   R.Assign(29,19,50,21);
   Control:=New(PButton,Init(R,'~P~revious Page',cmPrev,bfNormal));
   Dlg^.Insert(Control);

   R.Assign(54,19,73,21);
   Control:=New(PButton,Init(R,'P~r~int Page',cmPrint,bfNormal));
   Dlg^.Insert(Control);

   R.Assign(6,19,25,21);
   Control:=New(PButton,Init(R,'~N~ext Page',cmNext,bfNormal));
   Dlg^.Insert(Control);

   R.Assign(3,2,77,3);

Control:=New(PStaticText,Init(R,'                                    '));
   Dlg^.Insert(Control);

   R.Assign(3,4,77,5);

Control:=New(PStaticText,Init(R,'                                    '));
   Dlg^.Insert(Control);

   R.Assign(3,6,77,7);

Control:=New(PStaticText,Init(R,'                                    '));
   Dlg^.Insert(Control);

   R.Assign(3,8,77,9);

Control:=New(PStaticText,Init(R,'                                    '));
   Dlg^.Insert(Control);

   R.Assign(3,12,77,13);

Control:=New(PStaticText,Init(R,'                                    '));
   Dlg^.Insert(Control);

   R.Assign(3,14,77,15);

Control:=New(PStaticText,Init(R,'                                    '));
   Dlg^.Insert(Control);

   R.Assign(3,18,77,19);

Control:=New(PStaticText,Init(R,'                                    '));
   Dlg^.Insert(Control);

   DiskDialog:=Dlg;
  END;
```

```
FUNCTION MemoryDialog:PDialog;
VAR
 Dlg              :PDialog;
 R                :TRect;
 Control,Labl,Histry:PView;

 W1,W2            :Word;
 DosMem,XmsMem,EmsMem,UmaMem,A20Mem:LongInt;
 DosFre,XmsFre,EmsFre,UmaFre,A20Fre:LongInt;
 AllMem,AllFre    :LongInt;
 DosMemory        :Word ABSOLUTE $0000:$0413;
 St,S             :String;
 CPU              :Registers;
BEGIN
 DosMem:=0;DosFre:=0;
 XmsMem:=0;XmsFre:=0;
 EmsMem:=0;EmsFre:=0;
 UmaMem:=0;UmaFre:=0;
 A20Mem:=0;A20Fre:=0;

 R.Assign(0,1,80,23);
 New(Dlg,Init(R,'Memory'));

 R.Assign(4,3,75,4);
 Control:=New(PStaticText,Init(R,'|   Type of Memory         | Version |
Size    |    Free    | Status |'));
 Dlg^.Insert(Control);

 St:='| DOS Memory              |           |            |           | OK
|';
 S:=MakeHexString(GetDosVersion);
 Insert('.',S,2);
 Move(S[1],St[27],Length(S));
 DosMem:=DosMemory;
 DosMem:=DosMem*1024;
 S:=NiceNumber(DosMem);
 Move(S[1],St[37],Length(S));
 DosFre:=MemAvail;
 S:=NiceNumber(DosFre);
 Move(S[1],St[51],Length(S));
 R.Assign(4,5,75,6);
 Control:=New(PStaticText,Init(R,St));
 Dlg^.Insert(Control);

 St:='| XMS Memory              |           |            |           |
|';
 IF XMSInstalled THEN BEGIN
  S:='2.00';
  Move(S[1],St[27],Length(S));
  CPU.AH:=$88;
  Intr($15,CPU);
  XmsMem:=CPU.AX;
  XmsMem:=XmsMem*1024;
  IF XmsMem=0 THEN BEGIN
   XmsResult:=QueryXmsMemory(W1,W2);
   XmsMem:=W1;
```

```
  XmsMem:=XmsMem*1024;
  END;
  S:=NiceNumber(XmsMem);
  Move(S[1],St[37],Length(S));
  XmsResult:=QueryXmsMemory(W1,W2);
  XmsFre:=W2;
  XmsFre:=XmsFre*1024;
  S:=NiceNumber(XmsFre);
  Move(S[1],St[51],Length(S));
    IF XmsResult=0 THEN S:='  OK' ELSE S:='Error';
  Move(S[1],St[64],Length(S));
 END;
 R.Assign(4,11,75,12);
 Control:=New(PStaticText,Init(R,St));
 Dlg^.Insert(Control);

 St:='| A20 (High) Memory     |          |            |           |
|';
 IF XMSInstalled THEN BEGIN
  S:='2.00';
  Move(S[1],St[27],Length(S));
  IF QueryA20=1 THEN BEGIN
   S:='65,535';
   A20Mem:=65535;
   Move(S[1],St[37],Length(S));
   S:='0';
   A20Fre:=0;
   Move(S[1],St[51],Length(S));
  END ELSE BEGIN
   S:='0';
   A20Mem:=0;
   Move(S[1],St[37],Length(S));
   S:='65,535';
   A20Mem:=65535;
   Move(S[1],St[51],Length(S));
  END;
    IF XmsResult=0 THEN S:='  OK' ELSE S:='Error';
  Move(S[1],St[64],Length(S));
 END;
 R.Assign(4,9,75,10);
 Control:=New(PStaticText,Init(R,St));
 Dlg^.Insert(Control);

 St:='| Upper Memory          |          |            |           |
|';
 IF XMSInstalled THEN BEGIN
  S:='2.00';
  Move(S[1],St[27],Length(S));
  XmsResult:=AllocUpperMemBlock(65535,W1,W2);
  UmaMem:=393216;
  UmaFre:=W2;
  UmaFre:=UmaFre*16;
  S:=NiceNumber(UmaMem);
  Move(S[1],St[37],Length(S));
  S:=NiceNumber(UmaFre);
  Move(S[1],St[51],Length(S));
  CASE XmsResult OF
```

```
        0,$B0,$B1:S:='  OK';
        $80:S:=' Error';
      END;
    Move(S[1],St[64],Length(S));
    END;
    R.Assign(4,7,75,8);
    Control:=New(PStaticText,Init(R,St));
    Dlg^.Insert(Control);

    St:='| Expanded Memory      |          |           |              |
|';
    IF EmsInstalled THEN BEGIN
      S:=MakeHexString(GetEmsVersion);
      Insert('.',S,2);
      Move(S[1],St[27],Length(S));
      QueryEmsMemory(EmsMem,EmsFre);
      EmsMem:=EmsMem*1024;
      S:=NiceNumber(EmsMem);
      Move(S[1],St[37],Length(S));
      EmsFre:=EmsFre*1024;
      S:=NiceNumber(EmsFre);
      Move(S[1],St[51],Length(S));
      IF GetEmsStatus=0 THEN S:='  OK' ELSE S:='Error';
      Move(S[1],St[64],Length(S));
    END;
    R.Assign(4,13,75,14);
    Control:=New(PStaticText,Init(R,St));
    Dlg^.Insert(Control);


    R.Assign(4,2,75,3);

Control:=New(PStaticText,Init(R,'
                      '));
    Dlg^.Insert(Control);

    R.Assign(4,4,75,5);

Control:=New(PStaticText,Init(R,'
               '));
    Dlg^.Insert(Control);

    R.Assign(4,6,75,7);

Control:=New(PStaticText,Init(R,'
               '));
    Dlg^.Insert(Control);

    R.Assign(4,8,75,9);

Control:=New(PStaticText,Init(R,'
               '));
    Dlg^.Insert(Control);

    R.Assign(4,10,75,11);
```

```
Control:=New(PStaticText,Init(R,'├─────────────────────┼───────────┼──────────────
├────────────┼───────────┤'));
  Dlg^.Insert(Control);

  R.Assign(4,12,75,13);

Control:=New(PStaticText,Init(R,'├─────────────────────┼───────────┼──────────────
├────────────┼───────────┤'));
  Dlg^.Insert(Control);

  R.Assign(4,14,75,17);

Control:=New(PStaticText,Init(R,'└─────────────────────┴───────────┴──────────────
└────────────┴───────────┘'));
  Dlg^.Insert(Control);

  R.Assign(29,19,50,21);
  Control:=New(PButton,Init(R,'~P~revious Page',cmPrev,bfNormal));
  Dlg^.Insert(Control);

  R.Assign(54,19,73,21);
  Control:=New(PButton,Init(R,'P~r~int Page',cmPrint,bfNormal));
  Dlg^.Insert(Control);

  R.Assign(6,19,25,21);
  Control:=New(PButton,Init(R,'~N~ext Page',cmNext,bfNormal));
  Dlg^.Insert(Control);

  MemoryDialog:=Dlg;
END;


FUNCTION CPUBenchDialog:PDialog;
VAR
  Dlg              :PDialog;
  R                :TRect;
  Control,Labl,Histry:PView;
  CPUSpeed         :LongInt;
  St               :String;

  FUNCTION CPUBench:LongInt;
  CONST
   ToMove          =65535;
  VAR
   Buffer1,Buffer2:Pointer;
   Speed,I,EndTime:LongInt;
  BEGIN
   Speed:=0;
   GetMem(Buffer1,ToMove);
   GetMem(Buffer2,ToMove);
   I:=0;
   EndTime:=CurrentTime+19;
   REPEAT
    FOR I:=1 TO 5 DO Move(Buffer2^,Buffer1^,SizeOf(Buffer1));
    Inc(Speed);
   UNTIL CurrentTime>=EndTime;
```

```
    CPUBench:=Speed;
    FreeMem(Buffer1,ToMove);
    FreeMem(Buffer2,ToMove);
   END;

 BEGIN
  CPUSpeed:=CPUBench;

  R.Assign(0,1,80,23);
  New(Dlg,Init(R,'Motherboard Speed'));

  R.Assign(3,4,23,5);
  Control:=New(PStaticText,Init(R,'This Computer      ┤'));
  Dlg^.Insert(Control);

  R.Assign(3,7,23,8);
  Control:=New(PStaticText,Init(R,'Compaq 386/33 MHz  ┤'));
  Dlg^.Insert(Control);

  R.Assign(3,10,23,11);
  Control:=New(PStaticText,Init(R,'IBM AT 286/8 MHz   ┤'));
  Dlg^.Insert(Control);

  R.Assign(3,13,24,14);
  Control:=New(PStaticText,Init(R,'IBM XT 88/4.77 MHz ┤ '));
  Dlg^.Insert(Control);

  R.Assign(22,9,23,10);
  Control:=New(PStaticText,Init(R,'|'));
  Dlg^.Insert(Control);

  R.Assign(22,3,23,4);
  Control:=New(PStaticText,Init(R,'|'));
  Dlg^.Insert(Control);

  R.Assign(22,8,23,9);
  Control:=New(PStaticText,Init(R,'|'));
  Dlg^.Insert(Control);

  R.Assign(22,6,23,7);
  Control:=New(PStaticText,Init(R,'|'));
  Dlg^.Insert(Control);

  R.Assign(22,5,23,6);
  Control:=New(PStaticText,Init(R,'|'));
  Dlg^.Insert(Control);

  R.Assign(22,15,74,16);

Control:=New(PStaticText,Init(R,'└──────┬───┬───┬───┬───┬───┬───┬───┬
──┬─'));
  Dlg^.Insert(Control);

  R.Assign(27,16,74,17);
  Control:=New(PStaticText,Init(R,'5     10    15    20    25    30    35    40
55    60'));
  Dlg^.Insert(Control);
```

```
      R.Assign(22,11,23,12);
      Control:=New(PStaticText,Init(R,'|'));
      Dlg^.Insert(Control);

      R.Assign(22,12,23,13);
      Control:=New(PStaticText,Init(R,'|'));
      Dlg^.Insert(Control);

      R.Assign(22,14,23,15);
      Control:=New(PStaticText,Init(R,'|'));
      Dlg^.Insert(Control);

      St:=MakeBar(CPUSpeed DIV 1000)+' '+DecimalNumber(CPUSpeed);
      R.Assign(23,4,23+Length(St),5);
      Control:=New(PExtStaticText,Init(R,St));
      Dlg^.Insert(Control);

      R.Assign(23,7,50,8);
      Control:=New(PStaticText,Init(R,'███████████████ 20.969'));
      Dlg^.Insert(Control);

      R.Assign(23,10,34,11);
      Control:=New(PStaticText,Init(R,'████ 4.561'));
      Dlg^.Insert(Control);

      R.Assign(23,13,28,14);
      Control:=New(PStaticText,Init(R,'█ 1.0'));
      Dlg^.Insert(Control);

      R.Assign(3,2,12,3);
      Control:=New(PStaticText,Init(R,'Computer:'));
      Dlg^.Insert(Control);

      R.Assign(39,17,74,18);
      Control:=New(PStaticText,Init(R,'Speed relative to an IBM XT'));
      Dlg^.Insert(Control);

      R.Assign(29,19,50,21);
      Control:=New(PButton,Init(R,'~P~revious Page',cmPrev,bfNormal));
      Dlg^.Insert(Control);

      R.Assign(54,19,73,21);
      Control:=New(PButton,Init(R,'P~r~int Page',cmPrint,bfNormal));
      Dlg^.Insert(Control);

      R.Assign(6,19,25,21);
      Control:=New(PButton,Init(R,'~N~ext Page',cmNext,bfNormal));
      Dlg^.Insert(Control);

      CPUBenchDialog:=Dlg;
    END;


    FUNCTION DiskBenchDialog:PDialog;
    CONST
      MaxRW           =16384;
```

```
VAR
 Dlg             :PDialog;
 R               :TRect;
 Control,Labl,Histry:PView;

 DiskBenchArray :TDiskBenchArray;
 MaxTransfer    :LongInt;
 St             :String;
 Y,I            :Integer;

 PROCEDURE DiskBench;
 VAR
  Result,I,ToRead:Integer;
  EndTime,Counter:LongInt;
  Buffer         :Pointer;
  F              :FILE;
  ReadOverhead   :Byte;
 BEGIN
  ReadOverhead:=getprocessor;
  IF ReadOverhead<4 THEN ReadOverhead:=4;
  FileMode:=0;
  GetMem(Buffer,MaxRW);
  ToRead:=1024;
  Assign(F,'DSpeed$$.tmp');
  FOR I:=1 TO 4 DO BEGIN
   ToRead:=ToRead SHL 1;
   Rewrite(F,1);
   Counter:=0;
   EndTime:=CurrentTime+((ReadOverhead-I)*19);
   REPEAT
    BlockWrite(F,Buffer^,ToRead,Result);
    Inc(Counter,Result);
    IF Result<>ToRead THEN Rewrite(F,1);
   UNTIL CurrentTime>=EndTime;
   Counter:=Counter DIV(ReadOverhead-I);
   DiskBenchArray[I].WriteIt:=Counter;
   Close(F);

   Reset(F,1);
   Counter:=0;
   EndTime:=CurrentTime+19;
   REPEAT
    BlockRead(F,Buffer^,ToRead,Result);
    Inc(Counter,Result);
    IF Result<>ToRead THEN Reset(F,1);
   UNTIL CurrentTime>=EndTime;
   DiskBenchArray[I].ReadIt:=Counter;
   Close(F);
  END;
  MaxTransfer:=0;
  Reset(F,1);
  EndTime:=CurrentTime+19;
  REPEAT
   BlockRead(F,Buffer^,MaxRW,Result);
   Inc(MaxTransfer,MaxRW);
   Reset(F,1);
```

```
    UNTIL CurrentTime>=EndTime;
    Close(F);
    Erase(F);
    FreeMem(Buffer,16384);
  END;

BEGIN
  DiskBench;
  R.Assign(0,1,80,23);
  New(Dlg,Init(R,'Data Transfer Benchmark'));
  R.Assign(3,4,24,5);
  Control:=New(PStaticText,Init(R,'2048    Read      ┤'));
  Dlg^.Insert(Control);
  R.Assign(3,7,23,8);
  Control:=New(PStaticText,Init(R,'4096    Read      ┤'));
  Dlg^.Insert(Control);
  R.Assign(3,10,23,11);
  Control:=New(PStaticText,Init(R,'8192    Read      ┤'));
  Dlg^.Insert(Control);
  R.Assign(3,13,23,14);
  Control:=New(PStaticText,Init(R,'16384   Read      ┤'));
  Dlg^.Insert(Control);
  R.Assign(22,9,23,10);
  Control:=New(PStaticText,Init(R,'|'));
  Dlg^.Insert(Control);
  R.Assign(22,3,23,4);
  Control:=New(PStaticText,Init(R,'|'));
  Dlg^.Insert(Control);
  R.Assign(22,6,23,7);
  Control:=New(PStaticText,Init(R,'|'));
  Dlg^.Insert(Control);
  R.Assign(22,15,74,16);

Control:=New(PStaticText,Init(R,'└──┬──┬──┬──┬──┬──┬──┬──┬──
──┬──'));
  Dlg^.Insert(Control);
  R.Assign(26,16,74,17);
  Control:=New(PStaticText,Init(R,'200   400   600   800 1000 1200 1400 1600
1800 2000'));
  Dlg^.Insert(Control);
  R.Assign(22,12,23,13);
  Control:=New(PStaticText,Init(R,'|'));
  Dlg^.Insert(Control);

  Y:=4;
  FOR I:=1 TO 4 DO BEGIN
    St:=MakeBar((DiskBenchArray[I].ReadIt DIV 1024) DIV 40);
    St:=St+' '+NiceNumber(DiskBenchArray[I].ReadIt)+' Byte';
    R.Assign(23,Y,23+Length(St),Y+1);
    Control:=New(PExtStaticText,Init(R,St));
    Dlg^.Insert(Control);
    St:=MakeBar((DiskBenchArray[I].WriteIt DIV 1024) DIV 40);
    St:=St+' '+NiceNumber(DiskBenchArray[I].WriteIt)+' Byte';
    R.Assign(23,Y+1,23+Length(St),Y+2);
    Control:=New(PExtStaticText,Init(R,St));
    Dlg^.Insert(Control);
    Inc(Y,3);
```

```
  END;

  R.Assign(3,2,19,3);
  Control:=New(PStaticText,Init(R,'Buffer in Bytes:'));
  Dlg^.Insert(Control);

  R.Assign(45,17,74,18);
  Control:=New(PStaticText,Init(R,'KByte per Second'));
  Dlg^.Insert(Control);

  R.Assign(29,19,50,21);
  Control:=New(PButton,Init(R,'~P~revious Page',cmPrev,bfNormal));
  Dlg^.Insert(Control);

  R.Assign(54,19,73,21);
  Control:=New(PButton,Init(R,'P~r~int Page',cmPrint,bfNormal));
  Dlg^.Insert(Control);

  R.Assign(6,19,25,21);
  Control:=New(PButton,Init(R,'~N~ext Page',cmNext,bfDefault));
  Dlg^.Insert(Control);

  R.Assign(11,5,23,6);
  Control:=New(PStaticText,Init(R,'Write        ┤'));
  Dlg^.Insert(Control);

  R.Assign(11,14,23,15);
  Control:=New(PStaticText,Init(R,'Write        ┤'));
  Dlg^.Insert(Control);

  R.Assign(11,11,23,12);
  Control:=New(PStaticText,Init(R,'Write        ┤'));
  Dlg^.Insert(Control);

  R.Assign(11,8,23,9);
  Control:=New(PStaticText,Init(R,'Write        ┤'));
  Dlg^.Insert(Control);

  St:='Maximum Transfer Rate: '+NiceNumber(MaxTransfer)+' Byte';
  R.Assign(3,18,3+Length(St),19);
  Control:=New(PStaticText,Init(R,St));
  Dlg^.Insert(Control);

  DiskBenchDialog:=Dlg;
END;


FUNCTION VideoBenchDialog:PDialog;
VAR
  Dlg              :PDialog;
  R                :TRect;
  Control,Labl,Histry:PView;

  PortBench,BIOSBench:LongInt;
  St               :String;

  PROCEDURE VideoBench;
```

```
VAR
 EndTime,I        :LongInt;
 S                :String;
BEGIN
 FillChar(S,SizeOf(S),#32);
 S[0]:=#255;
 GotoXY(1,1);
 DirectVideo:=True;
 PortBench:=0;
 EndTime:=CurrentTime+19;
 REPEAT
  Write(S);
  Inc(PortBench);
 UNTIL CurrentTime>=EndTime;
 PortBench:=PortBench*Length(S);

 S[0]:=#1;
 GotoXY(1,1);
 DirectVideo:=False;
 BIOSBench:=0;
 EndTime:=CurrentTime+19;
 REPEAT
  Write(S);
  Inc(BIOSBench);
 UNTIL CurrentTime>=EndTime;
 BIOSBench:=BIOSBench*Length(S);
 DirectVideo:=True;
END;

BEGIN
 VideoBench;
 MenuBar^.DrawView;
 DeskTop^.DrawView;
 StatusLine^.DrawView;
 R.Assign(0,1,80,23);
 New(Dlg,Init(R,'Video Benchmark'));

 R.Assign(3,4,23,5);
 Control:=New(PStaticText,Init(R,'This System (Port) ┤'));
 Dlg^.Insert(Control);

 R.Assign(3,7,23,8);
 Control:=New(PStaticText,Init(R,'This System (BIOS) ┤'));
 Dlg^.Insert(Control);

 R.Assign(3,10,23,11);
 Control:=New(PStaticText,Init(R,'TSENG 4/486 (Port) ┤'));
 Dlg^.Insert(Control);

 R.Assign(3,13,23,14);
 Control:=New(PStaticText,Init(R,'TSENG 4/486 (BIOS) ┤'));
 Dlg^.Insert(Control);

 R.Assign(29,19,50,21);
 Control:=New(PButton,Init(R,'~P~revious Page',cmPrev,bfNormal));
 Dlg^.Insert(Control);
```

```
   R.Assign(54,19,73,21);
   Control:=New(PButton,Init(R,'P~r~int Page',cmPrint,bfNormal));
   Dlg^.Insert(Control);

   R.Assign(6,19,25,21);
   Control:=New(PButton,Init(R,'~N~ext Page',cmNext,bfNormal));
   Dlg^.Insert(Control);

   R.Assign(22,9,23,10);
   Control:=New(PStaticText,Init(R,'|'));
   Dlg^.Insert(Control);

   R.Assign(22,3,23,4);
   Control:=New(PStaticText,Init(R,'|'));
   Dlg^.Insert(Control);

   R.Assign(22,8,23,9);
   Control:=New(PStaticText,Init(R,'|'));
   Dlg^.Insert(Control);

   R.Assign(22,6,23,7);
   Control:=New(PStaticText,Init(R,'|'));
   Dlg^.Insert(Control);

   R.Assign(22,5,23,6);
   Control:=New(PStaticText,Init(R,'|'));
   Dlg^.Insert(Control);

   R.Assign(22,15,74,16);

Control:=New(PStaticText,Init(R,'└──────┬────┬────┬────┬────┬────┬────┬────
──┬─'));
   Dlg^.Insert(Control);

   R.Assign(27,16,74,17);
   Control:=New(PStaticText,Init(R,'5       10    15    20    25    30    35    40
45    50'));
   Dlg^.Insert(Control);

   R.Assign(22,11,23,12);
   Control:=New(PStaticText,Init(R,'|'));
   Dlg^.Insert(Control);

   R.Assign(22,12,23,13);
   Control:=New(PStaticText,Init(R,'|'));
   Dlg^.Insert(Control);

   R.Assign(22,14,23,15);
   Control:=New(PStaticText,Init(R,'|'));
   Dlg^.Insert(Control);

   St:=MakeBar(PortBench DIV 1000)+' '+DecimalNumber(PortBench);
   R.Assign(23,4,23+Length(St),5);
   Control:=New(PExtStaticText,Init(R,St));
   Dlg^.Insert(Control);

   St:=MakeBar(BIOSBench DIV 1000)+' '+DecimalNumber(BIOSBench);
```

```
    R.Assign(23,7,23+Length(St),8);
    Control:=New(PExtStaticText,Init(R,St));
    Dlg^.Insert(Control);

    R.Assign(23,10,57,11);
    Control:=New(PStaticText,Init(R,'█████████████████████     27.030'));
    Dlg^.Insert(Control);

    R.Assign(23,13,36,14);
    Control:=New(PStaticText,Init(R,'████████      7.280'));
    Dlg^.Insert(Control);

    R.Assign(3,2,23,3);
    Control:=New(PStaticText,Init(R,'Graphics Card:'));
    Dlg^.Insert(Control);

    R.Assign(33,17,74,18);
    Control:=New(PStaticText,Init(R,'1,000 instructions per second'));
    Dlg^.Insert(Control);

    VideoBenchDialog:=Dlg;
END;


FUNCTION ViewDialog(What:Integer):PDialog;
VAR
 Dlg             :PDialog;
 R               :TRect;
 Control,Labl,Histry:PView;
 VSB,HSB         :PScrollBar;
 St              :String;
 S               :PathStr;

BEGIN
  R.Assign(0,1,80,23);
  CASE What OF
       cmvConfig:St:='C:\CONFIG.SYS';
       cmvAutoexec:St:='C:\AUTOEXEC.BAT';
END;
 New(Dlg,Init(R,St));

 R.Assign(29,19,50,21);
 Control:=New(PButton,Init(R,'~P~revious Page',cmPrev,bfNormal));
 Dlg^.Insert(Control);

 R.Assign(54,19,73,21);
 Control:=New(PButton,Init(R,'P~r~int Page',cmPrint,bfNormal));
 Dlg^.Insert(Control);

 R.Assign(6,19,25,21);
 Control:=New(PButton,Init(R,'~N~ext Page',cmNext,bfDefault));
 Dlg^.Insert(Control);

 R.Assign(78,1,79,19);
 VSB:=New(PScrollBar,Init(R));
 Dlg^.Insert(VSB);
```

```
    R.Assign(1,1,78,19);
    Control:=New(PExtListViewer,Init(R,1,NIL,VSB,St));
    Dlg^.Insert(Control);

    ViewDialog:=Dlg;
END;

PROCEDURE TSysApp.HandleEvent(VAR Event:TEvent);
VAR
 P                :Pointer;
 CPU              :Registers;
 S                :PathStr;
BEGIN
 WITH Event DO
  CASE What OF
   evCommand:
    CASE Command OF
     cmPrint:Intr($5,CPU);
     cmNext,cmPrev:BEGIN
                    P:=Message(@Self,evCommand,cmClose,NIL);
                    IF Command=cmNext THEN Inc(CurrentWindow) ELSE
Dec(CurrentWindow);
                    IF CurrentWindow>MaxWindow THEN
CurrentWindow:=MinWindow;
                    IF CurrentWindow<MinWindow THEN
CurrentWindow:=MaxWindow;
                    P:=Message(@Self,evCommand,CurrentWindow,NIL);
                   END
     ELSE IF(Command>=MinWindow) AND(Command<=MaxWindow)THEN BEGIN
       CurrentWindow:=Command;
       P:=Message(@Self,evCommand,cmClose,NIL);
       CASE Command OF
        cmhProcessor:Insert(ProcessorDialog);
        cmhCoprocessor:Insert(CoprocessorDialog);
        cmhVideo:Insert(VideoDialog);
        cmhPort:Insert(PortDialog);
        cmlFile:BEGIN
                 Wait;
                 Insert(FileDialog);
                END;
        cmlDisk:BEGIN
                 Wait;
                 Insert(DiskDialog);
                END;
        cmsDOS:Insert(DosDialog);
        cmsMemory:Insert(MemoryDialog);
        cmbCPUBench:Insert(CPUBenchDialog);
        cmbDiskBench:BEGIN
                      Wait;
                      Insert(DiskBenchDialog);
                     END;
        cmbVideoBench:Insert(VideoBenchDialog);
        cmvConfig:BEGIN
                   S:=FSearch('CONFIG.SYS','C:\');
                   if S <> '' then
                      Insert(ViewDialog(CurrentWindow))
```

```
                         else
                             Not_Found;
                     END;
        cmvAutoexec:BEGIN
                         S:=FSearch('AUTOEXEC.BAT','C:\');
                             if S <> '' then
                                 Insert(ViewDialog(CurrentWindow))
                             else
                                 Not_Found;
                         END;
            END;
          END;
        END;
      END;
  TApplication.HandleEvent(Event);
  END;


BEGIN
  SysApp.Init;
  SysApp.Insert(ProcessorDialog);
  SysApp.Run;
  SysApp.Done;
END.
```

13.3 System Sleuth Professional

System Sleuth Professional is a trademark of Dariana, Inc. of Cypress, CA, Copyright (c) 1988, 1989 David Seifert. The System Sleuth Professional documentation is reproduced in this section with the permission of Dariana, Inc.

Introduction

About System Analyzer

System Analyzer is a passive diagnostic utility. Passive analysis programs like System Analyzer gather hardware and software information about a computer. These programs help determine what components are installed on a system. In fact, a lot of information can be collected even before the cover is removed from the machine. This saves valuable troubleshooting time.

To run System Analyzer, the following hardware and software are required:

Hardware:

- IBM PC, PC-XT, PC-AT, or 100% compatible computer.

- 256K of RAM installed and at least 192K of available memory.

- Monochrome/Hercules/CGA/EGA or VGA display adapter with appropriate display.

Software:

- MS or PC-DOS Version 2.1 or higher.

Getting Started

Installation

Before installing System Analyzer, make a working copy of the distribution diskettes. To do this, use the DOS DISKCOPY command. See the beginning of this chapter for installation instructions.

Type the following to run System Analyzer from the drive and directory containing the program and press (Enter):

```
SLEUTH
```

The System Analyzer has a menu system that can be activated at any time by pressing (F10). Most menu items have context sensitive help (press (F1) for context sensitive help).

Startup Conditions

Start System Analyzer and follow along as you learn how to use this unique diagnostic utility.

To start System Analyzer simply enter the SLEUTH command at the DOS prompt. If you want to run System Analyzer from a working copy in the A: drive, type the following at the DOS A: prompt:

```
A>SLEUTH
```

If you've placed the System Analyzer files in a subdirectory or on a different drive, you must change to the current drive and directory in order to start System Analyzer.

For example:

```
C:\ABACUS\486\SLEUTH
```

After a few moments, the opening screen will appear, showing the System Analyzer title window. This window also appears when you select About System Analyzer (Alt + F1).

Screen Layout

System Analyzer incorporates a drop-down menu system, sometimes called a point-and-shoot interface. System Analyzer functions can be accessed from the keyboard or a mouse. (For mouse support, be sure that an appropriate mouse driver is installed in the CONFIG.SYS file.)

The background field on which all activity takes place is called the Desktop.

To access functions with the keyboard, use the Shortcut keys. Each Shortcut key sequence uses the same general format: Alt +Keyname. This indicates that you hold down the Alt key and press the indicated key. The following illustration is an example of a desktop with an opened menu and display windows.

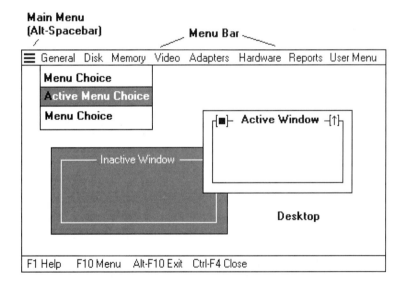

Desktop Screen Elements

The screen elements are as follows:

System Menu

Accessed by clicking on the system menu button in the upper-left corner of the screen, or by using Alt + Spacebar from the keyboard.

Menu Bar

Clicking on each Menu option or pressing [Alt]+First letter of the menu option activates its menu.

Information is displayed in Windows. Many windows can be opened on the desktop simultaneously. In fact, the number of windows you can open depends on the amount of memory on your system.

Windows can be layered, or Cascaded, on top of one another, similar to papers on a desktop. The upper-most window is called the Active Window. Cascading windows over others partially or completely hides the information found in the bottom-most windows.

Windows can also be Tiled. In this case the window size is adjusted so that each window has the same amount of viewing space; no windows overlap or obscure the windows around it.

Two types of windows can appear on the desktop: Active and Inactive.

The Active Window is the top, or current window. Like paper on a desk, the active window is the window you manipulate. If user interaction is required by the window, only the active window responds to user input.

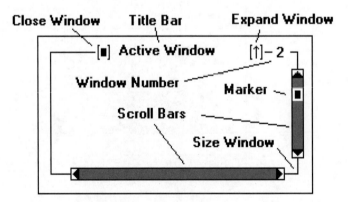

Active Window

This illustration shows an Active window display. An active window has several elements.

Title Bar

Shows the name of the window. The Title Bar performs tasks other than just displaying the Window name. The term "Title Bar" usually refers to the entire area above the top of a window. However, there are a few exceptions, which are noted below.

Close Window Button

Clicking on this button or pressing [Alt]+[F3] will deactivate or close the Active window, removing it from the screen. This area is NOT considered part of the Title Bar.

Expand/Contract Window Button

This button can appear as an Up arrow ([↑]) or an arrow pointing both Up and Down. Clicking on this button when it is an Up arrow ([↑]) resizes the window to full screen. If the button appears as an Up/Down arrow, it will contract or reduce the window to its original size. This area is NOT considered part of the Title Bar.

Window Number

The window number refers to the order in which the window was originally opened. If you are using the keyboard to run the program, [Alt]+Window Number will make that window the active window. To use [Alt]+Window Number, you can have a maximum of nine windows open at once ([Alt]+[1] through [Alt]+[9]). This area is NOT considered part of the Title Bar.

Scroll Bars

An active window is equipped with scroll bars, which let you display information that's hidden because of reduced window size. The Scroll bars become active when necessary. An active scroll bar will have a Marker. The Scroll bar Marker indicates the relative position of your view of the information in the window. For example, if the Marker appears in the middle of a scroll bar, an approximately equal amount of information can be revealed by moving the marker up or down. Clicking on the Up/Down arrows of the scroll bar moves the window display up, down, left, or right one line or column. You may also use the Up, Down, Left, and Right arrow keys ([↑] [↓] [→] [←]) on the keyboard for the same purpose.

Clicking on the Scroll Bar area immediately above or below the Marker will move the window display up or down one "window page" of information. The PgUp/PgDown keys ([PgUp] [PgDn]) on the keyboard perform a similar function.

You can move a Window around on the Desktop by pointing at the Title bar, clicking and dragging the window to the desired position.

Size Window

This area of the window is used to change the size of the window area. To do this, click on the area and, while the mouse button is depressed, drag the corner of the window to the proper size.

> Only the Active Window can be sized or moved on the desktop.)

Windows and Dialog Boxes

There are actually two types of window displays: Windows and Dialog boxes. A Window is used to display information. A dialog box lets you communicate with the system. In other words, dialog boxes allow the program to ask questions and let you input an answer. Unlike Windows, a Dialog box can be moved by dragging it around the desktop, but it cannot be sized.

System Menu Functions

Clicking on the three horizontal bars in the left corner of the Menu Bar opens the System menu (pressing [Alt]+[Spacebar] on the keyboard has the same effect). You can also access this menu by simply pressing [F10] followed by [Enter]. The System menu provides several options for customizing the way information appears on the desktop.

> Any available shortcut key sequences are displayed to the right of the menu option name.)

If a menu option is displayed in dimmed characters, that menu option is inactive (not currently available). For example, if you have no open windows on the Desktop, the menu options related to Windows will be inactive.

Help

Help is available at all times by pressing [F1]. However, you can also access the help system by using this menu option. If Help displays a message that no help is available, refer to this User's Guide for more information.

About System Sleuth

This displays the program name, program Copyright notice, and product version number in a dialog box. This is the window that's displayed when you first start System Analyzer. [Alt]+[F1] also displays this dialog box.

Setup Options

Three sub-menu functions are available through Setup Options.

Printer Setup

This sub-option allows you to define the way that System Analyzer communicates with a printing device. The dialog box is split into two main areas:

Device

These are the logical devices where you send a report:

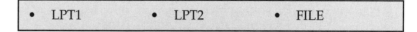

| • LPT1 | • LPT2 | • FILE |

TAKE NOTE

It's possible to send report output to one of the COMx: ports. Simply redirect the normal LPTx: printer output to one of the COM ports using MODE.COM prior to running System Analyzer. Refer to your DOS manual for more information on using MODE.COM.

File Name

Entering a name in this field sends the report to the selected printing device.

TAKE NOTE

Using the name CON as a filename sends report output to the video display. The output to CON does NOT pause for viewing while the report is being generated.

Printer Setup String

Entering control codes on this line sends commands to your printer prior to the report output function. System Analyzer expects printer control codes as a series of 3 digit decimal values. For example, the codes:

```
027 107 000
```

would set a Panasonic KX-P1180 dot-matrix printer in Near Letter Quality (NLQ) mode, Courier Font. Note that ALL printer control codes MUST be a 3 digit number: 001, 123, 010, etc. Refer to your printer manual to select the correct control codes for your printer.

User Menu Setup

Selecting this sub-option opens an interactive window to allow configuring the User Menu on the Menu Bar. Application programs (within memory limits of your system) can be included in the User Menu system.

It isn't possible to run internal DOS commands, such as DIR and COPY, through the User Defined menu. Use the DOS Shell to perform these functions.

There are three main data entry areas for the eight user defined menu options: Menu Item X, Command, and Parameters. Use the Tab key to move from one area to another. Pressing Enter signals the end of a data entry process and the dialog box will close.

Menu Item X

X = a menu option. Enter a brief description of the menu option here. Characters enclosed in the tilde "~" symbol are assigned as Shortcut keys. For example:

```
~C~hkdsk of C: Drive
My New ~M~enu
Do T~h~is Now
```

are all examples of how a Menu Item could be entered. In each case, the letters enclosed in tilde symbols will be the Shortcut key.

(Note: The User Defined Menu DOES NOT alphabetize menu options. They appear on the menu in the order in which you enter them.)

Command

The command line is the name of the application program you want the menu option to run and where it can be found. For example:

```
C:\DOS\CHKDSK.COM
D:\PROGRAMS\SYSTEM\TEST.COM
C:\UTIL\DT.EXE
```

The COMPLETE PATH NAME (Drive letter AND subdirectory names) MUST be included. If you don't provide the complete PATH and filename the menu option may not be able to complete its task.

Parameters

An entry in this area causes the entry to be appended to the program name in Command. In the first example above:

```
/F
```

on the Parameters line would append the "/F" command line switch to CHKDSK.

If you want to supply your own command line Parameters at option run time, simply place a question mark "?" in the Parameters area. When a menu option labeled like this runs, a dialog box will open, allowing you to enter your own command line parameters.

When you have finished entering menu options, select OK and the Dialog box will close.

TAKE NOTE

> On closing, User Menu Setup will write a file to the current drive and directory called SLEUTH.MNU. All User Menu information is stored in this file. If erased, no User menu options will appear during your next System Analyzer session.)

Display Colors

Display colors lets you change the colors from the display default settings. When selected, a dialog box opens. This box contains areas related to the desktop and its related components. All areas can be selected by clicking on them with the mouse or by using the Alt Key combination related to that area.

Items

Desktop Groups are divided into four areas:

• Desktop	• Menus
• Dialogs	• Windows

Selecting any of these will activate the Items area of the dialog, which shows all the features of that Group that can be changed.

Foreground colors and background colors can be selected for each item in the Group. The number of colors available varies according to the video adapter detected in your system. After all color modifications have been made, click on or select OK to complete the session.

TAKE NOTE

> On closing, Display Colors will write a file to the current drive and directory called SLEUTH.PAL. All color information is stored in this file. If erased, System Analyzer will revert to its default color settings.)

Move/Resize

This provides keyboard control of the position and size of the active window. When Move/Resize is active, the active window border changes to a single outline. Use the arrow keys on the keyboard to move the window. To change the window size, press the [Shift] and arrow keys. Press [Enter] to set the window size and position as selected or press [Esc] to cancel the operation and return the window to its previous size and position.

Next Window

Selecting this option makes the next Window number active. This option is useful if you're running the program without a mouse and more than 9 Windows are on the screen at once.

Zoom/Restore Window

This option performs the same functions as double-clicking on the active window title bar. A maximized, or full-screen, window is reduced to its original size. A small window is increased so that it fills the entire screen.

Close Window

Closes the currently active Window. The next window number will become active.

Tile Windows

Tiling places the windows next to each other without overlapping them. Each window is given the same amount of display room. Any time a window is expanded or a new window is added to the number open, the Windows mode returns to Cascade mode. You must select Tile Windows to arrange the windows. Windows may also be tiled by using the keyboard ([Shift]+[F4]).

Cascade Windows

The windows overlap (covering each other). The keyboard command [Shift]+[F5] changes the display to Tile mode.

25/50 Line Mode

Some video adapters can display text in 50 line mode. System Analyzer displays information in 50 line mode.

DOS Shell

Using DOS Shell starts a secondary Command processor in memory. This is the accepted method of running DOS commands, such as DIR and COPY. Typing EXIT at the DOS prompt returns you to System Analyzer. When running a DOS shell, there is no indication on the screen that you are still running System Analyzer. Since a secondary DOS session is in progress, you may find that certain application programs no longer have enough memory to run properly. This is normal. To free additional memory you must return to System Analyzer and Exit to DOS.

You may be wondering whether it's possible to use the DOS shell and start a second System Analyzer session. Although you can do this, you must use some clues to determine which Sleuth is which.

---

1. The About System Analyzer sign-on message appears when you start the second Sleuth session. Usually when you return from a DOS Shell, the desktop appears as it did before the DOS Shell was run. A new Sleuth session will display the original opening screen.

2. System Analyzer normally installs part of its code resident (as a TSR). The TSR map shows SLEUTH.EXE installed with only one Sleuth session in force. The clue is in how much memory the TSR entries are consuming. If one of the SLEUTH.EXE entries is using more than 100K of RAM, you are running more than one Sleuth session.

Exit

This menu option has the same effect as Ctrl + F4. Your System Analyzer session ends and you return to DOS.

Getting Help

Select F1 to activate the help function. Help is available within most parts of the program. When indicated on the last line of the screen, selecting F1 displays context-sensitive help for the currently active function or window. You'll see a reference to a section of the manual for further information.

Each help item listing contains two parts. The first is the reference to the command itself, its function, and use. The second is a reference to the section(s) of the Users Manual that explain the function in greater detail.

General

The General menu provides information about the basic hardware and software configuration of the system being examined.

System Overview

System Overview provides an overview of your system and its subsystems, such as CPU type, overall memory statistics, serial and parallel ports installed, etc.

General System Information

Includes basic system information, such as the kind of processor (CPU) being used in the system, the presence of a math coprocessor, which version of DOS is in use, the number and type of peripheral ports, and information about the BIOS ROM installed in the system.

CMOS RAM Information

Information shown here is contained in the battery-powered CMOS RAM of AT-Class systems.

Motherboard Switches

This reveals the settings of the motherboard DIP switch settings on PC and XT class systems.

TAKE NOTE

This option will NOT be available on Systems that adhere to the AT standard Real Time Clock register usage conventions.

Disk

The options on this menu all relate to the fixed disk drives installed in the system. This information pertains to local drives C: or higher. The information is available at both a physical device level and the logical drive level.

Overview

This provides information about the physical characteristics of the fixed drives installed in the system. If there are two drives installed, information is provided for each drive. This information includes the number of cylinders on each disk and the number of heads.

Partition Tables

Each physical hard drive attached to a system must have a partition table. This table is located on the first track of each hard drive. The table, which has a maximum of four entries, details how the drive is divided. Partitioning allows the physical hard drive to be divided into a number of logical disks.

Low Level Details

Each logical drive attached to a system has an area on its first track that contains key information about the format of the drive. This area is called the BIOS Parameter Block (BPB). The BPB introduces the operating system to the layout of the disk. These details include the number of File Allocation Tables (FATs), number of directory entries, number of heads in the hard drive and more. If there is more than one disk (logical) attached to the system, you will be prompted to press any key to see the BPB details for the next drive.

Usage Statistics

This option displays the amount of disk space that's used on each logical hard drive in a system. With a few exceptions, this report is similar to that of the DOS CHKDSK command.

Bad Track Map

Selecting Bad Track Map generates a listing of the bad tracks System Analyzer detects on the hard drive. A file is created in the root directory of the drive being tested that contains the list of bad tracks. To generate a bad track list, select Bad Track Map from the menu and follow the instructions in the dialog boxes. This list should be used to tell the low level formatting program which tracks are not able to store data and should be avoided. This list is generated by testing each sector on the disk's surface, whether previously marked bad or not.

View File

Selecting View File opens a dialog box and prompts you for a specific filename to examine. This option allows you to view any file on any disk on a sector-by-sector basis. Once you have defined a valid filename (including a path, if necessary), the display shows the contents of the first 256 bytes of the file. Each byte within the display is shown as a two character hexadecimal value, with ASCII equivalents shown on the right.

Memory

These menu options all relate to the system memory installed in your computer system. It provides information about the physical properties of the memory installed as well as the present contents of memory.

Overview

The basic system memory statistics are displayed. Submenus are available and can be selected like main menu options. The View Memory option requires user input.

Memory Managers

The right panel shows information about the memory managers and the amount of memory under their control. This information varies from system to system. Also included are statistics on Conventional, or DOS memory.

TSR Map

This option reports the names, load addresses, memory consumption and interrupts trapped by the Terminate and Stay Resident programs loaded into the system. The load address is specified as a four digit hexadecimal segment address. This is the significant part of the address where the program is loaded. The absolute load address is the displayed segment address with an offset of 0000. The length displayed is the size of the program's memory image in decimal.

TAKE NOTE

> A particularly well-behaved TSR will install itself in memory, then remove most references to its existence. In effect, it becomes part of the disk operating system. System Analyzer will locate a TSR of this type and describe it as a "Child of DOS".)

Device Drivers

This option reports the list of device drivers that are present in the system. Device drivers are the operating system's method of communicating with the hardware attached to the system.

EMS/XMS Verification

This option tries to allocate all available EMS or XMS memory, write to that memory, read the written data, compare the data with the original, and then de-allocate the memory. The purpose of this test is to determine whether all the pages of EMS and XMS can reliably hold data. A dialog box opens showing that the test is in progress. When completed, a window will open showing the results of the testing. If an error occurs, a line will be printed in the window explaining exactly what was wrong and on which logical page the error occurred. This information lets you determine which particular memory device is defective by consulting the hardware manufacturer's documentation.

View Memory

This option displays the current contents of any address in memory. Upon selection of this option you are prompted for a segment base.

Segment Base in HEX

This address should be specified as a 4 digit hexadecimal segment address. Enter the memory location to view the contents of the memory and click (OK).

Once the segment base has been specified, System Analyzer will display the 256 bytes of memory that start with the specified address. Each line of the display shows 16 bytes of data in 2 digit hexadecimal form. Following the hex bytes on the same line are the equivalent ASCII characters for the bytes in the file. The ASCII characters on the right of the display may look strange. This is normal for non-ASCII (binary) information.

Video

This menu relates to the display adapter and display attached to the system.

Overview

System Analyzer lists the type of display (monitor type) attached to the currently active display adapter (video card), if possible. Again, if a multimode adapter is present, and it is set in an emulation mode, the display (monitor) type may be different from the one stated by System Analyzer.

VGA Details

If System Analyzer determines that a Video Graphics Array Adapter is present, select (PgDn) to view detailed VGA information, such as the current video mode, the number of colors, video pages, and the amount of video RAM installed.

Adapters

Overview

This menu choice provides two standard levels of analysis of the contents of the expansion ROM area of the system's memory. Selecting this menu item displays a map of the memory range from address C000:0 through F000:0. The display shows the status of each of the four 16K "pages" of memory within each segment. The primary screen shows the I/O Card Area as a set of 4 16K pages within each of 4 64K segments. The offset address is also shown for each block. The color of the block (or shading pattern in monochrome) indicates whether that area of memory is currently being used by an expansion card.

C000 - F000 Segment Detail

If a valid ROM is located within a specified segment, the copyright notice from that ROM is also displayed. This information is helpful in determining not only what address space is being used but what device is using it.

Hardware

This menu provides IRQ Availability, I/O base port availability, an Interrupt vector table, a standard, or generic I/O port map, and Installation Assistant.

IRQ Availability

This window displays information about each of the 8 (16 in AT type systems) Interrupt Request channels available in a system. The information about each channel is displayed horizontally.

INT Vector Table

This option displays the segment and offset values (in hexadecimal format) for each of the 256 interrupt vectors supported by the Intel 86 family of microprocessors. These values are pointers (indirect references) to the address in memory where execution should be transferred when the interrupt is requested.

Installation Assistant

Installation Assistant simplifies installing new hardware, such as network adapters and other specialized I/O boards.

Selecting Installation assistant from the Main Menu displays the Installation Assistant screen. Note that the screen is divided into SECTIONS, or columns. Pressing the (Tab) key moves the cursor from one section to another. Use the Up/Down arrow keys to move from field to field within a section. While you are in this screen, pressing (Esc) at any time returns you to the Main Menu.

I/O Ports

To check I/O address availability, some user input is necessary. Enter a 4 digit hexadecimal address to check, then press (Enter). If you press (Enter) on a blank field, "0000" will appear in that field. When you have finished entering I/O Port base addresses to check, press the (Tab) key to move to the next section.

Memory Address Ranges

To check for the availability of an upper memory address range, you must supply a starting and ending 4 digit hexadecimal address. As in the I/O Ports section, if you press (Enter) on a blank starting address field, "0000" will be displayed. Type in a starting address and press [Enter]. The cursor will move to the ending address field and wait for you to supply a second 4 digit hexadecimal address. If you press [Enter] at this point, an address 4K greater than the starting address will be supplied. Press the [Tab] key when you are finished entering memory address ranges to move to the next section.

Test / Cancel / Save

Press [Tab] to move between these options. Pressing [Enter] when Test is highlighted will check availability on all I/O Port, memory address, IRQ and DMA channels.

Save

If it becomes necessary to check for the same I/O port or memory address ranges on several systems, use the SAVE option to save the information you have entered on disk. The default file save name is INSTALL.CFG. You may rename this file after saving to make it possible for a number of different saved configurations to reside on the same disk. However, there can be only one configuration file named INSTALL.CFG on the disk or parent directory where your System Sleuth files are stored.

If INSTALL.CFG is found when Installation Assistant starts, you will be asked if the saved configuration should be used. If you answer Yes to this question, information stored in INSTALL.CFG is restored to the screen. If you answer No, Installation Assistant will start with empty address fields.

Cancel

Use the Cancel option to return to the Main Menu. Selecting this option performs the same function as pressing [Esc].

I/O Ports - Standard Map

A list, which represents a generic list of port assignments for systems of the type being examined, appears. In other words, each type of system (PC,XT,AT,PS/2) has a different set of standard port assignments.

I/O Ports - Availability

The I/O Port Usage option lets you query an I/O address before configuring and installing a new card, which saves much guesswork. When I/O Ports - Availability is selected, you will be asked for a base port address. Most devices use I/O ports in groups of 8 at a time.

Select (PgUp)/(PgDn) to examine port addresses before and after the address you originally specified. Since the low I/O address range contains 65,536 addresses, numerous device combinations can use this space. Some of these devices, such as disk controllers and video adapters, interpret System Analyzer's I/O read signal as a command to perform some function. Use this option carefully. DO NOT ARBITRARILY QUERY I/O PORTS IN THIS AREA.

Reports

Report Options help prepare formatted reports of System Analyzer findings.

Create Custom Header

Allows you to place a heading at the top of each printed report page. You may enter up to three lines of descriptive text. To remove the default page header from all reports, leave the custom header lines blank and click or select (OK). Custom headers are only valid for the current report generation process. Only the default header is saved.

Select Report Items

Each available report item is indicated in the dialog box. Make your selections with the mouse, or press (Tab) and move the pointer through the various options. Press the (Spacebar) to select AND unselect each report item.

Print Report

Select this option to send the selected report to the output device chosen in Printer Setup.

User Menu

This menu displays all the user menu items input through the "Setup Options / User Menu Setup" function on the System Menu. The menu items displayed are read from the file SLEUTH.MNU. If a file isn't present at startup, User menu options won't be available. Refer to the Getting Started section for information on User Menus.

STEST

This diagnostic program performs intensive system tests. Type the following and press (Enter):

STEST

For help at anytime, press (F1).

The scan code is transmitted by the keyboard controller chip to the PC, where the code is converted to an ASCII value. The values are presented in rows.

Although the ASCII character set and the extended keyboard codes are standardized, scan codes vary depending on the keyboard. All three keyboard standards work with a different set of scan codes. This is shown in the following illustration which displays the scan codes for the PC/XT and AT keyboards.

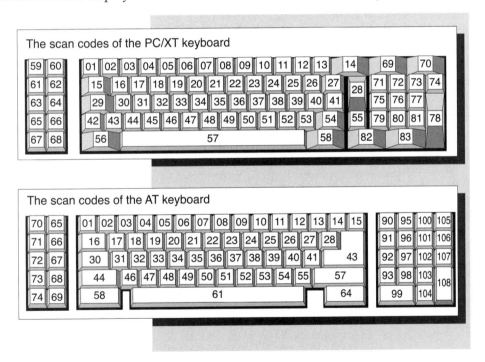

MF-II extended scan codes

Because of the AT keyboard controller, the MF-II keyboard also returns the same scan codes at port 60H as the AT keyboard, even though they are slightly extended. The MF-II supports three scan code sets that are different from any previous keyboards.

The following illustration lists the additional MF-II keyboard scan codes. A byte containing the value E0H precedes each code. This byte indicates an extended scan code that must be handled in a special way. This is because most of the scan codes are already reserved, and would otherwise be interpreted incorrectly.

Extended Scan Codes on the MF-II Keyboard		
Function keys	**Make**	**Break**
F11	57	D7
F12	58	D8
Gray cursor keys in separate cursor block	**Make**	**Break**
Home	E0 47	E0 C7
Cursor Up	E0 48	E0 C8
Page Up	E0 49	E0 C9
Cursor Left	E0 4B	E0 CB
Cursor Right	E0 4D	E0 CD
End	E0 47	E0 C7
Cursor Down	E0 50	E0 D0
Page Down	E0 51	E0 D1
Insert	E0 52	E0 D2
Delete	E0 53	E0 D3
All numbers are in hexadecimal notation		

In this instance, the break code equals the make code plus 80H and the initial E0H isn't changed. For the cursor keys of the gray cursor block that are used in combination with the Shift key, the Shift key must first be suppressed. So, the break code for the Shift key is sent before this scan code.

For the left Shift key, the prefix of this make code is E0H AAH and the prefix of the break code is E0H D2H. For the right Shift key, the make code is E0H B6H and the break code is E0H D2H.

Appendix B — Country Codes

DOS can be adapted to the specific requirements of the different countries. For example, you can adapt it to a country's date, time, and currency symbol. It's also possible to use country specific characters. The abbreviation Tsd. is the thousands separator (i.e., 1,000 for USA or 1.000 for Germany).

Country	Code	Date	Time	Dec.	Tsd.	Code Pg
USA	001	M-D-Y	ST:M:S.HS	.	,	437
French.Can.	002	Y-M-D	ST:M:S,HS	,	,	863
Latin Am.	003	D/M/Y	ST:M:S.HS	.	,	437
Netherl.	031	D-M-Y	ST:M:S,HS	,	.	437
Belgium	032	D/M/Y	ST:M:S,HS	.	,	437
France	033	D/M/Y	ST:M:S,HS	,		437
Spain	034	D/M/Y	ST:M:S,HS	,	.	437
Italy	039	D/M/Y	ST:M:S,HS	,	.	437
Switzerland	041	D.M.Y	ST.M.S.HS	.	,	437
UK	044	D-M-Y	ST:M:S.HS	.	,	437
Denmark	045	D/M/Y	ST.M.S,HS	,	.	865
Sweden	046	Y-M-D	ST.M.S,HS	,	.	437
Norway	047	D/M/Y	ST.M.S,HS	,	.	865
Germany	049	D.M.Y	ST.M.S,HS	,	.	437
Intern.	061	D-M-Y	ST:M:S.HS	.	,	437
Portugal	351	D/M/Y	ST:M:S,HS	,	.	860
Finland	358	D.M.Y	ST.M.S,HS	,		437

Appendix C

Device Designations

The following abbreviations are commonly used to address a device under DOS. They are used, for example, with the COPY command. All devices are identified by a colon to differentiate them from files. The colon is only required for the logical drives A: to Z:.

Addresses for DOS Devices	
Name	**Device**
A:	First diskette drive
B:	Second diskette drive
C:	First hard drive partition or RAM Disk
D:	Second hard drive partition/logical drive
E to Z:	Additional logical drives of the second hard drive partition or of additional device drivers
CON:	Console (display screen and keyboard)
PRN:	Output device of the first parallel interface (for example printer)
LPT1:	Output device of the first parallel interface (for example printer)
LPT2:	Output device on the second parallel interface (for example additional printer)
LPT3:	Output device on the third parallel interface (for example additional printer)
AUX:	Device on the first serial interface (for example mouse)
COM1:	Device on the first serial interface (for example mouse)
COM2:	Device on the second serial interface (for example Modem)
COM3:	Device on the third serial interface (for example an additional device)
COM4:	Device on the fourth serial interface (for example an additional device)
EPT:	Interface for IBM laser printer (Windows)
NUL:	Null Device/imaginary device

Appendix D — File Extensions

A file is designated by an eight character name and a three character extension. These extensions, indicating the type of file, have become standard.

PC File Extensions	
Ext	**File type**
$$$	Intermediate file, created through the use of the DOS pipe symbol
ACT	Communications-Account data file of the communication program Bitcom
ACT	Source code for the programming language Actor
AIO	APL file transmission format
AMG	System-Image file for Actor
APL	APL work file
APP	Application file for SQL-Windows and GEM-application program
ARF	Automatic action file, created by BASROM,FORTRAN and COBOL compilers of the IBM series; similar to batch file
ASC	ASCII text file
ASM	Assembler source text
BAK	Backup copy, contains preceding version of a file
BAS	BASIC source text, either in ASCII format or as token
BAT	DOS batch file, contains batch commands, DOS commands and program calls
BIN	Binary-file, for example from EXE2BIN
BLK	Block file of the demo program Show Partner with information about the edited blocks
BMP	Graphic-file in bitmap format (for example from Paintbrush under Windows)
C	C source-text
CAL	File spreadsheets from the Supercalc table calculations
CCL	Command language file of the communication program Intalk
CFG	Configuration file with information about hard- and software parameters from various programs, for example AutoSketch
CHK	File reconstructed from lost blocks by CHKDSK/f
CLR	Color-palette file of the Show Partner demo program
CLS	Library for Actor
CMD	dBase program
CMP	Word list for the spell checker of MS Word

PC File Extensions *(con't)*

Ext	File type
CNF	Configuration file for various programs
COB	Cobol source text
COD	Programs translated with Fortran
COL	Spreadsheet file of Multiplan
COM	Executable DOS program, which fits into a memory-segment
CPI	Character set table/Code-Page for DOS
CRF	Cross reference list created by MASM Assembler
CRS	Data for a Golfcourse of the "World Tour Golf" game
CTX	Data for the tutorial programs of various Microsoft products
CUR	Cursor file for MS Windows
DAT	Data file for various programs
DB	Paradox database file
DBD	Demonstration file for "Bricklin's Demo"
DBF	Data base in dBase format
DBS	Data base in SQL-Windows format
DBS	Word printer driver
DBT	Temporary data base file for SQL-Windows
DCT	Spellstar dictionary file
DEF	Windows Module definition file
DEV	Device driver for various programs
DFM	Palantir-Filer data input mask
DFV	Word print format style sheet
DIC	Dictionary file for various programs
DIF	Data Interchange Format, standardized file format for data exchange
DIR	Telephone directory for the dialing from Sidekick
DIS	F & A initialization file
DOC	Text file with and without format information (usually for Word for Windows)
DRV	Device driver for various programs
DTF	Data base for F&A and PFS
EMU	Terminal Emulation file of the Bitcom communication program
EPS	Encapsulated Postscript file
EXE	Executable program and DOS or Windows
F#	Formula definition for the input template of Paradox
FMT	dBase display template definition or format information of Textomat Plus
FNT	Fonts for various programs
FON	GDI loadable font file for Windows
FOR	Fortran source-program
FRM	dBase report format file or separately stored format for Textomat Plus
GEM	File created with the presentation and graphic programs under GEM
GEN	Ventura Publisher file
GX1	Snapshot file for the demo program Show Partner

PC File Extensions *(con't)*	
Ext	**File type**
H	Header file for the C compiler
HEX	Hex-file for DEBUG
HLP	Help file for various programs, for example Windows
HSG	Screenshot file in graphic format
ICO	Icon file for Windows, which contains the bitmap of an Icon
IDX	Index file
IMG	Windows and GEM picture file
IMP	Implementation file for IBM Pascal
INC	Include file for Microsoft Pascal
INC	Include file for Borland Turbo Basic
INI	Windows initialization file or Word printer initialization file
INT	Interface file for IBM Pascal or keyboard configuration of EuroScript
IT	Settings for the communication program Intalk
JOR	SQL Windows Journal file
KBD	EuroScript keyboard configuration
LAY	Superkey layout file, contains key assignments
LBL	dBase Label file
LIB	Library file for various programs
LOD	Load file for some copy protection systems
LSP	Lisp source text
LST	Listing file of the source code file assembled with MASM
MAC	Keyboard macro of Prokey and Superkey
MAP	Map file created by Link during the linking
MDM	Access modem file
ME	Extension of the READ.ME file with current information about the program
MEM	dBase memory file with variables
MEU	Information file or a menu group of the DOS Shell
MNU	Menu file, for example for the Norton Commander
MSG	Message file
MSG	Notice file for the calendar
MSP	Picture file for Windows Paint
NDX	Index file, contains the index for a data base
NET	Configuration file for the network version
OBJ	Object code file
OVD	Paradox Overlay file
OVL	Overlay file for various programs
OVR	Overlay file for various programs
OV	Overlay file for various programs
PAL	Paintbrush color palette
PAS	Pascal source text

PC File Extensions *(con't)*

Ext	File type
PCX	Paintbrush picture file
PCC	Picture cuts from Paintbrush
PFM	Windows printer font files (Printer Font Metric)
PGM	Overlay file for various programs
PIC	Picture file for various programs
PIX	Picture file for various programs
PIF	Program Information file for Windows for normal DOS applications
PJ	Project file for Super Project
PRF	Visicalc print file, contains a worksheet printed on the hard drive
PRG	dBase program
PRJ	Project file
PRN	Print file for various programs
PUB	Formatting information for PageMaker
PX	Primary Index file for Paradox
RC	Resource Script File with information for Windows
REC	Help file created with RECOVER
REF	Cross-Reference list of the Assembler
R#	Paradox report file
SC	Script file
SCN	Display screen file, contains a template for On-Line-Tutorial
SCP	Script file with macro for automatic program control of Bitcom
SCR	Access Script file or Screenshot file in txt format for Hotshot
SET	Paradox pre-set
SIK	Backup copy of a document for Word
SLD	Working file for AutoCAD
SOB	Part of the on-line tutorial from Microsoft
SOM	Contains settings for the sorting of data
SPL	Sqltalk spooling file
SQL	SQL Windows data-file
SYM	Definitions for the Symbolic Debugger of Windows
SYN	Word synonym file for the Thesaurus
SYS	Device driver, called by CONFIG.SYS
TIF	Tagged Image File, graphic format in which the colors have been converted to grey scales
TMP	Temporary file for various programs
TXT	Text file for various word processors with and without format information
VC	VisiCalc spreadsheet
WK1	Lotus 1-2-3 spreadsheet (V. 2 and higher)
WKS	Lotus 1-2-3 spreadsheet (V. 1 and higher)
WMF	Windows Metafile picture

PC File Extensions *(con't)*	
Ext	**File type**
WRI	Windows Write text file
X	Index file
XLC	Excel-Chart
XLM	Excel macro
XLS	Excel spreadsheet
Y	Paradox Index file
Z	Paradox Index file

The electrical assignments of the serial and the parallel interface, as well as the game port, are useful if you encounter problems with your interface.

Parallel interface

The parallel interface is generally used to connect an output device (printer, plotter, or something similar). In almost all computers the parallel interface is a 25 pin D style connector, and on the printer, it is a 36 pin Amphenol connector. So, the pin assignment for both connectors is displayed below. It's possible to solder a printer cable of this type yourself. While receiving (for example, the Atari Portfolio) the DATA lines are switched to input. For the data transmission to and from Atari Portfolio, a 1:1 Centronics cable with connectors on both sides must be used.

Status if a bit is set on the signal - line active				
Comp pin	Printer pin	Designation	Direction	Signal
1	1	STROBE	Output	Strobe to transmit a data byte
2	2	DATA 0	Output	Lowest data bit 0 (LSB) of the data byte
3	3	DATA 1	Output	Data bit 1
4	4	DATA 2	Output	Data bit 2
5	5	DATA 3	Output	Data bit 3
6	6	DATA 4	Output	Data bit 4
7	7	DATA 5	Output	Data bit 5
8	8	DATA 6	Output	Data bit 6
9	9	DATA 7	Output	Highest data-bit 7 (LSB) of the data byte
10	10	ACKNLG	Input	Display of readiness for data reception
11	11	BUSY	Input	Display that no data can be received
12	12	PE	Input	Display that no paper is available
13	13	SLCT	Input	On-Line-/Off-Line status of the printer

Status if a bit is set on the signal - line active *(con't)*				
Comp pin	Printer pin	Designation	Direction	Signal
14	14	AUTO-FEED XT	Output	Activation of the line-feed after every printed line
15	32	ERROR	Input	Display that an error occurred
16	31	INIT	Output	Caused by Reset of the PC, also initialization of the printer
17	36	SLCT IN	Output	Readiness for transmission (always active)
18	-	NC	-	Not Connected. This is important, because some printers have a voltage of +5 V on Pin 18
19	19	GND	Without	Ground for Pin 1 (STROBE)
20	20	GND	Without	Ground for Pin 2 (DATA 0)
21	21	GND	Without	Ground for Pin 3 (DATA 1)
22	22	GND	Without	Ground for Pin 4 (DATA 2)
23	23	GND	Without	Ground for Pin 5 (DATA 3)
24	24	GND	Without	Ground for Pin 6 (DATA 4)
25	25	GND	Without	Ground for Pin 7 (DATA 5)

The following signals aren't connected with the computer. The ground lines (GND) are usually connected with each other.

Comp pin	Designation	Direction	Signal
16	FG	-	Frame Ground
17	FG	-	Frame Ground
18	+5V	-	Voltage for external applications (i.e., printer switches)
26	GND	without	Ground for Pin 7 (DATA 5)
27	GND	without	Ground for Pin 7 (DATA 5)
28	GND	without	Ground for Pin 8 (ACKNOWLEDGE)
29	GND	without	Ground for Pin 9 (SELECT)
30	GND	without	Ground for Pin 10 (AUTOFEED XT)
33	SG	-	Signal Ground/Signal
34	NC	-	Not Connected
35	+5V	-	In some cases there is also +5 V here, otherwise the Pin is NC (Not connected)

Serial interface

In the serial interfaces there are two types of output: the 25 pin connector derived from the XT and the 9 pin AT connector. Since both are used in the 386 systems, the pin assignment is provided for both. With this information you can create an adapter.

Serial Interface Pin Assignment				
25 Pin	**9 Pin**	**Designation**	**Direction**	**Signal**
1	-	PG	without	Protective Ground
2	2	TD	Input	Transceive Data
3	3	RD	Output	Receive Data
4	7	RTS	Input	Request To Send
5	5	CTS	Output	Clear To Send
6	6	DSR	Output	Data Set Ready
7	-	GND	without	signal GrouND
8	1	DCD	Output	Data Carrier Detect
9 to 19	-	NC	-	Not Connected
19	-	NC	-	Not Connected
20	4	DTR	Input	Data Terminal Ready
21	-	NC	-	Not Connected
22	9	RI	Output	Ring Indicator
23	-	NC	-	Not Connected
24	-	NC	-	Not Connected
25	-	NC	-	Not Connected

VGA Standard Modes

Every VGA graphics card cannot represent one resolution. Instead, it has a series of display modes designated with a number and are usually the same for all cards.

Nr.	Mode	Color palette	Resolution	Text	Matrix
0	Text	16/262.144	320x200	40x25	8x8
0*	Text	16/262.144	320x350	40x25	8x14
0+	Text	16/262.144	360x400	40x25	9x16
1	Text	16/262.144	320x200	40x25	8x8
1*	Text	16/262.144	320x350	40x25	8x14
1+	Text	16/262.144	360x400	40x25	9x16
2	Text	16/262.144	640x200	80x25	8x8
2*	Text	16/262.144	640x350	80x25	8x14
2+	Text	16/262.144	720x400	80x25	9x16
3	Text	16/262.144	640x200	80x25	8x8
3*	Text	16/262.144	640x350	80x25	8x14
3+	Text	16/262.144	720x400	80x25	9x16
4	Graphic	4/262.144	320x200	40x25	8x8 CGA-compatible, double line raster
5	Graphic	4/262.144	320x200	40x25	8x8 CGA-compatible, double line raster
6	Graphic	2/262.144	640x200	80x25	8x8 CGA-compatible
7	Text	mono	720x350	80x25	9x14
7+	Text	mono	720x400	80x25	9x16
D	Graphic	16/262.144	320x200	40x25	8x8 MCGA-compatible
E	Graphic	16/262.144	640x200	80x25	8x8 MCGA-compatible
F	Graphic	mono	640x350	80x25	8x14 EGA-compatible
10	Graphic	16/262.144	640x350	80x25	8x14 EGA-compatible
11	Graphic	2/262.144	640x480	80x30	8x16 MCGA-compatible
12	Graphic	16/262.144	640x480	80x30	8x16
13	Graphic	256/262.144	320x200	40x25	8x8 MCGA-compatible

All resolutions with an asterisk (*) are EGA text modes with 8x14 or 9x14 character matrix and a vertical resolution of 350 lines.

The resolutions marked with a "+" are VGA text modes with a 9x16 letter matrix and a vertical resolution of 400 lines.

Default settings are 3+ for color monitors and 7+ for monochrome VGA monitors. If the card permits the interfacing of a TTL monitor, it's operated with the 3* resolution.

Nine pin connector

The assignment in the nine pin D Sub Video connector depends on its use as output connector for the Hercules, CGA, or EGA signals or for multiscan monitors for the input of the analog signals.

For the EGA output connector there are two bits for every color. MSB is the higher level (most significant bit) and LSB the lower value (least significant bit).

For the connection of a digital source to the multifrequency monitor, the assignments of the EGA connector are valid.

	Nine Pin Connector Layout				
Pin	**Digital in/output Hercules**	**CGA**	**EGA**	**Analog input multisync monitor**	**VGA pin**
1	Ground	Ground	Ground	Red	1
2	Ground	Ground	Red LSB	Green	2
3	-	Red	Red MSB	Blue	3
4	-	Green	Green MSB	Horiz synch	13
5	-	Blue	Blue MSB	Vert synch	14
6	Intensity	Intensity	Green LSB	Ground	6
7	Video	-	Blue LSB	Ground	7
8	Horiz synch	Horiz synch	Horiz synch	Ground	8
9	Vert synch	Vert synch	Vert synch	Ground	10

VGA connector

With the new video standard, IBM also introduced a new connector. To avoid confusion with the many existing connectors and to save space, 15 pins were accommodated in the space formerly occupied by 9 pins.

Since these pins are thinner, they must be inserted carefully. The connector can be found on VGA cards and monitors.

VGA Connector Pin Layout	
Pin	**Signal**
1	Red
2	Green
3	Blue
4	Monitor-identification Bit 2
5	-
6	Ground for Red-Signal
7	Ground for Green-Signal
8	Ground for Blue-Signal
9	No pin in the connector, no hole in the connector, protection against wrong insertions
10	Ground for synchronization signal
11	Monitor-identification Bit 0
12	Monitor-identification Bit 1
13	horizontal synchronization
14	vertical synchronization
15	-

Appendix H

Interrupt Channels

All components of a computer are coordinated in the PC through the interrupts. Every element (keyboard, interfaces, coprocessor, etc.) has a reserved channel through which it can be addressed. The interrupt channel is abbreviated as IRQ (Interrupt ReQuest channel).

In the XT model, there are eight interrupt channels, for ATs and 386 systems there are 16. There is also a non-maskable interrupt (NMI), which is reserved for parity checking and special assignments. In devices with ISA architecture, two devices cannot share an interrupt. This is possible with MCA.

Interrupt-Channels in ATs and 386es	
IRQ channel	**Function**
NMI	Parity check
0	Timer
1	Keyboard
2	Line to IRQ 8 to 15
8	Real-time clock
9	Substitute for IRQ 2 for 8-bit cards
10	Reserved
11	Reserved
12	Reserved
13	Coprocessor 80287
14	Hard disk controller
15	Reserved
3	Serial interface 2 (COM2)
4	Serial interface 1 (COM1)
5	Parallel interface 2 (LPT2)
6	Diskette controller
7	Parallel interface 1 (LPT1)

The assignment of the interrupts is controlled with two chips of the Intel 82598 A type. There is a hierarchy in which the interrupts are processed. At the highest level is the non-maskable interrupt, followed by channels 0 to 2.

Channel 2 is used as a connection to the second chip with the addresses 8 to 15. This is followed by IRQ 3 to 7. The IRQ 2 lost in the connection is made available to 8-bit cards as IRQ 9.

The use of the interrupts and their hierarchy is evident from the previous table.

The Interrupts 0, 1, 2, 8, and 13 aren't available for expansion cards. The IRQ channels 8 as well as 10 to 15 can be used only by cards with 16-bit connectors.

The interrupts are usually already assigned when you purchase your computer. Sometimes it may be necessary to change the interrupt assignment. If additional peripherals should be added to the already available interfaces (Btx card, scanner, mouse, graphics tablet) on a hardware level, problems can occur.

So, these cards often permit the setting of the interrupts that should be addressed by this card. If the settings are changed, the installation program must also be informed to ensure that the computer can address the peripherals.

Appendix

Error Messages

When a 386 computer is switched on, it performs a POST (Power On Self Test) that briefly checks all system components. If an error occurs, the computer starts to beep. The type of error can be identified by the number of beeps. The type of error message depends on the BIOS.

A short tone after the boot process signals everything is in order.

The numbers represent the tones produced by the PC. If no other indication is provided, all tones are of equal duration. Numbers separated by a dash indicate blocks of tones that are separated by a pause. An "x" means the number of tones can vary.

POST Messages and Tones		
Signal	**No. of tones**	**Error**
Phoenix-BIOS	AMI-BIOS	
1-1-3		CMOS-RAM
1-1-4	9	ROM-BIOS
1-2-1	4	System counter chip
1-2-2 and 1-2-3	1	DMA-Chip
1-3-x to 1-4-x and 2-x-x	3	64K basic-memory
3-1-1 and 3-1-2		DMA Slave
3-1-3 and 3-1-4		Interrupt Controller
3-2-4	6	Timer or Keyboard processor
3-3-4		Display screen-initialization
Phoenix-BIOS	AMI-BIOS	
3-4-x		Video
	no tone	Power
	continuous tone	Power
	Many short tones	Motherboard
	1 long, 1 short	Motherboard, Timer-chip or BASIC-ROM (IBM)
	1 long, 2 short	Video-Controller or display screen memory
	2 long	Parity of the memory chips

POST Messages and Tones *(con't)*		
Signal	**No. of tones**	**Error**
	2 long, 1 short	Synchronization of the monitor adapter
	3 short, 3 long, 3 short	Memory
	7 longer tones	Virtual mode
	8 longer tones	Writing into Video-RAM

The AT bus, in which the expansion cards are mounted, consists of two slots, of which one has twice 31 pins and the other twice 18 pins.

The longer part is the "8-part" of the bus. This is where cards, which don't use the shorter slot, can be inserted. The extension to 16 bits through the use of both slots, provides a higher throughput of data and is normally used by all VGA cards and hard drive controllers.

The following table lists the signals and their functions. The signals usually indicate their activity with a low level.

Pin	Description	Direction	Pin	Description	Direction
A01	IO CHCK	Input	A02	SD7	Input/Output
A03	SD6	Input/Output	A04	SD5	Input/Output
A05	SD4	Input/Output	A06	SD3	Input/Output
A07	SD2	Input/Output	A08	SD1	Input/Output
A09	SD0	Input/Output	A10	IO CH RDY	Input
A11	AEN	Output	A12	SA19	Output
A13	SA18	Output	A14	SA17	Output
A15	SA16	Output	A16	SA15	Output
A17	SA14	Output	A18	SA13	Output
A19	SA12	Output	A20	SA11	Output
A21	SA10	Output	A22	SA9	Output
A23	SA8	Output	A24	SA7	Output
A25	SA6	Output	A26	SA5	Output
A27	SA4	Output	A28	SA3	Output
A29	SA2	Output	A30	SA1	Output
A31	SA0	Output			
B01	Ground	without	B02	RESET DRV	Output
B03	+5V		B04	IRQ9	Input
B05	-5V		B06	DRQ2	Input
B07	-12V		B08	OWS	Input

Pin	Description	Direction	Pin	Description	Direction
B09	+12V		B10	Ground	
B11	SMEMW	Output	B12	SMEMR	Output
B13	IOW	Input/Output	B14	IOR	Input/Output
B15	DACK3	Output	B16	DRQ3	Input
B17	DACK1	Output	B18	DRQ1	Input
B19	REFRESH	Output	B20	SYS CLK	Output
B21	IRQ7	Input	B22	IRQ6	Input
B23	IRQ5	Input	B24	IRQ4	Input
B25	IRQ3	Input	B26	DACK2	Output
B27	T/C	Output	B28	BALE	Output
B29	+5V		B30	OSC	Output
B31	Ground	without			
C01	SBHE	Input	C02	LA23	Input/Output
C03	LA22	Input/Output	C04	LA21	Input/Output
C05	LA20	Input/Output	C06	LA19	Input/Output
C07	LA18	Input/Output	C08	LA17	Input/Output
C09	MEMR	Input/Output	C10	MEMW	Input/Output
C11	SD8	Input/Output	C12	SD9	Input/Output
C13	SD10	Input/Output	C14	SD11	Input/Output
C15	SD12	Input/Output	C16	SD13	Input/Output
C17	SD14	Input/Output	C18	SD15	Input/Output
D01	MEMCS16	Input	D02	IOCS16	Input
D03	IRQ10	Input	D04	IRQ11	Input
D05	IRQ12	Input	D06	IRQ13	Input
D07	IRQ14	Input	D08	DACK0	Output
D09	DRQ5	Input	D10	DACK5	Output
D11	DRQ5	Input	D12	DACK6	Output
D13	DRQ6	Input	D14	DACK7	Output
D15	DRQ7	Input	D16	+5V	
D17	MASTER	Input	D18	Ground	

Explanation

0WS

Signal that informs the main processor that the current bus cycle can be terminated without interruption with a wait cycle.

AEN(Output)

Signal that indicates whether the bus is controlled by the DMA chip (high level) or the main processor (low level).

BALE (Output)

Control signal for SD0 ... SD19 in connection with DMA cycles.

CLK (Output)

System clock, running synchronous with the CPU clock and set with Setup during "BUSCLK".

DACK0 ... DACK3 (Output)
  DNA Acknowledgment signal for the DRQ query (see DRQ0 ... DRQ3).

DACK5 ... DACK7 (Output)
  DNA Acknowledgment signal for the DRQ-query (see DRQ5 ... DRQ7).

DRQ0 ... DRQ3 (Input)
  DMA query-channel for the 8-bit data transmission.

DRQ5 ... DRQ7 (Input)
  DMA query-channel for the 16 bit data transmission.

DRQ4
  Used on the motherboard and for this reason doesn't appear on the AT bus. The query signals are kept on the high level until an answer is received. A low DMA number indicates a higher priority.

I/O CH CK (Input)
  Input/output signal control, indicates when a parity error of the input/output card is present.

I/O CH RDY (Input)
  Signal for extension of the input/output or memory-write/read cycle.

I/O CS 16
  Signal that indicates that the data transmission occurs with a wait cycle in the 16-bit mode.

IOR (Input/Output)
  Signal that activates the reading of input/output signals.

IOW (Input/Output)
  Signal that activates the writing of input/output signals.

IRQ3 ... IRQ7, IRQ9 ... IRQ12, IRQ14, IRQ 15 (Input)
  Interrupt signals for the operation of a peripheral device.

LA17 .. LA23 (Input/Output)
  Address bus up to 16 Meg.

MASTER (Input) This signal is set by an I/O processor that takes over the control of the bus (as "Master").

MEM CS 16 (Input)
  Signal that indicates that the data transmission is executing in 16-bit mode.

MEMR (Input/Output)

> Signal that indicates the read process of a memory location.

MEMW (Input/Output)

> Signal that indicates the write process of a memory location.

OSC

> Separate clock of 14.3 MHz for color graphics cards.

REFRESH (Input/Output)

> Signal that indicates that the memory refresh cycle for the DRAMs is operating.

RESET DRV (Output)

> Signal that has a high level when the computer is switched on during low power voltage or during a hardware Reset (cold start).

SA0 ... SA19 (Input/Output)

> Address bus, on which memory addresses up to 1 Meg are output.

SD0 ... SD15 (Input/Output)

> Bit channel from the data bus.

SHBE (Input)

> Signal, which indicates that the higher level byte is present on the data channels SD8 to SD15 of the data bus.

SMEMR (Output)

> Signal, which indicates the use of the memory below 1 Meg.

SMEMW (Input/Output)

> Signal, which indicates when a memory location in an area below 1 Meg is being written.

T/C (Output)

> This signal delivers a strobe when the termination time for a DMA channel has expired.

Appendix K Glossary

8086 processor

An Intel microprocessor developed in 1978. It features a full 16-bit data bus and can address 1 Meg of memory.

8088 processor

An Intel microprocessor developed in 1978. It features an 8-bit external data bus (for disk drives, etc.) and an internal 16-bit data bus. It was used in the original IBM-PC computers and can address 1 Meg of RAM.

80286 processor

An Intel microprocessor developed in 1984. It features a 16-bit data bus and can address 16 Meg of RAM (in Protected mode).

80386 processor

An Intel microprocessor developed in 1986. It features a 32-bit data bus and can address 4 Gigabytes of RAM (in Protected mode).

80486 processor

An Intel microprocessor developed in 1989. It features a 32-bit data bus and can address 64 Gigabytes of RAM (in Protected mode).

Address

The Intel processors (80xx) form an address from one of the four segment registers with another register or constant. The content of the segment address becomes the segment address and the other registers or the constant becomes the offset address. Both addresses are logical addresses related to a physical address. You can determine this physical address by multiplying the segment register by 16 and adding the offset address.

Address Bus

A line connecting the CPU with ROM and RAM memory. When the CPU addresses a memory location, first it must place its address on the address bus to set the switches for access to this memory location.

Application

A program designed for a specific purpose. Word processors, spreadsheets, and databases are applications.

ASCII

Acronym for American Standard Code for Information Interchange. ASCII is the standard for keyboard character codes, which applies to keyboards and printers. The ASCII standard covers key codes 0 to 127; individual computer manufacturers assign their own characters to codes 128 to 255. See also *Byte*.

AT

Acronym for Advanced Technology. The AT is essentially the "big brother" of the PC. It has a more powerful microprocessor, a higher processing speed in most cases, larger memory capacity beyond the 640K limit set by the old PC configuration, and higher disk storage capacity.

Bank switching

A method of expanding memory beyond the normal memory limits by quickly switching between two banks of memory chips.

Base memory

The first, or lower, 640K of the first megabyte of memory.

BASIC

A programming language (Beginner's All-purpose Symbolic Instruction Code). BASIC is popular with users as a computer language because it's easy to learn.

Batch file

A file containing a collection of commands. MS-DOS executes these commands in sequence when the user enters the name of the file. Some other terms are batch processing or batch job. Batch files can be created using the COPY CON command, EDLIN line editor, or a word processing program.

Baud rate

The unit used to measure the rate of data transmission, for example when communicating with another computer by telephone. A baud is approximately 1 bit per second.

Binary

A number system consisting of only two numbers (0,1), which are sometimes called bits. Unlike the decimal number system with its 10 numbers (0-9), the binary number system is better suited to the internal structure of a computer. Just as larger numbers can be composed in the decimal system, larger binary system numbers are constructed from several digits. Both number systems rely on the positional value of numbers. The numbers 0 - 9 in the 10 to the 0 power column have the value 0 - 9. The same numbers in the next column (10 to the 1 power) refer to 10 - 90, etc. In the binary system the column value increases as follows: 0, 2, 4, 8, 16, 32, etc.

BIOS

Acronym for Basic Input/Output System. BIOS is a program permanently stored in the memory of the computer and is available without an operating system diskette. For example, it performs the internal self test of the computer (counting up the memory available and testing for connected peripherals, such as disk drives). It also triggers the search for the operating system (MS-DOS) on the diskette in the drive.

Bit

The smallest unit in the binary number system. It can assume only two states (0,1) and therefore store only two different pieces of information. To store a character, several bits must be combined into a byte.

Boot/Reboot

The loading process that places the operating system in memory. A diskette used for booting a PC must have two "hidden" files available for telling the PC to boot, as well as the COMMAND.COM file.

Bus

A collection of communication lines transmitting signals between components on a circuit board or between the circuit board and expansion or other cards.

Byte

A group of 8 bits. While a bit can only assume two states (0 and 1), a byte can store from 0 up to 255 conditions. A character is usually stored in a byte. So a byte can store up to 255 different characters. The standard ASCII character set consists of 128 characters; the additional characters generally used in PC software increases the total number of characters to 255.

Cache

A special area of RAM to store the most frequently accessed information in RAM. You can greatly improve the speed of your system by using cache memory because it "optimizes" the cooperation among the different components of your system.

CD-ROM disk drive

A storage device that uses compact discs (CDs) to store data. Although a large amount of data can be stored on these discs, they're "Read Only Memory" disk drives.

CD-WORM disk drive

A storage device based on further development of CD-ROM drives. It's an acronym for "Write Once Read Many". These disk drives can write on the CD only once but read it as often as required.

Centronics

Standard connection between the PC and a printer. The connection of other devices to the PC occurs through interfaces. These interfaces use standardized connectors. There are serial interfaces, in which data is sent as individual bits, and parallel interfaces, in which a byte can be transmitted simultaneously. Both interfaces have their own standards: Centronics interfaces for parallel; RS-232 interfaces for serial. Most printers are attached through the parallel Centronics interface. It has the device designation LPT1: (Line Printer 1).

CGA

See *Color Graphics Adapter*.

Chip

Complicated electronic circuitry built into a small space. The early days of electronics required huge circuits. Chips compressed this same circuitry into a single silicon chip, which made it possible to develop small computers for the home. The most important chip in the PC is the microprocessor, which performs most of the basic tasks needed in a computer.

Clone

Another term used to describe an IBM compatible computer.

CMOS

A Complementary Metal-Oxide Semiconductor that pretends to duplicate the functions of memory chips or other processors. CMOS chips are used primarily in portable PCs that receive their power from batteries.

Color Graphics Adapter (CGA)

A bit-mapped graphics card that can display several colors at the same time (the amount depends on the CGA monitor you're using).

Controller card

A card (adapter) that connects the disk drive(s) to the computer.

Co-processor

Name for electronic components (see *Chip*), which relieve the microprocessor of some important tasks. For example, a math coprocessor often performs many of the math functions that can slow down the microprocessor during complicated graphics computations.

CPU

Abbreviation for Central Processing Unit. This is the main microprocessor of the PC. It's sometimes used to describe the PC's case.

Databus

A line used to transmit data between the CPU and RAM or ROM memory.

DIP switch

A series of small switches used by computers and peripherals to configure the equipment.

Directory

Due to the large capacity of the hard drive, files must be separated into various directories. They are arranged in a tree structure, in which the root directory can contain files and subdirectories. Each subdirectory can also contain files and subdirectories.

DOS

See *MS-DOS*.

Dynamic RAM Chips (DRAM)

A RAM chip that must be continuously refreshed. These chips vary in their access time, which is measured in nanoseconds.

Empty directory

A directory that doesn't contain any files or subdirectories.

Enhanced Graphics Adapter (EGA)

A high resolution graphics card with superior resolution compared to the CGA. The EGA combined the operating modes of the MDA and the CGA. This type of graphics adapter is capable of displaying all 16 colors in text mode with a resolution of 640 x 350 pixels.

Expanded memory

Memory above the 640K limit for DOS Version 3.3 (and earlier versions) which can be used for programs requiring large amounts of memory. Note that this area of memory requires special drivers and works only with software written for it.

Expanded Memory Specification (EMS)

A section of RAM above the 1 Meg limit set by PCs and XTs. Software and applications cannot work with EMS unless specifically written for EMS. See also the *LIM/EMS Standard.*

Expansion card

A printed circuit card that you can install to add new features and expand the current capabilities of your system.

Expansion slots

Slots or spaces inside the case for connecting cards to the motherboard. Most PCs contain these slots so it's easy to upgrade the system.

Extended memory

Area of memory above 1Meg that a computer using a 286, 386, or 486 processor can access.

File Allocation Table (FAT)

A portion of all DOS formatted diskettes containing information on the number and location of files and available storage space.

Ground

To make an electrical current connection to the earth or a conductor of equivalent effect.

Hard drive

A secondary storage device that uses several nonflexible disks. These disks, along with the recording heads and interfaces, are stored as a hermetically sealed mechanism.

Hercules Graphics Card

Also known by its acronym HGC. It features a text mode of MDA and graphics mode with a resolution of 720 x 348 one color (monochrome) pixels.

Hertz (Hz)

A unit of measure that equals a frequency of one cycle per second.

High-level format

A DOS formatting operation to include important sections, such as FAT, boot record, track free, and others on the hard drive.

IBM compatible

Clones of the IBM PC/XT/AT computers, following the IBM "industry standard." If programs and hardware configurations follow the IBM standard, this allows software to work with any computer.

Icon

Graphical representation of an object, including files, drives, directories, applications, etc.

Interface

Connection between a PC and various peripherals. Allows data to be exchanged between the PC and peripherals, such as printers. See *Centronics* and *RS-232 interface*).

Initialization

Another term for the process of formatting a diskette or hard drive so that it can be used.

Install

A process of attaching cards or other devices to the appropriate connectors or sockets.

Interleave ratio

Also called interleave setting. This is the ratio between the physical sectors of a hard drive, which are skipped for every sector used. If the hard drive has an interleave ratio of 3:1, the diskette writes to one sector, skips three sectors, writes to one sector, etc.

Jumper

Electrical connectors that allow you to customize a circuit board. It's a small piece of rectangular plastic with up to three receptacles.

K

See *Kilobyte*.

Kilobyte (K)

1,024 bytes and usually abbreviated simply as K (for example, 512K).

LIM/EMS Standard

A standard, introduced by Lotus, Intel, and Microsoft, that allows software to work with expanded memory above the normal 640K of RAM. Remember that software must be designed to run under the LIM/EMS standard to work with expanded memory.

Logical drive

A subdivision of a hard drive indicated by a specific letter. The first subdivision is usually designated as D because the primary partition is designated as C. Any other partitions can contain any number of logical drives designated by a different letter. Use the FDISK command to create partitions and logical drives.

Megahertz (MHz)

A unit of measure that equals a frequency of 1 million cycles per second.

Microprocessor

Another word for chip. When used in computer science, the term chip usually refers to the main microprocessor of the computer, which controls the basic functions.

Modem

An abbreviation for MODulator/DEModulator. This device converts the digital signals of your computer into electrical impulses (modulates) and transmits these impulses over telephone lines. Another modem then converts received impulses back into signals (demodulate) that another computer can understand.

Mouse

An alternate means of cursor control. The mouse is a small box with two or three buttons on top and a ball poking out the bottom. Moving the mouse on a table moves the cursor in the same direction on the screen.

Motherboard

Also called logic board. It's the large printed circuit board containing the CPU, support chips, RAM, and expansion slots.

MS-DOS

The standard operating system developed by the Microsoft Corporation for IBM compatible PCs. Your PC only becomes usable after the MS-DOS operating system has been loaded. It consists generally of a catalog of resident and transient commands, which can be accessed when required.

Multitasking

The process of running multiple programs or tasks on the same computer simultaneously. So you don't need to exit one application before starting different applications.

Parallel interface

Centronics interface, usually leading to a printer (see also *Centronics*). Parallel interfaces exchange data 8 bits at a time. LPT1: is the device designation for the first parallel interface. Additional parallel interfaces (if present) are accessed as LPT2: and LPT3:.

PC

Abbreviation for Personal Computer, which was originally an IBM product first introduced in 1981.

Peripheral

A device connected to the computer but external of the computer's CPU. These devices include printers and disk drives.

Protected mode

Advanced feature of the 286 and 386 processors where memory is protected and allocated for specific programs and extended memory.

RAM

Abbreviation for Random Access Memory. This is memory in which data can be stored temporarily. Unlike ROM, RAM can be written to and read from. The contents of RAM vanish when the computer is switched off. See also *ROM*.

Real mode

An operating mode where specific memory locations are given to programs and peripherals.

ROM

Abbreviation for Read Only Memory. ROM consists of information permanently planted on a chip (see *Chip*), which remains intact after the computer is switched on. When the user switches on the computer, the information from this ROM is read as needed. Unlike RAM, the user cannot write to ROM (hence the name).

ROM BIOS

The two ROM chips that contain BIOS code (Basic Input Output System) and system configuration information. See also *BIOS*.

RS-232 interface

Standard serial interface. Serial transfer involves the transfer of data one bit at a time.

Sector

A small portion of the track on a diskette. It's the area the computer uses to store data at specific locations on the diskette for retrieval. Normal PC sectors contain 512K of usable area.

SIMM

Acronym for Single In-line Memory Module. These are memory modules plugged into the motherboard or memory expansion boards. They usually store data 9-bits wide and add 256K or 1 Meg of RAM.

Slot

Name for a connector inside the PC where additional circuit cards can be inserted to enhance the capabilities of the computer. Lately some PCs on the market don't have these slots, and therefore cannot be easily enhanced.

Small Computer System Interface (SCSI)

An interface standard for hard drives and other peripherals.

Software Cache

See *Cache*.

VGA

Acronym for Video Graphics Adapter. It's a video display standard that offers a maximum of 256 colors simultaneously and offers better resolution than previous standards.

Utilities

Programs that either help the programmer program more efficiently or act as tools for helping the user in diskette and file management. Some utilities optimize the performance of a hard drive, others help the user recover deleted or destroyed files.

XT

Designation of a PC with a hard drive or a PC capable of running a hard drive.

The 486 Book — Index

T - W

Abacus
pc catalog
Order Toll Free 1-800-451-4319

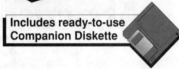

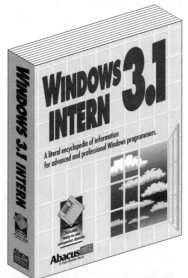

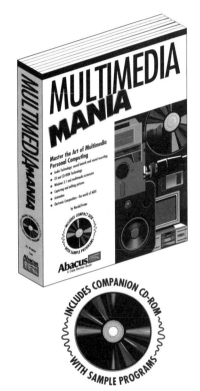

The Companion Diskette

The companion diskette features executable applications that display information about your computer and its configuration. The companion diskette saves you time because you don't have to type in the program listings presented in the book. And, we've included System Sleuth Professional from Dariana Technology, Inc., a $169.00 value.

The PCINFO program and source code developed in Turbo Pascal 6.0 and Turbo Assembler 2.5, both from Borland, are also included on the companion diskette. With this program, you can display information about your computer and its configuration. You can copy this program to your hard drive and start it from there.

5370 52nd Street SE · Grand Rapids MI 49512
Call 1-800-451-4319

The 486 Book Companion Diskette

Installation:
Insert the companion diskette in a disk drive. Log to that drive, and type the following and press Enter:

INSTALL

The INSTALL program will ask you for a source drive and a destination drive. Follow the instructions on the screen. The INSTALL program creates an ABACUS\486 directory, then creates subdirectories, into which the programs are inserted.

System Sleuth Professional installation:
Type the following to run System Sleuth Professional from the drive and directory containing the program and press Enter:

SLEUTH

The System Sleuth Professional has a menu system that can be activated at any time by pressing Alt. Most menu items have context sensitive help (press F1 for context sensitive help).
